Martin Bucer

Martin Bucer
A Reformer and His Times

Martin Greschat

Translated by Stephen E. Buckwalter

Westminster John Knox Press
LOUISVILLE • LONDON

Originally published as *Martin Bucer: Ein Reformator und seine Zeit*
© Verlag C. H. Beck, Munich, 1990

Book design by Sharon Adams
Cover design by Lisa Buckley

First edition
Published by Westminster John Knox Press
Louisville, Kentucky

This book is printed on acid-free paper that meets the American National Standards Institute Z39.48 standard. ♾

PRINTED IN THE UNITED STATES OF AMERICA

04 05 06 07 08 09 10 11 12 13—10 9 8 7 6 5 4 3 2 1

Library of Congress Cataloging-in-Publication Data

Greschat, Martin.
    [Martin Bucer. English]
    Martin Bucer : a reformer and his times / Martin Greschat ; translated by
    Stephen E. Buckwalter.
        p. cm.
    Includes bibliographical references (p.) and index.
    ISBN 0-664-22690-6 (alk. paper)
    1. Bucer, Martin, 1491–1551.   2. Reformation.   I. Title.

    BR350.B93G7413 2004
    284'.092–dc22
    [B]   2004041918

Contents

Preface

W ho in the world is Martin Bucer?" I can't keep track of how many times I was asked this question in the past years, usually following an initial query as to what I happened to be working on at the moment.

Few figures of the Reformation have been as neglected as this sixteenth-century theologian, churchman, statesman, and Christian. His name and at least some of his works may be familiar to scholars, but most people know little or nothing about the man who during his lifetime was one of the most important and influential figures not only of German but also of European church history. His authority rested upon his untiring, lifelong commitment—at a time of bitter conflicts and growing disunity among Christians—to union and reconciliation, not only among Protestants but even between opposing sides of the growing chasm within Western Christendom.

This inspired me to write a biography that presented Bucer in his time and context: as someone rooted in the assumptions and structures of the late Middle Ages who got swept into the greatest spiritual, social, and political upheaval of the sixteenth century. Only by firmly anchoring Bucer in the environment and times that sustained and shaped him can the biographer, in my view, avoid the fallacy of turning his subject into the center of events. History, in fact, did not revolve around Bucer. He was instead a child of the momentous, exciting, and diverse times in which he lived. I thus sought to describe Bucer as an individual living and acting within this wider reality; an individual who resolved to influence events and later actually found himself able to do so, if within certain limits.

Another question I was often asked was "Is it worth the trouble spending so much time on this forgotten and, in so many respects, remote figure of the past? Aren't there greater and more urgent problems than shedding light on the life and ministry of a sixteenth-century person, however important he may be?" I don't dismiss this criticism glibly, for years of hard work and research went into this book.

Yet I am convinced that we cannot authentically and effectively come to terms with issues of the present and the recent past unless we, while keeping guard against false analogy, become aware of their relative place within the broad sweep of history. This should not be misinterpreted as making a case for determinism of any kind, as if Bucer, Luther, Zwingli, or Calvin were responsible for the later course of church and political history—or maybe even for the unsound decisions of later generations. What I would like to underscore instead is that almost all the questions concerning how Christians understand themselves and their relationship to society in the modern era were stated anew in the sixteenth century, and that fresh answers were attempted as well at this time. How does one define a Christian? What is the proper relationship between recognizing statements of faith as true and living according to them? What is the church? What influence is it allowed to have, or maybe even entitled to claim, on surrounding society? And finally, how are the many intersections between church and state, between civic community and Christian fellowship, to be properly ordered? Bucer spent his entire life grappling with these and similar questions.

But he was by far not the only one. In fact, his statements and decisions were the outcome of unremitting dialogue, even altercation, with opposing positions, and studying how Bucer arrived at his conclusions provides us a glimpse into the broad array of religious and political positions that characterized this era. I hope that my presentation enhances readers' feel for this enormously, indeed often confusingly diverse spectrum of views. I focused my attention, of course, on the person of Martin Bucer and on his thoughts and actions as an individual. But my goal in doing so was to allow a whole epoch to come to life—in the form of a person whose life and work were an expression of the questions and struggles of his times.

Remembering the past dare not lead to the simplistic adoption, today, of solutions proclaimed or carried out in that past. It is much more important anyhow, when studying history, that we learn to listen more carefully to the questions asked by people of the past, trying to understand them on their own terms, than that we derive facile answers to modern problems. It is under these presuppositions that I—as a theologian, a historian, and a child of my own times—have undertaken to write about Bucer and his times.

We are all familiar with the truism that the dwarf sees further than the giant on whose shoulders he is standing. It remains to be seen whether this metaphor also applies to the present study, and whether I succeeded in appropriately working the achievements of past scholars into this book. In any case, I gratefully acknowledge my indebtedness to the selection of studies mentioned in the bibliography at the end of this book. I learned from all of them, even when I sometimes chose to emphasize things differently or came to differing conclusions. I express my gratitude particularly to two colleagues who went to the trouble of reading the manuscript of the German original: Professor Marc Lienhard of Strasbourg, an expert not only in Alsatian but also in European Reformation history, and the late Dr. Jean Rott, also of Strasbourg, the unsurpassed Nestor of Bucer scholarship. I made full use of their well-founded knowledge and their constant readiness to help. Both of them contributed corrections, suggestions, and even objections that required me to rethink parts of the book, reformulate them, or change them outright. The book owes a lot to them.

Rather than thoroughly revise the entire book for the sake of the English translation, I decided to add a chapter on recent research on Martin Bucer (chap. 10, "New Insights"). In it, I present the editions and monographs that have appeared since 1990, discussing their contributions and theses in order of their relevance to the successive periods of Bucer's life.

I am extremely grateful to Dr. Stephen E. Buckwalter for translating this book into English. It is a felicitous coincidence that he edits Bucer's German works at the *Bucer-Forschungsstelle* of the Heidelberg Academy of Sciences and Humanities. I thank him for his conscientious translation, from which readers will profit much, as well as for his numerous suggestions relating not only to form but also to content. Dr. Buckwalter also acknowledges the gracious help of John and Rachel Miller of Lawrence, Kansas; Professor Susan Boettcher of Austin, Texas; Dan Charles of Washington, D.C.; and Scott Amos of Charlottesville, Virginia, in checking significant portions of the translation.

Finally, I wish to express my very special gratitude to Professor Hans J. Hillerbrand for his diligence and determination in seeing that this English translation becomes reality, and I also extend my heartfelt thanks to Dr. Donald K. McKim, the Academic and Reference Editor of Westminster John Knox Press, for seeing the book through the press.

Martin Greschat
Münster, 28 February 2004
453rd anniversary of Bucer's death

Abbreviations

BB   Stupperich, Robert et al., eds. "Bibliographia Bucer-
                ana." In *Schriften des Vereins für Reformationsgeschichte.*
                Gütersloh: C. Bertelsmann, 1952. Vol. 169, pp. 37–96.

BCor   *Correspondance de Martin Bucer.* Edited by Jean Rott
                et al. 5 vols. to date. Leiden: E. J. Brill, 1979– .

BDS   *Martin Bucers Deutsche Schriften.* Edited by Robert
                Stupperich et al. Gütersloh: Gutersloher Verlagshaus
                1960– . To date: vols. 1–5; 6/1, 6/2, 6/3; 7; 8; 9/1; 10;
                11/1; 11/2; 17.

CR   *Corpus Reformatorum: Philippi Melanthonis opera quae
                supersunt omnia.* Edited by Karl Bretschneider and
                Heinrich Bindseil. 28 vols. Halle a. d. Saale: A.
                Schwetschke & Sons, 1834–1860.

BOL   *Martini Buceri opera latina.* Edited by F. Wendel et al.
                7 vols. to date. Paris: Presses Universitaires de France;
                Leiden: E. J. Brill, 1954– .

Pol. Cor.   *Politische Correspondenz der Stadt Strasburg im Zeital-
                ter der Reformation.* Edited by Hans Virck, Otto
                Winckelmann, Harry Gerber, and Walter Friedens-
                burg. 5 vols. Strasbourg: Trübner, 1882–1898; Heidel-
                berg: Carl Winter, 1928–1933.

Scripta Anglicana   *Martini Buceri Scripta anglicana fere omnia.* Edited by
                Conrad Hubert. Basel: Petrus Perna, 1577.

StA   *Martin Luther: Studienausgabe.* 6 vols. to date. Berlin:
             Evangelische Verlagsanstalt, 1979– .

TAE   *Quellen zur Geschichte der Täufer 7–8, 15–16 (Täuferak-*
             ten Elsass I–IV). Edited by Jean Rott et al. 4 vols.
             Gütersloh: G. Mohn, 1959–1988. Vol. 7 = Elsass I;
             vol. 8 = Elsass II; vol. 15 = Elsass III; vol. 16 = Elsass IV.

WA   Luther, Martin. *Luthers Werke. Kritische Gesamtaus-*
             gabe [Weimarer Ausgabe]. Schriften. 65 vols. Weimar:
             H. Böhlau, 1883–1993.

WA Br   Luther, Martin. *Luthers Werke. Kritische Gesamtaus-*
             gabe. Briefwechsel. 18 vols. Weimar: H. Böhlau, 1930–
             1985.

ZW   *Huldreich Zwinglis Sämtliche Werk.* 15 vols. to date.
             Leipzig: Heinsius; Zurich: Verlag Berichtshaus, Theo-
             logischer Verlag, 1905– .

Chapter One

Humble Beginnings

Sélestat

The Town

Where the Alsatian plain is at its widest, spreading over eleven miles from the Rhine River to the Vosges Mountains, just north of where the modern-day departments of Bas-Rhin and Haut-Rhin meet, lies the former imperial city of Sélestat. Its almost circular layout on the left bank of the Ill River survives to the present day, reminding us of medieval ramparts that once surrounded it. In the sixteenth century, the town lay next to a broad area of swamps and marshes to the south, through which the Ill meandered, splitting into various branches that repeatedly threatened the city with floods. On the north side, farmland, mostly vineyards, extended up to the town walls.

Several enthusiastic descriptions of Sélestat survive from the late Middle Ages. Beatus Bild—a butcher's son who, as a disciple and friend of Erasmus of Rotterdam, acquired European fame under the name of Beatus Rhenanus—drew the most clear-eyed and accurate portrait: Sélestat, he wrote, was a small town crammed with houses and interlaced with streams and waterways. In that respect, wrote Rhenanus, already a well-traveled man, his hometown resembled Holland, but "it could more readily be called a fortified camp than a town."[1]

Whether a firm fortification or a crowded town, Sélestat played a central role in Alsace as an imperial free city. Together with nine other towns, including Hagenau, Colmar, and Mulhouse, it formed the Decapolis, a federation of ten imperial towns intent on putting up at least token resistance to the powerful Alsatian territorial lords—the Duke of Lorraine, the Habsburgs, and the Bishop of Strasbourg. Although Hagenau, the residence of the imperial governor (*Vogt*), formally headed this federation, it was in Sélestat that all meetings of the Decapolis took place and that the federation archives were stored. Yet in difficult questions that went beyond specifically local concerns, the Decapolis tried to follow the course steered by Strasbourg, the powerful imperial city to the north.

Sélestat's population had reached four thousand by this time. Most of its inhabitants earned a living as farmers, particularly as winegrowers; the rest, as artisans. Shipping, which had thrived during the Middle Ages when the Ill was navigable as far upstream as Colmar, had declined at the beginning of the sixteenth century, and with it the transshipment port that had fueled Sélestat's rise to prosperity. The city now concentrated on its traditional role as a marketplace for the surrounding villages. It profited particularly from the enviable reputation of Alsatian wines throughout the entire Holy Roman Empire and beyond. Even in winegrowing regions elsewhere along the Rhine and Moselle valleys, in Franconia, or in Württemberg, the superior quality of Alsatian wine was beyond dispute. Traders traveled to Sélestat from far and wide, hoping to buy the prized wine at its source. Sales, however, began to stagnate at the turn of the century. A gradual change in taste was partly to blame. Greater difficulties, however, were posed by tariffs and duties that other cities, especially in the south, imposed in an effort to contain the flood of Alsatian imports. Towns like Sélestat that lay somewhat at the margins of Alsace's traditional winegrowing areas were hit especially hard. The "Oberpirger" wine of unparalleled quality grew elsewhere, between Thann and Colmar to the south. Increased demand had led to the expansion of viniculture toward the north, closer to Sélestat. But the "Niderpirger" produced here was not nearly as good. Poorer soil quality and adverse weather conditions led more often to failed vintages. Even though the negative effects of this long-term development were felt only gradually, by the end of the fifteenth century Sélestat's economy had clearly begun to stagnate.

Economic deterioration brought on social unrest, disturbances, and revolts, not only in the surrounding areas but in Sélestat itself.[2] In 1493, authorities uncovered and stifled a large-scale conspiracy that extended far beyond the city limits. It was triggered by a local economic crisis. Championing revolutionary demands, Hans Ulman, a member of the local patriciate, had succeeded in rallying impoverished masses under the banner of the *Bundschuh*, the peasant boot, which had come to symbolize the uprising. The episode was a signal of increasing social tensions in and around Sélestat. Discontent remained strong during the following decades, exploding finally in the Peasants' War of 1525.

The established order was beginning to crumble. A small class of merchants and wine dealers in Sélestat had achieved significant prosperity, yet many other townspeople struggled to survive. Social tensions grew into political discontent, for the patriciate held city government tightly in its grip. Eight mayors, or *Stadtmeister*, ruled the town hall, each of them governing for three months, assisted by seventeen councilmen, or *Ratsfreunde*. These twenty-five men constituted the town council and had the final say in Sélestat. To be sure, there were also fourteen guild masters, or *Zunftmeister*, elected to represent the fourteen artisan guilds of Sélestat. But the town council invited them to participate in its sessions only on selected occasions. The assembly of one hundred *Schöffen* appointed by the guilds was even less influential, convoked only in times of crisis.

As in other medieval towns, there was mandatory guild membership in Sélestat: burghers who wished to practice a trade had to seek membership in an artisan guild and pay the corresponding entrance fees and yearly membership dues. Journeymen and particularly apprentices were entirely under the authority of their master craftsman, in whose house they also lived. But the masters themselves fell into two categories, depending on whether they enjoyed full citizenship or were just *Soldner*, as Sélestat called its half-citizens. To be a full citizen who was eligible for a political office, one had to own a house with an adjoining courtyard or deposit an equivalent amount of money in the local bank. All master artisans, together with their employees, were responsible for defending the city and needed to possess weapons for this task. But the artisan guilds were more significant for the social and economic functions they fulfilled. They offered their members a certain degree of financial security in case of illness or invalidity. Most important, they regulated and controlled all aspects of production and trade in a very strict and precise way, and indirectly made it possible for the city council, which imposed innumerable regulations and ordinances of its own, to extend and enhance its control over the town.

The Church

Daily life in Sélestat, as in all other medieval towns, villages, and regions, was inconceivable without the church, which was intimately interwoven not only with the spiritual but also with the legal, political, and economic life of the town. Sélestat's very beginnings in the eighth century are inextricably connected with the Benedictine abbey of Sainte Foy (Saint Fides), around which the town grew and developed. For centuries the townspeople of Sélestat struggled for ecclesiastical independence and for the rights over the monastery, but they had to submit ultimately to the superior might of the Strasbourg bishop, who, along with the monastery and its extensive landed property, assumed the support of the abbot and his six monks. Only a couple streets away, north of the abbey, arose the impressive parish church of St. George, consecrated to the Virgin Mary since the Middle Ages. Its preachership was incorporated into the cathedral chapter of Strasbourg, giving this latter body the exclusive right to name the town pastor (*Rektor*) of Sélestat. In the immediate vicinity of St. George, toward the west and the north, not far from the city wall, were a number of church institutions charged with exacting the hated tithe from the laity: the tax offices of the local parish, the provost of Strasbourg cathedral, as well as the abbot of Hugshofen, all of which divided the fruit and wine tithe among themselves. But the abbey of Ebersmünster, the canonesses of Andlau, and the Hospitaller Order of St. John also had their own offices for the exaction of clerical taxes. It is not hard to believe one contemporary chronicler's report that there was "hardly a citizen" of Sélestat who was not financially liable to the church "in one way or another."[3]

Besides the Benedictines and the Hospitallers of St. John, mendicant orders such as the Franciscans and the Dominicans had their respective monasteries (the Dominicans a nunnery as well) in Sélestat, scattered along the southern half of the town in this order. Of these, only the Dominican convent has disappeared, its former plot now being partially taken up by the post office.

The list above gives us only an incomplete impression of the enormous swell of religious devotion that had late medieval Sélestat in its hold. Within its walls were also four Beguine convents, in each of which two to three unmarried or widowed women led a common life of prayer and meditation, according to the lay rule of St. Francis, but also took care of the sick and dying. Furthermore, beginning in the fifteenth century, lay confraternities proliferated. Their members rallied around a common patron saint, which they made the object of special devotion. The confraternity of St. Mary, or *Reidbruderschaft*, for example, committed itself to the veneration of Mary's immaculate conception, while the rosary confraternity, which developed in association with the Dominicans, made the recitation of the rosary prayer its special concern. Whereas these confraternities emphasized private spiritual edification, religious lay associations with a more communal dimension existed as well, such as guild confraternities, in which members of an artisan guild got together for religious and mutual aid purposes, worshiping a specific saint and maintaining his altar in the town church or in a monastery church but also attending to one another's temporal welfare. The winegrowers' patron was initially John the Evangelist, later John the Baptist. The guardian saints of the coopers were Simon and Jude. The larger guild confraternities did not provide an adequate framework for private piety, which increasingly found expression in smaller confraternities of journeymen of the same craft. The town council was understandably mistrustful of this process, given the prevailing social and political tensions.

Religion and the church were present everywhere and at every level. They imbued civic existence in its entirety and were, figuratively speaking, as indispensable and necessary as life-giving air. When the city gates were closed in the evening, one sang a "Salve Regina." If a storm was imminent, church bells were "rung against the tempest." Daily work, the year's seasons, special occasions in one's life, indeed all significant events in the town were intimately interwoven with the church and with the meaning it gave to life. Every church holiday celebration inevitably encompassed a communal celebration. Every communal feast was a church feast. The rhythms of the church were inseparable from the rhythms of life.

But precisely because popular piety was so vibrant and flourished in such diverse forms in Sélestat and elsewhere at the end of the Middle Ages, laypeople placed ever higher expectations on the church and its representatives. They wanted church leaders that actually lived in town, led morally exemplary lives, and were well trained in preaching and in pastoral care. While excoriating the clergy, the laity did not call into question the heart of church life, which was the Mass in all its forms, from the countless varieties of weekday votive masses to the elaborate ritual of the High Mass. The laity demanded of the clergy an intense and deep church life. This craving for a church that addressed laypeople's spiritual needs also manifested itself in reform movements of many kinds during the late Middle Ages, movements spearheaded by clergy and laypersons alike. In Sélestat these efforts aimed particularly at reforming the town parish.

Disenchantment with existing church structures, as diverse and widespread as it was, could be traced back to one root problem: the system of ecclesiastical benefices. Benefices, or prebends, were church positions financed by the revenue issuing from church property, including the numerous endowments laypeople had given to the church. Thus, church property in towns and villages produced income over which the respective town or village had no control, income that went directly to the holder of the benefice—usually a distant bishop, abbot, or cathedral chapter. The latter lived off of these benefices, in fact off of several of them at the same time, so that it was impossible for the absentee holders actually to fulfill their ecclesiastical duties at all these locations. They therefore would use part of their income to hire subordinate representatives such as "people's priests" (*Leutpriester*) or chaplains of even lower standing, most of whom were ill suited for performing church duties and could do little more than mumble their way through the Mass. And this was simply not enough for the increasingly articulate and pious laypeople in the towns and even in the villages.

The town minister position in Sélestat was, as already mentioned, financed by a benefice owned by the Strasbourg cathedral chapter. Toward the end of the fifteenth century, local townsmen were growing increasingly dissatisfied with the way Strasbourg was filling the position. They found the turnover exceedingly high and the pastors incompetent. There was a brief respite in lay complaints from 1492 to 1497, when Martin Ergersheim, the son of a prominent local family noted for his education and deep piety, held the *Leutpriester* position. But this only made tempers run all the higher when the cathedral chapter replaced him with an unsuitable candidate. The previous years had taught the laity that they did not have to take second-rate pastors for granted. The upper class of Sélestat burghers was, in fact, willing to invest a significant amount of money in obtaining the right to choose their own minister. They achieved a first breakthrough in 1503: the Strasbourg cathedral bowed to their demands, agreeing to receive the revenue of its benefice only if the newly elected pastor—unsurprisingly, it was Ergersheim—actually lived in Sélestat and carried out his pastoral obligations to everyone's full satisfaction. Martin Ergersheim certainly met the expectations of his supporters. He came from a respected Sélestat family, had studied at the famous local Latin school, and had a master's degree from the University of Heidelberg; he also could count on an important circle of humanist friends from which he picked his chaplains. Together with them, Ergersheim devoted an enormous amount of energy to his parish. He was known as an excellent and forceful preacher and as a devoted pastor. When he retired in 1518 on account of his age, the town council had by now almost exclusive say in the choice of his successor, who turned out to be another Sélestat native renowned for his scholarship and strong personal commitment: the Eichstätt preacher Dr. Paul Seidensticker (also known as Phrygio).

It turned out to be a much more difficult task to reform second-rank clerics—the so-called helpers, or chaplains. But also in this case, the deep religious longing of the laity and the determination of the council to obtain legal control over the local church complemented each other. The parish church presented no challenge in this respect: its three helpers were already appointed by the town minister. But at the beginning of the sixteenth century, Sélestat also had between thirteen and twenty other chaplains who lived off of the rapidly growing number of endowed Masses, yet, with one exception, none of them lived in town. Ergersheim, his colleagues, and the town council tried for years to reduce the endowments to six chaplainships, ensuring the respective chaplains a regular income, on the one hand, and giving the council important rights in the appointment of these positions, on the other. But it was not until more than ten years later, on May 16, 1521, that the town was able to achieve its aims, finally overcoming the resistance put up by the former benefice holders as well as by the Bishop of Strasbourg—and particularly the papal court in Rome.

The Latin School

The political self-confidence of its citizens, their deep religiosity, their determination to reform their church, and their openness to educational innovations all contributed toward creating a unique intellectual environment in Sélestat long before the end of the fifteenth century. At the heart of this environment lay Sélestat's prestigious Latin school.[4] The school's rise to fame began in 1441, when the council appointed Ludwig Dringenberg as a teacher—a Westphalian scholar deeply shaped by the piety and mysticism of the *devotio moderna*. One of the most significant and certainly the most famous of Dringenberg's pupils was Jacob Wimpfeling, who soon became a spokesman for a new kind of humanism. After Dringenberg died in 1477, Crato (Krafft) Hofmann carried on with his teaching. Among his former pupils could be counted the diplomats Jacob Villinger and Jacob Spiegel, the printer Matthias Schürer, the scholar Beatus Rhenanus, as well as Jerome Gebwiler, who led the Latin school from 1501 to 1509. After a one-year intermezzo with Oswald Baer from Brixen serving as head, Johannes Sapidus (Hans Witz) took over the school in 1510. This native Sélestatian, who had studied under Hofmann and Gebwiler, led the Latin school into a second golden age, with enrollment shooting up from 250 to over 900. Whereas the express goal of instruction had previously been to acquaint students thoroughly with the language and spirit of ancient Rome, Sapidus introduced modern trends, adding Greek language and literature to the curriculum. However, his support of the Reformation eventually cost him his position. The council fired him around the time the Peasants' Revolt was defeated, thus bringing one of the most splendid periods in the history of the school—indeed, of Sélestat itself—to an end.

All teachers of the Latin school, from Dringenberg to Gebwiler, imbued their students with a peculiar brand of humanism marked by unquestioned devotion to the church and a resolute commitment to ethics. School and church life were closely and conspicuously tied. In the first years of the sixteenth century, the town provided the Latin school with a new building located literally in the shadow of the church, with only a narrow alley separating the academy from the impressive west façade of St. George. This was no meaningless detail. The church relied on at least a small group of students to sing during High Mass every morning and to chant the "Salve Regina," as mentioned, every evening. Additionally, the students played an important role in Sunday-morning worship services. The teacher of the Latin school and his students came to church on Saturday evening to sing the vespers and to practice the liturgical songs for the following day. On Sunday morning the entire student body filed into the church and down the nave in a solemn procession and assembled in the choir. Many years later, Gebwiler still vividly remembered this as a stirring sight, declaring that "the town took special delight and pride in the students' singing in the choir on Sundays and holidays."[5] On Sunday evening they sang vespers at the same place. The students were also expected to sing during countless other church festivities, funerals, and commemorative Masses held for the dead on their respective anniversaries. Besides the salary he got from the town council, the school director received two and a half Rhenish guldens from the church for services performed—further evidence of the Latin school's strong links to the church.[6]

These external structures corresponded to inner attitudes. Wimpfeling, who influenced not only Gebwiler but also Martin Ergersheim, set forth his ideas on education in his book *Adolescentia* in 1510.[7] He aimed at nothing less than the renewal of the entire *corpus Christianum*, of Christian society. Ideas like those of Wimpfeling could also be found in the writings of other great Alsatians, for example, in the famous *Fools' Ship* (1494) by the Strasbourg civic secretary and municipal magistrate Sebastian Brant, or in the popular sermons of the fiery Strasbourg cathedral preacher Johann Geiler von Kaysersberg. They were all convinced of one thing: the renewal of society could be achieved only by training and bringing up new, better human beings. Pedagogy thus played a central role in their thought, and particularly in that of Wimpfeling. He was convinced that there could be no authentic ethical action without a purified and intensified personal piety. The priest had to teach exemplary moral conduct. Agreeing with the humanist consensus that the new "humanity" toward which they were aiming would express itself in a new and eloquent style, Wimpfeling attacked scholasticism and called for the study of Latin grammar and ancient rhetoric. He wanted young people to develop a taste for simplicity, authenticity, and practicality. He valued the classics only inasmuch as their study would supposedly usher in the anticipated Christian renewal. These ideas were not necessarily new. Indeed, Wimpfeling appealed over and over again to Petrarca and Gerson—although he read Petrarca selectively along moral lines and imbued Gerson with a generous dose of Alsatian conservatism. Nonetheless, Wimpfeling's unique ability to provide old texts with new relevance made him extraordinarily influential in the entire Upper Rhine Valley during the first two decades of the sixteenth century.

A further intellectual current complemented and enhanced the educational philosophy of the Sélestat school, shaping the thought of Jerome Gebwiler in a propitious way: the influence of the French humanist Jacques Lefèvre d'Etaples (Faber Stapulensis). Gebwiler became acquainted with Lefèvre during his study years in Paris, and the two soon became close friends. Gebwiler helped Lefèvre with his text editions and remained one of his most avid followers upon returning to Alsace. He also sent his most gifted students—among them Beatus Rhenanus, Sapidus, Michael Hummelberg of Ravensburg, and the sons of the Basel aristocrat Amerbach—on to Paris to study under Lefèvre. What did Gebwiler find so fascinating about this inquisitive seeker and incredibly well read scholar, who saw himself more as a philosopher than as a theologian? Both were deeply pious persons, and both believed that this piety had to express itself in practical deeds. Neoplatonist speculation played a key role in Lefèvre's thought, however, and not in Wimpfeling's. Lefèvre's conservative brand of humanism was far more sophisticated and multidimensional than Wimpfeling's simplistic moralism. As much as Lefèvre valued the study of language and the knowledge of grammar and rhetoric, what ultimately interested him was getting closer to finding the *one* truth underlying all those texts, but reflected only imperfectly and incompletely in them. For Lefèvre, the task of the humanist scholar thus took on an almost religious significance independent of its pedagogical usefulness. He never doubted that his brand of humanism was closely connected to the church. In fact, he was convinced that the humanist served the church, and indeed the entire world, by unveiling the plenitude and richness of Christian truth through his speculative work.

Jerome Gebwiler tried to introduce elements of Lefèvre's thought into his curriculum. In a pedagogical concept published later,[8] he distinguished three groups of students. First, there were those who were learning how to read and write—Latin, of course—as well as basic arithmetic. The next group studied the elements of Latin grammar and practiced reading simple authors such as Cato or Aesop. Gebwiler wished to go beyond that and also to acquaint students with etymology, syntax, as well as Latin verse and metric. The fundamental pedagogical innovation was reserved, however, for the third group: here Gebwiler wanted to introduce into the curriculum the *trivium*, usually taught at the beginning of university studies, and have the students learn rhetoric and dialectic, besides studying grammar and reading Latin texts as usual. Thus students practiced Latin style and composition, wrote Latin poetry, and were even encouraged to formulate elaborate letters modeled after those of Cicero, Pliny, or the Italian humanist Angelo Poliziano. Dialectic ultimately culminated in ethics. Students were to become more than experts in formal definition and abstract differentiation. They had to learn moral conduct—tangible, concrete behavior in accordance with ethical principles—in school. Therefore, after studying the fundamentals of Aristotle's *philosophia naturalis*, students examined his *philosophia moralis*.

What lasting effects did this educational philosophy have? Gebwiler wrote later in his Sélestat chronicle that many of his and his predecessors' students had learned the "basics of *grammatica*" in the Latin school.[9] While many of them probably did not learn much more than that, it is certainly possible that a few grasped quite a bit more and definitely grew in their learning.

This is the environment into which Martin Bucer was born and in which he was raised. This environment influenced him decisively, if not exclusively, for the first twenty-five years of his life.

Family Background and Early Childhood

There is not much we know about the Butzer[10] family. Is the "Claus Butzel" mentioned in a 1465 list of those paying the lowest taxes[11] an ancestor of Martin, perhaps even identical with his grandfather Claus Butzer? A certain Jörge Butzer is mentioned as a tenant in a 1474 contract reappraising the rent to be paid to the city hospital and poor asylum for a house located in the Schlangengasse.[12] Might this Jörge have been Claus's brother? In any case, Claus Butzer, who was registered in the citizenship list as a *Soldner* in 1480,[13] did live in this house, a rather elongated and narrow abode located at the western edge of town, not far from the city wall (on the street currently carrying the name of Impasse Plobmann but formerly called Butzengasse). Claus Butzer Jr., who himself was entered as a *Soldner* in the citizenship registry on January 16, 1487,[14] lived in his father's house together with his family. Later, his son Martin was born and grew up in this house.[15]

This information sheds light on the economic and legal status of the family. Claus Butzer Sr. and Jr. certainly did not enjoy full citizenship, being mere *Soldner*. They were coopers by trade, making the wooden casks and barrels in which the wine so essential to the region's livelihood was stored. Seen from a broader economic perspective, their profession was definitely a subsidiary one,[16] extremely sensitive to business cycles. Their income basically depended on the given level of wine production and sales, which was hard to foresee. Coopers belonged to the winegrowers' guild but did not carry much political weight within it, since wealthier winegrowers and dealers were also members. In other words, the Butzer family lived, and young Martin grew up, in rather pitiful economic conditions.

What would have been more understandable than to flee the town and seek one's fortune elsewhere? Martin's grandfather might well have attempted something like that.[17] We do know that his father left Sélestat in the 1490s, thus becoming "disloyal" (as his fellow citizens put it), since he moved away without renouncing his citizenship.[18] Where he went is not known. Whatever Martin's father attempted, he definitely did not succeed, for by the spring of 1501 he was back in town. His unlawful departure from Sélestat was forgiven and on June 22 he was readmitted into the winegrowers' guild. But by November 1501 he was gone once again, this time for good, heading off probably for Strasbourg and taking his wife, Martin's mother, with him. Strasbourg offered reasonable hope for further and more rapid advancement, being the center of Alsatian wine trade and allowing the coopers a guild of their own. To be sure, Claus's stay in Strasbourg is not documented until December 7, 1508, the day he was granted citizenship.[19] Claus died in Strasbourg in 1540, having spent the last years of his life in the city hospital, thanks to the mediation of his son, by then a prominent figure.[20] This information is not enough to prove that Claus Butzer was someone intent on climbing the social and economic ladder; the documented facts remain somewhat ambiguous. But if we also take into consideration the importance Claus placed on sending his son to the famous Sélestat Latin school, as well as the pains he must have taken to meet his son's insatiable demand for books,[21] we are justified in our impression that Claus worked hard to enable his son to fulfill ambitions and dreams that had never come true in his own life.

We unfortunately know nothing about Martin's mother. Bucer omits any mention of her. Her name was supposedly Eva, and tradition has it she worked as a midwife. But is it plausible that a job of such responsibility was entrusted to a woman who was apparently quite young and, besides, whose husband had abandoned the town illegally? Has she possibly been mistaken for Martin's grandmother? All we can say with certainty is that she died before her husband, for by 1538, Claus Butzer had remarried, taking Margaretha Windecker as his wife.[22]

Martin Bucer was born on the festivity of Saint Martin, November 11, and was probably baptized on the very same day, and christened according to medieval custom with the name of that day's saint.[23] It is generally assumed that 1491 was the year of his birth. There are no official records certifying this date, and Bucer himself does not confirm it anywhere. However, we do know with certainty that he entered his hometown's Dominican monastery when he was fifteen years of age, and the date of his entry can be deduced from other sources, so that the supposed year of birth is undoubtedly correct. What remains uncertain is whether Martin was his parents' first, their only, or their only surviving child.

While we have no irrefutable proof, it is more than probable that Martin Bucer attended the Sélestat Latin school.[24] School ordinances and later memoirs are not enough to reconstruct everyday life, but they do permit us to draw the following sketchy picture. It was the custom to enter school around the age of six or seven and to leave it by the time one was fifteen or sixteen.[25] In Alsace, classes usually began on Saint Gregory's day, March 13. Bucer was several months older than six by the springtime of 1498, so we can assume that he began to learn to read and write Latin at this time. It was not unusual for children of artisans to attend the Latin school.[26] Tuition was not exorbitant, and the school director occasionally reduced it for poor students.

We can only guess how quickly Bucer worked his way up from the lowest grade to the third, or highest, one. By the time he was admitted into this last group, it is certain that he had Jerome Gebwiler as his teacher, if not earlier. We also do not know whether Bucer already became acquainted at this time with people like Sapidus or Beatus Rhenanus, who later would be his close friends. We only know with certainty that Bucer's time at school was coming to an end in the summer of 1507. What had he gained from it? One thing is sure: not only was he able to read and even speak Latin fluently, but he was also capable of expressing himself with precision in this language. He had become familiar with the fundamental concepts of Aristotelian logic and the essential principles of this philosophical system. But most important, he had been influenced by a piety that expressed itself in practical terms and for which exemplary moral conduct was paramount. And all these elements were subsumed under a self-evident and emphatic commitment to the church. But what would the young Martin be able to do now? Which trade should he take on? At this time an event took place in the local Dominican monastery that soon had all Sélestat talking. And Martin's grandfather, Claus Butzer, who was watching over the youth's upbringing and education, reacted immediately.

The Dominicans

The Sélestat Monastery

The Order of Preachers (*Ordo Praedicatorum*), better known as Dominicans or Friars Preachers, came to Sélestat in 1282.[27] Before long, it gained a good reputation and even prospered financially. Of all the religious orders present in the city, it had the most impressive compound, in which one could find a stately 145-foot-long and 56-foot-wide church, several monastery buildings, and a vast garden extending along the Untermuhlbach, a branch of the Ill River. The Sélestat Dominicans owed their wealth to the many houses and the extensive landed property endowed to them particularly in the fourteenth century. In their church one could see the gravestones and epitaphs of the leading patrician families—the Wickersheims, the Müntzers, and the Botzheims—indicating which social class claimed a close allegiance to this order. As in many other medieval towns, the upper classes in Sélestat associated with the Dominicans, whereas the common people felt closer ties to the Franciscans.

The Sélestat Dominicans were not immune to the general decline all the mendicant orders experienced at the end of the fourteenth and throughout the fifteenth century. To be sure, the Observant movement, which sought to reform the order, had managed to get a foothold in Colmar, just south of Sélestat, already in 1389, and in 1464 the Dominican nuns of Sélestat joined the Observant reform. But the main Dominican monastery refused to submit, continuing with the "conventual" form of life that permitted a more liberal interpretation of the statutes requiring monastic seclusion as well as personal poverty. After the Dominican province of Teutonia split into two opposing groups, the Obervants and the Conventuals, during its chapter meeting in Colmar in 1464, it is no coincidence that the departing Conventuals continued their meeting in Sélestat.

It was the resolute Observant Vincent Bandelli who, as master general of the order, brought about the decisive turnaround. On May 18, 1505, he commissioned Petrus Siber, prior of the province, to reform the Sélestat monastery. He reiterated his command on June 10, 1507, thus finally

---

breaking the resistance of the Conventuals.[28] Monastic life was restructured according to Observant principles in the late summer or fall of 1507. It is reasonable to assume that the same procedure as elsewhere was followed, that is, a new prior and two monks from an Observant monastery were appointed to join the approximately nine monks already in Sélestat. It is possible that this new prior was Johannes Studach (or Studath) from the town of Guebwiller.[29]

Entering the Monastery

It was this event that drove the elder Butzer almost immediately, before the year 1507 was over,[30] to practically force his grandson into the Dominican order. At least, this is what Bucer reports sixteen years later.[31] Of course, we must consider the precise context in which he wrote his 1523 *Justification* (*Verantwortung*). Bucer had just abandoned the Dominican order and sought asylum in Strasbourg, asking the city council for protection. The city was in the midst of tremendous social and religious upheaval, and the council was trying to keep popular discontent toward the monasteries from getting out of control. It is unrealistic to expect that Bucer would—indeed, even could—give a fair presentation of his monastic past in such a situation. Hurting from personal accusations that supporters of the traditional church had launched against him, he bitingly attacked the institutions of the established church and did not even shrink from making the dubious denunciation that learning and scholarship were nowhere held in such low esteem as among the Dominicans!

We can safely assume that Bucer might have perceived things quite differently back in 1507. Unlike Luther, it was not grappling with religious questions that drove him into the monastery. We can also assume that his grandfather nudged him along this path. But then again, what choice did young Martin have? His family had not planned for him to learn a craft, which did not interest him to begin with. They lacked money for a university education. A further option was to become a priest, and Bucer's family might indeed have been intending this for some time. After all, sending a child to Latin school without further plans to continue on to university implied a future as a clergyman in store. Of course, this choice implied a very uncertain future, with the possibility of financial misery and social decline. Obtaining a well-paying pastorate position required a university degree or good social connections—it was even better to have both, as we saw in the case of Sélestat. If not, a clergyman was left to earn his livelihood as a "helper," in a poorly paid and not highly regarded chaplainship.

It is understandable that the elder Butzer, as he saw tremendous opportunities suddenly opening up in the Dominican monastery, could now allow himself to express open *abscheühen,* or loathing, toward secular priests. No longer forced to join the latter in their sad lot, young Martin was seemingly given the chance of a lifetime and admitted into the monastery. Furthermore, he was not required to give the monastery a significant endowment upon entry, as novices had had to do earlier.[32] Additionally, the earlier family dream that the boy would become a priest could still be fulfilled within the order. Finally, the Dominicans represented a possibility of social advancement that would have never been available to Martin elsewhere. To sum it up, their monastery symbolized what Claus Butzer described as *erbarkeit*—"respectability."

Upon admittance into the order, Bucer began a year as a novice. He received the tonsure and donned the white habit of the Dominicans, although without the scapular, the additional vestment worn over the chest and the back. The goal of this one-year probationary period was to acquaint the beginner with the monastic life in common, as well as with singing in a choir. The emphasis was on turning one's back to the world and devoting oneself to God completely. Before the year 1507 was over, Bucer was consecrated as an acolyte in the Strasbourg church of the Williamites (Hermits of Saint William of Maleval), thus receiving the lowest ecclesiastical orders, a prerequisite for theological studies.

In 1508 he professed the perpetually binding monastic vows of poverty, chastity, and obedience and became a Dominican monk in the full sense. Later, looking back, Bucer observed that he had had no other choice. But even his later negative perception of this event could not overshadow the deep impression that the monastic experience and its concentration on Mary, "the mother of God," made on him at that time. A huge painting of her could be seen at the Sélestat monastery. The representatives of the town's proud patrician class were portrayed humbly kneeling at her feet. The Dominican rule spoke of her as the special patron of the Order of Preachers, the only order that expressly bound itself to her through its vows. And the *Golden Legend,* a collection of saints' lives widespread throughout Europe, was full of miraculous stories reporting on how Mary had interceded before her stern Son on behalf of the Dominicans.[33] All this must have had a deep impact on a young man open to new ideas and impressions.

The Dominicans were a scholarly order. Their constitutions proclaimed study as one the principal aims of the order. This ideal was urged upon the monasteries again and again. But during a monk's first two years in a monastery, including the year as a novice, he was to practice only "piety, church services, and the reading of the Bible." If we apply this timetable to Bucer, this would mean that his superiors allowed him to begin the elementary study of philosophy in 1510. In this same year he was consecrated as a deacon—once again in Strasbourg, in the church of the Williamites.

Studies within the Order

It must be emphasized that we know very little about Bucer's time in the Sélestat monastery. By carefully studying the curricula of the Dominican order, the remnants of the library of the Sélestat Dominicans, and the list that Bucer made of his own books,[34] we can reconstruct his training very roughly. But even these little fragments of surviving evidence give a surprisingly clear reflection of the intellectual and spiritual atmosphere in which he lived and worked.

The elementary study of philosophy aimed at acquainting students thoroughly with Aristotle's thought, which constituted the very foundation of scholasticism. The great philosopher's writings were read in two consecutive programs of study, each of which concluded with an exam. First of all, his writings on logic, primarily the *Organon*, were studied. This *studium logicale*, according to the rules of the Dominican order, lasted three years. It was followed by the study of Aristotle's writings on natural science, in the course of which his ethics and metaphysics were also read. The normal length of this *studium naturalium* was two years. We can assume that Bucer took part in these programs of study from 1510 to 1514.

Two books from the Sélestat monastery library that Bucer took with him to Heidelberg convey more precisely the intellectual character of his introduction to the Greek philosopher: they were the best and most modern editions of Aristotle's works available at that time, compiled and commented on by Lefèvre d'Etaples and his student Jodocus Clichthoveus. Bucer also owned personal copies of Lefèvre's commentary edition of the *Nicomachean Ethics* as well as Aristotle's *On the Soul* (*De anima*) and his *Metaphysics*, both with the annotations of Thomas Aquinas. It is obvious that Bucer, even as a Dominican, still had strong intellectual bonds to the Sélestat Latin school.

The Order of Preachers commonly sent monks who had just completed their introductory studies to another cloister for a year. This was to ensure the best possible training, for not all monasteries counted adequate teachers in all areas. We do not know if the Sélestat monastery also took part in this custom; but we do know that Bucer visited Heidelberg and Mainz in the next period of his theological studies, as he recounts later.[35]

The detailed curricula of the Dominican order saw the study of Aristotle not as an end in itself but rather as an ancillary means leading up to and culminating in the actual study of theology.[36] The latter began with two years of elementary courses. During this time, budding Dominican scholars took a one-year lecture course on selected texts of the Old and New Testaments, followed by a survey course of the same duration on the *Sentences* of Peter Lombard—the fundamental medieval handbook of dogmatics. We do not know which commentaries students were encouraged to read along with these lectures. In any case, Bucer is probably referring to these two years of elementary theological work when he reports having studied in Heidelberg and Mainz. This would imply that he did biblical studies in Heidelberg in 1515 and took the survey course in dogmatics in Mainz in 1516. This assumption fits in well with the indisputable fact that Bucer was ordained a priest in Mainz. We do not know the exact day or year of this event, but he would have attained the minimum age prescribed by canon law for ordination to the priesthood by the fall of 1516, when he turned twenty-five. Even though exemptions from this requirement could be granted, particularly to the Dominican order, Bucer's ordination to the priesthood in Mainz can be most reasonably explained if we assume it took place while studying theology there.

If Bucer studied in the university towns of Heidelberg and Mainz, this does not mean he actually took university courses there. The Order of Preachers had self-contained study programs in the Heidelberg and Mainz monasteries, which gave its monks theological training provided by Dominican teaching staff within cloister walls. The degree to which Bucer might have had extramural academic contacts is unknown; it is certainly not implausible. For Bucer to have taken up theological studies immediately after completing his introduction to philosophy was at odds with a stipulation in the Dominican rule requiring monks to take a two- to three-year break between both study programs, during which they were to teach philosophy in a monastery. We can only guess the reasons for Bucer's brisk academic career. The mentioned ordinance might have been often circumvented, but it is just as possible that Bucer's superiors deliberately promoted his advancement. A further event bolsters the latter assumption: the chapter of the Dominican province of Teutonia elected Eberhard of Cleves as its new prior provincial during a meeting in Sélestat on August 15, 1515. Eberhard was more than an avid supporter of the

Observant movement; he was also the prior of the Heidelberg monastery and had been directly responsible several times for its study program, which aimed at grooming the intellectual leaders of the Dominican order. As an Observant, Eberhard of Cleves was interesting in recruiting as many gifted monks as possible and making of them priors, teachers, and professors intellectually qualified to take on the opponents of the Observant movement. The Conventuals had plans of their own to establish a *studium generale*, or house of higher studies, with a markedly modern, humanistic curriculum. What would have been more obvious than for the Observants to intensify their efforts to create their own intellectual elite, in order to spread the Observant cause throughout the province's monasteries and institutions of learning?

Whether this development influenced Bucer's academic path or not, in January 1517 we find him in the *studium generale* of the Dominicans in Heidelberg, well on his way toward obtaining a doctorate in theology—the highest academic degree of this period, granting him the right to teach in the theological faculty of a university.

The World of Humanism

Bucer did not spend time only on theology during these years in the monastery. About half his library, to be sure, as shown by 1518 inventory of his books, did consist of theological and philosophical works representing the thought of the great Dominican teacher Thomas Aquinas. But the other half of his collection covered rhetoric, history, grammar, as well as poetry, and thus was humanistic in the broadest sense.

This tension between scholasticism and humanism—or, more exactly, between Thomistic scholastic theology and an Alsatian humanism heavily influenced by Erasmus, and in which not only Bucer took part—cannot be resolved at the expense of one or the other. The tendency of scholarship to present them as mutually exclusive alternatives has no basis in the facts. Bucer's library is proof of this. A somewhat thin but very illuminating volume by Heinrich Bebel with the title *A Little Book on the Education of Youth*[37] is helpful in identifying the principle under which Bucer put his library together in the years 1515 and 1516. Bucer did not own the book, but the Sélestat monastery library had a copy. Bebel had been a professor of rhetoric and poetry at the University of Tübingen since 1497 and had been crowned poet laureate by the emperor Maximilian in 1501. He wrote his little book as a guide to those convinced of the importance of rhetoric but unsure which ancient authors they should read to achieve authentic eloquence. Of course, it was not the minister's job to preach grammar instead of the gospel from the pulpit, acknowledged Bebel. But the opposite was equally true: without a thorough training in rhetoric, which for Bebel included not just Wimpfeling's limited canon but ancient Latin literature in its entirety, there could be no meaningful scholarship of any kind.

Without having to go into details,[38] we can safely assert that Bucer acquired an astonishingly high proportion of the works recommended by Bebel. If we also include Lefèvre's modern Aristotle editions, mentioned previously, from the Sélestat monastery library—in which one could also find Poliziano's *Centuries* and a Greek dictionary—we have evidence enough, even on the basis of these pitiful remnants of a once huge library, that the Dominicans kept abreast of the high scholarship of the prestigious Latin school of the town.

Furthermore, Bucer's own development within this humanistic environment is worth examining more closely. Unquestionably, Bucer's older and much admired friends Beatus Rhenanus and especially Sapidus contributed significantly to his humanistic evolution. A similar process can be observed in Matthias Schürer's publishing program, from which Bucer bought many of his books. It is an uncontested conclusion that no one contributed more to the dissemination of humanism in Alsace than this Strasbourg printer.[39] The list of his publications allows us to trace the development of humanism from the initial predominance of Wimpfeling to the eventual supremacy of Erasmus. Bucer's own intellectual trajectory was paradoxically in some ways more progressive, but in others more conservative, than the route staked out by Bebel and Schürer. He was going beyond Bebel's list of recommended readings when he obtained Erasmus's *Praise of Folly* (*Encomium moriae*), and particularly when he bought the widely circulated Neoplatonist treatise *On the Divine Names* (*De divinis nominibus*) by Pseudo-Dionysius the Areopagite, edited and interpreted by Marsilio Ficino. Even more significant are the Schürer imprints that Bucer did *not* buy: neither Gerson nor Geiler von Kaysersberg, and not even the works of the patriarch of Alsatian humanism, Jacob Wimpfeling. Bucer was thus in accord with modern tendencies in German humanism that were pushing for a comprehensively new approach to tradition, though remaining within the boundaries placed by university and church institutions. In one respect, however, Bucer lagged behind. We do not find in him any trace of the widespread call to return to the church fathers, a call even echoed by Bebel. With the exception of Lactantius, who was admired more as a stylist than as a theologian, Bucer did not own a single copy of their works. This is clear proof of the unquestioned sway that the medieval tradition, particularly in the shape of Thomistic theology, still held over him.

The books that Bucer bought after 1516 show that he was becoming increasingly fascinated with the thought of Erasmus of Rotterdam. A new dimension of humanism was dawning upon him. But this development belongs more properly in his Heidelberg period.

Chapter Two

Between Erasmus and Luther

Heidelberg

A Student in Dominican Schools

In January 1517, Bucer returned to Heidelberg,[1] a city similar in many ways to Mainz, where he had just spent a year. Both were university towns. Each was home to a territorial prince respected and influential within the Holy Roman Empire—on the one side, a prelate, the prince-archbishop of Mainz; on the other, a secular prince, the elector Palatine. And each city not only lay at a crossroads of trade but also was a lively intellectual and political center in its own right in the midst of early modern Germany's pulsating heart.

At this time, Heidelberg had a population of about five thousand. The elector Palatine appointed the city's mayor (*Stadtschultheiss*), who wielded authority over a city council responsible for those inhabitants belonging neither to the elector's administrative staff nor to the university. This segment of the population included mostly artisans, fishermen, winegrowers, and small traders. Large-scale commerce was unknown, since craftsmen produced only for the local market. In terms of wealth and social status, the fishermen ranked above the numerous, mostly poor winegrowers, whose vineyards dotted the surrounding hillsides that today are covered by forests. The elector Palatine's court set the tone for the city. One-fourth of Heidelberg's inhabitants worked for the prince elector, from numerous noblemen and officials down to simple secretaries and domestic servants. The nobility's countless courts and palaces formed a prominent part of the city. The elector's civil servants and officials constituted a self-contained milieu with its own internal social order and jurisdiction.

21

Bucer had little to do with this side of Heidelberg, except for a few personal acquaintances among like-minded churchmen. We have no idea if he took notice of work on the fortification and embellishment of the now-famous Heidelberg Castle, which began in 1504. Bucer was at home in another world: that of the university, which also had a social order of its own and its own law court. Founded in 1386, and therefore constituting the oldest university in Germany, it had about six hundred students at the time. The prince elector had aimed to attract many different constituencies to the university and therefore made it a matter of principle that the two opposing movements of scholasticism be represented in the teaching body: the prevailing school of Nominalism, also known as *via moderna*, and the school of Thomism, or *via antiqua*, in which Bucer was being trained.

Bucer's superiors in the Dominican order sent him to Heidelberg, where he enrolled in January of 1517, primarily for the purpose of obtaining a university degree.[2] Such a degree was generally not required for teaching within a monastic order, and this was the case for the Dominicans. All that counted in the orders were internal exams and degrees that ultimately qualified one for admission to the institutions of higher learning known as *studia generalia*. However, an academic degree was necessary in order to assume one of the many university professorships that the mendicant orders started holding by the end of the Middle Ages. This led many territorial princes formally to incorporate monastic institutions of learning into the theological faculties of universities. This arrangement had advantages for both parties. Members of the mendicant orders could conveniently complete their doctoral studies in the same town in which their monastery and house of studies were located; the territorial prince could save the costs of one or several professorships, now assumed by the monastic order in question. In the case of Heidelberg, Elector Frederick I obtained permission from Pope Sixtus IV in 1473 to incorporate the Dominican monastery, not founded until 1476, into the university. This meant that Bucer was, on the one hand, formally a university student, subject to the institution's regulations, including its law courts, but on the other also a member of the internal house of studies, or *studium generale*, of his order, bound to its precise stipulations. The freedom to choose courses as one pleases and follow one's interests that a student of the humanities enjoys in German universities today was completely unknown to Bucer and his contemporaries. Training in all faculties followed an inflexible curriculum.

Bucer was enrolled on January 31, 1517, and as a Dominican was exempt from matriculation fees. Being a monk conferred on him further special rights. For example, in cases of minor misdemeanors he was not subject to the jurisdiction of the university rector but answerable only to the prior of the Dominican monastery. Most significantly, his matriculation made him officially a member of the teaching body of the university. This illustrates the special consequences that matriculation had for a member of a monastic order, on the one hand, and the essence of university study of theology in the Middle Ages, on the other. The university was training not future pastors but future scholars.

A secular clergyman would have needed to complete elementary studies in philosophy and obtain a master of arts, and after that attend five years of theological lectures, before attaining the *baccalaureus cursor* degree that would allow him to continue his studies and begin giving his own lectures on selected passages of Scripture at the same time. But Bucer had these qualifications already at the time of his enrollment. It was assumed that a monk sent to the theological faculty by his superiors had already completed elementary philosophical and theological studies within his own order.

Bucer's further training at Heidelberg was characterized by the combination of study and teaching typical of medieval universities. As a *cursor biblicus*, he was expected to lecture on 160 chapters of the Old and New Testaments in the space of two years—not an in-depth course but rather a survey lecture. The theological faculty specified the biblical passages he should expound, reminding him that he should not cover more than one chapter in a lecture. It is quite possible that Bucer began his teaching immediately after enrollment, which means he would have obtained the lowest theological degree of a *baccalaureus biblicus* by the end of 1518 or in the first months of 1519, probably upon passing an examination.

At the same time, Bucer was expected to attend lectures and take part in disputations within the *studium generale* of the Heidelberg Dominicans. The Dominican monastery in which he lived and worked was on the western outskirts of town, in a neighborhood sparsely populated by peasants and winegrowers. Their simple dwellings were dwarfed by the stately compound of the Dominicans, which included a church, cloister buildings, and a large garden. The monastery grounds abutted directly upon what today is Heidelberg's pedestrian Hauptstrasse, not far from the town's Speyer Gate (today near the Bismarckplatz). The monastery and its church were razed in the early 1860s and replaced with buildings (*Friedrichsbau, Alte Anatomie*) that today house the University of Heidelberg's Psychological Institute.[3] Life for members of the Dominican house of studies was regulated by statutes enacted in 1501. They provided that students be dispensed from choir obligations and the singing of canonical hours so that they might devote themselves exclusively to their studies.

However, taking part in the office for the mother of God, matins, and the daily Mass of the monastery remained compulsory. In addition, *studium generale* enrollees were required to take turns for a week at a time holding the first Mass in the chapel of the deceased Palatine countess (*Pfalzgräfin*) Margaretha, thus expressing the order's gratitude to the family of the prince elector for its generous financial support.

House of study members were also expected to sing the canonical hours on important church feasts as well as on the feasts of the patron saints of the order and of the Heidelberg cloister, which were Saint Anne, Saint Wendelin, and Saint Sebastian.

Bucer studied in this monastic and church-related setting. Students' primary academic duty was to attend the lectures of the *studium generale*'s director, which took place on all weekdays, except for brief breaks at Easter, during the grape harvest in the fall, and at Christmas. Michael Vehe, who had a doctorate in theology from the University of Heidelberg, led the *studium generale* beginning in 1515. In 1520 he additionally assumed a professorship at the university. Besides the daily lectures there were disputations every other day, during which one of the students—they took turns at this, in order of admittance to the *studium generale*—fulfilled the function of the *respondens*. The student who had joined the *studium generale* most recently also had special obligations of his own. We can imagine Bucer in this function, signaling the beginning of the lecture by ringing a bell three times, placing the opened book on the lectern for *regens* Vehe, removing it after the lecture, ringing the bell two times to call on the *sententiarius* to begin with his survey lecture on the *Sentences* of Peter Lombard, and finally indicating the beginning of a disputation also with two peals of the bell.

Bucer also had obligations teaching elementary philosophy courses within the Dominican order. We do not know which texts of Aristotle he discussed and which commentaries he used. But his 1518 book inventory[4] does help define with a certain degree of accuracy the intellectual world in which he felt at home during these years of theological study.

Theological Profile

It is natural to assume that Bucer would have owned several books by Thomas Aquinas, the great teacher of the Dominican order. How many books by Aquinas Bucer actually possessed, however, is astonishing: Bucer owned all of Aquinas's most important works, with the exception of his biblical commentaries. Furthermore, Bucer's other theological books stood squarely in the Thomistic tradition and included works such as Cajetan's treatise on Thomas's *Summa theologica*, Peter Paludanus's commentary on the fourth book of the *Sentences*, Paulus Barbus's (Soncinas's) *Metaphysics*, and Peter Crockaert's (Petrus Bruxellensis's) commentaries on Aristotle, Petrus Hispanus, and Thomas Aquinas. Bucer's studies at the Heidelberg *studium generale* were thus deeply rooted in the Thomistic school.

At the same time, Bucer was becoming increasingly influenced by the writings of Erasmus. His fascination with the great Dutch humanist may have already begun in Mainz in 1516. In Heidelberg, it clearly grew. Bucer's book list shows that he owned Erasmus's most important writings, such as the *Praise of Folly* (*Encomium Moriae*), which he might have acquired at an earlier time; Erasmus's edition of the Greek New Testament with his *Annotations*; the Dutch humanist's paraphrase of the letter to the Romans; his *Handbook of a Christian Soldier* (*Enchiridion militis christiani*); his *Complaint of Peace* (*Querela pacis*); the *Education of a Christian Prince* (*Institutio principis christiani*); an edition of his letters; as well as his *Defense against Jacques Lefèvre d'Etaples* (*Apologia ad Jacobum Fabrum Stapulensem*). In a parallel development, Bucer started buying books issuing from the printing press of Erasmus's publisher, Johannes Froben in Basel, in a clear shift of preference away from the Strasbourg printer Matthias Schürer. In a letter to his mentor Beatus Rhenanus in March 1520, Bucer wrote tongue-in-cheek that he was scraping money together by "guile and tricks" to buy all of Erasmus's works.[5]

What moved and excited Bucer so much about Erasmus's writings?[6] In part, it was certainly his brilliant style as well as the wealth of literary forms and aesthetically sophisticated figures of speech he used. More important for Bucer, Erasmus gave expression to the synthesis of Christianity and learning so typical of the new form of humanism. He criticized the church's obsession with externals and particularly a smug, complacent theology that had grown hollow and wasted time with sterile, hairsplitting sophistry, detrimental to both learning and piety. Erasmus also mocked ill-educated monks and their barbaric Latin. The basis of this criticism was, however, a positive vision of renewal that he summed up with the concept of "Christian philosophy" (*philosophia christiana*), a term that Bucer began using as well. It described a Christian way of life open to laypeople as well as clergymen, revolving around things quite simple and plain: following Christ in a life of piety, humility, peace, and love for one's fellow man. This faith turned its back on external church rituals and founded itself on the spirit of the Bible, thus giving the Christian more freedom and individual responsibility. It was a form of Christianity compatible with the vigorous learning and culture of this period and that did justice to the growing self-assertiveness of townspeople. These ideas put forth by Erasmus were indeed revolutionary, but the Dutch humanist was thinking of a gentle revolution that would succeed not through force but by intensified education as well as through ideas and books.

Much later in life, Bucer summed up what he had learned from Erasmus. In his eyes, the great humanist had swept away meaningless religious ceremonies with his linguistic eloquence and cogent reasoning, replacing them with simple faith in Christ. Erasmus had made clear that all that counts is obeying God's commandments, the content and aim of which is our neighbor's well-being. Finally, Erasmus restored the Bible and the church fathers to their deserved position in the center of Christianity.[7] Bucer's list reflects Erasmus's own intentions quite accurately. There can be no doubt that the young Dominican experienced Erasmus's thought as a sweeping liberation, and it is understandable that he became his avid follower and disciple.

But how could Bucer endorse these new convictions and still remain a Dominican monk, living in a monastery and studying scholastic theology? We will later see how Bucer settled this issue. For the time being, he found solace in the *Letter to Paul Volz* (*Epistola ad Paulum Volzium*) with which Erasmus prefaced the new edition of his *Enchiridion*. In it Erasmus acclaims the abbot of Hugshofen as a true monk *and* a true Christian. According to Erasmus, one could indeed live a life of scholarship and piety in a monastery, as long as one kept one's eyes set on things ultimate and did not cling to externals. It is also important to point out that Bucer lived in a monastery whose superiors were influenced by the spirit of Erasmus, or at least did not actively oppose it. In September 1518, Bucer wrote to Beatus Rhenanus that his prior, Bernhard Senger, who had lived in Basel, gave him his wholehearted support, and that the *regens* of the convent, D. Michael Vehe, at least had nothing against his lecturing the monks on Erasmus's *Praise of Folly* and *Complaint of Peace*.[8] Senger was also allowing him to perfect his knowledge of Greek under Johannes Brenz, to whom he went every other day in order to read Plato's *Symposium* in a small group. Another superior who was apparently influenced by the spirit of humanism was prior provincial Eberhard of Cleves.[9] Bucer could therefore cheerfully declare to Rhenanus that he did not care one bit what those fellow Dominicans completely opposed to humanism were thinking of him!

When Martin Luther came to Heidelberg in April 1518 to hold his famous disputation—the occasion on which he met Bucer—he stepped into the world of Erasmian humanism described above.[10] The vicar general of the Observant Augustinian Hermits, Johannes von Staupitz, had invited Luther to present his theology for discussion during a meeting of the general chapter of the order. The disputation took place on April 26 in the building of the arts faculty (*Schola artistarum*, to the east of the current Augustinergasse), in the immediate vicinity of the Augustinian monastery (today the location of the Universitätsplatz, between the "Old" and the "New" University). Representatives of the arts and theology faculties were present, as well as countless younger faculty and students who would later play a crucial role in spreading and establishing the Reformation in southern Germany, such as Martin Frecht, Theobald Billican, Johannes Brenz, possibly Erhard Schnepf as well—and of course Martin Bucer.

In a long letter to Beatus Rhenanus, Bucer excitedly recounted what he had seen and heard during the disputation, and what he had learned in a further personal conversation with Luther on April 27—"you know, the one who's been battering away at the indulgences, a problem we've dealt with far too little." Mixing report with interpretation, Bucer commented in detail on the first thirteen theses of the Wittenberg theologian, briefly mentioned the following three, and closed with a succinct discussion of the twenty-fifth thesis. Whether or not Bucer's letter accurately documents the disputation, which would imply that Luther's twelve philosophical theses against Aristotelianism had not been discussed, remains to be decided.

In twenty-eight skillfully arranged theological theses, Luther asserted man's incapacity to do good, denied free will, set forth a new understanding of theology based on the cross, and proclaimed salvation by faith in Christ alone. The pillars of his argumentation were theses 1 and 25: "God's law, that most salutary, life-giving teaching, is incapable of advancing man towards justice; on the contrary it hinders him"; "Not he is just who does many works, but rather he who without works believes much in Christ." He thus provided the basics of Reformation theology in outline: people are not justified in God's eyes through their works, but rather God justifies them by faith alone, that is, by trust put solely in Christ.

When reporting on Luther's "paradoxes," as he called them, Bucer took special interest in theses 1 and 25. He placed the greatest emphasis, however, on the first thesis. As far as the twenty-fifth thesis was concerned, Bucer stressed that human works were by no means being rejected, only trust in human works, since faith alone justifies. Although Luther had also affirmed this,[11] his primary emphasis lay on faith itself, from which the Christian's good works would follow. Initial differences were therefore beginning to emerge. Whereas Luther's theology was overwhelmingly based on faith in Christ, a faith that subsumed everything else, Bucer placed paramount importance on the ethical conduct that resulted from Christian faith. In this emphasis on the shape of Christian existence in the world lies the unmistakable legacy of Alsatian and Erasmian humanism.

Theological differences in the interpretation of law, that is, of the first thesis, are even sharper. Both Luther and Bucer agreed that God's law epitomized his holy and unconditionally binding will. Humans are incapable of meeting God's expectations. God's law therefore reveals our status in God's presence, said Luther, that is, our status as sinners. God's law makes our failure all the more obvious, crushes us and humiliates us before God, turning us into human beings completely dependent on God. If we deny this and succumb to the illusion of pleasing God with our works, we are actually turning away from God, since we are not letting go of ourselves but are rather trusting in our own capabilities and merits when relating to God. God's law is therefore a permanent accuser, driving humans away from themselves, leading them to trust only in God, who has revealed his love and forgiveness in Jesus Christ.

Bucer absorbed everything Luther said on human sinfulness, on human failure to fulfill God's law, and on the impossibility of becoming justified through works. He agreed entirely with Luther that Christians must place their trust solely in Christ, not in their own deeds and accomplishments. But Bucer was driving at a much broader understanding of law. God certainly accuses us and convicts us of our sins, but we have to go beyond this understanding of God's law, which remains external and foreign to us human beings. Christians, however, relate to God's law in a new way: they consent to it in their hearts and are moved by the Holy Spirit to live and behave according to it. Borrowing from Aristotle, Bucer described the way the law works in Christians as *Entelechia*, as an active and effective energy.[12] This was a crucial point for Bucer, for at this point in his letter to Rhenanus a cascade of concepts gushes out of his pen: God's law is *lex spiritus*, for the Holy Spirit rules us according to it; it is a *lex gratiae*, the law by which God's grace is active. Bucer expounded as well on the fruits of grace (*gratia*) and of faith (*fides*), on the law that pushes us toward life (*lex vitae*) and that makes all things new (*nova lex*).

Bucer's theological reasoning was unmistakably influenced by Erasmus, but in it we also find elements of Thomas Aquinas. He was thus no *tabula rasa* upon encountering Luther but interpreted the Wittenberg theologian according to his own background and theological agenda. Certainly, one reason Bucer was fascinated by Luther was quite simply the Witten-

berg Reformer's headstrong personality. But, as Bucer expressly emphasized, he was also attracted by the far-reaching agreement he perceived
between Luther's and Erasmus's ideas.[13] By this he probably meant their
joint recourse to the Bible and the church fathers, their christocentrism,
their emphasis on faith and a life lived according to faith. Bucer did see
the differences too. Luther impressed him as being more open and out-
spoken than Erasmus and certainly appeared to be theologically more radical, in fact, revolutionary. Opening the doors to Luther's ideas brought
into question—indeed, jeopardized—much more than just church ceremonies. Bucer understood this clearly and realized the far-reaching implications his encounter with Luther would have for himself; he therefore
implored Rhenanus not to let his disputation report fall into the wrong
hands. Bucer was at a crossroads, and sensing this, on April 30, 1518, he
formally drew up a will in the form of an inventory of all his books.

By the end of 1518 or beginning of 1519, Bucer obtained the degree of
a *baccalaureus biblicus*. The statutes of the theological faculty freed him from
teaching duties for one year so that he could prepare his two-year lecture
course on the *Sentences* of Peter Lombard by assiduously studying various
theological commentaries and *summae*. Bucer's theological views matured
further during this time. He expressed them publicly for the first time in
the summer of 1519, during a disputation of the theological faculty. It was
customary to hold one disputation a week during the summer academic
break between July 7 and September 8. A *sententiarius* or a *baccalaureus* usually drafted the theses to be disputed. One of these disputations, which
Bucer led and in which Theobald Billican acted as respondent, almost
ended in turmoil.[14] The bone of contention was Bucer's thesis that our fellow humans provide structure and orientation for our love of God (*chari-
tas ordinata a proximo*). At first sight mere scholastic hairsplitting, this was
actually an explosive issue, because it dealt a blow to a principle of scholasticism and constituted a frontal attack against the paradigmatic teacher of
the Preachers' Order, Thomas Aquinas.

Bucer's theses have not survived, but we can retrace them roughly. At
the start of the disputation Bucer was asked whether he was referring to
Christians' ethical obligations toward their fellow humans. This would
have agreed fully with ancient Christian tradition and was a point Erasmus
had underscored as well in his *Enchiridion*: Christians do not just live for
themselves but are to give themselves to God and neighbor.[15] But Bucer
aimed at more. He wanted to define the relationship between love of God
and love of one's fellow humans more precisely, reaching the bold conclusion that even if loving God was not the same as loving one's neighbor, the

two were practically coterminous. Bucer began with the presupposition that God commanded us to love our neighbors and that the person of whom Christ has taken possession is a new creation. Christians are so attached to God through Christ that they only see their neighbors and no longer themselves. They are now capable of truly loving their fellow human beings and are freed from having to pursue their own interests.

These reflections reveal that Bucer was indebted to Luther, but also that he had reached his own interpretation of Luther's Heidelberg theses. His differing understanding of God's law is once again evident. But it is also clear that he rejected all human efforts to influence God. When Bucer's fellow disputants argued in reply that we have to be concerned about our own salvation and—since all human abilities grow out of God's grace—love ourselves first, he dismissed this as the fundamental error of works righteousness and therefore a sin. Although Bucer was somewhat eclectic and vague in his procedure, at least the hint of a conflict with Thomas Aquinas was brewing. Thomas's theology centered on God's love for his creation and, in particular, for man. The greatest Christian virtue, love, could only be man's response to God's preceding, all-embracing love. Bucer agreed fully. In fact, he began with this same premise. But where Thomas connects love of God with love of self, Bucer diverged. Thomas, of course, did not mean selfishness or egocentrism. He wanted Christians to understand and accept themselves, along with their entire surrounding reality, as being loved by God. This implied that in loving themselves and this reality they were, in a way, loving God. But for Bucer this left human sinfulness out of account. According to Bucer, human beings, including Christians, were simply incapable of not perverting this kind of love into self-love. For this reason, Bucer insisted that God calls Christians away from themselves toward unconditional commitment to the other, to their fellow human beings.

Bucer was enormously pleased when he found these ideas confirmed in Luther's Galatians commentary, which he read for the first time at the beginning of 1520. In this commentary, Luther had attempted to develop his Reformation theology using humanistic language and reasoning. Correspondingly, he emphasized Christian freedom and loving one's fellow human beings. According to the Wittenberg theologian, the person who trusts in Christ is freed from the selfish need to assert his own merits when relating to God. Forgetting himself, he can concentrate fully on his fellow human beings and their needs. This love is concrete and down-to-earth, because human beings are truly accepted by God through faith in Christ and are therefore completely freed from any need to please God through actions. If we try to complement this path to salvation chosen by God by making additional demands on human beings, we entirely miss the mark.

But Bucer did place an idiosyncratic emphasis of his own by expressly discussing love of one's neighbor as an expression of Christian existence. Luther was much more cautious. He preferred to develop this idea from a christological perspective: Christ—and not man—reveals the gifts God has given us. If Luther emphasized the unsurpassed importance of the sinner's justification by God, Bucer stressed the intimate connection between justification and the gift of an ethically renewed better life all the more. It is for this reason that he perceived and developed theology as ethics. This remained a guiding principle of his thought and action from this time on.

Leaving the Order

At the same time that Bucer wrestled with these issues, storm clouds were gathering on the horizon of world and church politics. Even if little more than rumors reached Bucer's ears, it was unmistakably clear that the Reformation's opponents were assembling their forces. The legal proceedings against Luther on account of supposed heresy were being resumed in Rome, and the Reuchlin dispute was taking on a new dimension. This latter conflict affected Bucer directly, for the Cologne Dominicans under the leadership of the prior and grand inquisitor Jacob of Hoogstraten were at odds not just with Reuchlin but with the entire company of humanistic scholars.[16] They had made Reuchlin's cause their own, not necessarily out of sympathy for his theological and philosophical views but because they felt scholarship and learning themselves were at stake.

At this point, the knight and humanist Ulrich von Hutten managed to convince the powerful imperial knight Franz von Sickingen to begin a formal feud with the Dominican order on July 26, 1519, threatening to destroy Dominican monasteries if Hoogstraten did not cease the proceedings and assume Reuchlin's legal expenses in the amount of 111 Rhenish guldens. Sickingen, who had far-reaching political aims, did not care that much about Reuchlin but was certainly keen on winning the support of the humanists. After all, they did dominate public opinion at this time, before the much broader and more tumultuous wave of approval for Luther would sweep through Germany. Negotiations took place between Sickingen and the Dominicans, in which the prior provincial as well as the director of the Heidelberg house of studies played important roles. Finally, the decision was made in the provincial chapter meeting in Frankfurt at the beginning of May 1520 to ask the pope to revoke the condemnation of Reuchlin and to impose silence on both parties of the conflict. In addition, the chapter deposed Hoogstraten as inquisitor and prior.

In the meantime, however, Rome had become convinced, not least on the basis of what the humanists were loudly proclaiming, that Luther and Reuchlin were birds of a feather and that both of them deserved to be liquidated. Consequently, on June 15, 1520, the papal court drew up the bull threatening Luther and his followers with excommunication, and on June 23 it annulled the Frankfurt agreement. It took time, however, for news of this to reach Germany, a country carried away by an unprecedented wave of enthusiasm for Luther. His pamphlets, fresh off the presses, were selling like hotcakes, particularly his *Address to the Christian Nobility of the German Nation Concerning the Reform of the Christian Estate* (*An den christlichen Adel deutscher Nation von des christlichen Standes Besserung*). This booklet went through no fewer than ten reeditions or reprints in the course of 1520 alone. All of Germany seemed to be behind Luther in the summer and early fall of 1520. People hardly took notice of another important item of news: Charles I of Spain had been elevated to the throne of the Holy Roman Empire on October 23 in Aachen, becoming Charles V. As he headed from the Netherlands to the city of Worms, where his first imperial diet would take place in January 1521, he left pyres of burning books—Luther's books—in his wake: first in Louvain, then in Liège, afterward in Cologne, and finally, on November 29, 1520, in Mainz. On March 10, 1521, the imperial mandate against Luther's writings was proclaimed in Worms. Luther himself had already burned Pope Leo X's excommunication bull, as well as the collection of papal legal decisions known as the *Decretals*, at the Elster gate in Wittenberg in December. A storm was definitely in the making.

Like everybody else, the Heidelberg Dominicans were confused and worried by these events. Bucer was clearly not alone with his views within the monastery. But whereas Bucer's superiors were Erasmian, they definitely were not Martinian, as he had already written to Beatus Rhenanus on March 10, 1519.[17] The point of divergence was the attitude toward the papacy. But in the same way that Erasmus refused to join Luther's enemies openly, the Heidelberg Dominicans were also not prepared to take on Luther in a clear and decisive way. Tired of waiting, the papal legate expressly commanded the prior provincial of the Dominicans in November 1520 to preach against Luther and against the dissemination of his works.[18] The Heidelberg Dominicans felt even less comfortable with the action their order was taking against Reuchlin. How tolerant, open-minded, and, to a certain extent, uncertain they actually were can be seen in their willingness to promote Bucer's advancement within the order. At the meeting of the Dominican provincial chapter in Frankfurt in May 1520, Bucer's superiors recommended him for the office of "Master of Students" (*magister studentium*), even though he had come under suspicion as a committed Erasmian *and* Martinian ever since the summer break disputation.[19] With this office, Bucer's superiors were not only giving him a leading position in the cloister hierarchy, subordinate only to the director of studies and the prior, but were also paving the path for him to obtain the highest academic degree, that of doctor of theology. The rules of the order required one to have been *magister studentium*—that is, a director of studies under the *regens*—in order to be considered for the theological doctorate. Furthermore, when Bucer decided in the summer of 1520 to lecture not on Peter Lombard's *Sentences*, as the syllabus required, but on the Psalms, his students protested vociferously, but not one word of reprimand by his superiors is reported.[20]

Nevertheless, Bucer realized it would be a losing battle to stand up within the Order of Preachers for everything that had become important to him. We find remarks along these lines in his letters from March 1519 onward. But it seems Bucer waited until September 1520 before deciding definitively to leave the monastery.[21]

Feeling extremely isolated, Bucer had already begun in 1519 assiduously to seek contact with influential humanists, first admirers of Erasmus but then also sympathizers of Luther. He methodically set up a far-flung network of contacts: using Beatus Rhenanus as a mediator, he cultivated the acquaintance of Wolfgang Capito, cathedral preacher and university professor in Basel; he corresponded with Luther in Wittenberg but also with Luther's friend George Spalatin, a confidant of Frederick, the prince elector of Saxony; writing to Sélestat, he cultivated contacts with Jacob Wimpfeling and the diplomat Jacob Spiegel; he had good relations with a humanistic circle in Speyer, particularly with the cathedral vicar Maternus Hatten, who became a close friend. Finally, he had good relationships with Ulrich von Hutten and consequently with Franz von Sickingen, who was close to Hutten.

These contacts were more than just important to Bucer. They became vital when he became endangered personally. On November 11, 1520— his twenty-ninth birthday—Bucer wrote a troubled letter to Capito, cathedral preacher in Basel since the spring of 1520 and, more important, an influential friend of Archbishop Albrecht of Mainz. In this letter, he related having just heard that Hoogstraten had gotten his hands on letters in which Bucer made no bones about his opinion of Hoogstraten.

Hoogstraten was now threatening to make an example of Bucer as a follower of Luther the minute Hoogstraten was reinstated as inquisitor.[22] It was crucial for Bucer to be freed of his monastic vows as soon as possible, so that he would no longer be subject to the jurisdiction of the Dominican order. Capito first of all, but also Maternus Hatten and Jacob Spiegel, had the necessary connections in high places to see his petition through in Rome. Bucer assailed them with a flurry of requests through letters and personal visits. Hutten, as well, did his part in trying to convince Capito to help out the renegade monk. Bucer's prospects as a refugee were bleak. His last resort would have to be Sickingen's castles.

Probably doing his best to dissipate misgivings about his reputation, Bucer visited Papal Nuncio Girolamo Aleander several times in December 1520 and in January 1521. Aleander counseled him benignly to invest his gifts in a cause more sublime than Luther.[23] In February, Maternus Hatten finally succeeded in winning over an influential member of the papal court who, on his way back to Rome, would seek the annulment of Bucer's monastic vows on the grounds that he had been forced into the order as a minor. In all probability, Bucer did not flee the Heidelberg monastery until this point, seeking shelter in Hatten's home in nearby Speyer, where he had already stayed secretly several times in the past. At the end of March, news arrived that the papal bull releasing him from his vows had been issued. A race against time ensued, for Bucer's opponents in the Dominican order had also gotten word of his plan. Bucer did his utmost to see to it that the suffragan bishop of Speyer, Anton Engelbrecht, who was well disposed toward him, would be charged with absolving him of his vows. At the same time, Aleander warned the papal court emphatically against releasing the dangerous man from his commitment to the order. But his warning arrived too late. On April 15, 1521, the bishop of Speyer commissioned Engelbrecht to carry out the act of annulment. On April 29, 1521, Suffragan Engelbrecht solemnly released Bucer from his monastic vows in the town of Bruchsal, reassigning him to the status of a secular cleric.[24] He did this after Bucer had sworn that his petition was truthful and confirmed it with a witness unknown to us. No representatives of Bucer's home monastery in Sélestat showed up, in spite of being summoned. The Dominican house of studies in Heidelberg was not mentioned with a single word in the entire procedure. But this made little difference for Bucer: he was now a free man.

It is the Bucer of these troubled Heidelberg years who begins to take on precise contours and appears for the first time as an individual with distinctive features. The first descriptions of his physical appearance come from this period. One friend characterized him as being "gaunt," having "black hair and a dark complexion," as well as an "impassioned" personality.[25] Later observers never forget to mention the stately nose that dominated his face. In terms of his intellectual development, Bucer laid the foundations for his theology during these years. He had to fight his way through tough conflicts in order to arrive at and hold his convictions; this made him both intelligent and versatile. He was acquainted with the reality of power since earliest childhood and gifted at winning over the hearts of the powerful. He was not an opportunist. When he set his eyes on a goal, he tackled it energetically and confidently and at times, it seems, even ruthlessly, but never without carefully thinking through his aims. He thrived on personal relationships and contact with like-minded people but also on ever-new challenges—which is why we encounter him on the move again and again, always traveling somewhere. The second half of Martin Bucer's life was about to begin.

In Sickingen's Entourage

Ebernburg

In the final weeks before being freed of his monastic vows, Bucer spent most of his time in the castle of Ebernburg. He felt safe in this stronghold of Franz von Sickingen, high above the Nahe River and only a few miles from the town of Kreuznach, where Sickingen served as the elector Palatine's official, or *Amtmann*. Bucer was not the only one to seek refuge here—a whole band of prominent fugitives found asylum in the Ebernburg, among them Johannes Oecolampadius, Caspar Aquila, Johannes Schwebel, and not least Ulrich von Hutten himself, who coined the fitting phrase "shelter of justice" (*Herberge der Gerechtigkeit*) for Sickingen's fortress. The Ebernburg's location was strategic, Mainz being only twenty-five miles to the northeast, and the other important imperial free cities on the Rhine, Worms and Speyer, just a day's ride away for an experienced horseman.

Franz von Sickingen,[26] with whom Bucer would be closely associated for about the next two years, remains an intriguing figure. Mutually incompatible reactionary and modern elements can be found together in his thought. And what Sickingen's friends, particularly Ulrich von Hutten, tried to make of him is again something different. Hutten had met Sickingen in 1519 and ever since extolled him as the quintessential German knight, imbued with a deep and authentic piety and truly committed to his nation. Many, not just Bucer, admired Sickingen for having championed Reuchlin's cause. Finally, Luther's *Address to the Christian Nobility*

(*An den christlichen Adel*) seemed to assign Sickingen and the entire estate of imperial knights a social and religious role of crucial importance. But the truth was a lot more complicated—and considerably less flattering. It was unmistakably clear that imperial knights had been caught in a process of steady social and political decline for a long time. Their traditional governmental, military, and economic functions had slowly been taken over by the up-and-coming territorial princes, as well as by the imperial cities. The Reformation exacerbated the situation, causing new divisions in a group already made heterogeneous by differences in social and economic conditions according to region. Initially, though, the knights had reason to welcome the vision of a national and moral renewal of the empire that would reinstate them in their earlier position of importance. Hutten, in particular, added to this vision the ingredients of Sickingen's personal leadership and elements of Luther's theology, peppering the mix with sentiments of hatred toward clergymen, especially toward the papal court in Rome—sentiments that were not hard to find in Germany at the time. Hutten was hoping by these methods to win over the cities, which were still recalcitrant or even hostile toward the imperial knights. He conjured up a compelling vision: Franz von Sickingen in league with the emperor, a church deprived of its power and wealth, a pope bereft of his influence in Germany, and a nation united politically and morally under the banners of imperial knights, once again powerful and thriving.

Bucer was also attracted to these soaring dreams, although he accentuated different elements. He found especially convincing the idea of allying Sickingen with the emperor, as well as the goal of dismantling the power of the papal court in order to reform the church, enable the unfettered preaching of the gospel, and spread true Christian learning and piety. Sickingen's personal religious devotion and his interest in Luther's writing were proof enough for Bucer that this knight's commitment should be taken seriously. It is obvious, however, that he did not really grasp the more contradictory aspects of Sickingen's personality, who claimed a calling to serve God, the Holy Roman Empire, and justice, on the one hand, but on the other conducted feuds just like any other robber baron, ambitiously and ruthlessly grasping for power. Like most of Sickingen's friends and enemies, Bucer clearly overestimated him.

Bucer lived in Ebernburg castle for two months, from March until the end of April 1521, working closely with Hutten, whom he came to know in Strasbourg in November of the previous year.[27] Bucer functioned as a private secretary of sorts for Hutten, writing letters for him, organizing his book acquisitions and sales, and translating into German portions of his *Invectiva*, which Hutten would review critically. We do not know much more about Bucer's work for Hutten. There is no evidence for the improbable claim that Bucer also rendered voluminous writings by Hutten into German and completed them, and perhaps even began this task while still a monk in Heidelberg. Neither do we have the slightest reason to believe that Bucer is the author of two anonymous pamphlets that also appeared during these months. Both *Neu-Karsthans* and *A Beautiful Dialogue (Ain schöner Dialogus)*[28] may express Hutten's and Sickingen's religious and social ideals eloquently, but they differ from one another so enormously in language, argumentation, and even intellectual sophistication that they cannot possibly have been written by the same person. Some themes in *Neu-Karsthans*, which is definitely the more elaborate and skillfully written of the two works, are reminiscent of Bucer's theology, such as its emphasis that our actions should be guided by the wish to be useful to our fellow human beings and on love of one's neighbor and the Holy Spirit. But the differences are more significant. This pamphlet does not say a word about sin and forgiveness, about reconciliation, or about new life in Christ. And we do not have any further evidence that Bucer made himself an advocate of the common struggle of peasants and knights against the clergy under the leadership of Sickingen. All of these reasons belie Bucer's authorship of both works.

What Bucer truly felt is revealed in a long conversation he had with Glapion, the confessor of Emperor Charles V, in the first days of April 1521.[29] Glapion and the diplomat Paul von Armstorff came to the Ebernburg on friendly terms, hoping to neutralize Sickingen and particularly Hutten as political foes through this accommodating approach. Glapion specifically suggested that Luther not attend the imperial diet in Worms but come instead to Sickingen's castle, where one could calmly and safely discuss the best ways and means of reforming the church. It remains unclear whether the imperial confessor was merely interested in keeping Luther away from the diet or sincerely concerned about carrying out a moderate reform of the church, which for him would have meant a reform confined to Germany and leaving the doctrinal foundations of the church untouched. Glapion certainly interpreted Charles V's readiness to go along with such a reform too optimistically when he claimed that the imperial mandate against Luther's writings was drawn up only to deceive the pope's adherents. But Bucer was also conscious of not having done justice to Luther by depicting him, in the course of this conversation of several hours' duration, as a theologian planted squarely in the center of the church's traditional doctrine and interested solely in a national program

of reform. In his own way, Bucer was attempting what humanistic councillors would later try out in Worms, after Luther's refusal to recant: give
in partially in order to save the project as a whole and not waste this unique
opportunity to carry out a comprehensive reform of the church in Germany.[30] This vision remained one of Bucer's most important convictions.

Filled with these hopes, he rode toward Luther on horseback, aiming
to intercept him and convince him to come to Ebernburg castle. They met
at Oppenheim, only a few miles southeast of Mainz, probably on April 15,
1521. Luther flatly rejected Bucer's proposal. He certainly was not about
to jeopardize his safe-conduct, which was still valid for another three days.
But most important, he would never agree to a compromise when God's
revealed truth was at stake—not then, and not at any later time.

A Court Chaplain for Count Frederick

There are reasons to believe that Bucer witnessed Luther's appearance at
the imperial diet in Worms. But we lose track of Bucer after that, knowing with certainty only that by early May 1521 he was back in Worms
again, this time filling the office of court chaplain for Count Palatine
Frederick, the younger brother of Elector Ludwig V.[31] It is not entirely
clear how this connection came about. In any case, it had already been
arranged during Bucer's time in Heidelberg and before he had achieved
his dismissal from the Dominican order.[32] Apparently, Bucer was cautiously distancing himself from the path Hutten had taken and attempting, like Wolfgang Capito at the court of Archbishop Albrecht of Mainz,
to further the cause of true Christianity by persuading the mighty to take
gradual steps. Hutten was furious and accused Bucer of having betrayed
his calling and the grace given him by Christ by accepting such a post.[33]
Bucer's good rapport with Sickingen, however, was apparently not hurt by
this decision.

Whatever Bucer's hopes and expectations might have been, it did not
take long for him to become sobered and disappointed. Count Ludwig was
well enough disposed toward Bucer, but the gospel was certainly not one
of his priorities. Neither did Bucer find people in Ludwig's court eager to
give him a sympathetic hearing, so he soon felt isolated, cut off from all
like-minded contacts, and distanced from significant events. The count
Palatine had his official residence in Neumarkt in the Upper Palatinate
(Oberpfalz), a town Bucer described as "minutely small and incredibly
barbarous."[34] His situation improved at least in this respect when Ludwig
moved to Nuremberg on November 14, 1521, taking his entourage with

him. Emperor Charles V had asked the count Palatine to preside over the governing council (*Reichsregiment*) of the Holy Roman Empire, which conducted the emperor's affairs during his absence.

Bucer was now living in a large city. Nuremberg had a population of approximately thirty thousand inhabitants. It was politically the most powerful city of the empire and a center not only of craft and trade but also of culture and science. During that winter, the articulate and powerful patricians ruling Nuremberg took the first steps to further the Reformation in their city and, at the same time, keep it under their tight control.

We have every reason to assume Bucer enjoyed his stay in Nuremberg. Here he met people who shared his concerns, such as the famous humanist Willibald Pirckheimer; the provost of St. Lawrence, Hector Poemer; and the future Reformer of Nuremberg, Andreas Osiander. His hopes of obtaining a post as hospital preacher, however, were dashed by the city council on December 11. Bucer probably left Nuremberg in mid-March 1522. His destination is unknown. The months following are veiled in darkness.[35] There is evidence that Bucer was in the Duchy of Brabant, probably sometime in March and April, with Count Ludwig's knowledge, which could mean he was on a diplomatic mission. But Bucer also took the opportunity to preach there and had to flee because of it. In May he appears to have been working for Franz von Sickingen again, who sent him on an itinerant mission "for the sake of the Gospel." The precise content of this mission and the places to which Bucer rode are unknown. Bucer's mandate might have been part of Sickingen's broader efforts to unite the imperial knights, but this is only a guess. Bucer was in Strasbourg for several days at the beginning of July 1522, visiting his father, who had already imagined him to be dead. He could stay only briefly, though, since Sickingen had a new mission for him, which Bucer assumed to be in Saxony. We do not know if Bucer actually undertook this trip, nor do we know how long he was gone. It is not until November that we hear of him again, this time as a chaplain in Wissembourg. Sickingen's war entered a new phase after he lost a crucial battle near Trier, was placed under the ban of the imperial governing council, and renounced his feudal loyalty to the elector Palatine on November 10. At this point, he released Bucer from his duties.

Landstuhl

Hutten wrote to Bucer in September 1521, informing him that he could return to Sickingen's entourage anytime he desired. Sickingen was offering him a place to live, a dwelling for his parents, and a position as a pastor in the town of Landstuhl, and was also willing to pay his studies for one year in Wittenberg or at another university. In May 1522, Bucer took up Sickingen on this offer. He moved to Landstuhl, a small settlement at the foot of Sickingen's castle, some eighteen miles southwest of Kaiserslautern. He became the pastor of the town parish, over which Sickingen held the rights of patronage. Yet Bucer probably had little time to really concern himself with church issues in Landstuhl during the six months he lived here. He married Elisabeth Silbereisen, a former nun, during this time (probably in July or August). As Bucer later wrote,[36] she had been placed in a convent by her relatives when she was still a young girl. It is unknown where and when Bucer met her.

Bucer's statements on the Reformation movement sound tougher and more uncompromising in the summer of 1522 than in the previous year. Now, at the zenith of Sickingen's preparations, Bucer admiringly perceived "his knights" as blazing with zeal for the gospel. While claiming to reject all violence, Bucer expressed the fear that Christ would no longer tolerate the violence that the antichrist's servants committed against the common people by suppressing the preaching of the gospel. Bucer therefore saw a major upheaval as imminent. Christians could not stand on the sidelines under such circumstances and speak about caution and peace of mind. Whoever behaved in this way was letting the pope—and thus the antichrist—have his way. Bucer was evidently including Erasmus in his criticism, in a scarcely concealed fashion. Christians were called to confess Christ openly and to preach the gospel, even if it meant incurring the hatred of men and the accusation of inciting revolt. It was with these convictions that Bucer came to Wissembourg in November 1522.

Wissembourg

The Town

Wissembourg is tucked away in the northeastern corner of Alsace, some forty miles from Strasbourg and just south of the modern-day border between France and Germany.[37] The Lauter River skirts the southern edge of town and constitutes thereafter, on its way eastward toward the Rhine, the boundary between both countries. In the early sixteenth century the town formed—from a political, cultural, and economic standpoint—an integral part of the southern German region of the Holy Roman Empire. It was a free imperial city and a member of the Alsatian Decapolis. Its population of more than four thousand consisted mostly of merchants and artisans who lived off winegrowing as well as the market with which Wissembourg supplied its surrounding region. The town also produced and exported textiles. The municipal constitution resembled that of Sélestat, both being replicas of Strasbourg's civic order on a smaller scale. There were seven craft guilds, whose masters, together with fourteen "associates" (*Hausgenossen*) mostly representing the patriciate, constituted the town council. Eight burgomasters headed the council. They took turns governing affairs, two at a time for a period of three months.

Unlike Sélestat, Wissembourg citizens had not managed to stand their ground in the conflict with the Benedictine monastery in their midst. The abbey in whose shadow and under whose protection the town had developed was the wealthiest and the most powerful of all of Alsace throughout the Middle Ages. In the fifteenth century the city struggled fiercely and tenaciously to gain control over it. To make matters more complicated, the elector Palatine at the same time extended his territory to the very city gates, threatening Wissembourg's independence. An intricate situation resulted: town and abbey remained sworn enemies, but they faced a common foe in the electoral Palatinate. This external adversary did not weld the Wissembourg parties together but made each one suspect the other of secretly entering a deal with the elector.

In terms of its church landscape, Wissembourg was a typical medieval city. To the north of the massive abbey church stood the parish church of St. Johannes. The church of St. Michael, located in the eastern outskirts, also met the pastoral needs of the neighboring towns of Weiler and Schweigen. Both churches were incorporated into the abbey, which had exclusive say in filling the pastor posts. The abbey also controlled the collegiate church of St. Stephan, in which eleven canons regular lived. The Teutonic Order of Knights, Dominican nuns and monks, Franciscans, and Augustinians, each with their own monastery, and a house of Beguines completed the ecclesiastical scene.

Heinrich Motherer, who had good connections to prominent Wissembourg families, had been the pastor at St. Johannes Church since 1511. With their help, he managed by legal proceedings in 1517 to wrest control over the parish from the abbot and hand it over to the town council.[38] Knowing that he could count on support by the council—or at least by a significant part of it—Motherer enthusiastically absorbed Luther's teachings and proclaimed them openly from his pulpit. This same group of influential, reform-minded Wissembourg citizens also established contacts with Franz von Sickingen.[39] By pursuing these policies, which were extremely popular among the common folk of Wissembourg, the council was hoping to defeat, or at least decisively weaken, two opponents simultaneously:

the local abbot and the elector Palatine. When Bucer arrived in Wissembourg, he therefore found himself among kindred spirits.

Standing Up for the Reformation

Initially, Bucer had intended to stop over only briefly in Wissembourg, since he and his wife were on their way to Strasbourg, where Bucer was planning to leave her with his parents and then travel on alone to Wittenberg to continue his studies. But Heinrich Motherer insisted he remain in Wissembourg and assist him in preaching the gospel. Bucer finally agreed to become Motherer's chaplain for the next six months. Motherer dutifully reported the appointment of a new helper to the vicar general in Speyer.

Full of energy, Bucer went straight to work and started preaching once a day, and on Sundays and holidays even twice a day, morning and afternoon. In the course of his daily sermons, he systematically made his way through entire books of the Bible, beginning one day where he had left off the previous. After completing 1 Peter, he continued with the Gospel of Matthew. Only his deportation from Wissembourg at the beginning of May prevented him from concluding this series. Bucer later presented a compendium of what he had preached, in a pamphlet printed in Strasbourg under the title *Summary*.[40] During his time in Wissembourg, and in fact already while in Landstuhl, Bucer had become convinced that he was living in the end times. He believed he had only two options in this situation: to join Christ's side and live from his Spirit or to remain in the large and mighty camp of the antichrist. The abuse, suffering, and persecution endured by adherents of the Reformation therefore took on a deeper meaning.

Rooted in this theological interpretation of the present, Bucer developed his understanding of Christian existence in positive and negative terms. Christian existence for Bucer had its foundation in the Bible, God's law, the Christian's only rule and standard. Therefore, it was essential that not only the clergy but also laypeople become acquainted with and study the Bible. At the center of the Bible stood the message that God revealed himself in Jesus Christ and this message was to be received by faith. Bucer saw faith as trusting that God is loving and compassionate toward human beings. "There must be a rejoicing in God, trusting him freely and finding comfort in him as in a father, since he in fact cares for us and loves us more than a father his son or a mother her helpless infant."[41] Whoever is possessed of a faith like this is also possessed of the Holy Spirit and has handed himself over to God so completely that he cannot help but love God with all his heart and with all his strength, but also his fellow human beings as he loves himself. This had profound implications for understanding what the church is. For Bucer, the church was primarily and especially the community of those bound to one another by the same trust in God and the same spirit of commitment to their fellow human beings, to their neighbors. The Mass, at the heart of Catholic worship and essential to understanding the church as an institution that dispensed salvation, now took on a completely different meaning. No longer did the priest repeat Christ's sacrifice on the cross, thus reconciling the congregation with God, but rather a compassionate Father bestowed the free gift of his reconciliation on the gathered believers. For this reason, the Mass meant for Bucer "nothing else than receiving the body and blood of our Lord Jesus Christ, so that we may remember him who gave his body for us and poured his blood for the forgiveness of our sins—blood confirming the new and eternal testament that provides us with the grace of the Father and the forgiveness of all our sins."[42] Bucer accompanied these statements with bitter attacks against the traditional church and its representatives, particularly the monastic orders. Intertwining theological condemnation with social critique, Bucer accused monks of falsifying the word of God and putting human ordinances and ceremonies in the place of the clear biblical injunction to live entirely and unconditionally for the benefit of one's neighbor; instead, monks exploited and abused their fellow human beings! Not shrinking from inflammatory and provocative language, Bucer claimed: "There isn't anything spiritual about them and not even a touch of natural human decency in them; all they think about is to conduct themselves as unbridled and reckless lords, just because their fingers are smeared with a bit of holy oil and a lock of hair was cut off their heads. All they do is sell the body and blood of Christ and mumble or wail their way through the Psalms, without understanding a word and with their thoughts elsewhere. At the same time they suck the marrow out of the poor man's bones and ravish his wife and daughters. To sum it up: all unbelief, sin, disgrace and complete doom ensues from them."[43]

Bucer then drew up six theses summarizing his convictions and rejecting church ceremonies. Actively seeking a decisive confrontation with his opponents, he arranged for a public disputation to take place at noon on April 8, 1523. Even though Bucer had printed and publicized his theses from the beginning of March, and had gone personally to the Franciscans and Dominicans of Wissembourg to challenge them to this face-off, they simply ignored him. They knew very well that time was on their side, for

Bucer's situation had become extremely disadvantageous. Inflamed by his sermons, many in Wissembourg were ready to resort to violence to reclaim what their forefathers had endowed to the town's churches and monasteries.[44] Bucer refused to have anything to do with this. He had trouble, though, making his appeasing voice heard in the din of public uproar. For others in Wissembourg—and not just the monks—this just proved what they had suspected all along: that Bucer's preaching led to rebellion and prompted common folk to "not wish to obey Christian and temporal authorities any more, but rather desire to kill them and take what is theirs, counter to all honor, to God, and to the law."[45]

The town council continued to support Bucer, but some councilmen began to waver when the vicar general of Speyer summoned Bucer to appear for interrogation. It is not surprising that the church hierarchy took interest in Bucer: it was not about to leave a priest unchecked whom Papal Nuncio Girolamo Aleander had described as far more dangerous than Hutten, and who, furthermore, was married, supported Sickingen, and now openly advocated the Lutheran heresy. Soon afterward, the bishop strictly ordered the Wissembourg city council to expel Bucer. The council requested advice from Strasbourg on January 10. The Strasbourg council responded that it allowed its own preacher Matthew Zell to continue preaching in spite of the traditional church's objections, as long as he proclaimed only "the pure gospel." This encouraged the Wissembourg council not to waver in its support of Bucer. He harbored no illusions, however, about his vulnerability. He clearly saw that he was dangling from two thin threads: the groundswell of emotional support from the populace and his enemies' fear of Sickingen. The moment Sickingen fell, Bucer wrote in mid-January 1523, a mighty reaction would follow.[46]

The bishop of Speyer remained adamant and excommunicated Bucer. The Wissembourg delegates at the assembly of imperial cities (*Städtetag*) in Speyer negotiated with the bishop from March 31 to April 2, managing to have him postpone his definitive decision for one month. It was evident, though, that the bishop also knew time was on his side. His brother, Elector Palatine Ludwig V, set out in mid-April on a joint campaign with Landgrave Philip of Hesse and Trier Elector Richard von Greiffenklau to eliminate Sickingen once and for all. As expected, the defiant knight was defeated, dying in the ruins of his castle on May 7. Hardly a week later, on May 13, the elector Palatine's army occupied the village of Schlettenbach (now Niederschlettenbach), some six miles northwest of Wissembourg. The town council now urged Motherer and Bucer to leave Wissembourg secretly to avoid causing unrest in the populace. They, together with their pregnant wives, left that night, heading for Strasbourg. Soon afterward, on May 20, 1523, Wissembourg was forced to sign the Schlettenbach treaty, which reinstated the traditional privileges of the electoral Palatinate, subordinated the parish church once again to the abbey, and forbade any changes in religious and church matters. The attempt to introduce the Reformation in Wissembourg had failed for the time being.

Chapter Three

A Preacher in Strasbourg

Strasbourg

Economic, Political, and Social Background

Bucer—by now a penniless priest, excommunicated and persecuted because of his marriage and his agitational preaching—arrived in a city that was neither the largest nor the wealthiest nor politically the most important among German imperial free cities.[1] Cologne, Augsburg, and Nuremberg surpassed Strasbourg in all these counts. But the Alsatian metropolis boasted a propitious combination of all the factors that had given the aforesaid cities fame and prominence. Its population of almost twenty-five thousand made it, if not the biggest, certainly one of the largest cities in the Holy Roman Empire. It was among the empire's most important economic and cultural centers. And with the inception of the Reformation, Strasbourg began taking over, step by step, the political leadership that Nuremberg had exercised up to this point.

The Upper Rhine city lay at the vital junction of two significant trade routes: one issued from Lyon in the southwest and headed north and east via Frankfurt am Main; the other (and, with the shift of commerce from the Mediterranean to the Atlantic, increasingly important) route proceeded from northern Italy and headed toward the Netherlands and the up-and-coming metropolis of Antwerp. Strasbourg, and particularly its annual St. John's Day fair (*Johannismesse*), had become an important hub of commerce. Exquisite glass products and spices were imported from the Orient via Venice by land or by sea, hides from Switzerland, salt from Bavaria and Lorraine, furs from Poland and Russia—not to mention fish, essential during fasting periods, from many different regions. But Strasbourg's merchants

47

earned a living not only as intermediate traders but also as exporters of Alsatian goods such as grain, medium-quality cloths, weapons, jewelry, and, of course, the Alsatian wine so highly praised and esteemed in and beyond the Holy Roman Empire.

Power in Strasbourg was concentrated in the hands of a few wealthy families related to one another by consanguinity or marriage. The 1482 civic constitution granted the guilds a significant degree of political influence but did nothing to change the predominance of the richer guilds. Their overwhelming power remained unchallenged, since younger family members were required to join poorer guilds and ascend within them. Strasbourg's very elaborate political and social hierarchy allowed the ruling elite enough latitude to pursue its own goals.

Strasbourg's citizenry was organized into twenty merchant and artisan guilds and two guildlike societies of the noble *Constofler*, representing the patrician upper class.[2] The *Constofler* consisted mostly of urban and rural noblemen as well as of wealthy merchant families. But individual members of these classes also joined the more affluent guilds, so that the boundary between nobles and merchants was not clear-cut. Four *Stettmeister* were chosen from the patriciate for one year, each taking turns at leading affairs for three-month intervals. Their functions were limited, however, for the official head of the city was a guild member—the *Ammeister*, or master of the guilds. He was accompanied in this function by five *Altammeister*, or former *Ammeisters*. The city also had a Senate (*Grosser Rat*) and two privy councils: the Council of the Fifteen (*die Fünfzehn*) and the Council of the Thirteen (*die Dreizehn*). When meeting together with the Senate, the Fifteen and Thirteen were called collectively "the Twenty-one" (*die Einundzwanzig*), even though they were actually twenty-eight.[3] The six *Ammeister* were elected by the Senate and the Twenty-one. The thirty members of the Senate—ten patricians, including the four *Stettmeister*, and the representatives of the twenty guilds—were elected for two-year terms. Once a year, half the members retired, being replaced by an equal number of new members.

The actual government of Strasbourg lay in the hands of the two privy councils, the Fifteen and the Thirteen. The Fifteen consisted of five patricians and ten guildsmen and was in charge of domestic affairs, which included local church matters. The four *Stettmeister*, the *Ammeister*, four of the five *Altammeister*, and four further guild masters made up the Thirteen, which was responsible for diplomacy, including relationships to churches outside of Strasbourg.

A further body, subordinate to all these institutions, was the assembly of the three hundred *Schöffen* of the guilds. This assembly, consisting of fifteen masters from each guild, was convoked in times of crisis—such as 1529 or 1548—to vote on proposals put to them by the governing bodies. They met at the city hall, on the Martinsplatz (now Place Gutenberg). But more on that later.

This system, as complicated as it was, had one simple goal: to limit the power of the patriciate. It was impossible, however, to draw a clear line between the patricians and the wealthy guildsmen. In fact, the guildsmen majority was dependent on the cooperation of the minority of noblemen for the effective government of Strasbourg, since it was the nobles who had the leisure and money to devote themselves exclusively to politics. It comes as no surprise that the members of the urban elite ruling Strasbourg during these years had the following background: 42.9 percent of them were rentiers, 35.2 percent were merchants and goldsmiths, and only 13.3 percent were artisans.[4] However, it should be added that the apparent obsession of the ruling class with its own interests does not simplistically imply that it did not care for the general well-being of the population or have a sense of responsibility for the good of the entire city. The *Schwörtag*, an annual assembly in which all citizens renewed their civic oath of loyalty to the constitution in front of the cathedral, poignantly demonstrated the cohesion of the Strasbourg political body.

Nevertheless, social resentment remained an undeniable reality.[5] There were essentially three sources of tension. First of all, there was the mass of artisans' servants and journeymen who had no prospect of ever ascending to the rank of master. This whole group was almost entirely devoid of rights. Laborers and journeymen had to endure meagerly paid sixteen-hour workdays. Ever tighter city regulations made it almost impossible for them to change jobs. They were forbidden from forming associations or even gathering. Finally, there were countless regulations stifling and controlling their every step. The result was growing discontent and frustration.

A second group, no less embittered, was that of the lesser master artisans, caught in a difficult economic and social situation between the mass of oppressed workhands and journeymen, above whom they stood, and the wealthier master artisans, whom they could never join. The more affluent master artisans expanded their shops in capitalistic fashion, able to dictate cheaper purchasing prices since they always bought raw materials in large quantities and therefore could produce and sell more cheaply.

The smaller master artisans found it hard to survive under these circumstances. Of course, the whole idea behind the artisan guilds was to preclude unfair competition. There were, however, plenty of loopholes making it possible to circumvent guild statutes.

Third, all these artisans, no matter what their rank, were discontented with Strasbourg's ruling class. They were especially angry with the city's tax policies. In Strasbourg, as in other cities, most taxes and duties were collected in the form of indirect taxes on wine and staple foods. This system of taxes burdened the lower classes much more than it did the wealthy, particularly when poor harvests made prices soar.

Although this pent-up anger and discontent was significant, it would certainly be wrong to make too much of it. Neither at this time nor later did the class of artisans and craftsmen have a revolution in mind. But the muffled opposition of this large section of the population was enough to make the ruling oligarchy tread very carefully, especially since the surrounding villages and towns offered plenty of examples of insurgences, conspiracies, and riots, local as well as regional. At the same time, the ruling class was adept at averting unrest by invoking a cause that served both the wishes of the civic elite and the interests of the broader populace: the urge to do away with the exempt status of the church and its institutions in the city and to reduce all clergymen to the same level as the rest of the citizenry.

Anticlericalism

This was not an attack on the church, and even less on the Christian faith. Like the inhabitants of countless other cities and regions of the empire, the people of Strasbourg were extremely religious and devout. The fierce anticlericalism so widespread in the population had other roots. Laypeople saw daily how clergymen and monks lived free of the constraints and obligations that civic laws, and indeed the burden of having to earn one's own living, imposed on everybody else. Clerics led instead a life of luxury and comfort, paying no taxes other than a symbolic fee for the city's protection (*Schutzgeld*). They enjoyed countless privileges, among them economic ones, but particularly exemption from the city's laws. At the same time, they controlled ecclesiastical measures such as excommunication and anathema, which they could abuse to make their power felt over individuals, indeed, over entire cities. They were well off, if not outright affluent. And, according to a view widely held, there were simply too many of them in the city. Besides its cathedral, which included the high choir and the cathedral chapter reserved for members of the high nobility, Strasbourg had three collegiate churches with their respective chapters, as well as a canoness congregation. Additionally, there were nine parish churches; at least fifteen monastic establishments (eight for monks, seven for nuns); more than a hundred chapels; and with them a host of lower-rank priests, chaplains, and helpers. Rumors and accusations against the clergy were rampant. In particular, members of orders were looked upon as greedy and lazy and were charged with being stingy, slow-witted, undisciplined, and immoral.

These were, of course, exaggerations and false generalizations. But, for the first time, the clergy was under attack as a matter of principle and had to justify itself accordingly. Monks and priests represented practically the opposite of everything dear to the up-and-coming class of burghers who exalted hard work and economic achievement. The clergy did not keep pace with the vigorous growth of knowledge at this moment in history. Neither did they share the laity's urge to understand the world and the manifold changes, big and small, taking place within it. Finally and most important, the clergy did not meet the higher ethical standards that were emerging. The popular preacher Geiler von Kaysersberg had used his pulpit at the cathedral of Strasbourg to viciously castigate the grievous state of the church and its leaders for decades, comparing scandalous reality with the ideal of the early church. Wimpfeling and Brant had done the same in their lectures and writings. Inspired by Erasmus, local humanists spread an ethical ideal of their own, in alignment with the New Testament and the church fathers, emphasizing deep piety, learning, and freedom. Placed side by side with this ideal, the church certainly appeared decadent and corrupt. It was not so much that conditions had actually become worse as that the sensitivity and the ethical and intellectual expectations of the laity had increased. Even in circles little influenced by humanistic thought, there was a clear longing for higher moral standards and greater respectability. Priests and members of orders were increasingly perceived as a foreign body in the city, and lay citizens closed ranks to vie with them.

It was especially this civic patriotism that bound the Strasbourg oligarchy with the rest of the population. It would be incorrect to describe the city's rulers and its citizens as opponents of the church. What they wanted was to reform it and have as much control over it as possible. They wanted a say in the filling of vacant parish preacherships and more influence over the property and administration of monasteries, in which, after all, many of their own family members lived. Finally, the people of Strasbourg wanted the city's regulations and prohibitions to apply not just to the laity but to the clergy as well, and they expected the clergy to bear its share of civic obligations and duties. A plethora of diverse views, interests, and hopes were thus funneled into the Reformation movement: political and moral aims, religious convictions, social discontent, widespread anti-clericalism, and not least the craving for more intellectual freedom and spiritual responsibility. At the same time, it must not be forgotten that in Strasbourg, as well as elsewehere, it was primarily clergymen who absorbed the ideas of the Reformation and became its most fervent spokesmen and champions. Furthermore, instrumental in the success of the Reformation was the conviction that sinners are justified alone by God's grace, which released and set them free, pitting a liberating gospel against a law of increasingly strict ethical demands made on clergy and church.

Reformation Beginnings

As in other cities, Luther's ideas were spread in Strasbourg primarily through the printed word and by preaching.[6] Six of his works were published in Strasbourg in 1519, sixteen only one year later. The publication of Reformation literature, encompassing everything from strictly theological essays to polemical works and including booklets and pamphlets, increased exponentially in the following years in Strasbourg.[7] Opponents of the Reformation were able to keep pace at first but soon lost commercial appeal and the protection of the council. The way the great Franciscan controversialist Thomas Murner was dealt with is typical for all Catholic apologists. His rude polemical tract *The Great Lutheran Fool* (*Von dem großen Lutherischen Narren*) appeared on December 19, 1522, and was prohibited by the city council already on December 22. Except for Johannes Grüninger, all Strasbourg printers were now working for the Reformation.

We know little about the very first people to preach Lutheran ideas in Strasbourg. The only one able to hold his own was Matthew Zell, the staunch pastor of the cathedral congregation. After initially defending Luther, he proclaimed in the summer of 1521 that he would restrict himself to preaching the pure word of God. His popular style made his sermons a huge success, drawing crowds of more than a thousand listeners from all social backgrounds. First he preached from his pulpit in the St. Lawrence Chapel of the cathedral and then, because of the crowds, from the main pulpit in the cathedral nave. After he was forbidden to use it, carpenters made him a portable wooden pulpit of his own. Despite his brazenness, Zell was not expelled, probably due to the intense rivalry between the bishop, the cathedral chapter, and the city council. The bishop had canon law on his side as he called for Zell's dismissal. The cathedral chapter, however, protested against this measure and reached an agreement with the council to leave Zell alone as long as he proclaimed only the word of God and did not preach sedition. The bishop, however, remained determined to eliminate Zell and indicted him on twenty-four charges in December 1522, accusing him of heretical preaching, dereliction of duty, and the reckless introduction of innovations. Once again, an agreement was reached thanks to the council's support for Zell. At the same time, some had the impression the problem would take care of itself, since Zell's contract would expire regardless at the end of 1523.

However, an entirely new situation arose after the imperial governing council (*Reichsregiment*) issued a mandate on March 6, 1523, demanding that "only the holy gospel" be preached.

Opposing convictions and interests now clashed in an increasingly agitated and hostile atmosphere. Throughout it all, Strasbourg's ruling oligarchy kept clear goals in mind. As divided as council members were in their attitude toward the Reformation, they were certainly united in their desire to keep developments under their control and use them to further their own interests. For example, at the end of 1522, when negotiating with the monasteries over the renewal of the *Schirm*—that is, the city's protection of all monastic houses within its walls, as well as of collegiate churches and the high choir—the council compelled the clergy to assume citizenship. In the summer of 1523 it abolished the "perpetual rent" (*ewiger Zins*) owed to the church by usufructuaries of its houses and farmland. By paying the thirty or fiftyfold equivalent of this rent, tenants could now become owners. At the same time, the council introduced a new relief ordinance modeled after that of Nuremberg.[8] This ordinance was characterized by a combination of traditional concepts with Reformation ideas. In a Christian community, no one should suffer need. On the other hand, no one should be lazy and live off the toil of others. Begging was therefore forbidden, and needy townspeople were given aid only if the relief wardens appointed by the council had previously determined that they were really destitute and unable to work. The social disciplining of the population merged with a new bourgeois appreciation of work and achievement. Anticlerical implications as well were unmistakable: begging had entirely lost the aura of religious merit that previously surrounded it.

Matthew Zell pursued goals of his own. They can be discerned in his *Christian Justification* (*Christliche Verantwortung*) of the early summer of 1523. In this very first publication of the Strasbourg Reformation, dedicated to the city council, not only did Zell stand his ground but he also took the offensive, demanding that the gospel be preached openly and freely to all people, for only in this way could they be saved.

The Bible and the Holy Spirit are the foundation of the church, affirmed Zell. Therefore, the church's ordinances and ceremonies must be based on them and modeled after them. Finally, clergymen are not to be the masters but rather the servants of the church. Zell especially emphasized the clergy's responsibility for the common man. These ideas won the hearts of his listeners. Of course, there were also those who opposed the new faith, as well as a large number of the hesitant and undecided. A 1522 pamphlet declares:

> You want to teach me, son, to believe
> something other than my parents believed?
> That would be my eternal shame.
> I will not let myself be led astray.[9]

But Zell's adherents among the common folk and the educated pressed on impatiently, oblivious to all doubts and scorning any cautious attempts at mediation. A Latin pamphlet in the late summer of 1523 called on the city council finally to clean up the church, get rid of the hordes of priests, abolish the many Masses being celebrated, confiscate the property of the monasteries and collegiate churches, and vigorously support those preachers who sought God's truth and the well-being of their congregations rather than their own benefit.[10]

The city government, however, was not ready to take such far-reaching steps. The path it wanted to follow can be deduced from the important council mandate of December 1, 1523, which was essentially the city council's version of the decision of the imperial governing council (*Reichsregiment*).[11] Admittedly, only the gospel was to be preached. But the mandate also called for an immediate stop to all hostilities between clergymen and laypeople. All verbal abuse and particularly inflammatory, agitative speeches had to cease. All these would be punishable from now on. The council wanted tranquillity and order in the city. The council edict made it clear that the criteria all further developments would have to measure up to were "a truly Christian mind and evangelical truth, but also brotherly love, unity and peace."

The First Successes of the Reformation Movement

Bucer's Arrival in Strasbourg

It was in this convulsive, restless city that Bucer arrived in the middle of May 1523.[12] His most urgent concern was earning a livelihood. Initially, it was not certain that he would even be authorized to remain in the city. On June 9, Bucer pleaded with Huldrych Zwingli to find him a position in Switzerland. Bucer emphasized that his wife should be no obstacle, for "she knew how to live most abstemiously, would contribute to the edification of many, and be a scandal to no one."[13] For the time being, however, Bucer just seemed to run into closed doors in Strasbourg. While the council had assured him it would protect him against persecution, it rejected his application for citizenship. It also refused the petition of a group of laypeople and clergymen that Bucer be allowed to lecture them regularly in German on the Gospel of John. The council could not afford to get itself into further difficulties by sponsoring a married and excommunicated priest who had additionally discredited himself by supporting Sickingen.

The bishop of Strasbourg, to whom Bucer had reported his presence, forbade him from carrying out any church ceremonies and demanded on June 16 that the city council withhold its protection so that the renegade priest might be duly tried according to canon law. Bucer was summoned to appear before a small committee to which a friend of the Reformation, the influential former *Ammeister* Claus Kniebis, belonged. Bucer appeared before the committee, accompanied by his father. Instead of the expected cross-examination, he was given the opportunity to dictate his convictions to the minutes secretary. Bucer used the occasion to proclaim the legitimacy of marriage, including the marriage of former nuns and priests; describe the ban placed on him by the bishop of Speyer as a hasty and unjustified measure; and underscore that he wished nothing so much as to preach the gospel and discuss it further in lectures, and to do this with the consent of the authorities. He added: "I wish to look upon secular authority in every way as a layman should and do my utmost to obey it, regardless of whether my honor, my life or my property are at stake. Divine law obliges me and many to this."[14]

The city did not remove its protection. Bucer's situation, though, remained precarious. His renewed application for citizenship was rejected again in January 1524. Finally, on September 22, he was granted this privilege. He promptly enlisted in the guild of the "Gardeners," to which most of his parishioners at the church of St. Aurelien belonged. Back in the summer of 1523, this development was still completely unforeseeable.

Bucer had understandably gone to Matthew Zell as soon as he arrived in Strasbourg. In his first months there, he essentially worked as Zell's unofficial chaplain. It was in Zell's house (behind the cathedral, today at no. 5 on the Rue des Frères) that Bucer, after obtaining permission by the

council, held his daily one-hour lectures in Latin on the letters to Timo-
thy, on Titus, and on Philippians. And again, it was Zell who, because of
the ever larger crowds Bucer was attracting, let him use a bigger room in
his parish of St. Lawrence. In these facilities Bucer proceeded to give
classes on both letters of Peter and on the Gospel of John—this time in
German! The council did not do anything to stop him.[15] Bucer's situation,
however, was still far from secure.

The First Writings

During these months, Bucer published three books that impressively convey his theological stance and his visions for the future. Theologically
of greatest importance is the work *That No One Should Live for Himself
but for Others, and How We May Attain This* (*Das ym selbs niemant . . . leben
soll*).[16] Here Bucer outlines his theology in a systematic way for the first
time. The book consists of two parts: the first deals with God's ordering
of all life and all being, and the second discusses "how we may attain this."
Interestingly, the structure of this treatise coincides to a great extent with
that of Thomas Aquinas's *Summa theologica*. In the first part of his *Summa*,
Thomas discusses God as the foundation of all being and the cause of
everything that happens. In the second he deals with man as God's like-
ness, and in the third he writes about Christ as he who makes the new life
and being of man possible. Bucer followed this systematic pattern but condensed Thomas's first and second parts into one section of his treatise, in
order to underscore the fundamental significance of Christ and his saving
work all the more in the second section. This reveals how extensively
Bucer incorporated Thomas's legacy into his own theology.

Bucer also stood squarely in the tradition of Thomas Aquinas when
assuming a divine order of being that God has implanted in all his creatures in the form of a law—a law that makes all creatures seek the benefit
and well-being of the other and thus of the whole. For Bucer, loving one's
fellow humans was this law. He saw neighbor-oriented love as the prime
motive and driving force behind the entire universe. All created things
carry within them the urge to help and to benefit others, from lowest inan-
imate nature all the way up to the highest angels. His theology thus took
on a markedly ethical character. From these general premises Bucer drew
concrete conclusions for marriage and the hierarchical structure of society. Every human being is dependent on her fellow human beings, said
Bucer. This is particularly the case for human beings in their condition as
woman and man. It is only in coming together that they conform with

God's universal laws, becoming fully human in body and in spirit. There-fore, whoever forbade marriage (e.g., by requiring celibacy of priests) was an enemy of all things human and an enemy of God. Indeed, his criticism of church and society was driven to a great extent by the ontological norm of love of one's neighbor. Bucer did not question the existing hierarchical structure of society in the least. In fact, he still clung to the conviction that the clerical estate was above the others: "Because serving the spirit is supe-rior to serving the body, and what is general is superior to what is partic-ular, it thus follows that the apostolate—in which one does not serve several specific persons but rather the entire congregation, and this not in matters concerning the body but rather the spirit, from which eternal sal-vation ensues—is the most perfect of all offices, callings and ministries."[17] However, by formulating the norm of serving and loving one's neighbor, Bucer created a norm that was above all estates, a norm to which all estates had to measure up, both clergy and rulers, and merchants as well as crafts-men and farmers. Understandably, this theological approach led Bucer to work zealously his entire life toward establishing a new, better order of church and society, an order that truly reflected God's will. There was, therefore, always a political dimension to Bucer's theology.

However, the reordering of society that Bucer had in mind was strictly a *Christian* one. It was sin, after all, that had definitively destroyed the har-mony, so magnificently fashioned by God, of mutual love and partnership among all creatures. The only way out of the catastrophic deadlock of self-ishness, hate, and enmity was the one Christ had opened. For Bucer as for Thomas, Christ was not just the savior of the individual human being but also the restorer of God's intended order of creation. As mentioned above, this is the subject matter of the second part of Bucer's treatise. Not all peo-ple grasp the significance of what Christ has done, says Bucer. Only faith is capable of recognizing it. This implies that faith to a great extent means understanding and acknowledging what God, according to the Bible, has said and done. But this is only one aspect. Just as important is Bucer's pos-tulate that the believer receives the Holy Spirit, enabling him to center his life on the law God has implanted in creation—the law of loving one's fellow human beings. The Christian is thus called to struggle coura-geously so that God's salutary fundamental law may extend its reign in society. Bucer also repeats here what he had said in his Heidelberg theses: what it means to love God is spelled out concretely in our love for our fel-low human beings. This has nothing to do with trying to gain God's favor through works. It issues wholly and exclusively from the gratitude of the believer who acts in the assurance that God accepts and loves her in spite of her inadequacy and shortcomings. We can therefore, writes Bucer, "rejoice with all our hearts that it is our due to serve our fellow man and to show him the greatest compassion, for in so doing we display a modest share of gratitude to our most merciful Father and Savior and may continue, with hearts comforted, to look forward to His compassion, since we are endeavouring to carry out at least a small share of His will."[18]

The theological foundations that Bucer laid in this treatise echoed in manifold ways in the other two booklets he published in the summer and fall of 1523. This included his proclaimed readiness to allow himself to be killed if someone should prove that he was a false prophet adulterating God's law (Deut. 13:1–9). During this time Bucer displayed an extremely radical, even reckless attitude, based on his firm conviction that revealed truth was on his side. It is from this perspective that he defended his ministry in Wissembourg in the *Summary* discussed above. After this he wrote a *Justification* (*Verantwortung*)[19] in which he defended himself against rumors about him circulating through Strasbourg. Bucer's unconventional background—a former monk who married a former nun and had previously worked for the mutinous Sickingen—provided endless motives for gossip and for conjectures of the wildest sort. Certain sections of the Strasbourg population, Bucer reports, took malicious delight in reading the anonymous pamphlet *Schnaphan*,[20] which accused Bucer of grave sexual misconduct as well as the cynical abuse of Scriptural quotations in order to justify immorality, lawlessness, and violence. Bucer was outraged at these charges. "For the sake of God and truth, I ask of all those who love honesty and truthfulness not to believe such criminal and impudent liars—that's precisely what the people are who have said such things of me—and to allow me first to speak for myself. Even murderers are permitted this!"[21]

We cannot determine whether and to what extent this *Justification* had any effect on local public opinion. Ever since the late fall of 1523, the people of Strasbourg were preoccupied with other, more urgent topics. One of them was clerical marriage. On November 9, Anton Firn, the *Leutpriester*, or people's priest, at St. Thomas, married the woman with whom he had been living. For a consecrated priest who held a preaching position to marry publicly, and for Zell to conduct this wedding in the Strasbourg cathedral, was a deliberate provocation and demonstration.[22] On December 3, Zell himself married the phenomenal Katharina Schütz, the daughter of a master woodworker, who would later make history as a Protestant "church mother" of sorts.[23] Then, in 1524, the cathedral preacher Caspar Hedio and several other priests followed suit, and finally, in August, the prominent provost of St. Thomas, Wolfgang Capito, was married at a service in which Bucer gave the wedding sermon. By this time Bucer was no longer alone in his status as an anathematized and banned priest, for the bishop of Strasbourg solemnly excommunicated *all* the married priests of the city on April 3, 1524. This ban, however, had little effect. The entire city was in turmoil. Monks were leaving their monasteries. Supporters of the Reformation, Claus Kniebis among them (since 1520), seized the upper hand in the Council of the Fifteen. The city government always strove to maintain a semblance of unity on the outside, and this could convey the false impression that the entire ruling class actively supported the new movement, including the desertion of monasteries by monks and nuns, the inventorizing of monastic property for the purpose of later confiscation, the introduction of changes in the liturgy, and, most important of all, the insistence of the vast majority of the population that evangelical preachers be hired in place of supporters of the traditional church.

Preacher at St. Aurelien

Various strands were intertwined in this complex process: the initiative of the lay burghers of Strasbourg, the approval of the preachers, the intervention and ultimate success of the city council, and the delaying tactics of the religious traditionalists. Bucer's appointment as a preacher for the parish of St. Aurelien illustrates this phenomenon nicely.[24] It was mostly small urban farmers, the so-called *Gärtner,* or Gardeners, who belonged to this parish on the outskirts of Strasbourg. Their guild counted six hundred members and was therefore the largest, but also one of the poorest and least reputable, artisan guilds of the city. In January 1524, about thirty members of St. Aurelien asked the steward of congregational property to hire an evangelical preacher for the Sunday-afternoon and holiday worship services. The steward did not pass the request on to the collegiate chapter of St. Thomas, which was in charge of naming the preacher of St. Aurelien, but instead advised the Gardeners to file a petition with the council. The latter responded on January 27 by creating a committee that studied the problem and reported on February 3 that 120 families wished for an afternoon preacher and were, in fact, ready to pay for him out of their own pockets. The dean of St. Thomas chapter complained to the council that this was an encroachment of its rights. An agreement was therefore reached that the chapter should name a new, more qualified preacher. While the chapter tried its best to find a suitable candidate, the

Gardeners insisted on compliance with their original petition. On February 20, they also asked Bucer to preach for them in the afternoon of the following day in St. Aurelien. After consulting with several other preachers, among them Zell and Hedio, he agreed. Immediately after the service, in other words, on the evening of February 21, Bucer informed his "very special protector" Claus Kniebis what he had just done and requested that Kniebis defend his action before the council. Bucer affirmed that it had not been his intention to confront the council with a fait accompli, but in view of the circumstances, he had had no other choice. He expressly mentioned what he had preached his parishioners: the faith that enables and readies one to endure suffering and injustice. He was aware of how vulnerable his situation was, but he was also fundamentally convinced that the renewal of church and society would succeed only if the authorities and the ministers worked together closely and could trust each other.

On March 29, the representatives of the congregation of St. Aurelien declared to the chapter of St. Thomas that they had waited long enough. The chapter then agreed to make an exception and allow the council to fill the preacher position. It may be that Capito, as provost of St. Thomas, played a decisive role in granting this concession. In any case, the Gardeners chose Bucer as their preacher that very same day. The council, however, refused to confirm the vote, declaring to the congregation on April 4 that it would not appoint a married and excommunicated priest. It was not until August 24, when the seldom-convoked assembly of the three hundred *Schöffen* (leading guild officials) approved the council's decision to adhere to the gospel and to appoint parish preachers itself, that Bucer officially became the pastor of St. Aurelien.

After almost a year in Strasbourg, he had finally found a firm footing and joined those at the forefront of the struggle to introduce the Reformation. Admittedly, he was far from being the leader of this group. The preacher whom the people followed and who was capable of drawing masses of listeners was and would remain Matthew Zell (even though his sermons were sometimes a bit too long). The distinction of being the most influential theologian and churchman of the city went to Wolfgang Capito. He not only had a doctorate in theology and occupied one of the highest positions in the Strasbourg church hierarchy as a provost of the collegiate chapter of St. Thomas, but he was also an aristocrat through and through. He therefore caused quite an impression when he joined the Reformation in 1523, began preaching in German, got married, and took citizenship. Bucer fittingly said of him in the spring of 1524: "Truly, it is he who steers Christ's ship here."[25] But also Dr. Caspar Hedio, the cathedral preacher and distinguished translator of ancient Christian, humanistic, and Reformation texts into German, stood far above Bucer on the social scale. What distinguished Bucer from the mass of priests and chaplains, and accounts for his gradual development into one of the Reformation's most important figures, was his intellectual strength and agility, as well as his ability to harmonize medieval, humanistic, and Reformation theological ideas; his capacity for hard work; his incessant urge, born out of his theology, to improve existing ecclesiastical and social conditions; and, finally, his living piety, together with his sharp political intuition. Bucer's handwriting reflects exactly the increased pressure he was under. It had always been difficult to decipher. Now it became rushed and hasty to the point of illegibility (see p. 226).

The Turning Point

In the meantime, the mood of nervousness and restlessness pervading Strasbourg intensified. The preachers demanded that the city translate evangelical convictions into practical measures. They wanted God's truth to win the day in Strasbourg. While the council vacillated, the number of people acclaiming and backing the new teaching grew from day to day. But hostility toward the clergy grew as well. Bucer beseeched Capito in July 1524 to do everything in his might to overpower the opposition coming from supporters of the traditional church. He himself entered a debate with Thomas Murner over the Mass and published a Latin treatise at the beginning of August, *On the Lord's Supper* (*De caena dominica*), in which he sharply repudiated the idea that the Mass was a sacrifice.[26] But the real bone of contention soon became Conrad Treger, prior provincial of the Augustinian order. He had published a book of a hundred theses (*Paradoxa*) in Fribourg in Switzerland in March 1524, in which he not only placed the authority of the church and its councils above that of the Bible but also attacked Reformation preachers as ignorant fools who were leading the people astray. What made the Strasbourg ministers particularly angry was Treger's refusal to take part in any public disputation with them over his theses. Treger knew all too well that such a debate would be of advantage only to the preachers, and for this reason he adamantly claimed that only a bishop was authorized to summon such a dispute. When Treger, in a *Warning* (*Vermanung*) published in Strasbourg on August 20, went a step further and attacked not just the preachers but all the burghers of Strasbourg as heretics and rebels, emotions reached the boiling point. What began as heated discussions and angry gatherings at the entrances of monasteries turned into violent riots on September 5. Mobs started breaking into monasteries, looting and destroying religious images, pursuing notorious opponents of the Reformation and handing them over to the council, forcing it to take them into custody. Among those arrested was Treger.

Already before the outbreak of this revolt, the preachers had warned the ruling elites to be swift in introducing church reforms and addressing social concerns. They placed the blame for growing unrest entirely on adherents to the traditional church. "We demand only one thing of our opponents: that they no longer be allowed to belittle the honor of God, deceive the common man, and agitate the city with their godless lies, as they've done until now, without hindrance."[27] At the end of September the council requested an official statement from the evangelical ministers on the points of contention, which Bucer immediately drafted.[28] In twelve articles he summarized the teachings of the Reformation on the Bible and on justification and gave reasons for the rejection of the Mass and of all human ceremonies and inventions, including monastic vows, saint worship, purgatory, and the traditional liturgy. Just as vehemently as he emphasized that the gospel teaches obedience to government, he rejected the supposed authority of the pope and councils over the rest of the church.

Treger was released on October 12 and left the city. Overt opposition to the Reformation by supporters of the Catholic Church thus came to an end in Strasbourg. But Bucer, as well as Capito and Hedio, continued to battle Treger's ideas with the printed word.[29] In his treatise *Dispute with Conrad Treger* (*Handel mit Cunrat Treger*), Bucer gruffly asserted the exclusive authority of the Bible, in diametrical opposition to Treger's affirmation of church and councils as normative.

Yet how can one know that the Bible is the word of God and not human writ? "The Spirit, the comforter, who guides us in all truth according to Christ's promise, it is he who tells me this."[30] For Bucer, the Bible could and should claim unreserved authority, not because of a quality of supremacy attributed to it by man but as a result of the simple fact that it spoke to people and changed their hearts. He understood the church in the same way. Those whom the Holy Spirit had taught in this way, and therefore were elected by the Spirit (Bucer speaks of them for the first time as having been called by God before birth), constitute the true church of Jesus Christ. This true church, however, is hidden amid the mass of those who call themselves Christian and is thus not coterminous with any ecclesiastical organization, be it in Strasbourg, Rome, or elsewhere. In this respect, it is an invisible church.

Reforming the Worship Service

New problems were already besetting the preachers of Strasbourg as Bucer was writing those lines. Opposition to the Reformation by adherents to the traditional church may have been shattered, but the ministers were still far from their goal of reforming the church. Only the prerequisites for reform had been attained. The preachers' first goal was to create a standardized order of worship for the entire city. Convinced that this worship ordinance had to be squarely footed in the Bible, they presented their views to the theologians of Wittenberg and Zurich, hoping they could arrive at a conception that would be shared by the entire Reformation movement.[31] But already at this time the beginning conflict over the right understanding of the Lord's Supper began to eclipse all other topics. This is discussed in greater detail below. At this point it is important only to note that Bucer, who was particularly emphatic about the urgency of introducing a new liturgical order, was now acting in full accord with his colleagues. In the booklet *Ground and Cause* (*Grund und Ursach*), printed in the last days of December 1524, Bucer explained and justified the changes in the worship service.[32] Bucer prefaced his treatise with a letter to his former superior, Count Palatine Frederick, requesting that he give these ideas a hearing and scrutinize the alleged grounds critically, since they were intended for everybody, including laypeople. Eleven chapters followed in which Bucer discussed the liturgical innovations introduced in Strasbourg. All of seven were devoted exclusively to the Lord's Supper. A cool spirit of sternness and sobriety now pervaded worship in Strasbourg. Bucer did not just attack the idea that the Mass was a sacrifice; he also rejected priests' liturgical garments, the altar, and any form of ritual. Holy water and candles were to be done away with, as well as oil, salt, and consecrated water at baptisms. A simple table, prayers, psalms sung in German, a sermon—that was it. The Lord's Supper was celebrated every Sunday, and those attending were given the cup as well as the bread. The Strasbourg ministers were exceptionally rigorous in dealing with the numerous medieval church holidays, images, altarpieces, and side altars, abolishing them in their entirety. In this, the Strasbourg churchmen followed the model set by Zwingli and the church in Zurich. Whereas the Strasbourg liturgy retained the elevation of the eucharistic elements of bread and wine during the reading of the words of consecration as late as November 1524, this practice was now also dropped. Bucer gave a long-winded explanation for this measure, omitting to mention, however, that Zwingli as well had spoken out against elevation. Throughout all this, two things remained essential for Bucer: the clear teaching of the Bible and the conviction that external practices, ceremonies, and sacraments just diverted one's attention from what was ultimately important. "Since we have become dead to all earthly statutes through the death of Christ and have received only two earthly ceremonies and signs from the Lord, baptism and the Lord's Supper, we therefore admonish the people to pay more attention to *why* he instituted them for us than to *what* they are in themselves."[33] Only the future would tell whether this view could carry the day.

Liturgical changes in the worship services of the parish churches did not mean that the Reformation had triumphed in Strasbourg. The Catholic Mass—for the evangelicals, an intolerable blasphemy and abomination to the Lord—was still being celebrated in Strasbourg, most prominently in the cathedral itself and in the collegiate churches of St. Thomas, Old St. Peter, and Young St. Peter. Besides, there were still monasteries in which worship services continued to be held as in times past. The preachers fought these last bulwarks of the Catholic Church in Strasbourg by every available means. The city council, however, kept a low profile. It did require all clergymen to enlist in the roster of citizenship on January 3, 1525. But it did not make up its mind to abolish all Masses in the city until February 1529. As of May 1525, it had prohibited Masses in Strasbourg but expressly excluded from this interdiction the daily High Mass in the cathedral and in the three collegiate churches. The council had good reasons for giving in, if only partially, to the Reformation: the ruling elite realized all too well that they were in danger of being overrun by the peasants in the country and by their supporters in the city.

Rifts

The Peasants' War

From the beginning of the sixteenth century, growing social unrest in the countryside found expression in local and sometimes regional movements of uprising peasants, in Alsace as elsewhere. The Reformation message provided these movements with a new and exciting rallying cry.[34] The peasants' grievances over the manifold forms of economic, fiscal, political, and social oppression they endured, together with what they had traditionally described as their ancient law, probably also "divine law" and "divine justice"—these gained sudden new strength and momentum when combined, if not downright identified, with the gospel, understood as the unequivocal expression of God's will in the Bible.

One should by no means underestimate the peasants' religious motivation and sincerity. Their frustration with the half-hearted services rendered them by the poorly paid, indifferent, and often absent chaplains was certainly authentic. They demanded that evangelical preachers be hired, and they were ready to pay for them out of their own pockets. Bucer himself drafted and supported many such requests. Indeed, it was events in Strasbourg that provided the peasants with models they could imitate when dealing with the despised, affluent clergy, such as laying claim to their income, especially the tithe, for the benefit of the local parish and making it a point to use the Bible to vindicate their demands. Ties between country and town were close anyhow. Entire villages belonged to the city or to its collegiate churches. Others were fiefs owned by members of the patriciate. But wealthy burghers also owned land in the country and leased it to the peasants or lent money to them. Peasants from the surrounding countryside and villages came to Strasbourg regularly, not just on religious holidays but also during the weekly market days to sell their produce. On the whole, they had very close ties to Strasbourg's urban peasants, the aforesaid Gardeners, to many of whom they were related. For this reason, the Reformation movement spread early on from the city to the country, not just by means of pamphlets and sermons by clergymen but also through laypeople. Towns' craftsmen started showing up in the villages surrounding Strasbourg around February 1524, preaching. Their presence increased during the winter of 1524/25, coinciding with rising unrest in the countryside. The prohibition of this preaching activity by the city council on February 25, 1525, clearly did not stop it. These sermons and the twelve articles of the Swabian peasants, which also circulated widely at this time, created the right conditions for the peasants' uprising also to gain a foothold in Alsace at the beginning of April 1525.

The twelve articles are an interesting mixture of grievances, reform proposals, and revolutionary demands. In them the peasants lament the loss of their traditional economic and social rights, demand the reinstatement of earlier conditions, and call, in the name of the gospel and divine law, for a comprehensive reorganization of all of society. According to their wishes, God was to be given honor and earthly conditions were to be refashioned according to the injunctions of the Bible, in brotherly love and for the good of all. The peasants thus saw themselves as standing on God's side. At the same time, they thought it self-evident that the people of Strasbourg were their allies. The council did, in fact, send two of its members to begin negotiations with them on the twelve articles. It insisted, however, on speaking only to a committee elected by the peasants. The remaining peasants were to return to their homes in exchange for the promise of exemption from punishment. In answer to this, Erasmus Gerber, the leader of the peasant troops encamped at the abbey of Altorf near Mols-heim, asked the Strasbourg ministers on April 17 to come and talk with them.[35] The council gave its consent, probably favorably impressed with the declaration by Capito, Bucer, and Zell that they did not want to med-dle with the negotiations but rather confront the peasants "with what the word of God allows" and admonish them "to desist from such riotous assemblies." This is exactly what they told the peasants on April 18. On their way back to Strasbourg they drafted a letter to the peasants, repeat-ing their warnings in concise form. In it they reassured the peasants that they wished to help them, but that this was possible only if the peasant troops disbanded and allowed a committee representing them to negoti-ate with the city council in a conciliatory atmosphere. The council finally reminded them that they could not place themselves on God's side, for no revolt could be justified with the Bible.

Gerber succeeded in keeping his troops together in spite of these injunc-tions. This placed the Strasbourg government in a difficult situation, for the revolting peasants were establishing increasingly close contacts with the city's Gardeners and artisans. Eager to eliminate as many sources of conflict as possible and to consolidate its own power, the council decreed tax rebates and abolished, as mentioned above, most of the Masses. Tensions in the city approached their highest point when the peasants decided to march on Strasbourg to force the expropriation of those clergymen who had taken citizenship only recently just to benefit from the city's protection. Could the city in this situation continue to defend the right of anybody to become a citizen? The council consulted the *Schöf-fen*, the assembly of guild representatives, on May 11, and these procured the answer of the guilds on May 14. The vast majority chose to defend Strasbourg.

The city was spared this test of wills. The army of the duke of Lorraine caught up with the peasants near Saverne on May 17 and attacked them ruthlessly, causing a horrific bloodbath. A stream of refugees, mostly the wives and children of the defeated peasants, poured into Strasbourg, flee-ing the victors' vicious revenge. In the midst of this situation, Capito wrote a moving letter to *Ammeister* Kniebis, warning him of God's impending anger toward all who were now rejoicing. At the same time he pleaded for the council to be merciful, particularly toward the innocent: "I hear such gruesome reports that my ears are tingling. Disdain this by no means, my dear sir, and save the innocent!"[36] We know of no such statement by Bucer. This must not necessarily mean that he did not share Capito's feelings. Bucer did, however, remain remarkably silent during this period. The issues that really moved him were the struggle against the Mass and the papacy. He was outraged at the accusation that evangelical teaching had brought about the uprising. Exactly the opposite was true, he claimed in a letter to Beatus Rhenanus in August,[37] for the gospel and its proclaimers emphatically demanded obedience to the authorities from everyone. Long before the peasants' uprising, Bucer had become convinced, for pragmatic as well as theological reasons, that his goal of renewing the church and society could be achieved only in league with the government. He did not see quite as clearly that severing the Reformation movement from the religious and social concerns of vast portions of the population would also deprive his own plans of additional momentum from which they could have profited.

The Anabaptists

The defeat of the peasants and their allies did not signify the end of the Reformation in Strasbourg. But a spirit of disillusionment, passivity, and even total lack of interest in church issues undeniably started to spread— in the council as well as amid the population in general. This climate was propitious to the Anabaptists, who started arriving in Strasbourg as refugees as early as 1524 and were received quite warmly, particularly into the milieu of the Gardeners. These urban peasants also had a fiery lay preacher of their own, Clemens Ziegler, whom they refused to abandon. Ziegler himself, however, never joined the Anabaptists.[38]

Anabaptism grew out of many different sources and was anything but homogeneous. Two things about it, however, were clear. First, it represented a radicalization of Reformation positions, primarily those of Zurich but certainly of some Wittenberg positions as well. Second, Anabaptists preached and lived out an alternative to the mainstream of the Reformation, which the authorities had increasingly domesticated and channeled. Just how popular Anabaptist ideas were in Strasbourg, at least for a limited period, is made evident by the fact that those printers who were particularly sensitive to current moods preferred publishing Anabaptist pamphlets over ones written by the city preachers, and that the censors let them have their way. An anonymous pamphlet printed at the beginning of August 1528 also reveals the disenchantment of some Christians with the course the official church in Strasbourg was taking.[39] In a first section, the author complains that being evangelical apparently only means vilifying the Mass, clergymen, and monks and rejecting images in churches, church laws, and the pope. He then goes on:

> Love should be the only watchword
> for clearly identifying Christians.
> Now everybody goes his own way,
> to the detriment of the whole community.
> You notice this in the entire world,
> from the city mayor to the swineherd.
> Each claims to be the better Christian:
> under this cloak they disguise their evil,
> just as long as they can interpret everything,
> to support their own profit and enjoyment.
> But as soon as they can't, they promptly
> call it "rebellion" and "fanaticism."

At the time this text—written by Heinrich Vogtherr the Elder, who was at least an Anabaptist sympathizer—appeared, Anabaptist congregations with hundreds of members were already an integral part of the religious landscape of the city. These congregations, however, consisted almost entirely of refugees. The council's attitude toward dissenting religious views and beliefs was one of leniency, nonchalance, and to a certain extent even indifference, just as long as its political predominance was left untouched and peace and order in the city were not disturbed. This turned Strasbourg during these years into a refuge attractive to all religious outsiders and marginal groups.

The first to come were Anabaptists from Switzerland, who initially refrained, however, from proclaiming their views publicly. This changed in the course of 1526. Wilhelm Reublin's activities led to the development of a congregation inspired by his theological views. Soon a second Anabaptist congregation emerged, made up of followers of Hans Denck. Not too long after this, important additional Anabaptist leaders showed up in Strasbourg: Michael Sattler, Martin Cellarius, and Ludwig Hätzer. The Anabaptist movement was, of course, significantly broader than just these leaders and their respective supporters. There was the weaver Hans Wolff, for instance, from the little town of Benfeld between Sélestat and Strasbourg, who sometime in the spring of 1526 stormed Zell's pulpit during a sermon and tried to shove him away, hurling wild imprecations and announcing the end of the world at noon on Ascension Day, 1533. Bucer saw more than just religious fanaticism in all this. In all his dealings with

Anabaptists, he remained concerned not merely to have perfunctory conversations but rather to engage in serious discussion of fundamental theological issues with them.

A first opportunity for such an exchange finally arrived in December 1526. The first of these debates pitted Bucer and Capito on the one side against Michael Sattler on the other. Before long, decisive differences emerged. Whereas the Strasbourg theologians emphasized that love of one's fellow humans had to express itself in the assumption of political responsibility for the common good, Sattler gave utmost importance to the Sermon on the Mount, whose commandments Christians were called to obey unreservedly. Sattler's personal qualities, however, left a deep impression on Bucer and Capito, and they acclaimed him as a "martyr of Christ" upon hearing the shocking news of his brutal execution by the Austrian authorities several weeks later in Rottenburg on the Neckar River.

Talking to Hans Denck turned out to be much more difficult. Bucer perceived Denck as a dangerous deceiver, and he strove to expose him as such. For this reason, he made a point of confronting him in a public disputation in the Dominican church on November 22, 1526—against the will of the city council. It was decided that the topic of debate would be Denck's recent book *On the Law of God* (*Vom Gesetz Gottes*). Denck succeeded brilliantly in concealing his views through evasive answers, which led an outwitted and frustrated Bucer to accuse him of hypocrisy. Denck was expelled from Strasbourg on December 25, and on December 31 the council issued a mandate against Anabaptists, which was not published, however, until July 27, 1527.[40] The primary offense condemned in this mandate, the accommodation and harboring of Anabaptists, implies that most members of this movement in Strasbourg were outsiders who had sought refuge in the imperial city.

Wishing to warn the people of Strasbourg against what he perceived as Denck's dangerous teachings, Bucer published a booklet at the end of June 1527 in which he attacked seven theses drafted by the Worms preacher Jacob Kautz, whom Denck had just won over to his views. Bucer's *Faithful Warning* (*Getrewe Warnung*)[41] reveals how much he actually had in common with spiritualistic Anabaptists: as they did, he attributed a central role to the Holy Spirit, believed in God's election of the faithful, relativized the sacraments, and attached great importance to church discipline. Bucer drew a sharp line, however, when he saw Christ's saving work being diluted for the sake of turning him into an ethical model to be imitated. He also clearly rejected the Anabaptists when they self-righteously separated themselves from the rest of the community and when they refused to assume political responsibility in the form of governmental posts.

Bucer was in a heightened state of alert on this issue because his close colleague Capito began to dally with Anabaptism in the course of the year 1527. Martin Cellarius, whom Capito had taken into his home, succeeded in convincing the respectable provost of more and more of his ideas, which boiled down to an apocalyptic sort of spiritualism: the end times were at hand and the truly faithful were to turn inward and, in a process of gradually increasing spiritualization, detach themselves from all external church rituals.[42] Capito wrote a commentary on the book of Hosea that reflected these new ideas. Bucer was alarmed about this and entreated Zwingli and Pellikan in Zurich, Oecolampadius in Basel, and Ambrosius Blarer in Constance to do all they could to stop Capito from joining the Anabaptists. They succeeded in this. But the Anabaptists benefited immensely from the open sympathies displayed toward them by a churchman of such high reputation in the city and far beyond. These events contributed further to Bucer's emergence as the leading theological and intellectual figure of the Strasbourg Reformation.

A new wave of refugees brought about one hundred Augsburg Anabaptists to Strasbourg in the first half of 1528. For the first time there were revolutionary elements in town, shaped in their ideas by Hans Hut, a former follower of Thomas Müntzer. They preached the gathering of the faithful church in the end times and predicted that the persecution and oppression suffered at the present would abruptly change into their opposite, with the Anabaptists helping God out when he destroyed all his opponents on the day of wrath. Bucer was now ready to resort to harsh measures. He contemplated the death penalty for these militant Anabaptists and deportation for all the rest. The council, however, continued its policy of merely banishing undesirable persons.

The Controversy over the Lord's Supper

From the end of 1524, nothing engaged Bucer's attention more than the disagreement within the evangelical camp over the right understanding of the Lord's Supper.[43] This gradually became the topic most often addressed in his private and public statements. At first sight it is difficult to understand what this quarrel, conducted with ever growing hostility and accompanied by waves of bitter invectives and malicious allegations, was all about. For this conflict's central protagonists in Wittenberg and Zurich, and their respective supporters, what was at stake was the heart, indeed, the very essence of the Reformation. Before we look at this controversy more closely, it is important that we take a number of intrinsic and extrinsic preconditions into account. None of these was fundamental to this sharp theological split, but all were essential for understanding the course taken by this bitter struggle.

To begin with, all participants in the controversy over the Lord's Supper were former priests. That is, the Mass had stood at the very center of their ministry. Regardless of how rigorously and fundamentally they later rejected this theology, there can be no doubt that the question of the Lord's Supper occupied a much more significant place in their thoughts and emotions than any other theological topic. In addition, all those taking sides in this conflict or working out an independent position were acquaintances or even friends, especially those living in southwest Germany. Because of common intellectual roots and intersecting personal backgrounds, they were extremely well informed about the convictions and misgivings of "the other side" as it slowly began to crystallize here and there. Finally, what Zwingli and Luther were ultimately fighting about became evident only gradually. Only after cutting through layer after layer of accusations—that one side was betraying the Reformation and relapsing into Roman Catholicism, that the other was destroying the Word and Sacraments of God in the manner of enthusiasts and spiritualists—were the core theological issues at stake finally uncovered.

Bucer was an inextricable part of, and indeed thrived on, this network of personal contacts. Keeping in touch with people like Andreas Osiander in Nuremberg or Johannes Brenz in Schwäbisch Hall did not just give Bucer new ideas; these contacts challenged him to seek understanding and true theological agreements beween conflicting parties. Bucer's inclination, already encountered at an earlier time in his life, to seek and maintain contact with as many like-minded people as possible, became evident here. This turned Bucer into a man of compromise: someone seeking to settle differences once and for all in a conflict he felt was not only senseless but downright disastrous. At the same time, however, Bucer established contacts not just with opponents in the Lord's Supper controversy but also with people in places as far away as Silesia, and in France, Italy, and the Netherlands, in order to win people over to his *own* understanding of the Reformation.

It would be a misconception to interpret Bucer's readiness to dialogue during these years and his long-term endeavor to play down and, if possible, overcome the controversy over the Lord's Supper as evidence that he had no position of his own on this issue. The opposite is true. In the late fall of 1524, Bucer definitely abandoned the idea that the body and blood of Christ were physically present in the elements of bread and wine. A combination of motives was at work here.[44] He had always harbored doubts about the physical presence, he wrote later. In this he was possibly influenced by Erasmus. Initially, Bucer refused to give in to these doubts, since Luther himself seemed to cling to this understanding of the presence of Christ in the eucharistic elements. This changed, however, after Bucer read a sermon by Luther on John 6, in which the Wittenberg theologian put all emphasis on faith only—without intending to apply this biblical text to the Lord's Supper. But this is exactly what Bucer did. He thus underscored the importance of faith in the crucified and resurrected Christ, a faith that is strengthened through this sacrament, enabling all Christians, both individuals and entire congregations, to love their fellow human beings. What need was there, then, for the external elements of bread and wine, and even for this sacrament in the first place? That was exactly the question asked by Andreas Karlstadt, Luther's former colleague and now uncompromising opponent, in October 1524. Karlstadt published a series of pamphlets in Basel in which he tirelessly expounded his interpretation of the biblical words of consecration. According to Karlstadt, Christ was pointing at himself when he spoke the words "This is my body." We are therefore called to accept and receive Christ in spirit. This line of reasoning did indeed turn any external celebration of the Lord's Supper into something one could almost do without. Regardless of any appeal Karlstadt's interpretation may have had, Bucer could not help protesting vociferously, as an exegete and biblical scholar. Jesus himself had solemnly consecrated the Lord's Supper, and for this reason alone it could not be inconsequential. Besides, Karlstadt's exegesis was grammatically untenable. This was the situation when the Dutchman Hinne Rode came to Strasbourg on November 21, 1524, with a treatise-like letter from his countryman Cornelis Hoen. On the basis of comparison with other, similar biblical passages, Hoen interpreted the "is" in the words of consecration ("This is my body") as "means" or "signifies." In other words, the elements of bread and wine referred to the crucified Christ but did not contain his body and blood. This exegetical explanation, which Hinne Rode expounded and defended in greater detail, convinced Bucer thoroughly. And he was delighted when he found out that Zwingli endorsed this interpretation.

But leaving grammar and phraseology aside, what was this conflict ultimately about? At stake was the question of *how* God approaches man through Christ. The church's traditional response, that this took place by means of the sacraments, no longer convinced the Reformers. Did that not bind Christ and place him at the disposal of the church? Could he in this case still be the Lord to whom one was to entrust one's self in faith, and in whose hands one was to place one's entire life? What was the origin of this faith? All Reformers agreed that faith was a gift: not something that man could accomplish but rather a work of the Holy Spirit, brought about by God on the spur of the moment. How does God work in people when he changes their minds and convinces them of the truth of God's unconditional love in the life and ministry of Jesus Christ? Zwingli claimed that God acted directly and immediately.[45] God could also use external means, such as the preached word and the sacraments. These externalities, however, dare not be overemphasized, lest they usurp the place reserved for what is most important: God's gift. It was not least the attacks by his Catholic opponents, claiming Luther's interpretation of the supper as proof of the truth of their own views, that convinced Zwingli he was the lone defender of the fundamental Reformation credo of justification alone by faith in Jesus Christ.

Yet what guards such a faith from being a mere mood, an illusion, or a form of pious self-deception, if it is not qualified by something objective—something beyond man's disposal precisely because it is an external, objective authority, such as the preached word and particularly the word of the Bible? That was Luther's fundamental objection.[46] In the same way that God became man in Jesus Christ, God had bound his further presence and activity to the preached word of God and the dispensation of sacraments. The implications are enormously comforting: sinners plagued by self-doubt and fear can be certain that their Savior is there for them, not only in the preached word of God but in a very real and tangible way in the Lord's Supper, where Christ imparts himself freely to sinners in the elements of bread and wine. Whoever disputed this, thought Luther, was flatly denying the Reformation teaching of justification by grace, or, worse yet, was in league with Satan, who typically tried to turn all certainties of faith into subjective whims. This was precisely what Karlstadt was doing, said Luther. He condemned all others who opposed his views on this matter just as harshly, accusing them of dissolving what was indissoluble, of spiritualizing an eminently corporeal and concrete fact: that God had become man in Christ and that for this reason God comes to humankind tangibly and perceptibly in the elements of the Lord's Supper.

This is not the place to discuss the further altercations between Zwingli and Luther, which soon led to questions involving Christology and theology in general. This debate was certainly interesting, but Bucer made a point of not becoming involved in it. For both Zwingli and Luther, as the theological assumptions above demonstrate, the truth of the Reformation movement itself hinged upon the right interpretation of the Lord's Supper. For Bucer, this was simply not the case. He gave utmost importance to the Holy Spirit, who kindles in people's hearts trust that God will justify sinners, thus not only giving them joy and consolation but also moving them to love their fellow human beings. For this reason he never fully understood why Luther attached so much importance to the external signs and means to which God had bound himself. At the same time, he could not fully identify with Zwingli's uncompromising struggle against Luther's views. To be sure, Bucer found Zwingli's interpretation of the Lord's Supper to be the right one from an exegetical and, generally speaking, a theological standpoint, for he emphasized faith and the work of the Holy Spirit. In this respect, Bucer clearly stood in the camp of Zwingli as well as of Oecolampadius, who buttressed Luther's opponents in Basel. Bucer differed from Zwingli significantly, however, in that he never ceased to attribute the greatest importance to faith in Christ's reconciling act and the renewed life of the justified sinner—only these were decisive and therefore sufficient for church unity. All other issues were of only secondary importance for Bucer. Was it not possible to reach an accord at this level?

The Strasbourg preachers attempted an agreement of this type in October 1525, when they asked Gregor Casel, a common acquaintance well liked on both sides of the theological divide, to present their views in Wittenberg. In his instruction to Casel, Bucer tried to present the views of the Swiss theologians in a sympathetic light and pleaded for the mutual acceptance of differing views on the Lord's Supper. Luther responded with a harsh no. Unfazed by this reaction, Bucer concluded that he just had to work at finding the right wording that would satisfy both sides of the conflict. Solving the controversy over the Lord's Supper became his overriding concern, for he was convinced that it was nothing more than a trivial squabble over words that was distracting the Reformation movement's attention from more important things and destroying the unity much needed to confront supporters of the traditional church. But it was not just political and pragmatic reasons but also his theological convictions that led Bucer to be concerned about church unity. If all people, theologians and laypeople alike, are to read the Bible on their own and form their own opinions on what they've read—Bucer wrote in 1528—differing interpretations will inevitably result. But imperfect understandings of Scripture and even blatant errors are to be tolerated and do not jeopardize church unity, as long as they "do not overturn a child-like faith in God." "It is sufficient for our dear brethren if others agree with us on the fundamentals of the faith, those being: that we all are nothing and that God wants to save us and make us holy alone through Christ."[47] Bucer had thus taken up a position that strikes us as modern and that allowed him to enter into dialogue not only with Luther and his colleagues but also later with the Anabaptists and even with Roman Catholics.

However, Bucer himself thwarted this fruitful approach by taking it for granted that his and his Swiss friends' interpretation of the Lord's Supper was the only right one. Their opponents, the Wittenberg Reformers, were unfortunately wrong on this issue, but they were to be graciously tolerated in spite of this error, and everything possible was to be undertaken to set them right. With this understanding, Bucer wrote a defense, or *Apologia*, that he published in March 1526. Unfortunately, he interpolated his own interpretation of the Lord's Supper into two books by Wittenberg theologians that he published at the same time. In the first, Bugenhagen's commentary on the Psalms, which Bucer translated into German, Bucer inserted some remarks of his own on Psalm 111:5, without identifying them as an interpolation on his part. In the second, Bucer's Latin translation of the fourth volume of Luther's *Postils*, the Strasbourg theologian expressly corrects Luther's wrong understanding of the Lord's Supper in a series of separate annotations. The Wittenberg theologians were outraged. Luther was little convinced by Bucer's later claim that all he had wanted to do was invite readers to come to their own conclusions regarding the Lord's Supper. And Bugenhagen was even less persuaded by Bucer's attempt to place himself in the setting of late 1525, when there were no clear-cut, mutually hostile camps on this issue; nor did he take kindly to Bucer's reminder that he, Bugenhagen, had authorized Bucer to take liberties and use his own judgment in translating the Psalms commentary.[48] As far as the theologians in Wittenberg were concerned, Bucer had now manifestly proven himself to be a trickster and a hypocrite who talked about peace and understanding only in order to deceive his opponents.

Capito had warned Bucer ahead of time, foreseeing that his colleague's dubious methods would cause great harm. But no, wrote Capito to Zwingli on September 26, 1526, "our peasant" would not allow himself to be dissuaded.[49] This is a fitting characterization of Bucer. He was far from being someone who wanted to reach an agreement at any price. He could also vehemently demand that those positions he had determined to be true win recognition and be enforced. Would not everybody simply have to agree if one found clear and compelling wording?

This was just one side of his complex personality. At the same time, Bucer was further developing his already latent sensitivity to elements of truth in the arguments of his opponents. This changed the way in which he strove to solve the conflict over the Lord's Supper. He had not succeeded in making people ignore it as a trifling matter. Neither had he managed to carry the day merely on the persuasive power of his arguments, which had not convinced and won over his opponents as originally expected. It was therefore a question of finding the right formulation or wording that did justice to the views of both sides of the conflict. This is precisely what Bucer attempted to do as he now grappled with Luther's *Confession Concerning Christ's Supper* (*Vom Abendmahl Christi, Bekenntnis*),[50] which the Wittenberg theologian had described as his last word on this subject.

In the early summer of 1528, Bucer published a *Conciliation between Dr. Luther and His Opponents Regarding Christ's Supper* in the form of a remarkable dialogue.[51] Two merchants, one from Nuremberg representing Luther's views, the other from Strasbourg and a supporter of Bucer's interpretation, discuss the Lord's Supper. Predictably, the Strasbourg spokesman has better arguments at his disposal and ends up winning over his opponent. Bucer's purpose in writing this dialogue is thus clear: if he was not going to succeed in convincing Luther, at least he could try winning over some converts amid the latter's supporters. His second aim was to demonstrate that both sides coincided fundamentally in their respective interpretation of the Lord's Supper. Bucer felt he could prove this by taking up Luther's concept of a "sacramental union." The Wittenberg theologian had written that the bread and the body of Christ are definitely two completely different things; in the sacrament, however, they become an inseparable whole. By this Luther was trying to express his theological conviction that human beings, regardless of their worthiness and the strength of their faith, actually receive Christ, and that the Christ in the Lord's Supper is the same Christ who died for sinners on the cross. Both conclusions were unacceptable in this form for Bucer. Bucer tried to prove with logical and exegetical arguments that Luther was wrong when he believed that all who took Communion truly received Christ, irrespective of their faith. Neither was Bucer convinced that the raised Lord present in the Lord's Supper was simply identical with the crucified Christ. At the same time, however, Bucer emphasized that one could tolerate this mistaken understanding of the Wittenberg theologians, because Luther was finally no longer speaking of a Christ baked into the bread (*Christus impanatus*) but rather of a spiritual presence in the sacrament. And that was the decisive element for Bucer. "That is why we are reminded of the death of Christ: in order that we may believe and bear in mind that we are saved by means of his death. Wherever this happens, Christ is truly in our midst, we truly eat his flesh, truly drink his blood, and are true guests at his table; and even then we do not eat and drink mere bread and wine, but the bread and the cup of the Lord. The bread and the wine are then a true sacrament, a genuine sign and image, for the heart is spiritually and truly strengthened and edified by that which is represented and expressed externally through words and signs."[52] These sentences are clear evidence of the care Bucer took to express Christ's presence in the elements of the supper in particularly blurry terms. Luther accordingly rejected this interpretation in the harshest language. Bucer made no effort to accommodate, as far as Luther was concerned, persevering instead in views just as ungodly as they were mistaken. The fact that Bucer defended not only Zwingli and Oecolampadius but also the spiritualist Caspar Schwenckfeld and, in a sense, even Karlstadt convinced Luther beyond the shadow of a doubt.

Carrying Out the Reformation

Zwingli's Comrade in Arms

It is appropriate to look more closely at Bucer's relationship to Zwingli at this point.[53] Ever since Bucer's almost desperate letter to Zwingli in the spring of 1523, asking the Zurich reformer to procure him a position, correspondence between the two men had increased and become very personal. All issues of Reformation theology and practice became the subject of intense consultations between the Strasbourg theologians, led by Capito and Bucer, and Zwingli. These included topics such as images in churches, liturgical ordinances, the dissolution of monasteries, and degrees of consanguinity compatible with marriage but also encompassed fundamental issues such as baptism and the Lord's Supper. Events in Zurich during these years were seen as normative by the Strasbourg preachers, especially Bucer. A further factor was significant: a city council faction to which Claus Kniebis belonged was extremely interested in following the religious but even more the political course steered by this "democratic" city, which was a member of the Swiss Confederation. However, this was just one aspect of the question. No progress was being made toward reaching an accord that would allow Strasbourg to join a "Christian Federation" (*Christliches Burgrecht*) with Zurich, since opposition in the Strasbourg city council was too great. Neither were the Strasbourg preachers successful in convincing the council to carry through all the Reformation measures they deemed necessary. But it was not just these external factors that prevented the Strasbourg preachers from following Zurich's example entirely. Bucer's independence regarding Zwingli became evident early on and was much stronger than, say, Capito's. This did not mean Bucer was not willing to learn from Zwingli. But he certainly did not hesitate to formulate his own conceptions, object to Zwingli's arguments, and make his own suggestions as to how to proceed. Both were independent, self-reliant personalities who had common theological goals and supported one another against shared opponents.

The controversy over the Lord's Supper brought them even closer together. The actual differences between Zwingli and Bucer, as well as those between them and Oecolampadius in Basel, took second place to the need to close ranks. The disappointment was all the greater when this united stand began to dissolve after 1529. Initially, however, what they had in common prevailed. On no single occasion was this unity, at least as perceived from the outside, more evident than at the Bern disputation in January 1528, when Zwingli, Bucer, and Oecolampadius succeeded superbly in impressing their Swiss and southern German supporters with the power and effectiveness of the Reformation movement in this region.

Bern council elections in the spring of 1527 had paved the way for a possible victory of the Reformation.[54] Admittedly, the new city government left no doubt that it was going to maintain a firm grip over the local church. After considerable hesitation on the part of the authorities, Capito and Bucer were finally invited to a theological disputation organized by the council from January 6 to 26. The two were probably still in Bern immediately following that dispute, when the city magistrates decreed a number of sweeping changes in church matters on January 27, 1528, the most radical of which entailed the abolition of the Mass. Bucer and Capito had additionally made a lengthy stop in Basel in the last part of December on their way to Bern, taking time for thorough discussions with Oecolampadius and using the occasion as well to preach in the cathedral of Basel on December 26 and 27. They reached Bern at the beginning of January 1528. Their first contact with the Bern preacher Berchthold Haller, and especially with the Constance churchman Ambrosius Blarer, soon laid the foundation for lasting, close friendships. Bucer preached in Bern cathedral on January 22.

The Bern disputation consisted of three weeks of theological debates that took place in the Franciscan monastery in the presence of some 250 theologians. Admittedly, the vast majority of them sympathized with the Reformation before the disputation even began. Of the most prominent opposing theologians, not a single one attended except for Conrad Treger, who was present for only part of the debate. At issue were ten theses, five of which dealt with dogmatic fundamentals such as the meaning of the Bible, Christ, and the church, and the other five with church ordinances and ceremonies. Bucer intervened a total of sixty-two times in the discussion of the first group of topics. He was thus not only the most zealous disputant after Zwingli (who gave voice to his views 107 times) but also an eloquent speaker, skillful at gaining the sympathies of the public. In these debates, Bucer assumed a position entirely in line with what he had proclaimed up to this point: faith is all that counts; the Holy Spirit is of central importance; decisive for church unity is that all agree on the doctrine of justification—everything else can be tolerated, if necessary; there is no fundamental criterion other than the Bible; people become convinced of its truth through the work of the Holy Spirit. This sounds like a complete accommodation to Zwingli and his theology. Nothing could be further from the truth, however. Already in April 1524, when the issue of images in churches was acute, Bucer was unmistakably clear in telling the Zurich preachers that the biblical norm was only one side of the question, "for if the Holy Spirit is not instructing our hearts, Scripture can also become the letter that kills."[55] Bucer's theology is characterized by a fundamental tension between God's justice and law on the one side and the activity of the Holy Spirit on the other—ethical obligations toward our fellow human beings on the one hand and empowerment by the Spirit to fulfill these obligations on the other. Because of this, Bucer could emphasize different things in different contexts, following the guideline of love for one's neighbor but also keeping in mind what was necessary to promote this neighbor's faith. This made it easier for Bucer to approach other theological positions. But it never implied accommodating fully to another theological position, be it Zwingli's or—as we shall see later on—Luther's.

Education and Training

For Bucer, God's law was summed up in the commandment to serve our fellow human beings. Christians not only needed to be informed about this, but they also had to be educated and trained in this new way of life. Naturally, it was ultimately the Holy Spirit who played the decisive role. Nevertheless, church representatives and secular goverments had to do everything in their power to promote what was good and prevent evil in the city. Therefore, Bucer demanded of the ruling authorities that they permit the free preaching of God's truth, and also do away with false teaching and with forms of worship that contradicted God's commandments. Bucer placed great importance on the instruction and education of adults, and even more so of young people. For this reason he continued to give one-hour classes every day on books of the Bible at the Dominican monastery (today the *Gymnase Jean Sturm*). In addition, he and his colleagues arranged for catechism lessons for children to begin every Sunday afternoon in the summer of 1526. This was not enough: he also called on the city council to found German and Latin schools in order that the youth "be instructed and trained" in a form that is "Christian before God and also beneficial to the world." After all, as Bucer had already written in the summer of 1524, "the hope of benefit for all rests upon the youth."[56] These schools were to be funded with the income previously received by monasteries and collegiate churches. In 1526, the city decided to take on educational responsibility and entrusted three schoolmasters (*Scholarchen*), one of them Jacob Sturm, with this task. This commission, however, did not take action until 1528, when a Latin school was set up in the Dominican monastery under the leadership of Johannes Sapidus, and Otto Brunfels placed his own private school under the authority of the new educational commission. A major concern of Bucer's was also that the city of Strasbourg maintain a strict moral discipline. Hoping that church and city council would cooperate closely, he sought the establishment of a carefully structured system of church discipline that would include procedures such as personal admonishments but would not shy away from more drastic measures such as banning from the congregation. At the same time, the city council was to issue mandates that made disorderly and immoral behavior punishable.

Although Bucer's greatest emphasis was on morality, he did not lose sight of economic problems. In August 1524, for instance, he demanded that the city of Strasbourg spend more on its poor. At the same time, he spoke out vigorously against the exploitative practice of *fürkauff*, by which wealthy citizens bought up an entire crop or all the wine before the actual harvest or vintage in order to set arbitrary prices later on. Finally, Bucer never missed an occasion to criticize wealthy merchants harshly, be it in his very first written work in 1523, his *Conciliation* (*Vergleichung*) with Luther of 1528, or his attacks on this social class in 1549 in connection with the Interim. This same excoriation of the unchristian and antisocial craving for "mammon" can be encountered in Luther's and the other Reformers' writings. Bucer was trying to win the people of Strasbourg over to an all-encompassing vision of a Christian restructuring of society and it was his special wish that the city magistrates in particular commit themselves to carrying out such a vision. The central model to which

Bucer appealed over and over again was at least in part a reappearance of the traditional idea of seeking the general benefit of the community. Bucer's theology gave this model additional depth and weight. At stake were more than practical considerations of usefulness; at stake was God's law itself, which demanded an unreserved commitment to one's fellow humans and their needs. Therefore evangelization, preaching, edification, education, training, church discipline, and the enforcement of Christian day-to-day behavior by the magistrates were necessarily and logically intertwined from Bucer's perspective. Bucer was convinced that if the pure gospel were preached in Strasbourg, it would be clearly reflected in the morality of the lives led by its inhabitants.

All this was, of course, a program, a demand, and it had little to do with reality for the time being. But it did not leave Strasbourg untouched. When the city of Basel requested of the Strasbourg city council that Bucer be allowed to come to them for a limited period of time or, better yet, permanently, the council refused. It thus identified itself de facto with Bucer's goals.[57] When, soon after, a group of churchmen and laypeople asked the council to provide Bucer with a more centrally located apartment so that he would not have such a long way to his Bible classes in the Dominican monastery, the council consented immediately. Bucer was offered a house in the vicinity of St. Thomas Church (today no. 3, Rue Salzmann). It is not an exaggeration to observe symbolic significance in this move. Bucer was definitely no longer at the margins, but had found his place at the very ecclesiastical and political center of town.

A Biblical Scholar

During these years, Bucer published, in rapid succession, a number of commentaries on Old and New Testament books. All these exegetical writings were the fruit of the lectures he had given to educated churchmen and laypeople in the past years, which explains their broad approach and repetitiousness.[58] Capito proceeded in much the same fashion. He first gave a series of lectures on Habakkuk, Malachi, and Hosea and thereafter published a commentary on Habakkuk in 1526, then one on Hosea in German in 1527 and in Latin in 1528. In 1527, Bucer began an exegetical study of the Synoptic Gospels on the basis of Matthew. This commentary, dedicated to the Strasbourg city council, appeared in the spring of that year in two volumes. A commentary on Ephesians followed in the summer, and in April 1528 a commentary on the Gospel of John appeared with a preface to the Bernese ministers. In 1530, Bucer decided to merge both the commentary on the Synoptic Gospels and the one on John into a one-volume Gospel commentary without undertaking any major changes. In September 1528 he published a commentary on the book of Zephaniah, and one year later his exceedingly learned commentary on the Psalms. This last work appeared under the pseudonym of Aretius Felinus and was dedicated to the successor to the French throne. Most of these commentaries went through several editions.

Bucer's central goal as an exegete was to determine with the greatest possible clarity what the respective biblical author had intended to say. This required the ability to read the Bible in the original. Bucer not only had an excellent command of Greek, but he was also a first-rate Hebraist. But that was not enough. A biblical exegete, Bucer was convinced, must be extremely careful not to insert a conjured-up, supposedly more profound "spiritual" or mystical meaning into the message of the Bible. The allegorical interpretation of these texts only led one astray. Grasping the exact meaning of individual statements in the Bible would allow one to know what God intended in the past as well as today. He had chosen to interpret the Bible in this way, wrote Bucer in the preface to the commentary on the Synoptic Gospels, because "it is necessary that nothing other than the certain words of God be preached in the churches, words on which reason can rely beyond all doubt."[59] Bucer therefore placed much importance on finding out as much as possible about the historical circumstances in which the statements of the Bible were spoken and he made a point of consulting medieval Jewish commentaries when studying the Old Testament. Finally, Bucer tirelessly called on his readers to be self-reliant and to examine and judge for themselves, in order to come to their own conclusions as laypeople. On the whole, Bucer's biblical interpretations impress one as remarkably modern and progressive, although their style and systematic structure are less than engaging.

Bucer's aim was not just to write sophisticated and learned books. He did not just want to teach—he wanted to edify; he wanted to inspire his readers to do the right thing, to take the right kind of action. In this regard, he stood squarely in the tradition of Erasmus, of whose New Testament paraphrases he made avid use. Consequently, Bucer always combined the interpretation of a passage of Scripture with dogmatic and ethical observations, and also took the opportunity to bring the Bible to bear upon current issues, such as the Anabaptists and their understanding of baptism and secular government, on the one hand, or the right interpretation of the Lord's Supper, on the other. For Bucer, these were not extraneous questions foreign to the text. On the contrary, this was a consequence of how much he valued the Bible: if it contained God's truth, then it also had to contain the answers to all the questions with which the church was wrestling. Conversely, these problems were to be solved on this foundation, through the laborious study of Scripture, and not by means of speculations removed from the Bible.

Bucer pursued another important goal through his commentaries. As in his Latin translation of Luther's biblical expositions, for instance, on the epistles of Peter and Jude or the six volumes of the *Postils* (1525–1527), Bucer wanted to help the Reformation movement spread and to encourage embattled evangelicals in Italy, France, and the Low Countries. To outwit the censors and quietly disseminate Reformation ideas in countries such as France, Bucer not only used a pseudonym and wove Gallicisms into his Latin but also deliberately pretended to advocate the views of a humanistically educated adherent of the Catholic Church who was open to new ideas. Bucer's world went far beyond the city walls of Strasbourg and the borders of the Holy Roman Empire. It extended to the countries from which the big trade routes came that met in Strasbourg. Religious refugees from these countries arrived at Strasbourg early on—and not a few of them returned to their home countries as missionaries for the Reformation. "Strasbourg is the city of refuge for the expelled brethren," wrote Capito in July 1524 to the Leipzig doctor Heinrich Stromer. "Everybody who's persecuted somewhere comes here, and from here they are sent out again to serve the Word of God."[60]

The Abolition of the Mass

Manifold efforts at educating and training the population according to Christian principles, untold sermons, teaching and admonitions—all these could have only limited success, believed Bucer and his colleagues, as long as the forms of worship of the traditional church, especially the Mass, continued to be celebrated in the city. From the end of the Peasants' War, that is, the early summer of 1525, the Strasbourg preachers assailed the Mass without ceasing and pleaded with the council in ever new petitions to finally do away with this abominable "blasphemy."[61] Their arguments always ran as follows. The Mass is blasphemous because it claims to repeat Christ's unique sacrifice on the cross and even turns this act into a human work justly earning divine merit. The Mass has no basis in Scripture; in fact, it contradicts God's clear instructions on how to celebrate the Lord's Supper. Finally, the Mass does not promote Christian community but rather hinders it, and it does so in a complete and absolute fashion, ever since the truth has become manifest at least to a minority of Strasbourg citizens. This religious disunity of the population was an impending threat, argued the Strasbourg ministers in the spring of 1527, that would ultimately bring about "the doom of the city and of the common good."[62]

The city magistrates, including those members of the council who sympathized with the Reformation, saw things quite differently. The evangelical preachers and their supporters were, after all, just one of many groups in the city. A considerable number of citizens stubbornly clung to the traditional church. Most important, the bishop and the influential canons of the collegiate churches threatened the council and wielded enough power to cause the city a great deal of political trouble should it dare to flout the emperor's prohibition by going ahead with the suppression of the Mass. In addition, there were theological and pastoral aspects to the question. Jacob Sturm, for example, strongly criticized any attempt to change the old forms of worship in a moving statement drafted in August 1525.[63] The preachers' intimidating menaces and insults, he asserted, diverted attention from the essence of this sacrament, which was "brotherly love." Shouldn't we have patience with one another? "After all, there are Christians on both sides—may God have mercy!" Sturm was convinced that the rapid innovations of the past months had brought about only unrest, discord, and much damage, including the Peasants' War. For Sturm, it was a violation of people's consciences to presume one could amend in one year what had deteriorated in the course of centuries. Bucer countered in May 1526: "It is unchristian to say: 'Should we really change everything at once . . . ?' Who would not, if there was poison in his drink and he found out, immediately overturn his cup and empty it?"[64] The preachers once again pressed the council to abolish the Mass a year later: "If you are worried that there is only little faith in the church, demonstrate all the more a stronger faith and put to an end what prevents a true understanding of God's law and of faith in the church!"[65] The strongest argument of the ministers was the conviction that they were fighting for the cause of divine justice and truth.

Pressure on the council increased during 1528. Not only were the preachers warning and beseeching the magistrate, but now upper-rank citizens and groups within artisan guilds also filed petitions demanding the abolition of the Mass in order to save the city from God's wrath. Toward the end of 1528, the authorities became increasingly inclined to leave the decision on this matter up to the rarely convoked *Schöffen* of the guilds. This did not mean, however, that the authorities had reached a consensus. It is quite revealing, for instance, that Jacob Sturm, writing from Worms and on his way to the imperial diet in Speyer, implored his colleagues by no means to undertake any liturgical innovations. Conversely, Capito beseeched Claus Kniebis on January 3, 1529—that is to say, shortly before the decisive session of the council—to do everything in his might to ensure that the Mass finally be abolished. "This must now hold true: your city has to accept either the Pope or Christ completely and exclude the opposite."[66]

On January 9, 1529, the council called on the *Schöffen* to give this question careful consideration until February 20, when the voting was to take place. The results were 184 votes for the immediate abolition of the Mass, 1 against, and 94 in favor of postponing the decision until the diet of Speyer was no longer in session (of the three hundred *Schöffen*, twenty-one were not present). Although the council was quick to declare that the Mass had not been abolished, but rather its celebration suspended until it could be proven that it was a form of worship that pleased God, Strasbourg had definitely joined the Reformation through this decision.

Chapter Four

Spokesman of the Strasbourg Reformation

The Gospel and Politics

The Emperor, the Empire, and the Reformation

In 1523, two prince electors—the prince-archbishop of Trier and the secular elector Palatine—joined Landgrave Philip of Hesse in crushing the uprising of imperial knights led by the eccentric Franz von Sickingen. The same two princes, their differing stances toward the Reformation notwithstanding, joined ranks again two years later and annihilated the troops of rebel peasants. Both events illustrate a complex phenomenon: the political future of the Holy Roman Empire lay in the hands of the territorial princes.[1] Accordingly, their influence on the development and organization of the Reformation became increasingly great. Two goals were being pursued in this process, goals that often overlapped or merged in one and the same person. The first of these was the endeavor on the part of the prince to extend his own power and jurisdiction beyond the power and jurisdiction of others—be those the church or the local representatives of the imperial estates—by concentrating as many privileges and rights in his hands as possible. This expansion, however, implied a change in what it meant to "rule" over others. Ruling was no longer primarily seen as the static preservation of domestic law and order but took on a dynamic quality, aiming to achieve the greatest possible good for the many. This process could also be observed in the cities. There we increasingly see "governments" (*Obrigkeiten*) developing out of the "democratically" elected representatives of the community.[2] The second goal was the improvement and renewal of the church. This goal cannot be understood separately from the first, but neither can it simply be identified with it.

87

Issues of faith and questions regarding the correct understanding of revealed Christian truth were anything but marginal for the political rulers of the time. This relationship is precisely what makes the political positions and decisions of this period so complicated. In any case, the development of the Reformation in the territories and in the cities became increasingly assimilated into the efforts by the rulers to expand and consolidate their own political power. In most places this assimilation resulted in the standardization of doctrine and the organization of territorial church structures under governmental supervision and support. The imperial diet of Speyer in 1526 unintentionally helped bring about this development with its official resolution that, until the next council, "everyone should act as he deems accountable before God, Imperial Majesty, and the Empire."[3]

The rise and consolidation of princely territorial states within the Holy Roman Empire, a development that began around 1500, was at complete odds with the imperial idea and the vision of a centralized state with a monarch as its head as exemplified by emerging states in Spain, France, and England. Germany's political and ecclesiastical development, however, remained marked by the fundamental dichotomy of the holy Roman emperor on the one side and the territorial princes on the other. It was this fact that made the diffusion and success of the Reformation movement in the empire possible in the first place.

Any emperor who attempted to tighten the reins of power in much the same way as the princes were gradually and successfully doing in their own territories was bound to encounter fierce resistance on their part. At the same time, the imperial idea was so deeply ingrained in the political sphere that the relationship between imperial crown and princes cannot be simplistically reduced to one of antagonism. Tensions indeed became greater, however, with the elevation of a Spanish Habsburg to the imperial throne. Charles V embodied like no other ruler the idea of a universal monarchy, that is to say, one that encompassed many nations. The proud claim that the sun never set on his empire was not false. But for the time being, the overseas territories were much less significant for Charles than the European ones. Charles's territorial holdings managed to surround France and the Papal States in Italy effectively from all sides. This meant that Charles soon found himself involved in a fundamental, enduring struggle with these two European powers. A third factor he had to consider in his foreign policy was the consistent advance of the Ottoman Turks in the Balkan Peninsula, threatening Vienna and the very Habsburg heartland. On account of his overwhelming political might, Charles V was able to defeat his opponents on countless occasions. But it was precisely this indisputable superiority that incited Charles's opponents to rise up against him time and again, for his final victory could only mean the permanent defeat of his opponents—be they the French king, the German princes, the pope, or the Protestants. These political interests therefore often overlapped and intersected with the religious confrontation between the traditional church and the Reformation movement.

Essential to the self-understanding of the Holy Roman Empire was the assumed unity of the Christian faith. For Charles V, this idea was more than an ideological bond suited for cementing his diverse, far-flung territories. He fought against the Reformation out of heartfelt conviction. For this reason he placed Luther under the ban of the empire and had his writings burned after the diet at Worms in the spring of 1521. And it was under the same presuppositions that Charles's brother Ferdinand demanded from the delegates at the diet of Speyer in April 1529 that they revoke all innovations in matters of faith and be strict in carrying out the provisions of the Edict of Worms.

What role did the imperial cities play in this political setting? Their natural enemies were the territorial princes. The cities therefore sought protection against them from the emperor. The maintenance of a strong central power in the form of the empire was in the economic and commercial interests of the cities. This interest was one important reason why many cities, including Strasbourg, waited so long before they introduced the Reformation. It also explains their hesitancy to enter a political alliance with the Swiss, the traditional enemies of the Habsburgs. They hoped, in spite of the religious dispute, to preserve the traditional harmony with the emperor. The utter failure of this policy became evident at the diet of Speyer in 1529. The cities now had to make up their minds— for or against Charles V. Nuremberg, which had already introduced the Reformation years previously, decided in favor of the emperor. Strasbourg's religious and political development led it, as well as most southern German cities and a few territorial princes, to oppose Charles V.

The "Protestants"

At Worms in 1521, Luther had faced the emperor and the imperial estates alone. Now, eight years later, five princes and fourteen cities united themselves behind the famous "Protestation" of April 19, 1529, rejecting King Ferdinand's demands and arguing that majority decisions as framed in the imperial diet were inadmissible in questions of faith. For "in issues concerning God's honour and our souls' salvation and redemption each one of us must stand alone before God and is called alone to account, so that no one can excuse himself by appealing to someone else's inferior or superior decisions and provisions; beyond this, there are no other upright, well-founded, good reasons that oblige one to act."[4] Three days later these "Protestants" agreed to an alliance in order to defend themselves and their religious convictions against the emperor and his supporters, by force if necessary.

This unanimity and determination, alas, did not last very long. In the coming months, political and theological differences took precedence over the original common perception of threat. In Electoral Saxony and in the Margraviate of Brandenburg-Ansbach, the number of those refusing to make common cause with "sacramentarians" (*Sakramentierer*) and "fanatics" (*Schwärmer*) grew from day to day, with strong support from the theologians there, and particularly from Luther. They argued that if a war for the sake of defending the true faith should really come to pass, one could fight only alongside those with whom one ultimately agreed. Landgrave Philip of Hesse depended urgently on the political and military support of Saxony and therefore sought a pact with Saxon elector John "the Steadfast." At the same time, Philip pursued a second alliance between Hesse and the southern German and Swiss cities. Philip's plans could succeed only if the tiresome controversy over the Lord's Supper could be resolved. It had therefore been Philip's pressing concern for quite some time that a meeting between Luther and Zwingli take place.

The cities too, especially Strasbourg, were convinced that theological differences within the Protestant camp had to be put in the background in order to enhance the rapid creation of a common defense policy. They needed the support of the empire's princes, although they feared being exploited financially and even being dropped by them should political winds shift. The cities' relationship to the Swiss was also fraught with complications. Though the southern German cities had good and manifold relations to their neighbors in the south, they knew that a pact with the Swiss that did not take the princes into account would lead to the dangerous isolation of the southern Germans within the Holy Roman Empire.

For the time being, the Lutheran faction most decisively influenced developments. It met in Schleiz in southern Thuringia, some twenty-five miles northwest of Hof. Delegates agreed on seventeen articles of faith, drafted primarily by Philipp Melanchthon, that were to constitute the theological basis for any political alliance. These statements were definitely a summary of Wittenberg doctrine and included a flat rejection of

Zwingli's views. Using these theses as his starting point, Luther formulated fifteen articles at the close of the Marburg Colloquy on October 3, 1529. Fourteen articles attested to the matters that the parties agreed upon. The fifteenth then circumscribed the disagreement still persisting in the understanding of the Lord's Supper. Although the Marburg Articles included some formulations that could be understood as efforts to create rapprochement with the opposing side, it soon became clear that they represented anything but a theological agreement, especially from the perspective of the Wittenberg theologians and their supporters. Only a few days later this group met again in Schwabach, just a few miles southwest of Nuremberg, and sternly demanded of all other Protestants that they agree to the Schleiz articles in their original form as the prerequisite for a political alliance. But the southern German cities, especially Strasbourg and Ulm, felt they could only reject these "Schwabach Articles," as they were now being called. The same thing happened all over again at a meeting at the end of 1529 in Schmalkalden, a town administrated jointly by Electoral Saxony and Hesse. Instead of achieving its goal—the creation of a Protestant league—this meeting ended disastrously for the southern German cities. However, Strasbourg did manage to be admitted into the "Christian Federation" (*Christliches Burgrecht*) formed by Zurich, Basel, and Bern. Philip of Hesse also joined it in the summer of 1530.

Strasbourg's Position

Bucer was actively involved and assumed ever-growing responsibility in these developments. Side by side with Jacob Sturm, he exerted significant influence on the internal policy and even on the foreign relations of the Protestant camp in the following years. At the same time, we should not idealize the relationship between the men. The noble patrician Jacob Sturm, a member of the city council since 1524 and the determining figure of Strasbourg's foreign policy on account of his position in the Council of the Thirteen, was fundamentally oriented toward the empire, since he held fiefs from the bishop of Strasbourg and particularly the margrave of Baden and other territorial princes. Sturm's ascendancy pushed the council faction headed by Kniebis, which sought closer connections to Switzerland and especially to Zurich, into the background. Of course, Sturm did not want to betray this group. But an alliance with the Swiss was possible only if it included not only the southern German cities but also the territorial princes. Like Philip of Hesse, with whose politics he agreed wholeheartedly, Sturm wanted the dispute over the Lord's Supper to be excluded from all negotiations. And he was particularly vigorous in rejecting the pastors', and especially Bucer's, desire to have a say in the city's politics. Sturm's policy sought the greatest possible internal cohesion of his city, firm connections to the empire, and good relations with Charles V—in the degree that actual circumstances made all these goals possible.

If Sturm wished first of all to maintain Strasbourg's position of power and influence, Bucer had other, bigger goals. To be sure, he was also interested in pursuing the vision of a politically mighty city whose citizens lived in unity. But ultimately he saw Strasbourg only as a foothold for the much broader endeavor of spreading the gospel and establishing God's kingdom. That meant a great deal to Bucer—but not everything. His presuppositions did not allow him in any way to ignore, for the sake of politics, what he felt was God's truth. No doubt, God had ordained governmental authority and Christians had to obey its injunctions. But God's law was also binding for rulers. If they wished to be true rulers, pleasing to God, they had to serve God and shape society according to God's norms. And in this action they were dependent on the close and trusting cooperation of the theologians, who were the ones qualified to expound God's will.

Even though a fundamental tension—complete disagreement might, in fact, be more accurate—persisted between Bucer and Sturm on these issues, they shared goals in wide areas. These points of agreement can be summed up in three general points, as far as Bucer's activities during these years are concerned:

1. First of all, it was of utmost importance to create the broadest possible political and theological front uniting Protestants. Since the controversy over the Lord's Supper obstructed this coalition, everything possible had to be undertaken to overcome this conflict. Bucer had already attempted to come to an agreement with the Wittenberg theologians over this issue before 1529, as we saw above. It therefore cannot be said that only political pragmatism now drove Bucer to take action in this area. Of course, changed political circumstances were now favorable to such an endeavor.

2. It was equally important to press forward with all one's might and available means to spread and consolidate the Reformation in the Holy Roman Empire and beyond.

3. Finally, it was essential to equip the church in Strasbourg with the organization and structures necessary to consolidate what had been achieved thus far. This church could then serve as a foundation for further outreach.

It is these three aspects that we will now analyze in detail.

Working for Protestant Unity

Overcoming Isolation

Bucer participated in the Marburg Colloquy[5] of October 1–4, 1529, attending primarily as an appendage of the Swiss delegation. The main goal of the statesmen—in other words, of Philip of Hesse, but also of Sturm—had been to bring Zwingli and Luther together at one table. It was Philip's idea to urge Bucer to attend as well. The latter's efforts to reach an understanding in the eucharistic controversy had earned him a good reputation beyond Strasbourg's borders. Caspar Hedio was chosen to attend as a second Strasbourg theologian. He had maintained a good relationship with Melanchthon and was one of the few people to have close ties to Nicolaus Gerbel, the staunch Luther supporter in Strasbourg.

The Swiss—Zwingli and Oecolampadius, with their entourage—arrived in Strasbourg on the evening of September 6, after a thirteen-hour journey by boat down the Rhine from Basel. Joined by the Strasbourg delegation, they continued their trip on September 18, arriving in Marburg on September 27. Bucer hardly played a role in the theological conversations of the following days. However, Sturm brought Bucer into action on the afternoon of October 3, after negotiations collapsed. Sturm was apparently hoping that Strasbourg would abandon its commitment to the Swiss position. Luther, however, flatly rejected Bucer's statements. He not only claimed that one could not trust Bucer but also declared categorically: "Your spirit and our spirit do not coincide. On the contrary, it is obvious that we do not have one and the same spirit."[6] One more conversation did indeed take place between the Strasbourg theologians and Andreas Osiander from Nuremberg and Johannes Brenz from Schwäbisch Hall on October 4, during which Bucer proved ready to make considerable concessions to the Lutheran theologians. It is, however, highly unlikely that Bucer actually endorsed the Lutheran position on this occasion, as Osiander later claimed. They ultimately parted company unreconciled.

In the coming months, Bucer defended his understanding of the Lord's Supper on the one hand, but on the other he asserted that differing views on this issue must not be overemphasized at the expense of the many things the Protestants did, after all, have in common. Bucer had already made these two points in a memorandum on the Schwabach Articles he had written at the end of 1529 for Sturm to take to Schmalkalden.[7] There Bucer had affirmed that Christ does impart himself to believers in the Lord's Supper, but he is not *in* the elements of bread and wine. At the same time, the following holds true: whoever rests his hopes on and trusts

Christ alone and allows Christ to rule his life belongs to the fellowship of Christians, even if that person should err in individual doctrinal issues. Bucer particularly emphasized this view in the preface, dedicated to the professors of the University of Marburg, that he wrote for his *Commentary on the Gospels* published in April 1530. "If you immediately condemn anyone who doesn't quite believe the same as you do as forsaken by Christ's Spirit, and consider anyone to be the enemy of truth who holds something false to be true, who, pray tell, can you still consider a brother? I for one have never met two people who believed exactly the same thing. This holds true in theology as well."[8] In spite of the personal hurt caused by Luther's condemnations—hurt that can be clearly sensed when reading the preface—in the following years Bucer persisted stubbornly in this hermeneutical insight, much more typical of subsequent thinkers than of his own period. It was the basis for all his attempts to achieve agreement and understanding on each and every theological front. It was the same conviction that he had expressed to Zwingli in 1524: the common spirit is what counts, not the letter. For the Spirit of God, which opens us to faith and love, liberates us to understand genuinely and thus creates true unity. To persist in the letter, however, divides and destroys fellowship.

But Luther's supporters refused to allow themselves to be wooed by Bucer. Bucer gave the Strasbourg delegates to the Augsburg diet a German version of the aforementioned preface,[9] but the Lutheran theologians brushed it aside as irrelevant as soon as it fell into their hands. In any case, in Augsburg a situation completely different from that in Speyer the previous year seemed to be taking shape. Charles V, whom the pope had just crowned emperor in Bologna on February 24, 1530, announced in his invitation to the imperial diet of Augsburg that he wanted the supporters of the Reformation to submit and explain their views to him. This request led to feverish efforts on the side of the Protestants to set forth and defend the innovations brought about by the evangelical movement. But then Johannes Eck published 404 theses of his own in which he accused evangelicals of having separated themselves from the early, true church not just in external details but in all fundamental articles of the Christian faith. This attack was more than just a theological challenge. It had dangerous legal implications for the status of Protestants within the empire and had to be taken seriously. Philipp Melanchthon, the main theologian among the Wittenberg delegates in Augsburg, therefore dropped plans for a written defense of evangelical innovations and decided instead to draft a comprehensive confession of doctrine. In this confession, and particularly in the twenty-one dogmatic articles constituting its first section, Melanchthon vigorously emphasized that the Reformation in Electoral Saxony and its supporters were in full agreement with the teachings of the early church.

In view of this goal, any efforts on the part of the Strasbourg delegates to convince the Saxons to join them in a common theological and political front were perceived as bothersome and inexpedient—particularly since the Strasbourg theologians were considered to be clear allies of Zwingli and of the "seditious" Swiss, who did not accept the political predominance of the territorial princes in the empire. And since Strasbourg did not want to ally itself exclusively with the Swiss cities, it as well as other southern German cities stood politically isolated. Efforts by Strasbourg's political representatives to be allowed to endorse the Saxon confession with the single exception of its article on the Lord's Supper met with failure. The Strasbourg delegates thus urgently sent for Bucer and Capito to come to Augsburg to write up a separate confession as quickly as possible. The twenty-three articles they drafted[10] essentially follow the pattern of Melanchthon's confession without reproducing its dual structure of statements of doctrine on the one hand and defense of innovations on the other. With regard to the Lord's Supper, Bucer drew up a very lengthy, long-winded article that sought to accommodate the concerns of the Lutheran camp. But the other southern German cities were unhappy with his wording. Strasbourg invited the delegates of the free imperial cities of Memmingen, Lindau, Constance, Ulm, Biberach, Isny, Kempten, Heilbronn, Frankfurt, and Wissembourg to meet on June 30. Strasbourg wooed these delegates, hoping to obtain their endorsement of its confession. But even though Bucer went to the trouble of drafting a new eucharistic article, this one much shorter and somewhat vaguer, only Constance, Lindau, and Memmingen were willing to sign the confession, besides Strasbourg—which is why it was given the name *Four Cities' Confession*, or *Confessio Tetrapolitana*. No other city was inclined to support the Strasbourg statesmen and theologians, who were obviously isolated. Zwingli himself set forth his own confession, his *Account of Faith* (*Fidei Ratio*). Thus, the dissonance in the Protestant camp was just as evident as the vulnerability of the Strasbourg position.

In August 1530, however, a new development on the political scene allowed Bucer to overcome the walls of Lutheran resistance that had obstructed his advances until then. The deliberations of a commission of Catholic theologians resulted in the flat rejection of all the Protestant confessions in their entirety. The emperor endorsed this decision. Furthermore, exploratory conversations that a small committee had conducted with Melanchthon and Eck, in hopes of bringing both sides closer, came to nothing. The situation was becoming threatening for the Protestants. These threats became reality on September 22, 1530, with the closing decree of the diet of Augsburg: Charles V gave the Protestants until April 15, 1531, to return to the established church. Their failure to do so would be met with force. These circumstances lent new persuasiveness to the voices of those pleading for concord within the Protestant camp. Indeed, Sturm and Bucer succeeded in convincing Prince Ernst of Lüneburg and the Saxon chancellor Gregor Brück that Strasbourg was genuinely interested in reaching an agreement. Most important, after much hesitation Melanchthon finally agreed to a lengthy meeting with Bucer on August 24. Bucer had realized long ago that his project to settle the eucharistic controversy was condemned to failure if he did not succeed in getting Melanchthon on board. Instrumental in swaying Melanchthon had been a scholarly treatise by Oecolampadius in which the Basel theologian impressively demonstrated that the Greek and Latin church fathers were far from unanimous in their teaching on the presence of Christ in the elements of bread and wine. Bucer summarized the results of his conversation with Melanchthon in nine theses he dispatched to Luther and to the Strasbourg magistrates. The Strasbourg Council of the Thirteen reacted immediately by sending Capito to Basel and Zurich to begin negotiations on these articles.

Oecolampadius gave his consent, but Zwingli proved to be considerably more skeptical, even though he did not reject Bucer's articles entirely.[11] Not a word was heard from Luther. Bucer decided to ride on horseback to the castle of Coburg, the southernmost point of Electoral Saxony, where Luther was staying during the duration of the Diet of Augsburg. Since Luther was under the imperial ban, he could not leave Saxon territory, but he wished to be as close as possible to Augsburg. Bucer and Luther conducted long and hard conversations, especially on the Lord's Supper, from September 26 to 28. Like Zwingli, Luther presented objections to Bucer's theses. It soon became evident that Luther was not about to give ground in any way. But Bucer succeeded in one respect: he overcame Luther's distrust. The Wittenberg theologian encouraged him, in fact, to continue in his efforts to bring about an agreement. Consequently, Bucer rode on, traveling through southern Germany and Switzerland in October 1530, trying to convince statesmen and theologians of the relevance of his articles for a settlement. These theses essentially affirmed that Christ truly gives himself to the faithful in bread and wine, without being bound, however, to the actual elements. At the same time, Bucer repeated his conviction that both sides had been in agreement for quite some time already. Bucer was received warmly at the different stops of his itinerary: in Ulm, Memmingen, Isny, Lindau, Constance, and even in Basel and Zurich. The most important of these stays was the one in Zurich, where Bucer set forth his views to the city council on October 12, using the article on the Lord's Supper in the Tetrapolitan Confession as his point of departure. Zwingli was remarkably taciturn. Of course, he realized that Bucer's primary goal was to convince Luther. Zwingli did not oppose Bucer in a fundamental way, but neither was he by any means willing to express agreement with him. This did not prevent the Strasbourg theologians from drafting a statement by the end of the year 1530, dedicated to Ernst of Lüneburg, that would constitute the basis for the resolution of the eucharistic controversy. This statement was a first breakthrough in overcoming the theological isolation of the city.

Rapprochement with Luther

Although Luther had expressed strong reservations about Bucer's suggestion for a concord, at least he seemed to be generally well disposed toward that endeavor.[12] Things stood differently for Zwingli. On February 21, 1531, he wrote an angry letter to Bucer that implied the end of their friendship.[13] Zwingli considered his own views to have been watered down much too extensively and Bucer to have conceded far too much to Luther. What really roused him to indignation, however, was his impression that Bucer had opportunistically turned himself into a lackey of Strasbourg's political goals. Zurich was well aware of the fact that Sturm and Strasbourg were avidly seeking an alliance with Electoral Saxony. Did that not sufficiently explain Bucer's rapprochement with Luther? Bucer was shocked, indeed deeply hurt, by Zwingli's accusations. Of course Bucer was interested in the unification, the theological and political consolidation of Protestantism. But wasn't that Zwingli's goal as well? And this goal was obviously not going to be achieved without an alliance with the territorial princes and a settlement with the Lutherans. Bucer was understandably resentful that his former companion in arms defamed the difficult and intricate efforts to reach a theological settlement as a betrayal of principles. He wrote back to Zwingli: "I will no longer harass you with my plans for concord and apologize for having wearied you up to now with so many expenditures of energy on the part of my colleagues as well as my own toil and effort."[14] This letter provided a dignified, clear response. But it also signaled the definitive break with Zwingli.

In the meantime, a Protestant defensive league had been voted into existence in Schmalkalden in the final days of December 1530. Strasbourg was admitted into the league on account of the statements in the Tetrapolitan Confession. The city's representatives were at the same time encouraged to convince the Swiss to join on the basis of the Tetrapolitan Confession. However, this theological openness disappeared by the time the Schmalkaldic League held its second meeting, in March and April 1531. Voices in the Lutheran faction were demanding the acceptance of the Augsburg Confession of Faith as an essential prerequisite for a joint military alliance. The Swiss could naturally only reject this demand as unreasonable. But an opportunity for serious negotiations on this issue would never arise, for on October 11, the Zurich forces were utterly defeated by the Swiss Catholic cities in a battle near Kappel. Zwingli remained on the battlefield, dead among the fallen. Oecolampadius perished one month later in Basel, a victim of the plague. Especially the death of the latter was a hard blow for Bucer, who lost not only a friend but the most important pillar in his efforts to win over the Swiss and convince them to agree to a settlement with the Lutherans.

Meanwhile, the emperor tried to drive a wedge between the supporters of the Saxon confession and the southern German cities, who once again were being mentioned in one breath with the Swiss. And once again the city of Strasbourg and its supporters had to fear theological and political isolation within the empire. After all, weren't there powerful factions in the Lutheran camp who perceived them anyhow as "sacramentarians" and false brethren? And wasn't the danger present as ever that the territorial princes would come to an agreement and leave the cities to their fate? Didn't the negotiations that the electors of Mainz and the Palatinate were starting to carry out with the Protestant princes point exactly in this direction? Would Philip of Hesse be strong enough to persevere in his alliance with the cities? And, last, what was to be made of the objective agreement— a favorite theme of Bucer's—between Strasbourg's Tetrapolitan Confession and Saxony's Augsburg Confession? Would it provide a foundation strong enough that the necessary coalition of Protestants could be built upon it?

It was to debate these questions that delegates of the southern German imperial cities assembled in Ulm on March 23 and 24, 1532.[15] Thanks to Bucer's tireless efforts, they finally agreed that at the negotiations between Protestant and Catholic princes about to begin in Schweinfurt on April 1, they would sign the Augsburg Confession if necessary. Melanchthon's *Apologia* of the Augsburg Confession, published in 1531, paved the way to this important concession. For the first time, the Wittenberg theologian publicly set forth an understanding of the Lord's Supper in which the presence of Christ was bound *to*, but not *in*, the elements of bread and wine. Bucer picked up this idea at Schweinfurt when expounding the fundamental agreement of all Protestants in doctrinal matters, including the Lord's Supper.[16] To be sure, Bucer persisted in maintaining that unbelievers do not receive Christ and that the "how" of Christ's presence remained a mystery. But in any case, he succeeded brilliantly in raising the quarrel over wordings and formulations to a higher theological level, explaining the meaning and significance of the sacraments thoroughly within the general context of Reformation theology. As he emphasized, they are a "visible reminder" of the fact "that God promises to us that he will be a kind-hearted God and Savior and that he will keep us as his children and heirs," a reminder "by which he binds himself to us and offers us his loving-kindness in such a way that when it is given to us to understand this rightly, we in our own turn surrender and offer ourselves entirely to God, from which a godly, very heavenly and eternal life follows."[17]

However reluctant and averse the southern German cities might have been to adopting the Lutherans' Augsburg Confession, doing so not only gave them the protection of the Schmalkaldic League but also allowed them to claim the benefits of the imperial truce. Beset by the Ottoman Turks, Charles V was forced to court the assistance of the very same Protestants he had intended to suppress by force only two years earlier. Bucer immediately put all his energy into negotiating a pact with the emperor that was not exclusively defensive. The decisive question, of course, was whether the territories and cities that joined the Reformation after the conclusion of the cease-fire would also benefit from the emperor's protection. From Bucer's standpoint, this was clearly the case. Anything else would mean confining the gospel and obstructing the spread of God's truth, as Bucer asserted in several lengthy memoranda. Who would want to be responsible for that? "Christ did not wait for us to come to him and call him," Bucer wrote in June 1532, "but went looking for us when we were still enemies of God, and he brought everything to bear, even his soul, in order that we be helped. Therefore we should also love our fellow men in this way."[18] The Nuremberg moratorium (*Nürnberger Anstand*) of August 1532, an agreement to suspend the issue of religion until a future council, left the aforementioned question of the political protection of newcomers to the Protestant fold unanswered. Nevertheless, this settlement represented a meaningful success for the Schmalkaldic League: for the first time the holy Roman emperor officially treated Protestants as partners.

Spreading the Reformation, consolidating and safeguarding what had been reached thus far, and establishing the greatest possible unity and cohesion among Protestants—these were, as mentioned above, three aspects of Bucer's central goal during these years. It was the last of these three tasks that proved to be the most difficult and troublesome during the year 1533. Bucer's public endorsement of the Augsburg Confession during the Schweinfurt assembly caused a great deal of irritation among the Swiss, and it completely shocked many of his supporters and friends in the southern German cities. At the same time, however, Luther did not give him the slightest support, sharply and ruthlessly condemning whoever was not on his side as "sacramentarian," "Zwinglian," or "fanatic" (*Schwärmer*). Bucer nevertheless continued to work tirelessly at calming the conflicting parties, taking the edge off opposing positions, trying to find the right balance between both sides in order to reconcile them. In April and May 1533, he once again undertook a major trip through southern Germany and Switzerland, setting forth his theological standpoint and attempting to win his audiences to it. His itinerary included Basel, Schaffhausen, Dissenhofen, Constance, Bischofszell, St. Gall, Zurich, and Bern, from which he returned to Strasbourg via Basel on May 25. Bucer was received cordially at every stop and his ideas were given a serious, or at least a polite, hearing. It was unmistakably clear, however, that Oecolampadius's successor in Basel, Oswald Myconius, and Heinrich Bullinger, who had assumed Zwingli's legacy in Zurich, remained unconvinced by, and were even openly skeptical toward, Bucer's plans.

What little basis in fact Bucer's image—still widespread today—as a slippery tactician and a wordy opportunist actually has is demonstrated most impressively in the way he responded to Luther's missive to the Frankfurt city council, published in January 1533, which was full of crude and ugly allegations against Bucer. The Frankfurt pastors' *Defense* (*Entschuldigung*), published in March of the same year and drafted by Bucer, is remarkably succinct and sober.[19] The drafts Bucer wrote in preparation for this pamphlet do reveal how deeply hurt he was by Luther's brutal polemics. The fact that Bucer did not return in kind cannot simply be attributed to tactics. Bucer realized clear-sightedly that, in view of the hardening of theological lines of battle, anyone working for concord and understanding would risk being accused of not really being sure what he believed and of ultimately not believing what he claimed to teach. Bucer was willing to expose himself to this misunderstanding. "In any case," he wrote, "we must seek unity and love in our relationships with everyone—regardless of how they behave towards us."[20] Bucer displayed the same calm self-assuredness in the face of obstacles and ability to remain above the fray in a letter of February 10, 1533, to Margarethe Blarer, in which he wrote of Luther: "Now I finally know that the man is seeking God."[21] This path was made easier for Bucer by the fact that since 1533 he could count on Melanchthon's support, and even his friendship.[22]

Consolidating His Standpoint

This state of affairs is the background for two treatises Bucer wrote in 1534 that are fundamental to his understanding of the Lord's Supper. The first one, entitled *Report from Holy Scripture* (*Bericht aus der Heiligen Schrift*), appeared in March.[23] In it, responding to the events in Münster that had led to the establishment of an Anabaptist kingdom, Bucer explained his understanding of the church, the ministries, and especially the sacraments, in twenty-eight chapters. His views on these matters had matured in the course of his altercations with Anabaptists and spiritualists in Strasbourg but also in connection with the organization of new church structures in cooperation with the secular authorities. These were fundamental ideas for Bucer and accordingly he dedicated this book to the city council of Augsburg. While this city faced other problems than those that had affected Münster, both had factions fighting for control over the city, and in both the success of the Reformation was far from certain.

Attaining doctrinal unity and avoiding division were central concerns of Bucer. From a theological standpoint this meant—as Bucer expounded in his *Report*—listening to Scripture, believing and trusting Christ alone, and loving one another. For the life of the Christian fellowship this meant specifically that a church needs order and discipline, that laypeople are to participate in congregational life as elders, and that secular authorities are to work in close cooperation with churchmen. All these ideals implied that external, "objective" means of grace—especially the ministry and the sacraments—took on a new importance for Bucer compared to his earlier years. It would be admittedly wrong to speak of a fundamental breach in his thought. Throughout the previous years Bucer never wavered in attributing a central role to the Holy Spirit and in affirming that Christians lived a renewed life as a consequence of the liberating effects of the Spirit. However, Bucer's deeper appreciation of Luther's understanding of the Lord's Supper and his expressed conviction that Anabaptists and spiritualists threatened to dilute all established theological and ecclesiastical norms unless a firm institutional dam could be erected, coupled with a thorough study of the Greek church fathers, led Bucer from this time on to emphasize more strongly than he had previously the incarnation of Christ, that is to say, the reality of God drawing near and giving himself to humankind.

This new emphasis is a recurring theme throughout Bucer's *Report from Holy Scripture*. As far as church ceremonies are concerned, it is only logical that Bucer now writes: "The sacraments are divine acts of the church, instituted by God so that through them God's gifts and our salvation—accomplished by our Lord Jesus Christ—may be, on the basis of God's promise, administered and given with words and visible signs to those whom the church recognizes as fit, on account of God's promise, for this salvation."[24] Of course, Bucer was quick to add, this gift can become effective only if received in faith. The mere outward performance of sacraments remains futile. The emphasis, however, lay on God taking the initiative and approaching humankind. Applied to baptism—the main subject matter of this treatise—this meant that infant baptism was meaningful and necessary. "God wants to be the God of our children in Jesus Christ. Because this is such a great work of God's grace he promises it to them as well as to us. He wants them to participate in the death of Christ and in his salvation; therefore they should be baptized."[25] And regarding the Lord's Supper this emphasis meant that "God wants to help us, that is, give himself to us, within and through his church, with and by means of the words and sacraments. . . . For this reason nothing in the body and blood of Christ is changed, displaced or destroyed, and our souls are fed not with bread and wine but with our Lord Jesus Christ himself; we would certainly feel this adequately and sufficiently in ourselves if we were only obedient to the Gospel as we should, had true fellowship in Christ, and proper devotion to his Word and to the sacraments."[26]

Bucer's book and particularly the statements he made there on the Lord's Supper attracted much applause from figures as diverse as Melanchthon and Osiander, and even from Luther in Wittenberg as well as Bullinger in Zurich. Bucer's second treatise of the year 1534, his *Defense against the Catholic Axiom* (*Defensio contra axioma Catholicum*), which appeared in September, also met with a similarly sympathetic reception.[27] In this work Bucer responded to the strong attacks by Robert Céneau, bishop of Avranches and professor of theology at the Sorbonne in Paris, who had assailed the Protestants' understanding of the Lord's Supper as well as the doctrinal dissension among them. In this book, dedicated to the cardinal and archbishop Antoine Duprat, Bucer skillfully asserted not only that all Protestants agreed on the eucharistic issue but also that learned Catholics were in concord with them on this matter, underpinning his claims with quotations from the church fathers and Thomas Aquinas. Bucer affirmed that Christ gave himself for us on the cross once and for all. Believers receive this gift in the Lord's Supper in such a manner that Christ really imparts himself fully and entirely to them when the elements of bread and wine are distributed, and he does so in order that they also offer themselves in a life of service and love toward their fellow human beings. Finally of importance in this treatise is that for the first time Bucer introduced the distinction—so important in later negotiations for eucharistic rapprochement—between believing (*pii*), unworthy (*indigni*), and unbelieving (*impii*) recipients of the Lord's Supper. Bucer was convinced that nonbelievers could not receive Christ; they get only bread and wine—a claim that had always been Bucer's standard position. But now he was also ready to concede that Christ also communicates himself to the unworthy precisely because they are not totally lacking in faith. Bucer thus reinforced the idea that salvation was being offered in an objective way through the sacraments.

The same effort Bucer made in this book to bridge positions and—in spite of hardening dogmatic fronts—stimulate a conversation between Protestants and Catholics he had made one year previously on a smaller scale, limited to Germany. His *Preparation for the Council* (*Fürbereytung zum Konzil*)[28] of September 1533 was coupled with the yearning, widespread throughout Germany, for a national council. It also constituted a response in its own right to Erasmus's plea for unity in his book *On the Lovely Concord of the Church* (*De amabili ecclesiae concordia*). Once again, Bucer presented his views in the form of a dialogue, this time between a supporter and an opponent of the Reformation. The rhetorical method chosen was not arbitrary. It corresponded fundamentally with a characteristic feature of his personality and his theology, a feature we have already encountered: the idea that the path to truth is charted through hard struggles to reach a common position and unity. This way requires talking and communicating with opponents—opponents of whom one nevertheless must assume that they are also led by God's Spirit and are ultimately pursuing the same goals. Bucer's certainty of knowing the truth did not preclude efforts to win over opponents lovingly. It is out of this conviction that Bucer wrote in a very personal letter to his good friends Margarethe and Thomas Blarer in Constance, not long after the *Preparation* appeared: "My striving certainly aims at one thing (although admittedly often without the necessary warmth and prudence): that Christians accept and embrace one another in love. For all moral flaws and faulty judgments have their origin in the failure of the Spirit of Christ to have an effect because of insufficient unity. I certainly have experienced quite distinctly in my own person what love and, if not hate, at least antipathy are capable of."[29] In the same way as he had approached Luther publicly for the first time in his *Conciliation* (*Vergleichung*) of 1528, he was now approaching supporters of the Catholic Church. Back then he had attempted to reach out to the more reflective among Luther's supporters, and now he was pursuing a similar goal, expressly distinguishing between pious Catholics on the one hand and the ensemble of the pope and his supporters on the other.

Admittedly, Bucer's proposed settlement brushed off all too smoothly and harmoniously such difficult and long-lasting problems as the supposed primacy of the pope and disagreements on the understanding of church ministries, and therefore also of the Mass. But we must ask ourselves on the other hand: Which leading theologian of the Reformation possessed at this time the inward freedom to write a book like this? Who else, other than Bucer, would have been capable of publicly proclaiming and drawing the necessary consequences from the following statement, which runs through the book like a scarlet thread? "I do hope, however, that there are many dear children of God on both sides, improperly named after men and thus kept divided. Instead, we should attempt as much as possible to find and use all ways and means in order that all God-fearing persons in all camps become united in Christ, our Lord."[30]

Offshoots of the Strasbourg Reformation

Western Europe

Bucer's frame of reference and his goals—so much is clear—extended far beyond the Strasbourg city limits; in their hopes for effect, they were indeed aimed more broadly than only at the Protestant camp and, ultimately, even the empire. He cultivated contacts just as much with people in Italy as in the Netherlands, in northern Germany and even in Denmark, as well as in Silesia and the surrounding regions.[31] Of course many of these relationships were not very deep, which does not mean that Bucer had not sought them intentionally; and most of them did not bring with them any actual influence on the conduct of these persons by Bucer or by the specific emphases of the Strasbourg Reformation. However, it is unmistakably clear that Bucer's thought by this time had assumed a European dimension that distinguishes him from many other Reformation theologians. This far-reaching focus is not the least of the reasons for which many of Bucer's theological statements—both the more carelessly made and the more deliberately formulated—seemed so unacceptable to many of his supporters and friends at this time and in the following years, since they thought only in local and regional terms.

During these years Bucer attempted twice to influence the spread of the gospel in Western Europe by means of high-level politics. Both attempts ended in failure. These efforts are nonetheless extremely typical for his way of thinking and for his ultimate goals. The first situation arose in 1531 with the attempt of Henry VIII of England to annul his marriage, and the resulting opportunity to convince him to join the Schmalkaldic League.[32] Bucer was initially disposed to allow Henry a bigamous marriage, a concession he was ready to make out of pastoral considerations and for the good of the kingdom. But then he retreated from this position step by step, assuming an opposing stance similar to that of Wittenberg. Bucer's brief intervention in this debate gives us a slight hint of the extremely thorough and comprehensive study of the subjects of marriage and divorce that he was engaged in at the time. We will treat this topic in greater detail later on. The mostly negative judgments of continental Reformers to Henry's marriage affair led to a cooling of relations with England. This state of affairs, however, did not dissuade Bucer from establishing closer and lasting contacts with leading English churchmen.

Relationships with France seemed to develop more promisingly.[33] Political reasons motivated King Francis I to seek contacts with the German Protestants. His envoy Guillaume du Bellay, brother to the archbishop of Paris, traveled—accompanied by the Strasbourg physician Chelius, or Geiger—throughout the Holy Roman Empire after the spring of 1534, trying to win support for a larger religious colloquy. Bucer also prepared a major memorandum on this topic, essentially endorsing the position adopted by Melanchthon. There were, however, two important differences between Bucer and his Wittenberg colleague. For one thing, Bucer very skillfully weaved the theological authority of Thomas Aquinas into his arguments for concord, especially concerning the Mass. Second, Bucer was basically willing to recognize the primacy of the pope and recognize the Catholic bishops—if these would actually fulfill their official duties as a service in the spirit of Christ and as intended by Christ. Finally, Bucer wrote a personal letter to the French king on February 8, 1535, in which he lashed out at the deplorable state of affairs in the traditional church and bravely interceded for the persecuted French Protestants.[34]

Paris did not react to Bucer's advances. Placards with acrid invectives against Catholic worship, particularly the Mass, that a radical Protestant group posted in Paris and the French interior on the night of October

17/18, 1534, led not only to a carnage costing the lives of guilty and innocent alike; this event also convinced Francis I that the Reformation was to
be equated with riots, revolution, and immorality. The Anabaptist reign
of terror in Münster seemed to confirm him in his prejudices. From now
on, Francis persecuted the Reformation's followers in France. German
Protestants interested him solely as possible political allies.

This whole affair had unpleasant consequences for Bucer. His memorandum to Francis I became public and triggered a storm of outrage. Now
not only did traditional opponents of his plans for concord, such as
Bullinger in Zurich, attack Bucer sharply, but friends such as Thomas
Blarer in Constance did so as well. They asked: Was this where Bucer's
quest for reconciliation was ultimately to lead? Did he aim to place the
church back under the authority of the pope? Bucer's attempt to defend
himself fell on deaf ears: "We cannot, after all, give up on those in the other
churches who invoke Christ; therefore, we must see how we can come to
an agreement with them, determine what we can concede to them and what
we, for their sake, can revoke on our part."[35] His opponents' mistrust
remained unassuaged by his remarks. Their lasting suspicion was a further
impairment to Bucer's efforts, already difficult enough, to convince not
only Constance and the Swiss but the southern German cities as well to
unite themselves with Strasbourg's theological and political stance.

Ulm

Bucer's strong influence on the development of Protestantism in the
imperial cities of southwestern Germany has already been referred to,
above. We have reported on his frequent trips to this region as well as on
his discussions with preachers and statesmen there. His vast, still mostly
unpublished correspondence with the representatives of these cities gives
ample testimony to the tight network of communication uniting them and
to the degree to which Bucer was a sought-after counselor in the entire
region. His responses to the numerous queries reaching Strasbourg char-
acteristically accommodated themselves very skillfully to the particular
conditions and prerequisites of the individual petitioner. But they also
reveal Bucer's permanent attempt to stay in the background, showing his
correspondents the way but taking care not to dominate them. Good
examples for this diplomatic style can be seen in the way Bucer helped the
cities of Ulm and Augsburg establish the Reformation.

To be sure, political and theological ties between Ulm[36] and Strasbourg
existed already prior to 1529. But it was really the signing of the Speyer

Protestation by both imperial cities that year, and the resulting political isolation, that made them move closer together. Ulm, with its fifteen thousand inhabitants, was smaller and weaker than Strasbourg and was in considerably greater danger, for its territory abutted on staunchly Catholic Bavaria in the east and on Württemberg in the west. From 1519, Württemberg was ruled by the Habsburgs. That was one of the reasons why the patrician council led by veteran burgomaster Bernhard Besserer worked hard at avoiding an unequivocal commitment in religious issues, in spite of the pressure from factions in the city that clearly supported the Reformation. These groups, led onward by the fiery, even uncouth evangelical preacher Konrad Sam, a friend of Zwingli's, impetuously urged the city to abolish the Mass and establish evangelical church structures. The council did not yield to these demands until it sensed that the outside political support it needed to end its vulnerability was forthcoming. Then, on November 3, 1530, it called on the guilds to vote on the acceptance of the harshly anti-Protestant closing decree of the Augsburg diet—not before having depicted to the people of Ulm in no uncertain terms what dangers it was exposing itself to if it dared vote against the emperor. These dire warnings notwithstanding, 1,576 citizens voted against accepting the decree, and only 244 in favor. In the spring of 1531, Ulm became a member of the Schmalkaldic League, and on April 14 the council called a committee of nine into being that was charged with formally introducing the Reformation. From the very beginning Ulm planned on steering a middle course between Luther, whose views were rejected by most of the local citizenry, and Zwingli, whom the city could not afford to endorse openly. As a result, Ambrosius Blarer of Constance, Johannes Oecolampadius of Basel, and Martin Bucer were chosen to assist the committee as outside theologians. By May 21, all of them had arrived in Ulm. All three had been friends for quite some time already and were lodged jointly in Konrad Sam's large house (found today at Pfauengasse 13). Every single one of them contributed in a significant way to the creation of Protestant church structures in Ulm. But it was Bucer who did most of the work and was actually in charge. For the first time he was given the opportunity of putting his dream of a comprehensive restructuring of society along Christian lines into practice. And Bucer certainly made use of this opportunity.

As a very first measure—the committee of nine had decided this in consultation with the three out-of-town theologians—eighteen articles summarizing the fundamentals of Reformation theology were to be proclaimed to the rural population of Ulm's large surrounding territory. Articles 1 to 6, clearly drafted by Bucer, had Christian doctrine as their subject and concentrated on explaining the position that sinners are justified by God's love alone. The next eight articles discussed the errors of the traditional church's theology and worship forms. The final four articles were devoted to temporal authority and vigorously proclaimed the government's right to reorder society along Christian lines, including its right to replace the traditional episcopal marriage courts (based on papal canon law) with the magistrate's own secular marriage courts (to be based on Scripture, that is, divine law). Most of the ideas presented up to this point are already familiar to us from previous writings by Bucer—ideas that were shared, of course, by Konrad Sam, Johannes Oecolampadius, and Ambrosius Blarer. It is in the subsequent annotations that Bucer added to explain the eighteen articles that the Strasbourg theologian takes full advantage of the opportunity to develop a comprehensive conception of the church. To begin with, he demands that preachers be selected with the utmost care and be kept under scrupulous control. He assigns this task to a committee of church wardens (*Kirchenpfleger*), to be made up of pastors and city council members. Bucer's stipulations also provide for the convening of yearly church synods, the visiting and inspection of rural congregations regularly, the creation of schools, the establishment of catechetical instruction, the constitution of marriage courts, and finally the assurance that the magistrate assumes its responsibility for maintaining a high level of moral discipline in the city.[37] Bucer thus placed great importance on the introduction of the "Christian ban" (*christlicher Bann*): whoever publicly transgressed the Ten Commandments was to be admonished three times by "ministers of discipline" (*Zuchtherren*) according to Matthew 18; if he nevertheless persisted in this behavior he was to be excluded from the Lord's Supper and thus from the congregation.[38] Oecolampadius had succeeded in convincing Bucer that the decision over such a measure had to be taken by the congregation itself. Correspondingly, the draft ordinance prepared by the three outside preachers provided for the committee of eight ministers of discipline to be made up of three men from the congregations, two pastors, and only three council members. This model, however, was not put into practice. The Ulm magistrates were not in the least sympathetic to the idea of creating a church disciplinary body almost entirely exempt from their control. After all, they had not freed themselves from the pope and his irksome legal privileges just to share power over the church with the preachers! The definitive church ordinance finally adopted in August 1531 thus determined that of the eight ministers of discipline, four had to be city council members—accompanied by two representatives of the congregations and two of the pastors. The powers of this committee were also curtailed decisively, allowing it only to admonish and to warn Ulm citizens, but not to excommunicate them. Bucer was bitterly disappointed over this decision, since it fundamentally thwarted his vision of a thoroughgoing, all-encompassing Christianization of society.

The actual process of carrying out practical Reformation measures in Ulm went more smoothly. After the rural congregations had been acquainted with the eighteen articles in a series of sermons, the urban priests were asked to give their opinion on these articles on June 5, 1531. On June 6 the members of monastic orders were called to take a stance. On the following day it was the village priests' turn to be examined. The general results were not encouraging. Of the city's thirty-five priests, only five expressed themselves unequivocally in favor of the Reformation. The rest of the secular clergy and the vast majority of the forty-four members of orders responded noncommittally or in a way indicating that they had not understood the articles. Only Conrad Köllin, prior of the local Dominican monastery, proved to be an eloquent advocate of the traditional church's position. The examination of the village clergy produced similar results. But in this case as well, an able and energetic spokesman of the established church was found in the person of Dr. Georg Osswald, the minister of Geislingen. He had already caused a minor riot after unreservedly condemning a sermon held by Bucer in Geislingen as a "wicked heresy." Now he proceeded to draft eighteen counterarticles of his own, over which he and Bucer disputed publicly on June 27. But that event was merely a belated skirmish that occurred after the main battle had already taken place.

For on June 16, the Mass was abolished in Ulm. A few days later the city council ordered images and side altars removed from the churches and provided for the Lord's Supper to be celebrated in accordance with the teachings of the Reformation. Bucer left Ulm on June 30, journeying on to the nearby imperial towns of Memmingen and Biberach, together with Oecolampadius, in order to study the situation of the churches there. He returned to Strasbourg on July 18, 1531, where he proceeded to compose a *General Announcement* (*Gemein Außschreiben*) justifying the Reformation measures taken in Ulm. In this small treatise he put special emphasis on refuting all of Osswald's arguments in great detail. On August 1 the burgomaster and the council of Ulm sent this document and an accompanying letter to a total of thirty-seven cities and territorial princes. The new church ordinance already mentioned above came off the press a few days later. Once again, Bucer was the main author. The ordinance was based on the draft the three preachers had prepared. But Bucer significantly expanded certain sections as a result of the debates with opponents of the Reformation. He added one article devoted exclusively to marriage issues. Reprinted in this publication were also a number of older council mandates concerning moral discipline. With the publication, at the end of September 1531, of the *Little Manual* (*Handbüchlein*), a handbook of worship forms compiled primarily by Blarer and Sam, the Reformation in Ulm could finally be considered complete.

Bucer continually maintained his close ties with Ulm in the coming years, particularly with Martin Frecht, Sam's successor. Among other things, they discussed the problems posed by the spiritualists Caspar von Schwenckfeld and Sebastian Franck, both of whom had many followers in Ulm, even including some in positions of power. Another issue that arose frequently was the antagonism between the pastors and the council. Bucer was often asked to give advice in ticklish issues of marriage and divorce now arising as a consequence of the reorganization of matrimonial law (hitherto adjudicated by episcopal courts but, according to Reformation demands, now to be exercised by civil courts). Following Strasbourg's example, Ulm set up a marriage court consisting entirely of civil lawyers. Since these were overtaxed by the problems brought before them, however, it was decided to reconstitute the court on October 27, 1533. Now it was to be composed of five preachers and only two members of the council. Frecht, who like all Reformers considered the administration of marriage law to be a civil and not an ecclesiastical task, was appalled at this affront. Bucer, however, saw this change as an opportunity to bring his views on the subjects of marriage and divorce to bear in Ulm and elsewhere. For this purpose, after already having written several smaller memoranda on this topic, he now drafted a two-hundred-page treatise *On Marriage and Divorce according to Divine and Roman Law* (*Von der Ehe und Ehescheidung aus göttlichem und kaiserlichem Recht*),[39] which he sent to Frecht at the beginning of December 1533. In this major work he skillfully, if at times a bit speciously, delineates the fundamental agreement between Scripture and Roman law and, on this foundation, discusses the essence of marriage and how marriage is to be contracted properly. This is followed by a detailed presentation of the legitimate grounds for divorce as well as the right to remarry thereafter. Bucer's elementary theological conviction that all human beings have a natural inclination, instilled in them by God, to serve and love their fellow human beings was a cornerstone of his marriage thought. Bucer thus formulates an understanding of the fellowship of marriage that significantly enhances ideas previously set forth by Erasmus. Bucer's deliberations were quite modern for their time; in fact, they definitely had revolutionary qualities about them. For example, Bucer did not only permit divorce on account of adultery, inferred on the basis of Matthew 19:9; for him, the irreversible breakdown of a marriage was sufficient to allow separation and remarriage—not only for the man but also for the woman. "You cannot force conjugal love. . . . Therefore, in this regard let's not try to be wiser than God himself, who wishes that those who no longer are of a single heart be separated."[40]

Bucer's broad-mindedness admittedly had the consequence that his views on marriage and divorce did not receive full support anywhere. Frecht was not the only one to express his reservations; Ambrosius Blarer in Constance and Simon Grynaeus in Basel also had serious doubts, although they could agree in some points. What dealt a deathblow to Bucer's entire project was the refusal of Ulm burgomaster Bernhard Besserer, in March 1534, to defend the Strasbourg theologian's uncommon marital ideas in future negotiations with other southern German cities. Dealing with the territorial princes and the Lutherans was difficult enough. Why should Ulm saddle itself with additional problems? Bucer's modern ideas on marriage and divorce would be forced to await the context of more propitious times.

This episode is nevertheless helpful in illustrating how hard it is to reduce Bucer's personality and theology to one plain formula. We see him vigorously championing the rights and the freedom of the individual at the same time that he vests temporal authority with far-reaching powers over the leadership and organization of the church. These thrusts were not mutually incompatible for Bucer. The ecclesiastical and political situation in Ulm and elsewhere made the cooperation of the magistrate with the church indispensable. In fact, it was much more than that: God himself had given the authorities a mission and entrusted them with a special responsibility, and the pastors had every intention of reminding the authorities of this charge. However, at no time did Bucer believe one could build the church exclusively by relying on temporal government. He always remained convinced that the faith of individuals and their empowerment by the Holy Spirit were of ultimate importance, since the Spirit was to permeate and reshape the entire world and be served by all structures and orders of creation. This conviction, held dearly by Bucer, also guided him in his efforts to help establish evangelical church structures in Augsburg.

Augsburg

In no city of the Holy Roman Empire was early capitalism, represented by the Welser, Paumgartner, and especially by the Fugger families, so pronouncedly developed as in Augsburg.[41] And nowhere did social inequality stand out so glaringly and harshly as in Augsburg. The existence of a sizable urban proletariat, particularly among the weavers, was an undeniable reality. In addition, nothing short of an army of beggars, who made up 10 percent of the population, was present in this city. As a result, religious questions were not only closely intertwined with social ones, but the latter tended to eclipse the former. Furthermore, the Reformation movement in the city lacked a leading personality accepted and legitimized by all factions. The impulsive and gruff Michael Keller, an unequivocal supporter of Zwingli, enjoyed the support of the lower classes only. The ministers that Strasbourg had sent to Augsburg—no fewer than five in the course of the year 1531—were also able to win over only a limited section of the populace. None of these preachers was in a position to mediate between opposing factions, and even less to unite them. To be sure, a majority in the Augsburg city council clearly leaned in favor of the Reformation. However, they possessed no united Protestant front at home to fall back on and were exposed to outside political pressure by Catholic Bavaria and the Habsburgs, not to mention the clout wielded by the Augsburg bishop himself, whom the wealthy merchant families of the community firmly supported. As a consequence, the council did everything in its power to avoid committing the city to a specific course toward Reformation.

Bucer therefore saw his task—a task he took in hand energetically through letters and personal visits—as twofold. First, he had to create unity among the pastors, not just theologically but also on a personal level. He had to help the city find a theological consensus somewhere between Zwingli and Luther: a difficult task, for the latter had attacked the Augsburg preachers directly and indirectly several times since 1530. The second challenge facing Bucer was the problem of convincing the council not only to make use of its right but also to assume its responsibility to care for the well-being of the church—which implied taking drastic measures to introduce the Reformation.

In June 1531, Bucer came to Augsburg from Ulm for a few days, and he used this opportunity to preach an emphatic "peace sermon."[42] It was of little use, as he found out later from the letters that his friend Gereon Sailer, an Augsburg physician and diplomat, wrote him. The squabbles between the ministers continued, with personal, theological, and social differences and conflicts overlapping and thus exacerbating the dissension. An uninterrupted stream of letters of admonishment, instruction, and encouragement addressed to the Augsburg pastors issued from Bucer's pen. He even drafted small compendiums of his theology for them, particularly concerning the Lord's Supper. All this activity was to no avail.

A council newly constituted in January 1534 gave fresh impetus to local supporters of the Reformation. It arranged for a large disputation with adherents of the Catholic Church to take place. The latter, however, refused to have anything to do with it. But the evangelicals were reticent as well. Once again, Bucer was asked to come to Augsburg. His commentaries on the epistles of Paul could wait, Sailer wrote to him on April 24, but it was absolutely essential that his presence in Augsburg not be delayed.[43] His outstanding gifts as a disputant, as a reconciler of hostile camps, and as a leader in the struggle against the papists—these were urgently needed. Bucer did not come until November 6, however, and remained for only one month. In the meantime, on July 22, the council had prohibited Catholic preaching and abolished the Mass in most of the churches. The Mass continued to be held only in the local cathedral and in seven further churches, under the direct jurisdiction of the bishop. Bucer's principal aim in Augsburg was to unite the preachers on the basis of his conciliatory statements on the Lord's Supper. Again, he had only limited success. He did, however, achieve a major breakthrough the next time around, when he stayed in Augsburg at the invitation of the council from February 26 to April 22, 1535, and then again in May of that year. By means of the sermons he held in St. John's Church, many individual conversations, and, last but not least, the support of the council, Bucer was able to convince the local pastors to endorse ten articles he had drafted.[44] These included a summary of his theological principles and also promulgated the strict subordination of the clergy to the city authorities. Bucer was essentially contributing to the establishment of a state church system. This seemed the only way possible to bring about the necessary unity and cohesion of the Protestant camp in Augsburg.

The events of 1535 were just the beginning. Plenty of difficulties still needed to be surmounted, and Bucer, the "actual superintendent" of Augsburg,[45] would still have to heed countless calls for help before the victory of the Reformation could be finally secured, in the summer of 1537, with the enactment of a new church ordinance. In the meantime, however, decisive groundwork was carried out. For one thing, reconciliation with Luther and his Augsburg supporters succeeded because of Bucer's ten articles. Now nothing prevented Augsburg from joining the Schmalkaldic League. The city was admitted into the alliance on January 20, 1536.

The other issue that occupied Bucer during the entire time of his involvement in Augsburg was that of the right of temporal authority to carry out church reforms. In dealing with this question, Bucer thought in a context much broader than merely that of Augsburg. The Augsburg city council had already requested a number of legal opinions on this issue in 1533. On this occasion, Sailer urged the Strasbourg preachers to also draft a memorandum. Bucer therefore dwelled heavily on this topic during his stays in Augsburg. Since the ideas of the spiritualist Sebastian Franck as well as those of Luther found many supporters in Augsburg, Bucer felt compelled to explain his own differing views more extensively. Fulfilling this task meant disproving convincing objections: Was not the gift of faith something entirely spiritual, internal, and therefore out of bounds for any external authority? If one allowed civil authority to decide in spiritual matters, would that not mean getting caught in a new popery and most detrimental tyranny? Not necessarily, felt Bucer. To bolster his case, he encouraged the Augsburg preacher Wolfgang Musculus to translate Augustine's letter to the Roman general Boniface[46] into German. Bucer wrote the preface and afterword for this booklet, which was given the programmatic title *On the Office of Government* (*Vom Ampt der Oberkait*).[47] About two months later, on May 17, 1535, Bucer published a more detailed presentation of his views on civil authority in his *Dialogues or Discussion* (*Dialogi oder Gesprech*).[48]

Once again, he selected the genre of the hypothetical dialogue, this time among three friends, two of whom represented the views of the Zwinglians and the spiritualists, respectively. And once again, Bucer skillfully presented his own view, step by step and in great detail, as representative of a position averse to both extremes—which made it the only correct one. As he wrote, it is the duty of government to carry out God's will. The Old Testament, the laws of the Christian Roman emperors, and even papal ecclesiastical law teach this unequivocally. During the years in which Bucer was so concerned with consolidating and organizing Reformation church structures, he made a point of resorting expressly to this legal tradition, for it offered him an abundance of material for enhancing and developing his own theological conviction that divine justice and law lay at the foundation of society.

Consequently, it was only logical that Bucer conceded full legal authority to subordinate authorities such as city councils, which were subject to the emperor, and thus also assigned them the duty of carrying out church reforms. God clearly demanded that everything evil and harmful be eliminated. And God made those to whom he had given power responsible for consummating these activities. But did this action not imply the revocation of due obedience to the emperor? Bucer denied this possibility. In the same measure as every subject is called to obey the authorities in all temporal matters—including bishops who are territorial princes—so the imperial cities were bound to the orders of the emperor. However, when the issues at stake involved the will and the commandments of God, it was God whom one had to obey, rather than any human authority.

But did this power of the state over the church not infringe too far, indeed, much too far on the sovereignty of Christian faith, on the freedom the Holy Spirit grants? Was Bucer now about to abjure this entire framework merely for the sake of establishing a civic community that was religiously uniform and Christian through and through? As much as Bucer cherished such a community as an ultimate goal, we do injustice to his thought if we reduce it to this one aspect. The dialectical tension between law and spirit that manifests itself so often in Bucer's thinking was also present here. Certainly, faith in Jesus Christ and the justification of sinners through this faith remained of central importance. But this justification did not mean that the person made new by the gift of grace and empowered by the Holy Spirit, who now consciously accepted God's law and sought to live according to it, was necessarily infallible or free of sin. Quite on the contrary, such a person was in need of support and guidance; put in other words, he needed to be *educated.* In its role of education, civil authority assumed its most important function for Bucer; it was intended to play a central role in carrying through Reformation measures and in developing a system of church discipline. Civil authority provided the orientation necessary to put the ideal of a renewed ethical life into practice. "Fair punishment is thus nothing else than pure love, mercy and salvation, not just for the troubled congregation, which by means of the punishment is freed from the nuisance and scandal of pernicious ruin, but also for the ethically lax, who in this way are put in fear and consequently persist all the more in the truth, and finally even for those whom one punishes."[49]

Bucer's extraordinary confidence in the civil authorities, which finds such ample expression in this treatise, is appropriately understood only if we take two factors into account. To begin with, when Bucer said "civil authorities" (*Obrigkeit*), he did not mean the modern, anonymous, and almost omnipotent state apparatus we know today but rather the weak statelike entities that were slowly developing and seeking new forms of sovereignty in the early modern period, and that therefore appeared to be quite open to the idea of assuming responsibility for the church. Second, Bucer was deeply convinced that his own theological views were in league with God's will and God's law, which held sway over the entire world. To proclaim and help bring about God's rule—that was Bucer's ultimate concern, and not the delusion of thinking "that we owe our own existence to ourselves and have a choice to either commit ourselves to God or not, according to our whims."[50] This conviction gave Bucer dignity and self-assurance when dealing with the mighty and powerful, taking precedence over any readiness to accommodate to their demands. And this conviction also allowed Bucer to see the development of the Reformation in Germany and Europe in a broader perspective and concentrate all the more on consolidating what the evangelical movement had achieved so far in Strasbourg.

Organizing the Church

Reforming the Church

The evangelical pastors did not wish merely to destroy. They also wanted to reform the church and make it better.[51] The ministers explained their plans to the Strasbourg city council in a detailed manner in the spring of 1529.[52] Now that the Mass was finally abolished, conditions were ripe for the transformation of the city of Strasbourg into a truly Christian community. The preachers, and Bucer in particular, placed their hopes on being able to work in close cooperation with the authorities.

Never had the city held as many worship services centered on sermons (*Predigtgottesdienste*) as it did in this period. Two such services were held Sundays in every parish church. In addition, Bible lessons took place at noon in the cathedral and in the church of St. Aurelien, and an evening service as well in the cathedral. The council did not make up its mind to remove images and side altars from churches until it had joined the "Christian Federation" (*Christliches Burgrecht*), a defensive alliance with Basel, Bern, and Zurich, on January 5, 1530. The public disturbances that accompanied this iconoclastic measure led Bucer to write up a brief defense of the removal of images in May.[53] And just a few weeks later he decided to respond to the attacks Erasmus was launching against the Reformation, and particularly against the Strasbourg Reformation. Bucer did so by asserting that the authorities had the right and the duty to take part actively in spreading the gospel and helping it take root in society.[54] Besides, according to Bucer, the positive fruits of Reformation efforts had become unmistakably evident in many places, including Strasbourg. Bucer was exaggerating, of course. Or, to put it another way, he was taking much for granted that had yet to take place in Strasbourg, since he was presuming the authorities would support his endeavors unquestioningly. Indeed, the council had issued a major mandate on the issue of moral discipline on August 25, 1529. However, the marital court established by the city council on December 16, 1529, did not include any pastors among its members—unlike new marital courts in most southern German cities. Neither did the new marriage ordinance of 1530 take them into account. On the other hand, Reformation supporters succeeded in having three church wardens (*Kirchenpfleger*) assigned to every one of Strasbourg's seven parish churches; they were responsible for supervising church discipline as well as correct evangelical doctrine. These wardens were laypeople; one of them was a council member, another was one of the *Schöffen*, and the third was chosen from the rest of the citizen body.

The city council did not proceed according to a carefully predetermined plan. It improvised in its tactics, cautiously reacting to the ever-changing political circumstances. But this indecision on the part of the council, and particularly its apparent commitment to the sole principle of not allowing anybody else to take decisions out of its hands, made the evangelical preachers all the more impatient and zealous in urging the council to carry through finally with the pursuit of Reformation goals. Bucer described everything at stake for the city in the small treatise *On the Shortcoming of Religion* (*Vom Mangel der Religion*), written in August 1532.[55] In it, Bucer painted a dismal picture of Strasbourg. He claimed that local citizens, including members of the ruling bodies, were lukewarm or even indifferent to questions of faith. Sermon attendance and overall hallowing of the Sunday were less than satisfactory. Typical for the mood of the city were not the desirable pious earnestness and strict moral discipline of the Christian community; instead, the day-to-day behavior of its citizens was characterized by extravagant spending, feasting, gambling, drinking, immoral behavior, and even unabashed contempt for the church and its representatives. Bucer protested: "Finally, we can and should not tolerate anybody here—without risking God's severe wrath and the doom of the city and the church—who refuses to vow not to blaspheme our Christian religion and refrain from enticing anybody away from hearing the Word of God, from encouraging other believers to do so, or from praying for God's grace together with other Christians."[56]

Using these demands and complaints by Bucer as their starting point, the pastors and church wardens presented a major petition to the city council in November 1532 that contained numerous suggestions designed to bring about the changes that corresponded with their vision of what the church ought to be.[57] What the preachers presented to the council was nothing less than a far-reaching plan for the Christianization of all of society. It began with the Christian education of children and youth and included enforced church attendance for all city inhabitants, the inculcation of disciplinary mandates by the magistrate, and even drastic measures to improve church discipline. The congregations of the surrounding villages were also taken into consideration, with the demand that they be inspected once a year. The foundation of this entire project was the demand made on the city council that it establish and bring pure Christian doctrine to bear in Strasbourg. "For as far as the teaching of Christ is concerned, almost all say and do whatever they please, without any basis in Scripture, without their action corresponding to their faith, and without any scruples." Therefore, as the pastors' petition declares, "it is no wonder that good morals and piety are going from bad to worse, people are leading one another astray and corrupting one other."[58]

When writing this, they particularly had the Strasbourg Anabaptists and the spiritualists in mind. The preachers wished very much to dispute publicly with them, in order to refute their ideas and convince the populace of the errors of these movements and of the truth of the church's teaching. This aspect became especially important for Bucer in the coming months. Strasbourg's tolerant policies had made it possible for a significant number of these "sectarians" to seek and find asylum within its walls. Their presence transformed the debate over defining characteristics of the church into an acute issue for the pastors. Did the Anabaptists and spiritualists all belong to the church, regardless of what they believed? The pastors certainly did not feel that they did. But how could they be excluded from—or better yet, won back for—the church? Merely by preaching the pure gospel and patiently wooing these seduced Christians? Bucer was convinced that such measures were not enough. Rather, God's revelation had to be staunchly asserted as the sole truth and then imposed in the city with all available means, including governmental force. Tolerance in issues of doctrine and faith was tantamount to negligence and disobedience toward God's clear commandments. And Bucer's entire concept of a thoroughly Christian society understandably stood and fell with the clarity and uniformity of Christian teaching. Bucer therefore invested all his energy in the establishment of a standard, obligatory norm of Christian doctrine in Strasbourg with the help of the authorities. Not until he had achieved this goal could he hope to win back the Anabaptists—or demand their expulsion.

The "Sectarians"

A new wave of refugees, arriving since 1529, made the number of Anabaptists and spiritualists in Strasbourg rise dramatically.[59] At their pinnacle, these movements numbered some two thousand members. The occurrence of famine and failed harvests was one reason why so many of them took refuge in Strasbourg. A second important reason was the lenient, indeed almost indifferent attitude of the city council toward dissidents. Apocalyptic expectations now became widespread. Prophets such as Lienhard and Ursula Jost or Barbara Rebstock proclaimed dreams and visions that conveyed images of enormous hostility toward the established social order and its expected destruction in the urgently awaited end times, whose imminent arrival was assumed. These ideas, which found a cogent spokesman in the furrier and itinerant preacher Melchior Hoffman from Schwäbisch Hall, were especially popular among the lower classes, whereas the more educated and well-off citizens of Strasbourg took a liking to the mystical and spiritualistic ideas proclaimed in Strasbourg by the Silesian aristocrat Caspar Schwenckfeld von Ossig. In addition to these two main groups, a smaller group was composed of the followers of the local "Gardener" Clemens Ziegler. He became withdrawn from the world after the disillusionment of the peasants' uprising and took on spiritualistic views. Somewhat similar was the theology of the fellowship begun by Hans Denck and Jacob Kautz, although it was significantly different from all previously mentioned groups in one respect: these men and their disciples were Anabaptists, that is, they taught and practiced the baptism of adults upon the confession of faith. Further Anabaptist groups were the strictly biblicist "Swiss Brethren," who had originated in Zurich, and—theologically close to the latter—the followers of Pilgram Marpeck. Finally, Strasbourg harbored supporters of Hans Hut, who were influenced by apocalyptic and revolutionary ideas. Although it was hard to draw clear borders between these different groups in some respects, the religious and theological differences between them were generally harsh and ultimately irreconcilable. These "sectarians" were thus far from constituting a cohesive group. What united them, however, was solely but significantly their rejection of any form of the official church associated with the state. As a consequence, the representatives of this official church, Bucer foremost among them, perceived the Anabaptists as dangerous opponents.

Throughout these years Bucer complained repeatedly about the growing influence of the sectarians and the fateful consequences their activities had for the creation of new evangelical church structures in Strasbourg. For instance, in November 1532 he wrote to his close friend Ambrosius Blarer: "Pray for our church. The heretics are ruining it incredibly. Through our misguided leniency they have gained such strength that this evil can be neither done away with nor properly remedied."[60] This lament was an exaggeration, to be sure. But it aptly reflected the deep disillusionment that befell Bucer several times during these months. His letters reflect his conviction that the individuals who governed the city simply let matters drift. The religious zeal of the early 1520s had to a large extent given way to passivity or even indifference. As a result, Bucer thought, people who took their Christian faith seriously joined the Anabaptists or spiritualists out of disappointment with the fruits of the Reformation. The official preachers felt like powerless fighters for a lost cause. Admittedly, Bucer and his colleagues continued to urge the council to take action. At the same time, he sought to confront his opponents. In the late fall of 1531, he used his lectures to refute Michael Servetus's attacks on the doctrine of the Trinity succinctly and precisely.[61] This statement, which was spread in handwritten form, won the approval and recognition of his friends. On December 9, 1531, Bucer was finally able to dispute with Pilgram Marpeck inside town hall, but "behind closed doors." The confrontation,[62] which continued in written form until the beginning of 1532, when Marpeck left Strasbourg, revolved primarily around the issue of infant baptism, which was discussed by both participants in great detail. Bucer supported his arguments for infant baptism essentially on the basis of analogy with circumcision in the Old Testament, seeing it as an expression of God's fundamental order—God approaches us unreservedly and unconditionally *before* we do anything on our part. Marpeck rejected this argument, insisting on personal faith as a decisive prerequisite for baptism.

Bucer was not left unmoved by the deep piety and exemplary moral conduct of this Anabaptist leader and his congregation. But he disapproved of their self-imposed separation all the more. How much more could be achieved, especially regarding church discipline, if all would work together instead of against each other? "Unfortunately, we do not yet have much we can boast about," affirmed Bucer, "even though, God be praised, our teaching is the true, authentic teaching of Christ, in spite of how poorly it is being followed."[63] Clinging to God's truth and preaching it were the matters that ultimately counted the most for the Reformation. And where these took place, each one would inevitably be confronted with his own pitiful inadequacy before God and with his failings, and therefore also be inclined to tolerate the same shortcomings lovingly in his fellow Christians. Accordingly, the strongest accusation Bucer leveled against the sectarians was that by departing from true doctrine, they betrayed true piety, which lovingly seeks the welfare of one's fellow human beings and of the entire community. As Bucer had written to Margarethe Blarer as early as September 1531: "Heresy is not this or the other delusion or opinion, but rather a craving of the flesh by which one presumes, in conduct or doctrine, to undertake something apparently better than the divine custom in the common church, and therefore proceeds to separate oneself from the church and join a particular band or sect. . . . They claim to be holier than everybody else but flagrantly miss the goal of love, which alone lies—as God Himself—at the essence of all piety. Therein lies the poison."[64]

The Synod

In their major petition submitted to the council on November 30, 1532, the pastors and church wardens had demanded that Christian ethical standards and religious discipline shape daily life in the city, that true doctrine be preached and asserted with official sanction, and finally that Anabaptists and spiritualists be publicly refuted. In response to this petition, the council created a commission to which Jacob Sturm, Martin Herlin, Andreas Mieg, and Sebastian Erb belonged.[65] When the unrest and disturbances created by Melchior Hoffman's preaching assumed alarming proportions, this body finally came under pressure to take some action. The lay theologian and furrier Hoffman was arrested on May 20, 1533. Previously, on April 12, the council had approved the commission's proposal that a city synod be held. The definitive program for this synod was assembled in the following weeks. It was to begin by laying down the principles of true Christian doctrine and having all Strasbourg preachers and teachers commit themselves to these. After that, the leaders of the sectarians were to be cross-examined on the basis of this doctrinal outline. Finally, all rural ministers and remaining clerics were to be scrutinized. The ruling authorities thus played a large part in determining the course of further ecclesiastical developments in Strasbourg from the very beginning. By proceeding in this way, they particularly precluded the possibility of radical groups gaining any sort of decisive influence. In May 1533 the pastors and church wardens presented a program for conducting the synod[66] that they had coordinated beforehand with the council's commission. Accordingly, the program harmonized entirely with the policy outlined above. The text, drafted by Bucer, centered on a summary of church doctrine in the form of sixteen articles.

At six o'clock on the morning of June 3, the four members of the council's commission, now functioning as presidents of the synod, gathered in the choir of the Church of the Penitent Magdalens (today Église Sainte-Madeleine) together with the twenty-one church wardens and all the teachers and preachers of the city. They discussed the sixteen articles in great detail and finally endorsed them—in spite of the objections of Anton Engelbrecht, Hans Sapidus, and Wolfgang Schultheiss, who saw this action as an inadmissible encroachment on the church's sphere of influ- ence and on the conscience of the individual by temporal authority. We will return to this problem when discussing the written debate between Bucer and his opponents that continued until the end of 1533. The synod concluded its first session on June 6, after the pastors and teachers had had the opportunity to conduct their "censure," that is to say, to report what they found objectionable about their colleagues' moral conduct and administration of office. The groundwork for inspecting rural congrega- tions and for dealing with sectarians had been laid.

The main session of the synod took place June 10–14, once again in the Church of the Penitent Magdalens. The censure of the village ministers was carried out without any difficulties, and they promptly endorsed the sixteen articles. Subsequently, the sectarian leaders were questioned, prin- cipally Clemens Ziegler, Melchior Hoffman, and Caspar Schwenckfeld. Bucer, who played the main role in these interrogations, did not find it hard to defend the newly established doctrinal foundation by bringing his eloquence and his debating gifts to bear. However, it is just as evident that he did not succeed in convincing his opponents, and even less in com- pelling them to join his camp.

The following months went by without any action on the part of the council. So the preachers took the initiative once again, making use of their presence in the synod commission, of which Bucer and Capito were members, to have it present the draft of a church ordinance.[67] They also urged the council to have the synod resume its official sessions. The com- mission's draft, entitled *Deliberations of the Church Wardens, Pastors and Assistants* (*Bedacht der Kirchenpfleger, Prädikanten und Helfer*), afforded a glimpse in outline form of Strasbourg's future church ordinance—and of the enormous influence over the church the city council would ultimately wield. All final decisions now lay in its hands, from supervising doctrine to appointing ministers, from the weekly meeting (*Konvent*) of pastors and church wardens to the broader task of church discipline—which, inter- estingly enough, no longer included the ban and exclusion from church fellowship. Finally, the council was also responsible for making sure Sun- days were appropriately hallowed and for keeping watch over sumptuary matters, such as too luxurious dress, as well as keeping tabs on the general state of morals in the city.

The third session of the synod, which met on October 23 and 29, 1533, did not bring any significantly new contribution. The council for its part

advised the preachers to come to a settlement of their doctrinal differences. Once again a commission was created, charged with inspecting the
writings of Hoffman and Schwenckfeld. All other matters were placed on
hold for further study. On December 26 the council warned the pastors
to stop agitating from their pulpits for the continuation of the synod.[68]
The ministers refused to comply. Caspar Hedio warned in a sermon held
before the council on January 14, 1534, and published soon after: "Dear
Strasbourg, spare no pains to guard yourself against doctrinal dissension.
If not, your doom will be near at hand!"[69] The preachers once again presented their demands to the magistrate on January 28, barely disguising
their threat to resign collectively should no decisions be made, particularly concerning a binding standard of Christian doctrine.[70] This time the
council did not persist in its policy of vain promises and delaying tactics,
sobered by the events taking place in Westphalia: the Melchiorites had
seized power in the city of Münster, ruthlessly expelling the "godless,"
that is to say their opponents, from the city. The Strasbourg council
wasted no time elevating Bucer's Four Cities' Confession of 1530 and his
sixteen articles of 1533 to the rank of official Christian teaching on March
4, 1534. These actions were followed by a decree on April 13 requiring all
Anabaptists in Strasbourg either to make their peace with the church on
the basis of these statements of faith or leave the city within eight days.
Four more mandates were issued in June 1534 providing for the immediate baptism of all infants and the expulsion within fourteen days of those
sectarians unwilling to swear an oath confirming their endorsement of the
newly established statements of doctrine. These measures indicate that,
at least in principle, the new church had firmly taken root in Strasbourg.

Results

This synod, with its activities extending over several months, doubtless
represented the pinnacle of Bucer's influence in Strasbourg. It was not least
due to his tireless efforts that the synod laid the groundwork for firmly
organizing the church in the free imperial city on the Ill River. Admittedly,
Bucer would still have to endure plenty of disappointments and setbacks
on the way to this goal. And the results of the synod were far from being
identical with his vision of a city thoroughly Christian in every way.

Nevertheless, Bucer was now regarded as the leading personality of the
Strasbourg church. On September 13, 1534, Capito issued the judgment:
"Bucer is the bishop of our church."[71] And the Strasbourg preacher
Theobald Schwarz (also called Nigri) wrote to Wolfgang Musculus in

Augsburg as early as July 8, 1533: "I wish so much that you could have seen and heard what grace God bestowed upon Bucer as he responded to all the objections of his opponents. Many (I know I am saying the truth) who previously could not stand even hearing Bucer's name are now beginning to like him sincerely. Even some Papists who up to this point thought only badly of the Gospel agreed with him and are starting to abandon their views. Glory be to God!"[72]

In preparing and carrying out the synod, Bucer had relied entirely on the close cooperation of the city authorities, as repeatedly noted above. This relationship was by no means a contradiction of what he had believed previously, but rather the evident continuation of a conception he had developed many years before. In it, lofty theological principles went hand in hand with ideas of a very pragmatic nature. Bucer had always been convinced that he would not succeed in organizing the Strasbourg church anew without the help, and much less against the will, of the authorities. Consequently, he not only accepted existing power structures, he even sanctioned them. However, he placed enormous emphasis on the responsibility of civil authority before God. Bucer hoped in this way to ensure the church a great deal of influence. The fact that the leading members of the council were rather clueless about how to tackle the theological decisions facing the city attested to the correctness of Bucer's appraisal. When the Tetrapolitan Confession and the Sixteen Articles—in other words, Strasbourg's future doctrinal norm—were discussed in the council on March 29, 1534, not even committed supporters of the Reformation were capable of uttering an informed opinion of their own on these documents. The patrician Hans von Blumenau's statement was typical: he declared he did not want to be against it! "Whatever suited milords, that would also suit him," report the minutes.[73] To be sure, if Bucer based the independence of the church on the theological illiteracy of the council, which appears to be the case, he was focusing his gaze too much on persons and not paying sufficient attention to the structural changes that his promotion of a state church system was helping bring about.

Bucer's understanding of the church changed in the process. Indeed, he remained convinced that essentially only the elect, who had the Holy Spirit, belonged to the church; and since only God knew who they were, one was to concentrate on preaching the gospel to all, administering the sacraments to all, and submitting all to discipline. But much of what Bucer himself had believed previously—and which he now encountered in a similar form among Anabaptists and spiritualists—seemed at least to recede into the background. Among these matters were his eschatological frame of mind and his conviction that spiritual fellowship was one of the essential characteristics of the church—views that he had held passionately in the past, for example, while a preacher in Wissembourg. In those early years he had criticized unjust social conditions in the traditional church sharply, unfazed by the accusation that his and his friends' actions were splitting the church. Now, when the sectarians behaved similarly, he called on them to act lovingly toward their fellow Christians, be patient with corrupt practices not yet eliminated, and particularly not to split off or separate themselves from the church. There is *one* principle, however, that Bucer stuck to consistently: his conviction that he had discerned God's truth and had to stand up for it. For this reason, he wanted to renew the church and give it a new organization. And it was because of his conviction that he also attached ever greater importance to formulating church doctrine and defining the office of the minister. Finally, this inner conviction was also the reason for which he struggled so fiercely against "Epicureans" and sectarians in Strasbourg.

"Epicureans" were commonly understood at the time as people given to sensual pleasure and holding no religious beliefs.[74] The term was polemical and deliberately derogatory. It certainly did not correspond to the way in which the people to whom Bucer applied the name understood and described themselves. What these Epicureans wanted above all was freedom, both intellectual and religious. They therefore opposed any imposition of norms by the church, which for them performed no function other than the limitation and restriction of their freedom of conscience. Quite a few of those whom Bucer was now fighting had been his earlier companions, for instance, Otto Brunfels, Hans Sapidus, and Anton Engelbrecht, the fellow Dominican who had freed Bucer of his vows back in 1521. The discussions that took place in the course of the synod thus became mixed with a good dose of personal disappointment and even resentment on both sides. It is no coincidence that the debate boiled down to the issue of whether the civil authorities might hold sway over the church's organization and daily life. Engelbrecht and some of his friends were finally willing to yield to Bucer and to political reality inasmuch as they were ready to grant not the authorities as such but Christians holding office the right to influence civic policy according to their religious convictions.[75] For Bucer, such a concession was not sufficient. In a gruff and inflexible manner he proclaimed that on the one hand theologians needed to tell those in power which path they had to follow; on the other, pressure and force on the part of the authorities were meaningful ways of educating people on becoming Christians. He wrote: "For it has been quite beneficial for many, as we have learned by experience and still remain convinced, to have been compelled first through fear and pain in order to then become wiser, or to have followed with deeds what already had been learned with words."[76]

There is no doubt that the position held by Engelbrecht and his associates was more modern and promising for the future. When comparing the two stances, it is easy to find Bucer at fault. It cannot be ignored, however, that for all his moral narrow-mindedness and for all his austerity that left little room for laughter, *joie de vivre*, and the sensory delights of Alsatian wine and cuisine, Bucer was not mistaken in seeing the views of the Epicureans as the tip of the iceberg of an increasingly widespread attitude of religious relativism and indifference—an attitude his theological and religious presuppositions forced him to fight fiercely.

His other opponents were the sectarians. These were, besides Schwenckfeld, with whom Bucer would have plenty of disputes in the coming months and years, the Anabaptists, especially Melchior Hoffman and his followers. Bucer published his *Proceedings against Hoffman* (*Handlung gegen Hoffman*) in 1533, against the will of the city council.[77] At the end of that year a publication defending infant baptism (*Quid de baptismate infantium sentiendum*)[78] appeared, in which Bucer attempted to win over to his views Bernd Rothmann, at the time the leading figure of the Reformation movement in Münster. In both treatises Bucer expounds arguments already familiar to us: he defends infant baptism by appealing to the precedent of Old Testament circumcision and rejects Hoffman's claim that Christ was exclusively divine and that man can ascend to him through his deeds, asserting in response the traditional church doctrine of the two natures of Christ as well as the Reformation teaching on justification by faith.

To begin building the church upon the foundation of the official standard of doctrine that had finally been established, Bucer published a catechism in the spring of 1534.[79] Even though he presented the entire contents—the Apostles' Creed, including statements on the sacraments, as well as the Ten Commandments and the Lord's Prayer—in question-and-answer form, the booklet was far too difficult for children and youth. The exposition was much too lengthy, almost exclusively theological, and of an exceedingly academic nature. Correspondingly, this catechism never took root in Strasbourg.

The new church ordinance was finally printed in December 1534.[80] It was a thoroughly revised version of the text that had been presented to the synod commission in the fall of 1533. As already mentioned, the views of the city council carried the day in this version of the ordinance. The council appointed pastors, kept watch over them as well as over the church wardens (*Kirchenpfleger*), and even supervised the *Kirchenkonvent*, or meeting of pastors and church wardens, that took place every two weeks, and of which Bucer was made the chairman. Not a word was said in the ordinance about church discipline or the ban. The council did indeed order all disciplinary mandates issued since 1523 to be read aloud in the guild halls on February 7, 1535, and made them binding for all citizens. This decree, however, did little to lessen the disappointment of Bucer and his friends. Previous years had shown what precious little came of such decrees. Not surprisingly, the preachers' complaints about religious apathy, blatant disregard for the work of the church, and immorality in Strasbourg continued. Bucer was very far from seeing the groundwork laid for a comprehensive and truly Christian reshaping of society in Strasbourg— even after the synod.

The discussions and exchanges that took place in the course of the synod provide us with a vivid portrait of Bucer's personality at this time.[81] Bucer's friends praised his intelligence and skill in debating, his certitude of judgment, his persuasive gifts, but also his personal modesty. His opponents spoke of the deft ways in which he used a plethora of formulations and wordings at his disposal to confuse and refute others. They accused him of being self-willed, judging others prematurely, and pursuing his goals with obstinacy. Bucer was beyond all doubt a domineering person who put much value on keeping others at a distance. Never did he try less to appeal to the populace than at this moment. His moral rigidity bordered on pitiless ruthlessness as soon as he became convinced that he was dealing with individuals or groups who were resisting God's evident truth. But at the same time he was capable of winning people over in a charming and engaging fashion. It is incorrect to assume that in doing so he was behaving selfishly. Personal advantage and gain never played a role in Bucer's personality. Neither did he lose his earlier natural gregariousness and compelling desire to exchange thoughts with like-minded people and friends. His intense correspondence with Ambrosius and Margarethe Blarer exemplifies this trait eloquently. But all these dimensions of his personality were eclipsed by his overwhelming zeal in preparing the way for God's rule in town and country. This zeal won him few friends—but many critics, distrustful onlookers, and not least fierce opponents. In this respect, Bucer was also a lonely man during these years.

Chapter Five

A Champion of Protestant Unity

Roads

In Bucer's days roads were self-contained, colorful worlds of their own, teeming with a garish multitude of people and animals—a vivid reflection of early modern society in all its vulgarity and its glaring contradictions. Eyewitness reports of the times give us a glimpse into this harsh reality, but perhaps even more poignant are its portrayals in the altarpieces, paintings, and etchings by artists of the time. We see the peasant guiding his heavy-laden horse or donkey to market, accompanied by his wife, child, and dog. We see the merchants traveling with their heavy wagons drawn by two teams of horses and frequently escorted by squads of armed horsemen. Footloose mercenaries march along, their halberds on their shoulders, as well as impoverished wandering scholars and students in search of a living or just a cheap place to spend the night. Finally, we see monks traveling in groups of two from one monastery to the next, their eyes downcast. (Bucer had traveled in this way as a Dominican many years ago from his home monastery of Sélestat to Strasbourg, Mainz, and Heidelberg, and later from there to Frankfurt, Basel, and Speyer.) Every once in a while a lonely horseman or a light carriage overtakes the people on foot. And then we see the outcasts of society: vagrants, jongleurs, fugitives, cripples, and people blinded or maimed horribly in some other way, alone or in hordes, assailing and importuning travelers with their loud screams and begging. Life, love, and death were ever-present on these roads. The furtive pair of lovers hidden in the wheat field or in the tall grass just feet away from the road was a beloved motif of artists. More rarely did they draw or paint the travelers who had collapsed in exhaustion, died of hunger, or frozen to death.

These roads were ordinarily not paved and were therefore hollowed out and deeply rutted from much use, muddy to the point of miring all traffic in the springtime and fall, and dangerously icy in the winter. To have firm ground under their wheels, the wagons had to swerve constantly to the left or to the right of the actual highway. The path cut by travelers thus twisted and meandered its way across the countryside. The large number of crucifixes lining the sides of the roads also struck foreigners visiting the Holy Roman Empire. These, as well as wayside shrines, were especially numerous as one approached the vicinity of villages and cities. No less typical, however, was the gruesome sight of places of execution outside city gates, with gallows and wheel, rotting cadavers, and crows circling above.

Traveling on roads like these was not just strenuous—it was dangerous. One did not travel for pleasure. Highwaymen were a constant threat to be reckoned with, especially on secluded paths winding through deep hollows or thick forests. Bandit knights held up merchants. But also other kinds of travelers, small groups, and particularly people traveling alone could never feel safe from bands of thieves or stray mercenaries ganging up on them and killing them for their money, clothes, and horses. A person like Bucer was susceptible to additional, special dangers. For example, when the district governor (*Landvogt*) of Lower Alsace found out that Capito and Bucer had stayed overnight near Ammerschwihr on their way back from the Bern disputation in 1528, he regretted not having gotten wind of it soon enough to capture the two.[1] The *Landvogt* declared he would have happily rewarded anyone disclosing the Reformers' whereabouts on time with one hundred Rhenish guldens. As a consequence, the Strasbourg council refused repeatedly to allow Bucer to travel without armed escort. It was not always possible, however, to provide such protection. There were plenty of occasions on which Bucer would have to travel alone or in the company of merely one or two colleagues on horseback. The horse was clearly the fastest means of transportation of the times. The former Dominican probably learned how to ride during his stay in Sickingen's castles. It is in this period that we first see Bucer undertaking trips on horseback on behalf of this imperial knight.

But even if we leave the omnipresent dangers listed above out of account, traveling remained toilsome and arduous enough. Road conditions caused the axles and wheels of carts and wagons to break repeatedly. Lighter carriages overturned—and travelers could count themselves lucky if all they ended up with were scrapes and bruises. Horseshoes got detached and horses became lame, forcing their riders to dismount and lead them by the reins all the way to the next town. Inns and hostels were crowded and filthy and were frequented by people of ill reputation, and guests had good reason to fear being robbed while sleeping. During the day, travelers were completely at the mercy of the inclemency of the weather: they got soaked to the bone by rain, their entire bodies got spattered with mud and slime, and in the winter they were chilled and numbed by wind, snow, and ice. One can imagine the gratitude and relief travelers must have felt upon catching sight of the steeples, towers, and gates of a city in the distance, especially if they could count on friends or acquaintances welcoming them there.

From now on, these realities would characterize Martin Bucer's day-to-day life not just temporarily, but for months at a time. Hours of intense theological debate, especially in the cities of southwestern Germany and in Switzerland, were preceded and followed by many days and nights on such roads. To be sure, Bucer had already done quite a bit of traveling previously, but now hardly a year went by in which he did not spend at least several months outside of Strasbourg.[2] From October 1534 to January 1535 he traveled through southern Germany on horseback and then northward to Kassel, covering more than one thousand miles. From February to June 1535 he visited the southwest German cities again, traveling some seven hundred miles. He covered roughly twelve hundred miles from April to June 1536 when traveling through southern and central Germany and later continuing on to Wittenberg. His trip to the league's diet in Schmalkalden from January to March 1537 and a further round-trip through southern Germany and Switzerland from May to August of the same year seem almost modest in comparison. Combined, they still represented over eight hundred miles of travel. In April and May 1538 we find Bucer in Switzerland. He rode almost four hundred miles on horseback during those weeks. From October to January 1539 he visited Hesse and Saxony. This involved traveling at least some fifteen hundred miles. And on an additional trip to these territories from November 1539 until January 1540 he covered another nine hundred miles. These estimates are all based on modern highway distances. We can safely assume the distances actually covered by Bucer were even greater. Furthermore, this summary does not take into consideration a number of smaller trips Bucer undertook during these years. All of this means that Bucer practically covered 7,500 miles during the six years—1534 to 1539—under consideration, in other words, about 1,250 miles a year.

Nor did he by any means travel for pleasure. But his passionate desire to unify all Protestants, particularly regarding their understanding of the

Lord's Supper, compelled him to take these troubles and dangers on himself. Just to keep negotiations from stalling, he had to be almost everywhere at once: reinforcing like-minded theologians in their views, encouraging those faltering and wavering, refuting and doing all he could to win over critics and opponents. In many places, fundamental decisions became increasingly dependent on his presence and his vigorous intervention. Bucer had now become a crucial figure of the Reformation. In fact, during these years he was doubtless *the* champion of Protestant unification.

The Wittenberg Concord

Preconditions

Once again, political events were propitious to efforts by individual theologians, especially Martin Bucer, to heal the severe rift in the Lord's Supper issue still afflicting the Protestant camp. At the beginning of 1534, Landgrave Philip of Hesse undertook a daring attempt to recapture Württemberg and restore it to its legitimate ruler by ancestry, Duke Ulrich, expelled by the Swabian League in 1519. Philip was able to count not only on the help of the Schmalkaldic League but also on the consent and support of a remarkable coalition of enemies of the Habsburg dynasty from both within and outside the Holy Roman Empire. Among these improbable allies was the strictly Catholic Bavaria, which felt threatened by the Austrian regime in Württemberg. The pope was also informed about Philip's venture. A most important participant was finally French king Francis I, a fierce enemy of Charles V and of all Habsburg designs for world dominance. He provided troops and finances in exchange for rights over the Habsburg territory of Montbéliard. The Austrian troops, badly equipped and poorly led, were defeated without much effort near Lauffen on the Neckar River on May 13, 1534. King Ferdinand, Charles's brother, was busy repelling incursions by the Turks in Hungary at the time. He thus had to agree quickly to the peace of Kaaden (near Eger/Cheb in northern Bohemia), signed on June 29. The treaty attempted a comprehensive solution to the problems at hand. Its main points were: Duke Ulrich got his territory back as an Austrian intermediate fief; that is to say, should Ulrich's lineage die out, Württemberg would revert to the Austrians. In exchange, Saxon elector John Frederick gave his consent to Ferdinand's election as "king of the Romans"—something he had refused until now. In addition, the harsh legal processes that the imperial Chamber Court was conducting against the Protestants for their violations of existing legislation were to be suspended. Finally, the parties to the treaty agreed to allow no "sacramentarians" in Württemberg—a formulation that came dangerously close to equating supporters of Zwingli's understanding of the Lord's Supper with spiritualists and Anabaptists. This stipulation brought about feverish efforts to finally reach some kind of an agreement on the Lord's Supper among all Protestants.

For there were naturally quite a few theologians and laypeople in Württemberg who felt at least an affinity to the Swiss position, beginning with Duke Ulrich himself. Also concerned were southern German free imperial cities such as Augsburg, Ulm, Memmingen, Lindau, Isny, Kempten, and Biberach, which were now hoping to have a reliable ally in the Duchy of Württemberg and were therefore urgently interested in seeing the eucharistic controversy solved. Finally, all sensible people knew that the only way to find a fundamental solution for the problem was for the Wittenberg and Zurich theologians themselves to reach a settlement. It is on these three different regional levels that Bucer took direct and indirect action in the coming months and years.

During this period, Bucer became one of the leading, if not the leading, figures within German Protestantism. It is true, he never enjoyed the phenomenal intellectual and theological authority that Luther commanded. Melanchthon's theological and church-political influence as the author of the first Protestant dogmatics (*Loci Communes*) and of the Augsburg Confession (*Confessio Augustana*) of 1530 was also in some ways more far-reaching. Besides, Melanchthon had the support of Luther (if sometimes tense) and of the Saxon elector. Bucer, however, was capable of winning the commitment of and mobilizing a significant portion of those Protestants, especially in southern Germany, who had been forced to come to terms with reality beyond their limited local and provincial boundaries. Bucer thus became the decisive motor of progress toward an agreement in this camp. He now ceased repeating that the eucharistic controversy was just a squabble over words, at least when he was speaking with the Wittenberg theologians. It was Luther who dictated the conditions for a theological and ecclesiastical agreement—and Bucer conformed. He still remained just as convinced as before that only unity among Protestants would pave the way for the full success of the Reformation in all of the Holy Roman Empire and in Europe—that is to say, for the sweeping realization of Christ's rule. Bucer's consequential use of formulations that could be interpreted and understood in many different ways was held against him already as a sign of insincerity. This harsh judgment fails to notice that Bucer was convinced from the start that the contesting parties concurred in matters essential and crucial but simply were not able to come to an agreement on side issues. It also is unmistakably clear that during these years Bucer remained unwaveringly true to the position he had already developed in writings mentioned above, such as in his book "to the Munsterites," as he called it: the *Report from Holy Scripture* (*Bericht aus der Heiligen Schrift*).

Bucer had only indirect influence on the eucharistic settlement reached in Württemberg, the Stuttgart Concord on August 2, 1534. His friend Ambrosius Blarer and the Lutheran Erhard Schnepf agreed on a formulation that the Lutherans had suggested during the Marburg colloquy of 1529.[3] The decisive statement in it was the affirmation of the real, that is to say, the corporeal presence of Christ in the Lord's Supper. Zwingli had rejected this formulation back in Marburg. The fact that Bucer now gave his cautious consent to it aroused a great deal of mistrust, particularly in Heinrich Bullinger of Zurich, who regarded himself as the custodian of Zwingli's legacy. Bucer was indeed able to gain the confidence of the southern German cities at a meeting in Constance in December 1534. The Swiss, however, refused to show up, merely sending a written statement expressing their skepticism and reservations.

Bucer left Constance in great haste before the meeting was over, dashing northward to Kassel, for Philip of Hesse had finally succeeded in getting the Saxon elector and the Wittenberg theologians to agree to begin unification negotiations once again over the Lord's Supper. Melanchthon and Bucer discussed not only eucharistic issues but also other theological topics intensely with one another from December 27 to 29. They got on very well and were pleased to note that they agreed extensively on the issues that had been controversial up to that point. Of course, they both realized this was not enough—it was winning Luther over that was going to be crucial. The latter had given Melanchthon a written instruction rigidly expressing his own uncompromising views. But Melanchthon's position had changed in the meantime.[4] He now believed that Christ was present in the Lord's Supper to the extent that he gave himself to the communicants when the elements of bread and wine were administered. This cautious dissociation from the idea that Christ's body and blood were tied up with the elements of bread and wine coincided exactly with Bucer's concern. It is therefore not surprising that both could agree in Kassel that Christ is certainly present in the Lord's Supper inasmuch as he is united to the bread and the wine "in a sacramental way" (*auf sakramentliche Weise*). Bucer and Melanchthon were ready to leave it at that, not delving further into *how* this union took place and refraining from proposing new consensus formulations. Luther's drastic wording—namely, that in the

Lord's Supper one held Christ in one's hand and in one's mouth—was left untouched as an extreme statement, but at the same time it was emphasized strongly "that the body of the Lord as such can neither be reached nor understood by reason, but faith must rather be active here."[5] Finally, Bucer drafted a friendly response to Luther's harsh instruction, informing the Wittenberg theologian that he misjudged the Strasbourg Reformers' understanding of the Lord's Supper, since in reality they agreed with Luther completely.

Bucer was overjoyed and full of optimism when he returned to Strasbourg in the first days of the new year 1535. Capito took off for Zurich soon after in order to pass on the promising news to Bullinger and attempt once again to woo the Swiss. Bullinger, however, remained skeptical. Doubts and reservations also came to the fore elsewhere in Switzerland. Was it not better to wait first and examine carefully how matters would develop? After all, all parties to this dispute had experienced enough disappointments in the past. In this situation, Bucer was able to achieve significant progress toward creating a climate of rapprochement with Wittenberg by convincing the Augsburg theologians to endorse ten articles he had drafted. Luther was pleased by these theses, which—as mentioned previously—were a summary of Reformation doctrine, beginning with the Trinity, continuing with justification by faith, dealing thereafter with the sacraments and the obligation of government to work at establishing a Christian commonwealth, and concluding with attacks on Anabaptists and spiritualists. The Wittenberg Reformer realized that his opponents could not simply be labeled "fanatics" (*Schwärmer*) or hypocrites.

Of course, this did not mean an end to all misunderstandings and disagreements. In April 1535, Luther's friend Nikolaus von Amsdorf published a biting piece against "Zwinglians and Anabaptists," among whom he decided to include the Strasbourg theologians. Bucer was outraged and embittered by the accusation that he and his colleagues were only feigning concord with the Lutherans and in reality held quite different views. This insinuation hit the very nerve of his union efforts. Nevertheless, he managed to tame his anger, in part through Melanchthon's coaxing, and responded to Amsdorf clearly and resolutely, but without any acrimony, in a series of "Axioms" (*Axiomata apologetica*). Bucer definitely wanted unity. He could do without any additional difficulties on the path toward this unity.

Further developments proved him right. In October 1535, Luther suggested to the southern German theologians that the two sides conduct verbal negotiations over all issues of doctrine, particularly the Lord's Supper.

The encounter was to take place in Eisenach on May 14, 1536. Bucer did his utmost to convince the Swiss and the southern German theologians to participate, refusing to accept skepticism and doubt over the outcome as excuses. "Truly, I would not be able to desist from it any longer with a clear conscience," he wrote in April 1536, "for I have already come so far in this matter with a clear conscience, with true grounds in Scripture, and with the consent and the encouragement of my superiors and brethren."[6]

However, doing away with the last reservations and the remaining resistance turned out to be no easy task. To be sure, on December 1, 1535, Swiss theologians meeting in Aarau agreed on a formula asserting the presence of Christ in the Lord's Supper. In addition, the First Helvetic Confession (*Confessio Helvetica prior*)[7]—which an assembly of theologians in Basel drafted on February 4, 1536, with a view to the coming council convened by Pope Paul III, to take place in Mantua—certainly left enough leeway for rapprochement between Protestants. Capito and Bucer, both of whom were present in Basel, brought to bear all the influence at their disposal, especially upon the formulation of the eucharistic article. On the other hand, the Swiss put just as much effort into emphasizing their independence and repelling all foreign influence. It is with this in mind that Bibliander decided to publish the correspondence between Zwingli and Oecolampadius in March 1536. Bucer wanted to make sure that this did not create new difficulties and therefore wrote a brief preface to the publication. What he accomplished was exactly the opposite of what he intended. The Swiss were not persuaded by his claim that it was primarily in opposition to the traditional Catholic interpretation that Zwingli had attached utmost importance to faith in the Lord's Supper. Ultimately, the Swiss refused to participate in the colloquium with Luther. Furthermore, this publication once again aroused deep mistrust among Luther and his supporters. What was Bucer really up to? Was he still imagining he could simply put Luther's and Zwingli's views together? No question about it—the negotiations were going to be difficult.

The Agreement

The southern German church representatives and theologians departed for Eisenach in separate groups in the final days of April. Bucer came from Augsburg by way of Frankfurt. Luther, however, was not able to attend. He had been frequently ill in the past months, tormented by lithiasis and plagued by sleeplessness and severe depressions. Unfazed, the delegation left Eisenach without a moment's hesitation and headed directly for Wittenberg. It arrived on Sunday, May 21, 1536.[8]

On Monday morning the southern Germans presented letters to Luther that he was to read before negotiations began. At three in the afternoon of that very same day, all assembled at Luther's house in the former Augustinian monastery to conduct the first deliberations. The atmosphere was icy. Luther attacked his guests immediately, expressly including Bucer, and asserted that meaningful talks could take place only if the southern Germans first publicly recanted their false understanding of the Lord's Supper and henceforth taught that unbelievers as well as believers actually received the body and the blood of Christ in their mouths with the Lord's Supper.

This opening left Bucer obviously bewildered. Capito stepped in skillfully and started explaining the Strasbourg theologians' understanding of the Lord's Supper. Bucer then regained his accustomed eloquence and took the initiative once again, remaining the central spokesman of the southern German delegation until the end of the negotiations. He resolutely confronted Luther with the fact that just repeating old insults and preconceptions would make the long trip to Wittenberg a waste of time. What the Strasbourg preachers and the theologians in other cities actually taught could be discerned quite clearly from their writings. Did it not make more sense to believe them, rather than the usual slanderers and squabblers, of which there would always be more than enough? And as far as the recantation demanded by Luther was concerned, the Strasbourg delegation would certainly not be afraid of admitting errors publicly. But never would they recant what they had not proclaimed in the first place: that supposedly only bread and wine are given to the congregation in the Lord's Supper. Bucer also described Luther's statement that the body and blood of Christ are received with the mouth in the Lord's Supper as extremely misleading. He emphasized that unbelievers certainly only received bread and wine.

The deliberations were then suspended because Luther felt ill. At his request they were not continued until the afternoon of the following day. The controversial point in question was now whether unbelievers (*impii*) receive Christ—something that Luther affirmed and Bucer denied. Johannes Bugenhagen found a way out of the impasse by once again bringing up a formula suggested by Bucer in 1535 that distinguished between unbelievers (*impii*) and the unworthy (*indigni*). The important thing was to make sure that Christ's real presence in the Lord's Supper did not depend on the faith and the worthiness of participants. Whether or not Christ was also present for those who did not believe anything at all, that is to say, for unbelievers, was ultimately left undecided. The wording chosen did justice both to Luther's insistence on the comforting certainty that Christ truly gives himself to the conscience-stricken and to Bucer's interest in emphasizing the fellowship of humankind with God and the new life resulting from this fellowship that enables believers to build the church and reshape the world.

Following this, Luther asked every one of those present personally if he believed what had been stated at this meeting: that the congregation did not just receive bread and wine in the Lord's Supper. All affirmed this and emphasized that they agreed with Luther's remarks. After that, Luther and his supporters left the room to confer with one another briefly. Upon returning, Luther declared: "Worthy lords and brethren, we have now heard every one of you answer and confess that you believe and teach that the true body and the true blood of the Lord are given and received in the Holy Supper, and not just bread and wine. . . . You take exception to including unbelievers, but you do confess, as Saint Paul does, that the unworthy receive the body of the Lord. . . . We do not want to quarrel over this. Since this is how matters stand with you, we are in agreement, we recognize and accept you as our dear brethren in the Lord, as far as these articles are concerned."[9] Melanchthon was then charged with putting this agreement into writing.

It was a moving occasion, especially for Bucer. This was the moment he had been working toward for years, overcoming countless setbacks, disappointments, vituperations, and his own feelings of hopelessness. To be sure, it was not an unqualified success. Further points of doctrine had not been discussed yet, and the settlement just attained had to win recognition back home, in the southern German cities and particularly in Switzerland. But the first significant breakthrough had been achieved: Luther and his supporters had been won over. Bucer had made concessions to Luther without having betrayed his own theological standpoint—which can be described as that of an exhibitive real spiritual presence of Christ in the Lord's Supper. Bucer had thus neither simply acquiesced to Luther nor glossed over real differences. The result was a concord in the true sense of the word—an agreement on fundamentals that still left enough leeway for differing emphases.

Negotiations continued on May 24, with discussions over infant baptism and church discipline. This agreement as well was fixed in writing. The atmosphere had become much more relaxed by now. The meetings took on the character of an exchange of views and no longer sounded like an interrogation. In the afternoon, schooling and education were discussed. On the following day—it was the Ascension of Christ—a worship service was held in which Luther preached. The southern Germans took offense at the candles, the Mass vestments, and the elevation of the elements during the Lord's Supper—all practices they had done away with long ago. On May 26 and 27 the talks continued, this time on the right and duty of the civil authorities to carry out church reforms. Both sides remained at odds on this issue. Bucer was not able to persuade the assembly to consent to his far-reaching ideas on this topic. The Lutherans drafted and signed a separate statement.

On May 27, Bucer also gave a detailed account of the confession of the Swiss Protestants (*Confessio Helvetica prior*). His comments were received sympathetically. Even before the departure of the southern Germans, Luther encouraged Bucer to continue negotiations with the Swiss cities on the basis of the concord just reached. On May 28 all the delegates endorsed the text of the Wittenberg Concord with their signature— except for Johannes Zwick from Constance, who had no authorization by his city council to do so. Before having the Concord published it was agreed that both sides should first drum support for it among their respective constituencies, "so that no one should find fault with our action and say we wanted to rule over the church and pass resolutions on behalf of others without asking them first."[10] The southern Germans departed from Wittenberg on May 29.

They stopped over in Frankfurt from June 2 to 5, where Bucer wrote down his report on the conference.[11] His aim was to summarize what had been accomplished and at the same time plot out the future course of action. The Concord was only the beginning. The point now was to win support for it in all of southern Germany, but especially in Switzerland.

Results

Getting the Wittenberg Concord approved was understandably easiest in Strasbourg itself. On June 22, Capito and Bucer drafted a lengthy statement, addressed to their colleagues, in which they set forth and justified the eucharistic settlement. The official presentation of the Concord took place a week later, on June 29, in the chapter house of the former Dominican monastery before the assembled larger council (*grosser Rat*), pastors, teachers, and church wardens. It was followed by a brief discussion and ultimately by the signing of the Concord by the clergymen present. Only

Paul Volz, Wolfgang Schultheiss, and Anton Engelbrecht—all of whom had practically become outcasts since the synod in 1533—refused to affix their signatures to the settlement. It was probably on the following Sunday, July 2, that the congregations of Strasbourg were officially informed about the agreement.

Getting the southern German imperial cities to endorse the Concord proved to be more difficult. Almost all of them ultimately gave their assent to the treaty, but only after Bucer had coaxed and urged them unceasingly. His efforts to convince the city of Constance, however, did not avail in the least. Not only the council, on which Johannes Zwick's brother Konrad sat, but even old friends such as Ambrosius and Thomas Blarer resisted the Concord. A number of different ideas and interests played a role here. For one thing, the city looked increasingly to Switzerland for political orientation and support. Second, it was exceedingly mistrustful of Bucer, ever since he had written the aforementioned memorandum for the French king permitting bishops to retain their traditional political and legal rights. The city of Constance had freed itself precisely from the yoke of the bishop, after much struggle, as a consequence of the Reformation! They therefore obstructed Bucer's attempts at union now and also urged the Swiss, especially Zurich, not to embark on such negotiations.

It was naturally the Swiss Protestant cities that put up the stiffest resistance. Bucer pursued two courses in order to overcome this opposition. In the first place, when expounding the Lord's Supper to the Swiss, he asserted the fundamental agreement between the Wittenberg Concord, on the one side, and the eucharistic ideas of Zwingli and Oecolampadius as well as the First Helvetic Confession (*Confessio Helvetica prior*), on the other. Second, he attempted to win over individual cities, particularly Basel and Bern, on the strength of his charismatic personality, his undisputed theological authority, and his lucid ability to debate. He achieved significant results on both courses but failed to make a decisive breakthrough.

Any talk of Christ binding himself to the elements of bread and wine was rejected immediately and emotionally by the Swiss, allergic to anything only mildly suggestive of a natural union. But that was precisely what he did not mean, asserted Bucer over and over again. It was a "kind of" union, a "sacramental" union, an ultimately inexplicable union. And it was definitely not a union in which—Bucer now resorted to images drawn from Alsatian cuisine—Christ was present "like wine in a jug or meat in a pastry shell."[12] It was now of crucial importance that the Swiss declare unmistakably that not only bread and wine were distributed in the Lord's Supper, that they stop accusing the Lutherans of perniciously mingling the glory of the risen Christ with the earthly elements, and that they finally leave the bitter conflicts of the past at rest. Bucer had his mind set on the future, and he was therefore urging the Swiss to hold a national synod on the topic. This could be an opportunity for opposing camps to clash, wrestle with one another, and—Bucer was convinced of the outcome—emerge from the debate united.

Bucer formulated these ideas in the spring of 1537 in a letter addressed to the Zurich theologians in particular and the Swiss in general. His own situation was extremely difficult at the time, for the Swiss had gotten wind of a letter he had written to Luther on January 19, 1537,[13] in which he all too candidly expressed his irritation over the indecision and smug self-satisfaction of the Swiss. The latter were irked additionally by Bucer's "Retractions" (*Retractationes*)—a text he inserted into the section discussing Matthew 26:26 and John 6:63 in the third edition of his commentary on the Gospels (1536), self-critically recanting earlier statements on the Lord's Supper. This especially outraged the Bernese theologians, for they understood these retractions to be a falsification of the results of their very own disputation of 1528. To be sure, Bucer succeeded splendidly in explaining himself in Bern in September 1537. Ultimately, however, his appearance did not dissipate unexpressed indignation over the fact that an outsider—"this Strasbourger!"—had attempted to lead them and their church by the nose in such a patronizing way.

The facile claim that Bucer was on Luther's side certainly does not do justice to this dispute. It is true, however, that Bucer's encounter with the seriously ill Wittenberg reformer in Gotha on March 1, 1537, left a lasting impression on him. Luther downright implored Bucer to continue his mediation efforts. Understandably, this filled Bucer with renewed strength of purpose. After his personal success in Bern, he thus drafted an enlarged German version of his retractions under the title *Corrections* (*Verbesserungen*). This text impressively documents Martin Bucer's character, revealing his ability to admit and renounce mistakes ("The righteous accuses himself first, then others"),[14] his innermost conviction that the controversy over the Lord's Supper could be solved if both sides (which at this moment meant the Swiss in particular) sincerely wished to solve it, and his unselfish and unflagging work for concord and understanding, work that he undertook without sparing his own energies. Bucer knew what he was talking about when he wrote to Archbishop Thomas Cranmer of Canterbury at this time in reference to Simon Grynaeus of Basel: "He has yet to experience how difficult it is convincing even open-minded people of something that is truly good—indeed, people without the slightest mistrust towards things good and just."[15] Most significant, Bucer's ecclesiastical and political frame of reference once again proved to be much more far-reaching than that of most of his contemporaries. Particularisms and parochialisms of any kind went against his grain. It was during these years at the very latest that Bucer developed a Europe-wide consciousness. He was not only acutely aware of the situation of Protestants in other countries, he also had a clear sense of the most significant ecclesiastical and political powers and movements of his day. Bucer was convinced that Protestants had to become active in this wider arena, joining forces and purposefully engaging in these broader conflicts. He struggled for this tenaciously and unremittingly.

But this was something the Swiss Protestant cities were precisely not interested in. They were self-contented. And Bucer was not able to pry a single city out of this complacence, not even Bern or Basel. To be sure, both cities made some effort to accommodate to the wishes of the Strasbourg theologians at the Zurich conference from April 28 to May 4, 1538; the cities even responded to Luther in friendly terms. But Bucer was not able to elicit more from them. They neither accepted nor rejected the Wittenberg Concord. Especially Bullinger and the Zurich theologians stubbornly and doggedly opposed any concessions. What he and those in his camp really thought can be deduced from a caricature circulating at the time: it displays Bucer and Capito holding a weir-basket in which Luther is sitting. The Pope drives the fish toward Luther while a clown-like figure makes fun of this perverted cooperation. In the satirical verses accompanying the drawing, "Truth" has the last word:

> *der glöubig wirt stiff an mir blyben*
> *und üch blinden lan butzwerck tryben.*[16]

(the believer will firmly stay at my side
and leave you blind people to your silly games)

The Alemannic word *butzwerck* (play, mockery, humbug)—with connotations such as *sich putzen* or *aufputzen* (to smarten oneself, spruce oneself up, put on a show)—unmistakably aimed at insulting Bucer. He never abandoned his hope, however, of one day winning over the Swiss for a eucharistic concord after all. But new and more ambitious projects of union laid claim to his time and energy for the coming years. From now on, Bucer would be engaged in a daring attempt to reach a rapprochement and a settlement with the Catholics of the Holy Roman Empire.

Organizing the Church in Strasbourg

Morality and Church Discipline

At the same time that Bucer and the Strasbourg pastors were doing all they could to convince the civil authorities to take stricter measures against immorality in Strasbourg and enforce church discipline, the council found time to discuss the enlargement of the city brothel in great detail. "After all, we have to let the world be the world a bit," jotted down the civic secretary wryly.[17] This incident is exemplary for the practical limits constraining Bucer's and his colleagues' lofty goals. Issues perceived by the preachers as simply crucial for setting up Christ's reign in Strasbourg were appraised by the council from a strictly pragmatic viewpoint. Doubtless the preachers were radical and uncompromising in pursuing their goals— as could be expected of them. Those in power were forced indeed to come to terms with this, but they were still determined not to allow the preachers' position to have the slightest influence on Strasbourg's fate.

Accordingly, from 1535 onward, the city council turned down all requests coming from the preachers for it to clamp down on moral misconduct, and especially for it to enforce church discipline. The utter failure of the pastors' entire efforts became evident. Progress was made neither on the personal nor on the institutional level. The church wardens (*Kirchenpfleger*) did not even come close to carrying out what Bucer and his colleagues expected of them. It did not help much that Bucer defined their function as a ministry essential to the church. These men saw themselves ultimately as city officials and not as church servants, not least because of their appointment by the city council. Incapable of grasping Bucer's aim of creating an independent, self-assured church, they perceived their task within the traditional framework of political and moral surveillance by the civil authorities. Consequently, they did absolutely nothing. At the same time, Anabaptist groups started growing once again in Strasbourg. They attracted a lot of followers not only on account of their pious lifestyle but particularly because of the strict discipline they practiced.[18]

Bucer did not waver from his earlier goal of establishing "the rule of Christ" in Strasbourg, but from the late 1530s onward he began working at it with somewhat different tactics. He continued to place his full confidence in cooperating with the city council, as we shall see shortly. At the same time, however, Bucer began encouraging individual congregations to become more self-reliant and to take responsibility into their own hands—a topic to be discussed further below. It is important to note that

Bucer did not see these two thrusts as mutually exclusive. Bucer believed that his goal, the establishment of Christ's rule in society, could become reality only if church and magistrate worked together. He was skeptical enough, however, to realize that this cooperation would work effectively only if the actual power of the civil authorities was countered by a truly independent church.

The second synod of the Strasbourg church, which met in the former Dominican monastery May 26–28, 1539,[19] made even the greatest of optimists realize that they could expect precious little help from the council in setting up Christ's reign in the city. Decisions on matters deemed urgent by the pastors were ultimately dragged out until the summer of 1544. The synod did adopt a confession of faith essentially in agreement with the first version of Bucer's sixteen articles (1533). It additionally brought about a greater standardization of liturgy. Both church and state agreed to give infant baptism a prominent place in the worship service. Differences arose, however, as soon as the subject changed to church discipline. Now as ever, the council remained unwilling to make fundamental concessions of any kind. Even the formal adoption of confirmation was rejected on May 18, 1540. Confirmation had actually already been carried out in several parishes from 1538 onward by means of a ceremony in which the pastor laid his hands on the heads of children, blessing them after they had completed the catechism, successfully passed an exam, and given a personal confession of faith.

Ever since the late 1530s, Bucer took great pains to awaken and foster feelings of individual accountability and self-reliance among Strasbourg's Christians. The magistrate saw this as an attempt to split the local church into two classes of Christians, and it obstructed Bucer's plans accordingly. Of course, Bucer was not seeking such a division. But, for him, clearly the worse option was for the church to become a mere object of civic and political administration, lacking an independent spiritual life and a discipline of its own. Bucer was convinced that in this area fundamental changes had to be introduced. He thus worked at this comprehensively— from an academic and from a pastoral perspective. We will analyze both in this order.

Scholarship and Education

The individual Christian should be able to give account of his faith to himself and to others. Bucer made this demand early on, as did the other Reformers. But Bucer also worked at putting this principle into practice

from the very beginning. Clearest proof of this was his successive exegesis of the Bible, carried out continuously from year to year—not just for
theologians but also for all educated and interested laypeople. In 1536 two
ponderous Latin tomes appeared in print, the product of some of the lectures Bucer had been giving for the past years. One of them was the third
edition of his commentary on the Gospels; the other was his commentary
on the book of Romans.[20]

Already Bucer's contemporaries perceived the Romans commentary as
his most important exegetical work, and they heaped their praise upon it.
It deals with the central topic of the Reformation: faith in Christ and the
justification of sinners. But Bucer was quick to add that it also dealt with
"the precepts surrounding the true duties" of the Christian.[21] The book
thus intended to inform and educate from a theological and an ethical
point of view, especially pastors and teachers lacking formal education but
charged with "passing on the philosophy of Christ to the common folk."[22]
Bucer's frame of reference in all this was not limited to Strasbourg and the
Upper Rhine Valley. As the dedication of the Romans commentary to
Thomas Cranmer, archbishop of Canterbury, indicates, Bucer had all of
Europe in view.

The same sweeping vantage point brought itself to bear on Bucer's
understanding of theological tradition. He described not only how Paul
and other biblical witnesses, particularly John the Evangelist, were in
agreement with the Reformation message. He went to great pains to convince his readers that this had also been the traditional teaching of the
church for many centuries. Bucer thus got a conversation going between
the apostle Paul and the humanist Erasmus of Rotterdam; he got the
church fathers of the east, including the beloved John Chrysostom, and
the west, Augustine at the fore, talking with the Reformers and the "better scholastics," with Thomas Aquinas in the lead. Admittedly, this was
not possible without occasionally doing injustice to one or the other or
without at times playing down differences too extensively. Bucer was certainly aware of this. But his vision of the church compelled him to endure
these contradictions. It was manifestly clear that at the present, a living,
personal faith could not be reduced to a single form of expression, and this
made dialogue necessary between dissenting parties (a dialogue, of course,
that assumed obedience to the words and commandments of Christ as
Lord of the church). Bucer was convinced that the debate with past theological tradition and with one's opponents had to take place in exactly
the same way. Polemic was not enough, for it did not take this understanding of the church into account. But the same was also true for set-

tlements reached at any price. What was necessary was something much more difficult: demonstrating that differing assertions could harmonize if one set one's mind on the edification of the church and of all of Christendom, thus contributing to the furthering of salvation and of a truly Christian life in the church. Faith in Christ and the justification of sinners remained the foundation for all this. But by placing not these doctrinal statements but rather their ethical consequences in the forefront, that is, by developing piety as the concretion of the gift of justification, Bucer could remain open to the rich heritage of theological tradition and use it convincingly in his efforts to reach unity. Bucer followed this line of thinking assiduously in his theological and ecclesiastical work of the following years and decades.

Bucer's commentaries aimed to teach, train, and cultivate in a comprehensive fashion. They did not only make theological statements—they also educated in the broadest sense. These commentaries had grown out of lectures and were indeed a summary of what the schools in Strasbourg were capable of achieving. Bucer had put a lot of energy into the development of schools quite early, as we saw above. Now, in the 1530s, the educational system in Strasbourg experienced a huge improvement. This was largely due to Bucer.[23] He had always been convinced that all young people should be sent to school, girls as well as boys, the gifted as well as the less gifted. In 1535 there were eight schools in Strasbourg with instruction in German, two for girls and six for boys. In addition, there were three Latin schools. In 1534, Bucer was able to create a boarding school in Strasbourg for the tuition-free training of future pastors. Instrumental in making this possible was the support of Ambrosius Blarer in Constance but especially the financial backing offered by the patricians Peter and Jost Buffler from the free imperial city of Isny. The Buffler foundation thrived in no time. Soon there were some thirty youth from all of southern Germany and Switzerland living and studying in the boarding school on a regular basis.

At the same time, Bucer worked at simplifying and standardizing the instruction given to these youth, which took place in the former Dominican monastery of Strasbourg, and coordinated it as well with other courses taught in Strasbourg, such as his biblical lectures at St. Thomas. Efforts to turn the school into a university, however, were obstructed by the city council, which deemed it too expensive and, after the recuperation of Württemberg for the Reformation, superfluous, for the university at Tübingen could now reassume this training function. Bucer succeeded nevertheless in 1539 in merging all the Latin schools of the city into one major educational establishment that met on the premises of the former Dominican monastery. Jean Sturm became the rector of this new academy. Sturm came from Schleiden in the county of Manderscheid in the Eifel region, where he had been born in 1507, and had been trained superbly in the Netherlands and in Paris. The academy, which opened in Easter 1539, soon flourished under his leadership. In 1544 it already had 644 schoolboys and students, who were taught in ten different classes. There was one teacher for every age-class and, in addition, just as many professors. Outstanding scholars were won over as teachers from among the religious refugees arriving in Strasbourg. Besides theology, the subjects taught included law, some medicine, rhetoric, dialectic, poetry, and, of course, Latin, Greek, and Hebrew. The school's pedagogical goal was to cultivate and promote languages, the humanistic study of classical antiquity, and a Christian piety anchored in the church. Bucer and Jean Sturm agreed fully on this goal, which corresponded with the latter's motto of a "learned and eloquent piety." Bucer contributed significantly to the rise and successful development of this academy. He drafted its statutes, worked hard at finding excellent teachers, and, most important, secured long-term funding for the project through a contract with the chapter of the collegiate church of St. Thomas. The relationship between Bucer and Sturm deepened in the course of the years. Jean Sturm turned from a mere supporter of Bucer into a very close friend, even while preserving his independence of judgment from the respected Reformer who was sixteen years his senior.

The same is true for another foreigner whom Bucer attracted to Strasbourg in 1538, but whom he could not convince to stay for more than three years: John Calvin.[24] The obviously gifted Frenchman, only twenty-nine years old and already renowned, lived first in Bucer's house and then with other refugees in a larger building in its immediate vicinity. The backyards of both houses abutted, giving the two the opportunity to get together frequently and become more closely acquainted with each other. At the time, Calvin was the pastor and organizer of the French refugee congregation that met at St. Nicholas. In addition, he taught at Sturm's academy. Finally, he accompanied the Strasbourg delegation to the religious colloquies in Hagenau, Worms, and Regensburg convoked by the emperor. (These will be the object of our thorough attention later on.) The Strasbourg preachers were impressed at the way in which Calvin built his congregation. He placed great importance on fostering the independence of individual members, on kindling and promoting faith in each of them, and on having them assume their individual responsibility for the congregation. Intensive Bible study and a strict church discipline were the means he used to reach these goals. Calvin also succeeded in winning back a remarkable number of Anabaptists to the Protestant fold. It is no coincidence that he entered his name in the membership list of the tailors' guild on July 29, 1539—a guild known for the many Anabaptists and their sympathizers in its midst. The woman whom Calvin married in Strasbourg, Idelette de Bure, was the widow of an Anabaptist he himself had converted.

Calvin and Bucer not only had a good rapport with one another, they also had much in common theologically. They both emphasized the gift of the Holy Spirit, called for a life characterized by love of one's fellow man, and insisted on church discipline. The young Calvin found in Bucer a trustworthy counselor and a friend who was almost like a father. In the following years, this relationship of mutual trust survived in spite of tensions and many crises. For Calvin certainly did not hesitate to criticize Bucer severely, for example, for his willingness to make generous concessions to the Catholics, or for the vagueness of his statements on the Lord's Supper. But Calvin also could find remarkable words of praise for his senior and mentor. For instance, in 1539 he applauded the Strasbourg reformer as biblical exegete: Bucer is a man, wrote Calvin, "who on account of his profound scholarship, his bounteous knowledge about a wide range of subjects, his keen mind, his wide reading, and many other different virtues, remains unsurpassed today by anyone, can be compared with only a few, and excels the vast majority."[25] The extent to which Bucer and the Strasbourg church influenced Calvin and thus the Reformation in Geneva cannot be determined with final certainty. It is worth noting that much of what we encounter in Geneva was developed and tried out first in the Alsatian imperial city: the liturgical order, the singing of psalms, the multiplicity of ecclesiastical offices, the weekly meeting of pastors, and the school of higher education. Geneva also succeeded at something that Bucer had attempted in Strasbourg untiringly but ultimately in vain: building a congregation equipped with a strict discipline that did not shrink back from ban and excommunication.

Piety and Fellowship

A congregation like the one described could only result from education and training. This meant encouraging individual Christians and instilling a sense of responsibility for the congregation in them. But it was just as important that the congregation as a whole develop into a closer-knit fellowship and learn to see itself as capable of acting on its own. From the mid-1530s onward Bucer unmistakably concentrated his efforts at reforming the church in these areas. This did not necessarily mean opposing the secular powers. Bucer was just as insistent now on the duties of the civic authorities toward the church as he had ever been before. But it was evident to him that action on the part of the magistrate was not enough. "Appreciation and a sense of concern for what the 'fellowship of saints' is supposed to be are disintegrating from day to day," wrote Bucer to Ambrosius Blarer on April 4, 1538. "Even the pastors appear to understand less and less what true pastoral care is."[26] Bucer was intent on doing something about this.

A new, revised version of his catechism appeared in November 1537.[27] This new catechism not only was significantly shorter, it was also more practice-oriented and included sections "for the very young and the simple-minded." The most interesting thing about it, however, is that it commits young people to accept church disciplinary measures: "I will gladly let myself be admonished and punished, I will also gladly admonish my fellow man, and I want to cherish church discipline and consolation highly and make assiduous use of them."[28] Bucer thus succeeded in making a slight dent in the indestructible hull of governmental opposition to his plans. Even if the authorities would continue to obstruct any attempts at carrying through a sweeping church discipline in the city, here at least was a means of pursuing this same discipline with methods voluntary and pedagogical.

A demand that Bucer made in a memorandum from the early summer 1538—that every Christian should be willing and able to confess his or her faith personally—pointed in the same direction.[29] This was also the central focus, but on a much larger scale, of his major work *On True Pastoral Care* (*Von der wahren Seelsorge*), published at about the same time.[30] The church, wrote Bucer, ensues when individual people who believe in Christ and trust him alone grow together, forming a fellowship. Not only leadership and teaching are necessary for the growth of such a fellowship but many other offices as well, especially pastoral care and ministering to the needy. These ecclesiastical offices were to be filled by elders, that is, people who had proven themselves to be convinced Christians, regardless of social standing.

Bucer thus did not formulate a sophisticated doctrine of ecclesiastical offices as Calvin did later. He did not define the specific tasks of the different offices and meticulously differentiate between them. Bucer's aim, instead, was twofold. To begin with, he affirmed that the Holy Spirit was at work in a fellowship of believing Christians—something he stressed over and over again. This implied that members of such a fellowship would be vigorously active, assuming responsibility for their fellow human beings and for the entire church. Aside from this effort to foment the readiness of Christian fellowships to act on their own initiative, Bucer pursued a second goal: to afford the church a measure of codetermination through the ecclesiastical office of elders, who were to be chosen from among church members and then solemnly installed in this function. These elders were to guard over church interests when dealing with the civil authorities, and also to help church discipline be truly enforced in the entire Christian fellowship. "From this follows, first of all, that Christians must serve the Lord above all things and with the greatest diligence. For they are members and tools of Christ, and Christ must live in all of them, and not just they for themselves. Everyone is to do this according to his own calling and capacity, by the measure in which Christ lives in him. Christians must serve the Lord above all things and with the greatest diligence, so that all His lost sheep are sought faithfully, led to Him, and brought back into the fellowship of His church."[31] Bucer took pains to refute in great detail theological, political, and ethical objections to his plans. Essential to his understanding of the church as a fellowship of believing Christians created by the Holy Spirit was not only that it was to be an active and diverse fellowship willing to take its organization into its own hands. Even more important was its earnest determination to practice church discipline. Hesitating or being cautious in this matter was for Bucer tantamount to indecision regarding the central question of faith and trust in Christ. "We must make up our minds whether we are really willing to be Christians or not."[32]

It goes without saying that the city council did not take kindly to Bucer's treatise. Hardly a work of the Strasbourg reformer, who by this time had attained great fame far and wide, was ignored more deliberately than this one. His book struck the council at a sore spot, for its own interests lay in preventing the rise of a church that was independent from the state and had its own ecclesiastical jurisdiction. Bucer went through the same experience again two years later, when the council obstructed his efforts to turn the ecclesiastical court of pre-Reformation days into an autonomous church disciplinary court.

Bucer pursued goals that he perceived as theologically fundamental with a tenacity and versatility that are fascinating. Among these were the renewal of Christian life and church discipline as the outgrowth of a truly Christian fellowship. Alas, these evidently could not be realized in Strasbourg. Therefore, his hopes and expectations were all the greater when chances of carrying them out elsewhere seemed to loom on the horizon. It was with this anticipation that he traveled to Hesse at the end of 1538, responding to Landgrave Philip's invitation.

Hesse

The Landgraviate

The Landgraviate of Hesse[33] was a territory without natural geographical boundaries, extending from the rivers Werra and Weser in the northeast to the Odenwald Mountains and the Rhine River in the southwest. It was not only completely surrounded by numerous other dominions; these also cut deep into the Landgraviate, severing its territorial integrity at many places. It bordered on the Electorate of Mainz to the south and on the Electorates of Trier and Cologne to the west. To the north it abutted on the bishopric of Paderborn and the Duchy of Brunswick. Toward the east it faced the Duchy of Saxony. In other words, the Landgraviate of Hesse, at the heart of the Holy Roman Empire, accurately reflected the empire's own territorial compartmentalization and political disunity inasmuch as the Landgrave participated in the countless local and regional conflicts in the attempt to increase his influence and might.

When Philip of Hesse came to power in 1518—he was not quite fourteen at the time, making it necessary for Emperor Maximilian I to declare him prematurely to be "of age"—the Landgraviate was far from being a political unity. Philip found himself at the head of a cluster of extremely diverse territories, many of which had not come under the domination of Hesse until one or two decades before. At bottom, the Landgraviate consisted of four discontinuous regions, separated from each other by other territories and themselves riddled with a smattering of enclaves. To begin with, there were the Lower and the Upper Principalities of Hesse. The former included Kassel as well as the Werra, Fulda, and Eder river regions; the latter comprised Marburg and the areas surrounding the rivers Lahn and Ohm. Both principalities were not reunited until 1500. Only half a century earlier Hesse had achieved a certain degree of cohesion through the acquisition of the counties of Ziegenhain (in the region of the Schwalm River) and of Nidda (in the Vogelsberg region), which closed the gap between Lower and Upper Hesse. The rich county of Katzenelnbogen became a part of Hesse in 1479. It consisted of the lower county of St. Goar on the Rhine and the upper county, to the east of Oppenheim, with Darmstadt at its center. There was no land corridor connecting these two parts of the county with one another or with the rest of Hesse.

This constellation of facts allows only one conclusion: at the time of the rise of the early modern state, any ruler who found himself at the head of such a territorial hodgepodge and cherished even the slightest political ambitions faced the urgent task of consolidating and making uniform his territory from a political and administrative viewpoint, and, not least, in terms of the beliefs and the attitudes of its inhabitants. Philip of Hesse pursued such a policy with dogged determination.

Circumstances were particularly favorable to his endeavor. Hesse had succeeded in prevailing against its external enemies, especially against the Electorate of Mainz. Internally, resistance by the nobility was declining. A well-trained and efficient civil administration consisting of councillors and secretaries supported Philip unconditionally—since they depended upon him entirely. Finally, Philip was financially strong and autonomous enough to achieve his goals against the will of the nobility and the representatives of the cities. Significant sources of revenue were at his disposal: the customhouse on the Rhine at St. Goar collected duties for him and, most important, he profited immensely from the "guilder wine tariff" (*Guldenweinzoll*), which Emperor Maximilian I conceded to him in 1505. It stipulated the payment of one golden guilder for every *Fuder* (cartload, equivalent to some 250 gallons) of wine that went through Hesse. This included Alsatian wine transported on the international trade route heading east through Frankfurt am Main.

Still another factor worked to Philip's advantage: the Reformation movement. Of course it was preceded by authentic efforts at reform, and there can be no doubt as to the sincerity of Philip's own personal embracing of Luther's teaching and the cause of the Reformation around 1524. But it is just as evident that Philip did not hesitate to translate his religious convictions into pragmatic political measures. For him, the official endorsement of the Reformation clearly would help strengthen the political and spiritual cohesion of the Landgraviate.

The first steps taken in this direction, however, were vacillating and irresolute. An assembly of theologians as well as representatives of the nobility and the cities met in Homberg an der Efze in October 1526. It was not a church synod in the pure sense of the term, but neither could it be simply called a provincial diet.[34] In any case, it became clear that the Landgrave was eager to introduce the Reformation in his territory. The first Reformation blueprint, however, failed immediately, not least of all because Luther himself vetoed it. It was the work of the French evangelical refugee François Lambert d'Avignon, who had wanted to create a church made up of congregations whose members were wholehearted Christians and were willing to submit to a strict church discipline. From 1527 on, Philip followed a second model that was much more realistic and thus much more successful. It was primarily Adam Krafft who put it into practice, justifying his later fame as the "Reformer of Hesse." Krafft, whom Philip appointed as his court chaplain in 1525, followed the Reformation model of Electoral Saxony. Therefore, beginning in 1527 monastic property in Hesse was inventoried and placed under the control of the Landgrave. The latter also appointed pastors, ordered the inspection of congregations, and organized poor relief. The Mass was abolished and church ceremonies were renewed—with Wittenberg once again serving as model. Finally, it was also in the year 1527 that Philip founded his own academy of higher studies in Marburg, the city in which he had his residence. It was the first Protestant university.

Organizing the Church

By the early 1530s, the territorial church of Hesse had become well organized from an administrative point of view—and the Landgrave was firmly in control of it. The church was divided into six superintendencies: Marburg, Kassel, Rotenburg, Alsfeld, Darmstadt, and St. Goar. Synods were in charge of discussing and deciding all issues concerning the church as a whole, though their decisions had to be approved by the Landgrave. A state law regulated all matters concerning the pastorate. All pastors of Hesse were on the official payroll of the Landgraviate, receiving uniform salaries. These circumstance and the types of tasks that the Landgrave assigned the church quickly led the pastors to see themselves—and to be seen by others—as a part of the civil administration of Hesse. They cooperated closely with those state employees who were in charge of poor relief or schools, and their task could be defined as one of Christian and moral education of the populace.

There was no lack of rules for the enforcement of church discipline, some of which even provided for expulsion of noncomplying members from the congregation. This matter, however, was seen as pertaining exclusively to the church; the state refused to endorse church measures or to support them in any way. In consequence, church discipline in Hesse existed only on paper. Only if there had been autonomous congregations with a vibrant spiritual life of their own would such a church discipline have been able to function without state support. The territorial church of Hesse may have been well organized and efficiently integrated into governmental structures, but it did not have such congregations, nor were the circumstances described above conducive to their development.

The situation in other princely territories that had joined the Reformation was not much different. In all these territories, as in Hesse, Anabaptists constituted an attractive alternative because of the emphasis they placed on personal conversion, the strict discipline they practiced in their congregations, and their conspicuous disapproval of, indeed outright disdain for, the state church, which they saw as immoral and spiritually bankrupt. Anabaptism was particularly attractive in Hesse because Landgrave Philip remained fundamentally opposed to the death penalty for heretics. On the other hand, the authorities of Hesse were deeply concerned about the challenge the Anabaptists represented by separating themselves religiously and socially from the established order, especially since the territory of the Landgraviate was splintered and lacking political cohesion to begin with. If Anabaptism was a marginal problem elsewhere, here it challenged the very foundations of the state. On September 1, 1536, the chancellor of Hesse, Johannes Feige, informed Philip in no uncertain terms that it was high time the Landgrave himself attend to this grave problem "and postpone all other issues, for difficult decisions must be taken in this matter—decisions that either mean taking action that is benign or action that causes suffering. Otherwise great evil threatens all of us."[35]

This was no exaggeration. To be sure, Hesse had been successful in curtailing the growth of Anabaptist congregations after 1533. But from 1537 on, all efforts in this direction were useless.[36] Officials and pastors in the border regions between Hesse and Thuringia, that is to say, in the ecclesiastical territories of Fulda and Hersfeld, as well as in Upper Hesse, observed that particularly the common people displayed growing sympathy for the Anabaptists and were eager to join their movement. Furthermore, all governmental organs were forced to admit their helplessness. It was in the midst of this situation that Philip asked the Strasbourg city council to send Bucer. There were two qualifications that made him just the right person for this task: first, his untiring and unwavering insistence—not to be swayed by opposition or obstruction of any kind—on church discipline; second, his unmistakably clear protest against any kind of division or separation from the church. And Bucer brought both points home in a long discussion with several Anabaptist leaders from October 30 to November 1, 1538, in Marburg. The result was a huge success for the Strasbourg reformer.

Bucer proceeded in Marburg in exactly the same way as he had done in Strasbourg years ago during the first synod: he carried out disputations in public; he vigorously emphasized that not a pious life but the merits of Christ and love constitute the foundation of the church; but he stressed just as vehemently that the church could not exist without discipline and the ban. He used careful logic in his arguments and was demanding on his listeners, but he also was inviting while exhorting them. Most important of all, he tried eloquently to win the Anabaptists back to the Protestant fold.

Bucer did, in fact, set them thinking. He achieved a major breakthrough on November 2 in the course of a prolonged conversation with Peter Tesch, an Anabaptist leader known and respected in Hesse and beyond. Tesch declared himself and his supporters willing to return to the mainstream church if it would truly exercise discipline—and if the Anabaptists were given plenty of time to readjust to its pastors and congregations. Bucer guaranteed the fulfillment of both requests, having been given full powers by Philip.

On November 25, 1538, a synod that met in Ziegenhain, some six miles east of Treysa, resolved to reorganize church discipline. At the same time, Tesch and other former Anabaptists traveled through Hesse trying to convert their earlier partisans—with considerable success. All this was about more than just improving morals and enforcing church discipline. In the Ziegenhain disciplinary ordinance,[37] Bucer once again formulated his traditional ideal of a self-reliant congregation pulsating with life. Church discipline was an essential component of such a congregation. Just as essential were church members who assumed responsibility for the congregation, in other words, elders. Finally, it was important that church members and especially the youth be cared for from an educational, pedagogical standpoint, which is why Bucer also introduced confirmation here. He knew all too well that education and discipline only had a future in active congregations whose members were committed Christians. But did not a state church that was run like an organ of government and administered by civil servants stand precisely in the way of such a development?

The Ziegenhain disciplinary ordinance was published in January 1539, along with a new church ordinance and an excerpt from Bucer's catechism of 1537. Bucer had already left Hesse in December 1538. While his vision of the church certainly left an imprint, his ordinances did not meet with any success. Bucer admonished Philip again and again to finally put the Ziegenhain resolutions into practice. Philip gave the corresponding orders—and everything stayed the way it was. Living congregations were not going to result from administrative decrees and indifferent bureaucrats—in a letter to Philip in 1540, Bucer described the majority of the Landgrave's civil servants as "crude people of the flesh" and his pastors as "very negligent."[38]

The Jews

As territorial states in Germany developed and took on more definite contours, and as the Reformation movement became institutionalized through doctrinal formulations and church ordinances, awareness of groups that did not conform with the strived-for ideal grew. This was particularly the case for the Jews of the Holy Roman Empire.[39] Many princes began drafting ordinances regulating the affairs of Jews in their respective territories (*Judenordnungen*). They did this in order to standardize the different regulations already in existence and to bring them all under princely control. Furthermore, the princes sought to glean benefits from the protection of Jews by assigning them functions in the administration of the state's finances. Third, they pursued the goal of bolstering their own subjects against Jewish economic competition. The primary aim of the Protestant pastors and theologians, for their part, was to imbue the entire population with Christian doctrine and to educate it along these lines. Therefore, while some saw the Jews as the object of Christian mission, other sought at the same time to single them out on account of their persistent nonconformity. The respective goals of church and state could thus be brought into at least partial agreement with one another. This was particularly the case for a territorial lord who saw himself as responsible for not only the physical well-being but also the salvation of his subjects, and who was influenced by a theology that emphasized the religious duties of civil authority and aimed at establishing a truly Christian society. This was precisely the background of the 1539 ordinance for the Jews of Hesse.

The Landgrave's warrant protecting the Jews of his territory (*Schutzbrief*) expired in 1538. Philip thus commissioned Bucer with drafting a memorandum specifying under which conditions Jews should be allowed to remain in Hesse. He was given seven articles to start from, five of which provided extremely favorable economic incentives for them to remain in Hesse, while the remaining were more conventional in their goals, prohibiting Jews from discussing their faith with Christians and forcing them to attend sermons aimed at their conversion. Bucer vigorously rejected all these articles except for the last two. After formulating a statement of his own, he first sought the approval of the leading theologians of Hesse and after this sent his draft to the Landgrave in December 1538.

Bucer's recommendation of policy toward Jews (*Judenratschlag*) accurately reflects the direction his theology had taken from the early 1530s on. Accordingly, we find in it a summary of his thoughts—already developed in the *Dialogues* (*Dialogi*)—concerning the right and the duty of civil authority to set up a Christian social order in obedience to God's law. This had the following consequences for Jews[40] in Hesse: they were allowed to hold their own worship services, but they were not to seek converts to their faith and especially were to refrain from "blaspheming Christ." The government had the duty to see to it that the gospel was preached to all subjects and was obliged to punish anybody who showed disdain for it. Whereas the *Dialogi* of 1535 had spoken of committing manifest unbelievers to do useful work, and a further memorandum of the same period suggested punishing obstinate Anabaptists with forced labor, Bucer now translated this general idea into the specific recommendation that Jews be prohibited from performing any kind of trade and that the civil authorities should engage them "in the humblest, most arduous and most trying tasks"—such as burning coal, sweeping chimneys and sewers, or getting rid of animal carcasses.[41] Bucer concludes the *Judenratschlag* with the appraisal that such harsh punishments would serve as a deterrent and as a corrective measure. New in this memorandum was Bucer's wholesale adoption of anti-Jewish stereotypes. Never before had the Strasbourg reformer uttered such biased and sweepingly negative judgments over Jews. He possibly was influenced in these statements by the attitudes of some of the leading theologians of Hesse, who at first advocated expelling all Jews from the Landgraviate. Bucer's vilifying declarations, as unacceptable as they are, are mild, however, when compared with Luther's later invectives seething with hatred against Jews.

Bucer was firmly convinced that the issue at stake was allowing God's strict but salutary law to rule everyday life—God's law that promoted what was good (that is, God's revelation) and stifled everything opposed to it (in other words, evil). That is why he opposed expelling the Jews from Hesse. This would have implied for him that once again the civil authorities were not willing to take God's law and God's order seriously. But for the same reason, he did not allow himself to be impressed by the critical objections that Landgrave Philip, Jewish representative Josel von Rosheim, and others made against his memorandum. On December 27, 1538, he wrote to Philip of Hesse: "Therefore, wherever a truly godfearing government exists, the members of the family of faith should always be given preference, and the despisers of faith treated disadvantageously. And civil authority, who, after all, must not carry through its own, but rather God's judgments, should consistently treat unbelief in such a way that it arouses contempt."[42] This was hardly a humane guideline, and it certainly was not an enlightened opinion. But it does exemplify the fact that, for Bucer, state policy toward Jews was only one aspect of his broader vision of pushing ahead vigorously with the establishment of God's rule—a rule already pre-arranged in creation.

The major *Judenordnung*, or legal ordinance regulating the affairs of Jews in Hesse, that eventually appeared in the summer of 1539 did not conform with Bucer's goals. This does not mean that Bucer's ideas did not influence it in any way. The text did, in fact, represent a compromise. The ordinance did not unequivocally legalize the presence of Jews in Hesse but made it dependent upon the goodwill of the Landgrave. Philip did allow the Jews to engage in trade and commerce (against Bucer's advice); he also permitted them to work as moneylenders in restricted circumstances and under strict supervision. Philip translated some of Bucer's religious demands into legal precepts: the abjuration of all "blasphemy" against Christ or against the Christian faith; the prohibition of the Talmud; a ban on the construction of any new synagogues; the prohibition of any religious dialogue between Jews and Christians; the obligation to attend sermons aimed at missionizing them; the death penalty for Jews and Christians living together. A third aspect is important: Bucer had demanded that the fee Jews paid in exchange for their protection be proportional to their respective wealth, in order that they not be exploited mercilessly. Philip's ordinance turned this precept into a tool for regulating the immigration of Jews or for arranging for their expulsion.[43]

The Jews of Hesse were extremely unsettled by this *Judenordnung*, for it was entirely open at the outset which direction would carry the day: a policy of limited pragmatism or one strictly subordinate to the whims of the Protestant church. Quite a few Jews decided to leave Hesse at this point. This cannot be simplistically attributed to Bucer's theological and ecclesiastical activity in the Landgraviate. On the other hand, neither is it possible glibly to dissociate Bucer's thoughts and convictions from this ruinous development. Bucer must bear his share of blame for Christendom's calamitous sins against the Jewish people.

Philip's Bigamy

From October 1538 on, Philip and Bucer began cooperating more and more closely. They not only held similar ecclesiological views but also felt a strong personal affinity. Of course, this did not change the fact that

Philip remained a territorial prince, a "lord," and Bucer was consequently his "servant." But Bucer did not allow himself to be inhibited by this distinction. After all, he served a God who was Lord over the entire universe. The fact that Bucer was on friendly terms with Philip but remained completely independent in his theological thinking may have induced the Landgrave to turn first to the Strasbourg theologian when seeking a way out of his marital quandary.[44]

Gereon Sailer of Augsburg, an intimate associate of Philip and a friend of Bucer, arrived in Strasbourg on the evening of November 4, 1539, and informed Bucer about Philip's intention to incur a bigamous marriage. Bucer was appalled. Such an action would cast doubt upon any attempts to enforce church discipline, renew the life of Christians, and create a new society. It would ruin the reputation of Protestantism and thus hinder its spread in Germany and Europe—not to mention bigamy being a capital offense. In spite of all of this, Sailer informed Philip that he would probably be able to count on Bucer's help. This was a complicated matter, with pastoral, political, and theological implications. It should be clear to modern readers, of course, that at the time it was not considered unusual for a person in power to have a mistress. And did not the Old Testament appear to sanction polygamy through countless examples? Could it therefore be prohibited in an absolute way? Was it not ultimately more upright to marry a mistress in addition to one's first wife than to have countless extramarital affairs? Matters were made more complicated by the fact that Philip of Hesse constituted the mainstay and pillar of the Schmalkaldic League. For Bucer, however, this was not the dominant factor to be considered. Never—not at this time or later—did he let himself be guided primarily by political considerations. At the same time, however, he never lost sight of them completely.

In December 1539, Bucer drafted a detailed memorandum listing the "arguments in favor and against" (*Argumenta Buceri pro et contra*)[45] a bigamous marriage. The only truly Christian marriage, wrote Bucer, is a monogamous one. Only in exceptional situations, that is to say, in order to prevent fornication (1 Cor. 7:2), can a second marriage be allowed. The latter, however, must be kept secret, in other words, disguised as a concubinage in front of the public; this second "marriage" must also retain the legal status of a concubinage. Those involved in it, however, can be assured that in God's eyes they are not living in adultery and sexual immorality. This is what Bucer had also explained to Philip privately in November. Philip, however, apparently heard only what he wanted to hear: that Bucer considered bigamy a possible choice for the Landgrave and that he was going to try to convince Luther and Melanchthon of its legitimacy. Philip did not say a word to Bucer about the promises he, the Landgrave, had made to the mother of his mistress Margarethe von der Sale. Philip had, in fact, promised her that the intended marriage would be a legal one in the full sense of the term, and that the Reformers would publicly support its legitimacy.

At the beginning of December, Luther and Melanchthon drafted statements of their own with conclusions similar to Bucer's. Even the elector of Saxony declared himself to be favorably disposed toward the plan. The wedding took place on March 5, 1540, in the castle chapel in Rotenburg on the Fulda River. Melanchthon and Bucer, who happened to be in the region because of a forthcoming assembly at Schmalkalden and were not told a thing beforehand by Philip, suddenly found themselves in the awkward situation of being unwitting wedding guests. Unsurprisingly, the matter did not stay secret for long. By June it was known even outside Germany, dismaying the Protestant camp and filling Catholics with triumphant indignation ("so this is what the evangelicals are really up to!"). Of course, it would be cynical to deny that not few of those who raised their voices in accusation lived in concubinage themselves or held mistresses. This does not change the fact, however, that the Reformers, and Bucer in particular, seriously compromised themselves. Even if we discard any moral narrow-mindedness when assessing the counsel they gave to Philip, their sophistic concession of bigamy for alleged pastoral reasons was, from an ethical standpoint, dubious at best.

Philip was definitely not into fine moral distinctions. If the Bible apparently allowed bigamy, and if bigamy did not contradict the will of God in Philip's particular situation (as the leading Protestant theologians had told him), why could he not speak openly and freely about it? The Landgrave was not prepared to conceal his action, and the von der Sale family was understandably even less willing to hush up the marriage. In this way, the disastrous affair took its course.

Luther and Bucer made it clear to Philip that they had permitted the bigamous marriage only on the condition that it be kept secret. Luther now called on the Landgrave to deny everything, while Bucer, for his part, gave him the advice to be ambiguous and vague! Philip felt cheated. And he especially felt double-crossed when none of his earlier allies stood by him after the matter became public—not even the Saxon elector or Duke Ulrich of Württemberg. Philip was now forced to come to an agreement with the emperor. This whole affair had a very unpleasant personal sequel for Bucer. A long-winded, anonymous "Dialogue" (*Dialogus Neo-*

buli) defending Philip's bigamy appeared in the summer 1541. The author turned out to be pastor Johannes Lening of the town of Melsungen, in northern Hesse. But people everywhere—including in Strasbourg—were convinced it was Bucer who had really drafted the unsophisticated work. Foul rumors and scornful rhymes ridiculing Strasbourg's reformer started circulating. The civic secretary of Strasbourg, Michael Han, and the vast number of his supporters taunted Bucer publicly with this matter through the spring of 1542. In the meantime—on June 13, 1541—Philip reached a secret settlement with Emperor Charles V. He thus ushered in the demise of the Schmalkaldic League and of German Protestantism.

Chapter Six

The Reformation of the Empire

Imperial Policy

"Where are the most Holy Father, the Pope, and the very Christian King of France to be found? In spite of their great titles and names they are incapable of rescuing a thing. Poor and simple Christians are now being murdered wretchedly: men, women, and children, young and old. Whoever is able, runs away, abandoning his country and leaving behind his entire possessions. For no one is there deliverance . . . Where are the glorious fighters of heretics now? . . . As long as their opponents are poor people and innocent books, which cannot talk back and do no harm to anyone, then they are extraordinarily capable of waging war and of fighting, indeed they are lions. But when it comes to fighting the Turks, they are all just rabbits!"[1] With these words Johannes Turmair, or Aventinus, a humanist true to nation and emperor and a former Bavarian court historian who died as a Protestant in Regensburg in 1534, captured the despondent mood widespread in the Holy Roman Empire in the 1530s. Of course, most Germans hardly expected any real help from the pope or from the French king in combating the Ottomans. German observers were more inclined to place them in the enemy camp. And did they not have every reason to expect even less from militant opponents of the Reformation? The situation was serious: the enemy of Christendom was infringing upon the very borders of the Holy Roman Empire. Many people in Germany, irrespective of their theological leaning and confessional allegiance, began asking whether the time had not arrived to put internal religious conflicts aside, or at least defer them in order to join forces in facing the Turkish danger behind a united front.

The vast majority of Protestants, in fact, were on the emperor's side in this respect. This attitude happened to coincide felicitously with the political goals of Charles V, but this coincidence does not imply perfect agreement between the parties.[2] Merely in terms of geography, the emperor had a much broader perspective than did the German Protestants. For instance, he realized quite accurately that the Ottomans were not only a threat to Vienna and the Habsburg patrimonial territories but had also become the dominant naval power in the Mediterranean. People in Germany barely took notice of the battles and struggles taking place down there. The developments they followed with great fear, indeed almost passionately, were those taking place in the southeastern corner of the empire. In 1529 the Turks stood at the gates of Vienna. Even though this encroachment turned out to be a mere action of military reconnaissance and not an actual attempt at conquest by "the infidels," the event struck horror in the hearts of Europeans. In 1532 the Ottomans came as far as Styria, and in 1541 they incorporated central Hungary into their empire. Charles's brother Ferdinand succeeded in negotiating an eighteen-month-long cease-fire with the Turks on November 10, 1545, but not before having paid them 10,000 ducats in tribute.

The Ottomans' connections to France made them especially dangerous for the emperor. In fact, Francis I and the Turkish sultan formed a veritable alliance in 1536, thus thwarting Charles's plans to launch a crusade. This action by the French sundered the unity of European Christendom much more dramatically than did the conflict between Protestants and Catholics. The pope (Paul III since 1534) tried to stay above the fray between the French king and the German emperor, for an emperor with too much power threatened the pope's ecclesiastical interests as well as his political goals in Italy. But Charles's military campaign against the French, and particularly his war against the Turks in the Mediterranean, failed miserably. Charles V and Francis I agreed to a ten-year cease-fire in the Treaty of Nice in June 1538. But as early as 1542, a French army invaded the Low Countries. At the same time, Ottoman and French naval fleets carried out joint maneuvers in the Mediterranean.

The emperor found himself in sore need of allies in order to prevail against this alliance. This situation meant in the first place trying to call forth from his isolation the English king, Henry VIII, who had declared himself the head of the church in his country in 1534, and attempting to make him an ally of the German empire. Charles also needed the pope's support, especially in order to convoke a council that would finally begin tackling the task of reforming the church—something all groups regarded as urgently necessary. A council was also Charles's only hope of reconciling his empire's "protesting" estates—the supporters of the Reformation—with the Catholic Church and consequently obtaining their support for his political goals. This endeavor involved a number of complicating factors: Charles had to make sure not to wrong the German Catholics; they had formed an alliance of their own in Nuremberg in June 1538 against the powerful Protestant Schmalkaldic League. At the same time, he had to avoid giving his Protestant subjects the impression that he was actively assisting the Catholics. Finally, he had to woo the Protestants away from their French allies, winning them over as fellow warriors in the struggle against the Turks.

The implications were twofold. Charles V was forced, on the one hand, to make an increasing number of concessions to the Schmalkaldic League during the 1530s in order to obtain the financial and military help necessary for meeting his goals. On the other hand, he expressly and consistently restricted the concessions he made to the Protestants, declaring them valid only for the period leading up to a council, but not thereafter. By doing so, he was making himself and his politics dependent on someone—the pope—over whom he ultimately had no influence, in spite of all his power.

On June 2, 1536, Pope Paul III summoned a council that was to begin its sessions in Mantua on March 23, 1537. He did this not out of spiritual concern but rather because he realized that the church finally had to confront the nagging problem of religious schism in order to regain its earlier political influence. It is thus not surprising that sudden changes in political developments induced the pope to change his mind about this church assembly just as suddenly: the council was postponed five times in the course of four years. These delays were hardly due to resistance on the part of the Protestant estates, but rather were because of the French king's rejection of the pope's plan. Francis I definitely did not see the need for a council. He found himself quite capable of managing heretics in his country on his own. And he understandably had little interest in helping Charles V resolve the confessional divide within Germany that was presenting the emperor with so many thorny problems. In Germany, but not only there, the fickleness of papal policy brought forth reactions ranging all the way from deep disappointment to unabashed satisfaction. In any case, Paul III eventually ruined his reputation in all camps because of his repeated postponements of the council. When he once again convoked a council in 1541, the initial reaction was absolute indifference. Because of this reaction, the council changed its goals fundamentally: it aimed no longer at bringing the Protestants back to the traditional fold but rather at strengthening and consolidating the Roman Catholic Church.

In Germany, people began asking themselves: If a truly universal council was not feasible and the pope was not willing to carry through with the reform of the church, did not the obvious next step consist of proceeding *without* the pope and convoking a national German council in which the imperial estates, the electors and princes as well as the representatives of the clergy, the nobility, and the cities, could discuss confessional issues among themselves and pass the corresponding resolutions? It is not surprising that this idea became increasingly popular in the late 1530s. And with Charles V also supporting it, it soon became a political factor to be reckoned with.

To understand this development, one must remember that countless princes and their advisers were tremendously alarmed by the political situation in Germany: at the same time that Ottoman armies were standing at its borders, the empire found itself divided into two opposing confessional camps, each with a military alliance of its own, each armed and ready to engage in a fratricidal war at any moment. What many found particularly unbearable—if not entirely absurd—about this situation was that it could not be attributed entirely to fundamental theological and ecclesiastical differences between supporters of the Reformation and their opponents. In fact, many of those involved were not even aware that Western Christendom was about to split into two confessions. Contacts and connections between both camps were intense, not least because the reigning families and dynasties in Germany were often interrelated. Therefore, was it not reasonable to assume that if both sides would make a sincere effort and display goodwill, they would be able to emphasize what they had in common and what united them, instead of what was dividing them?

This attitude was accompanied and supported by a religious and theological trend that attached central importance to the Bible and the work of the Holy Spirit and perceived the inward renewal of man and resulting exemplary ethical conduct as fundamental to Christian existence, as well as for the renewal of society and the church. Unquestionably, this position was deeply influenced by humanism, and particularly by Erasmus of Rotterdam. His book on the *Restoration of Church Unity* (*De sarcienda ecclesiae concordia*, 1533) was quoted and appealed to repeatedly during these years. However, this widespread devotion to a biblical humanism in combination with varying degrees of spiritualist emphasis can hardly be reduced to the influence of a single man. A much broader intellectual and religious movement, which in Italy and elsewhere became known under the concept of *evangelismo* (only inadequately to be rendered as "evangelism"), contributed to the lasting influence of Erasmus's brand of humanism beyond the death of the Dutch humanist.

As mentioned previously, political leaders often tried to make this theological and intellectual trend work to their advantage. Rulers of territories such as the Duchy of Jülich-Cleves, the Electorate of Brandenburg, and the Duchy of Saxony tried to carry out church reforms that steered a middle course between the Reformation and the papacy. But even within these two opposing camps, quite a few people—mostly political leaders but also theologians—favored the achievement of a balance, indeed, the pursuit of a definitive settlement between both sides. And the only reason this minority movement influenced politics on a larger scale lay in Charles V's participation. He needed church unity, for he needed a united empire to assist him militarily and financially in fighting the French and the Ottomans. Since he could expect no help from the pope, Charles decided to venture official theological negotiations between Catholics and Protestants. Whether he realized the depth of the theological chasm separating both sides is a moot issue. It is more probable that he, like many of his contemporaries, was convinced of the necessity of comprehensive ecclesiastical and particularly moral reforms; everything else, such as theological differences, was simply perceived by such observers as an agglomeration of exaggerations and misunderstandings.

This was the background for the Truce of Frankfurt (*Frankfurter Anstand*), sealed on April 19, 1539, which prolonged the peace that the warring confessional factions had already agreed to in Nuremberg back in 1532. The Frankfurt settlement was reached after almost two months of tough negotiations, and it included the following compromise. The ceasefire would initially last six months. In the course of this period, two meetings would take place: one in Worms in May, to discuss support for the emperor's military campaign against the Turks, and one in Nuremberg in August of the same year, to explore the possibility of overcoming theological, particularly ecclesiological, differences. This religious colloquy was to be "free," that is, not subordinate to papal authority. In addition, all legal proceedings against Protestants in the imperial Chamber Court (*Reichskammergericht*) were to be put on hold during these six months. This court, with headquarters in Speyer since 1527, was the court of appeal and the highest judiciary authority for all princes, nobles, and cities that were subject to the emperor alone—and it certainly had created many problems for the Protestants in the past, most recently by imposing the imperial ban

(*Reichsacht*) on the northern German city of Minden. The Truce of Frankfurt had just one catch for Protestants: only present supporters of the Reformation could claim the benefits of the cease-fire. Expressly excluded from it were any parties who might join the Protestant movement later. Bucer now became extraordinarily active—at the highest political level—within the framework described above.

Religious Colloquies

Leipzig

At the end of 1538 and the beginning of 1539, Bucer attended negotiations in Leipzig, the most important city of the Duchy of Saxony.[3] Georg Witzel wrote later that the Strasbourg reformer came disguised as a merchant.[4] Bucer attended on his own initiative, but several factors almost forced him to attend this meeting. For quite some time the various political leaders and estates of Albertine Saxony had been discussing the religious course that the Duchy should steer after the death of strictly Catholic Duke Georg, who died without heirs. Everybody, including high-ranking church leaders, was convinced that church reforms were necessary and that practical measures needed to be taken. Yet it was not only religious issues that had to be solved but concrete economic and political ones as well. Merchants and craftsmen were abandoning the Duchy and moving just a few miles to neighboring Ernestine Saxony in order to be able to express their Lutheran faith openly and freely. Powerful groups in Albertine Saxony, however, remained interested in safeguarding the independence of the Duchy and therefore opposed church reforms modeled in any way after those of the neighboring, more powerful Electorate of Saxony.

Thus a plethora of motives and interests compelled the Saxon chancellor Georg von Carlowitz to invite political leaders from Ernestine Saxony and Hesse to secret discussions, of which the Duke knew nothing. Landgrave Philip supported Carlowitz's endeavor—the prince of Hesse could only profit from these developments in the Duchy. Philip therefore sent his own chancellor, Johannes Feige, along with Bucer to Leipzig. Electoral Saxony sent Melanchthon and Chancellor Gregor Brück. The Duchy of Saxony was represented by Carlowitz and the councillor Ludwig Fachs, as well as the former Lutheran Georg Witzel, who had converted to Catholicism.

To restore church unity, to do away with all abuses by following the example of the church fathers of the first centuries, to renew Christian life—these were top priorities on Georg Witzel's agenda. All these goals played an important role in Bucer's thought as well. For the Strasbourg reformer, however, they hinged on the central conviction that any reformation worth its name had to be founded on the Bible and on the doctrine of the justification of sinners through faith in Jesus Christ alone. This unshakable point of departure ensured Bucer the freedom to make extensive concessions to his theological opponents. Ultimately, Bucer was certain that Christ himself would find a way of prevailing, if one only allowed him enough freedom of action. God's truth would carry the day without fail if only God's followers would stand up for it resolutely enough and in the right way. These are the arguments Bucer used when urging his fellow Protestants to join him in negotiating with the Catholics. For we are also willing and able to defeat our opponents, he declared, "with the sword of the councils, statutes and ordinances of the Early Church."[5]

A heated theological discussion between Bucer and Witzel thus took place in the week from January 2 to 7, 1539, in Leipzig. This half-private, half-public debate began in the so-called Paulinum (where the *Universitätshochhaus*—the modern university high-rise building erected in the time of the German Democratic Republic—now stands) and was continued in Ludwig Fachs's private home. Since Bucer and Witzel were willing to defer controversial doctrinal points until a later time, Melanchthon and Brück withdrew from the negotiations; in their opinion, doctrinal unity was a prerequisite for structuring the church anew. In the course of 1539 and in the years beyond, Bucer would set forth and develop in great detail an argument that he had essentially presented in Leipzig already on this occasion: If one could succeed in getting the leading statesmen of the Holy Roman Empire, indeed, maybe even the majority of the imperial estates, to agree to a comprehensive church reform based on the norm of the early church, would not that be a decisive success? Would not even the Wittenberg reformers have to fall in line with the rest of the empire and submit to such a Germany-wide legal church ordinance? This effort was Bucer's goal from now on. It was an audacious endeavor, for it required Bucer to be active at the highest political level.

At the end of the Leipzig colloquy, both sides agreed on fifteen articles that Bucer himself probably drafted.[6] They dealt with justification, penance and confession, baptism, the Mass, confirmation, the papacy, various ceremonies, and finally the invocation of saints, the commemoration of the dead, as well as the role of government in the church—all themes relevant to the practical life of the church. Differences in doctrine were largely ignored. Therefore every reason exists to see this text as a church ordinance relevant to the life of all Christians, going far beyond problems specific only to the Duchy of Saxony. In it Bucer makes no doctrinal concessions to Catholicism. He did admit to having remained silent on crucial controversial theological issues such as baptism, confirmation, and especially with regard to the Mass and the papacy. This course of conduct on the part of Bucer was the object of harsh criticism back then and remains so today. This condemnation, however, does not do full justice to Bucer's insight that giving prominence to church customs still held in common and appealing to liturgical practices and ceremonies of the early church, on the one hand, and to the widespread yearning for moral renewal and a more personal piety, on the other, would create a pragmatic foundation for a dynamic, never-ending process of reform within the church. This may have been only an illusion, but it is one to which significant people in all periods of history have devoted themselves, including the ecumenical movement of the twentieth and twenty-first centuries. For this was Bucer's concern: not to discuss dogmatic issues—as important as they were—purely as such but rather to explain and develop their significance and necessity in the context of ethics, and then of tradition and religious practice; that is to say, in the context of the day-to-day life of the church.

The text of the Leipzig agreement between Bucer and Witzel circulated widely in the following months and years, not just within the empire but as far as Rome. It did not, however, have any direct effects. One of the reasons for this was the Truce of Frankfurt (*Frankfurter Anstand*), which opened up entirely new prospects for a broadly imperial church reform, prospects that Bucer had every intention of making use of.

From Frankfurt to Hagenau

The Truce of Frankfurt did not meet with Bucer's approval. Not only he but many other supporters of the Reformation as well criticized the fact that by imperial law only current members of the Schmalkaldic League were included in the cease-fire granted by the peace agreement.[7] He sharply reprimanded the shortsightedness and complacency of the League members, who were apparently more interested in safeguarding what they had reached than in taking the risk of expanding and laying new foundations for Christ's reign.

Bucer welcomed one aspect of the Truce of Frankfurt wholeheartedly, however, and he defended it passionately and with great skill: the emperor's promise that a free religious colloquy between the confessional parties would take place—a colloquy that, as Bucer hoped, would turn into a national church council, a Germany-wide assembly of imperial representatives without the interference of the pope and the imposition of his supposed supremacy. "I certainly believe that we could come to an agreement on those things that are truly fundamental to the Christian faith, and leave the rest unresolved in Christian freedom, if we would only focus on God with all our hearts, not allow Rome to stop us, and could come to some kind of an arrangement regarding ecclesiastical property."[8] These lines summarize Bucer's point of departure as well as his goals. If one kept one's eyes fixed exclusively on God, expecting help and salvation only from God, then one would be forced to admit that sinners are justified through faith in Jesus Christ alone. This remained a fundamental assertion for Bucer. If Catholics would agree with this assertion—and Bucer was convinced most of them would, if one would only explain it to them correctly—an authentic common foundation could be reached upon which one could discuss all other theological and ecclesiastical issues.

Bucer hence once again made the distinction, already known to us, between central and subordinate articles of faith. But as broad-minded as Bucer could be in this respect, he was all the more uncompromising when it came to the pope and the papal curia. Their dominant influence had to be eliminated if the church were ever to be reformed truly. Bucer was convinced that Rome was interested not in reforming the church but rather in defending the current sad state of affairs, and that it was even ready to squelch divine truth in order to maintain the status quo. A further issue of fundamental importance was that of church property. An enormous variety of problems confronting the church as an institution at the beginning of the sixteenth century (that is, as an organization involved in every aspect of daily life) ultimately derived from the question of its property. The matter of property included problems associated with the whole system of benefices, or prebends, and the chronic absenteeism of parish pastors; it also concerned the vast property of monasteries and collegiate churches that was withheld from the common good and thus from socially responsible use, and it included the use of this property for the offspring of the city patriciate and especially of the nobility. Everybody in the early sixteenth century had experienced this reality in diverse ways, including Bucer—among other places in his hometown Sélestat. In this respect the problem of church property was anything but a purely academic issue. It was certainly characteristic for Bucer's approach to church reform that he paid just as much attention to these practical questions as to fundamental theological issues. The dialectical relationship between divine law and God's Holy Spirit so typical of this thought also manifested itself in his handling of this issue. Bucer could not speak about the gospel and about God's truth without referring to God's statutes, norms, and ordinances at the same time.

Bucer advertised the program outlined above in a book of dialogues, *On the Truce of Nuremberg* (*Vom Nürnbergischen fridestand*), published in the summer of 1539 under the telling pseudonym of "Konrad Treue von Friedesleben."[9] The work was dedicated to Ruprecht von Manderscheid-Blankenheim, the nephew and political and ecclesiastical adviser of the archbishop of Cologne, Hermann von Wied. This book represented only one small part of Bucer's broader campaign for a German national church council, a campaign he carried out with tremendous zeal and under persistent concealment of his true identity. No other German reformer could present the diversity and, in some cases, the contradictions of conflicting positions, and at the same time bring these closer to one another, with the same eloquence, journalistic skill, and theological plausibility as Martin Bucer. With these intelligent and trenchant works capable of arousing, intensifying, and taking advantage of public moods, the Strasbourg reformer was now definitely trying to influence a wider public.

In the pseudonymous work *On the Truce of Nuremberg*, Bucer creates a fictitious conversation in the imperial city of Speyer among three men: a nobleman, personifying a resolute if somewhat impulsive supporter of the Reformation; a prior, embodying a reflective Catholic open to reforms; and the secretary of a prince. The secretary presents Bucer's views in such a lucid and reasonable way that he ends up convincing the nobleman and the prior of the need to carry out a national church council. In January 1540, in Aschaffenburg, Bucer, using the same pseudonym, wrote another dialogue in which the same characters conducted a detailed conversation over the question of ecclesiastical property.[10] This book was dedicated to Georg Schenk von Tautenberg, the imperial governor of Frisia, who died shortly after its composition, however, on February 4, 1540.[11] In this work Bucer once again called for a Germany-wide church council. He wanted this dialogue to be understood as a contribution to the discussion of a problem that would certainly be on the order of business of such a council: What was to become of the vast property of the church? Bucer made it clear that Protestants had no intention of allowing Catholics to cite church tradition for their case. Bucer saw this tradition in a positive way, as church law correctly understood—that is to say, church law cleansed and purged by the Bible. The fictitious nobleman emphasizes this view as well: much too often the Protestants speak, he says, "as if the Christian church would have been lying in a grave ever since the times of the Apostles, not coming back to life until we finally raised it."[12]

For Bucer, the Bible and church tradition proved that the church had a legitimate right to own means and resources in order to accomplish its goals and provide its services; but they also proved that these means and resources had been entrusted to the church *only* for the purpose of reaching these goals. Consequently, Bucer could throw the Catholic accusation that the Protestants were sacrilegious robbers of church property back at supporters of the traditional church themselves. After all, the canons and cathedral chapters, the monks, nuns, bishops, and cardinals, were all living off this property as if it were their own, without serving the congregations with teaching, preaching, and pastoral care. Bucer made the following suggestion for reform: every congregation should receive as much ecclesiastical property as necessary for the support of the pastor it had chosen. The civil authorities were to supervise this process, receiving their own share in exchange. "For we maintain that the necessary service that they render to the church deserves a salary just like any other useful service."[13] Henceforth monasteries were to live off of their own work, especially by providing relief for the elderly, the poor, the sick, foreigners, and handicapped persons. Just like all other ecclesiastical goods, monastic assets were to be secularized, including the extensive landed property of ecclesiastical foundations and the territories of bishops. To be sure, Bucer had no intention of expropriating the current holders of church offices; neither did he wish to deprive the nobility or the civic patriciate from the usufruct of these goods. All the above persons, however, were to cease exercising church functions. In this respect, the renewed church was going to be a poor church.

Bucer did not leave it at that. When it became a settled matter in May 1540 that the coming religious colloquy would take place in Hagenau, some thirty miles north of Strasbourg (Speyer, another likely location, happened to be in the throes of the plague), Bucer once again drafted a dialogue, slipping into the role of a reasonable Catholic canon who explains the usefulness of a national council to a fellow canon, who happens to be a somewhat less reasonable supporter of the pope.[14] The self-critical canon complains about how the Protestants are becoming stronger each day, whereas among Catholics one observes "how the more time goes by, the more dilapidated we become; we do not have any learned people; respectability and virtue cannot be found in our midst."[15] Only those who derived enjoyment from their own demise were placing their hope on the pope. The reflective prelate continues: whoever wishes peace and tranquillity instead of civil war and the downfall of their existence must now vigorously demand a comprehensive reform of the church by means of a national council.

After the Hagenau conference eventually ended without any results, Bucer once again published a booklet in August 1540, this time under the pseudonym "Wahrmund Leuthold," vigorously championing the Protestant cause and advocating the unmet goals of the colloquy.[16] This time he unabashedly contrasted the Protestants with the Catholics, depicting the former as peace-loving, wishing to reach an agreement with the other side, and sincerely seeking the renewal of the church, but the latter as warmongers intent on defending current abuses just because the pope wanted this. Catholics have no arguments in their favor, claimed Bucer, for Christ, the Bible, the church fathers, and even the decrees of the early church councils speak on behalf of the Protestant position. Because of this, the papists do not take the risk of disputing with Protestants and refuse to give a public account of their views. "We are thus forced to have our greatest enemies as judges over us, as lords and patrons!"[17] How long could such a situation persist?

At the same time that Bucer attempted to influence public opinion in favor of a national church council, with pseudonymous publications addressed at a wide audience, he pursued the same goal in private letters to the territorial prince upon whom he had the greatest theological, ecclesiastical, and personal influence: Philip of Hesse. Two points of view appear repeatedly in Bucer's letters to the Landgrave. On the one hand, Bucer emphasizes that conditions in the Holy Roman Empire had never been as favorable for bringing about a national council free of papal influence. A majority of imperial cities and princes clearly leaned toward the Schmalkaldic League; those still wavering could be won over easily, since Protestants were equipped with better theological and historical arguments. It was necessary only to begin discussing controversial dogmatic issues; "thereafter, the power of the Lord will take over with his Holy Word and produce so many results that we will have much for which we can be grateful to the Lord."[18] On another occasion Bucer asserted his certainty that "we will neatly chase the Antichrist out of all of his haunts, one after another, without striking a blow and without waging war."[19] This statement clearly shows that Bucer did not downplay theological differences. In this respect he saw eye to eye with the Wittenberg theologians.[20] He also shared with them the firm conviction that Catholics would gradually and inevitably become convinced of the fundamental theological insights of the Reformation, as soon as they had taken the first steps in acknowledging the lordship of Christ, not the pope, over the church, and had given their agreement to the teaching that sinners are justified only through faith in Jesus Christ.

A second element Bucer emphasized incessantly in his letters to the Landgrave was the stern demand that territorial princes take religious issues seriously and not be interested primarily in increasing their own power and extending their own territory, but rather in "extending Christ's rule."[21] He thus called on Philip to try to influence the imperial estates in the same way Bucer had done through his publications, by urging them to put pressure on Emperor Charles V and his supporters to carry through with his promise to organize a religious colloquy "that would signal the glorious beginning of a true reformation of the church."[22] Bucer certainly did not expect any backing from the emperor for his ambitious plans, but rather opposition and resistance. And it was far from clear that Charles V would allow himself to be outmaneuvered by Bucer.

King Ferdinand solemnly inaugurated the conference in Hagenau on June 12, 1540; Bucer arrived on June 22. The atmosphere was edgy and hostile. The two sides were unable to agree on a joint procedure. Whereas the Catholics wished to pick up negotiations where Melanchthon and Eck had left off during the diet of Augsburg in 1530, the Protestants demanded first that the other side provide proof for its claim that the Augsburg Confession contained doctrinal errors. Since an agreement could not be reached, Ferdinand adjourned the colloquy on July 28 and decided that it should reconvene in Worms, some seventy miles north of Hagenau. There, scholars from both sides would be given the opportunity to dispute on even footing in the presence of the emperor. This transposition thus amounted to the promise of a free confessional negotiation. It needs to be mentioned, however, that powerful pressure groups in Wittenberg and Rome were not entirely disappointed with the failure of the Hagenau meeting. In both camps concerns ran high that too many concessions could be made to the respective adversary. Bucer, however, worked hard at building bridges between both sides, engaging in conversations with Catholic representatives. Among the people with whom he became more closely acquainted in Hagenau were the aforementioned archbishop of Cologne, Hermann von Wied, and especially his assistant Johannes Gropper.[23]

Worms

Emperor Charles V was not present, but imperial chancellor Nicholas Perrenot de Granvelle solemnly opened the colloquy on November 25,

1540, in the historic city on the Rhine. Bucer had already arrived, on November 1.[24] Both sides had agreed back in Hagenau to create two commissions, each consisting of eleven members and charged with drafting a document that would serve as the point of departure for negotiations. Nothing came of this procedure,[25] for the Catholics soon realized that they were anything but united among themselves. Electoral Brandenburg and the Palatinate clearly leaned toward Protestantism. Eck's theological stance was incapable of winning over a majority within the Catholic camp. Even the papal nuncios Giovanni Morone and Lorenzo Campeggio did not agree with one another. Whereas the members of the Schmalkaldic League impatiently called for the beginning of theological negotiations, rallying around the revised form of their confession (*Confessio Augustana variata*) that Melanchthon had presented in September 1540, the Catholic representatives did all they could to prevent these very negotiations from getting off the ground. In an atmosphere laden with enormous mutual distrust and characterized by political trickery and deceit, Granvelle finally succeeded in convincing each side to name a theological spokesman. For the chancellor, it was not just a matter of preventing a victory of the Protestant estates; even public exposure of the bickering and dissension among Catholics was something he needed to avoid. Philipp Melanchthon and Johannes Eck thus carried out detailed and prolonged discussions on the topic of original sin from December 24, 1540, until January 17, 1541. In the evening, they drafted a joint statement in Granvelle's quarters. The very next morning, the chancellor closed the colloquy in the name of the emperor and announced that theological negotiations would continue at the imperial diet to take place in Regensburg in the coming spring.

The skillful politician Granvelle had thus achieved a significant success for Charles V: an agreement between Catholics and Protestants in the form of a text that had met the approval of at least a few theologians and statesmen. Bucer helped bring this about in a decisive way. In Worms he once again got together with Johannes Gropper, who was there as a delegate of the archbishop of Cologne. The two had not only become acquainted in Hagenau but had also conversed quite intensely and thought alike on quite a few theological and ecclesiastical topics, including justification by faith. If one takes a closer look at Gropper's *Manual of Christian Education* (*Enchiridion christianae institutionis*) of 1538, it is easy to see why Bucer perceived him as a kindred spirit. Gropper also sought to conduct theology on the basis of the Bible and the church fathers and was wary of any doctrinal narrow-mindedness. He emphasized man's constant dependence on God's grace, which then empowered the Christian to lead a new life. Gropper took giant steps toward the Protestant position when he understood faith as trust and therefore spoke of Christians' certainty of salvation, since Christ cancels their guilt but also enables them to act according to a higher ethical standard. This conviction is also what led Gropper to reject any doctrine proclaiming man's justification by faith in Christ *alone*. He found this wording misleading, for it appeared to neglect the ethical commitment of Christians. Bucer agreed with Gropper's emphasis on ethics, as we have seen above, and both theologians also attached great importance to the work of the Holy Spirit.

Bucer and Gropper were convinced that they ultimately agreed theologically. Both sides appeared to mean the same things and pursue the same goals, even though they used different terminology and formulations. Affinity and trust between the two men and their positions thus grew. At the same time, though, this growing consensus made differences and antagonisms appear all the more pronounced when unity could not be achieved, making each side feel deceived and outwitted by the opposing side.

Initially, however, harmony and consent prevailed. The two men visited each other frequently in Worms and carried on negotiations of their own—at the same time that the official colloquy was getting nowhere. Then, on December 14, 1540, Gropper and Gerhard Veltwyck, the secretary of the chancellor,[26] revealed to Bucer that Granvelle was calling for secret negotiations. Bucer and Capito, on the one hand, and Veltwyck and Gropper, on the other, were to draft a joint statement that would serve as the basis for religious negotiations at the coming imperial diet.

This information put Bucer in a quandary. Up to this point he had not expected Charles V to provide the slightest support for the reform of the church—and certainly not for his planned national council. Bucer adhered to this opinion as late as November 22, when he wrote to Philip of Hesse: "The Imperial court is the greatest enemy of the freedom and justice of the German nation."[27] But now Granvelle was suddenly telling Bucer of the need to bolster Charles V, who was interested in peace and understanding, so that those in favor of war would not carry the day. Bucer asked both Jacob Sturm and the chancellor from Hesse, Johannes Feige, for advice. Both responded favorably to Granvelle's plan. On December 20, with negotiations already under way, Bucer asked Philip for a backdated official mandate to engage in them, which the latter promptly sent him.

Bucer was well aware of being involved in a risky undertaking. Both he and Capito were "quite conscience-stricken, wondering whether we are actually serving the Devil with these talks, while intending to serve Christ," as he wrote to the Landgrave on December 20.[28]

A combination of political, theological, and pastoral motives induced him to proceed in this venture nonetheless. From a political viewpoint, the Catholic camp appeared to fall apart into opposing groups as soon as even slightly friendly advances were made in its direction. The secular princes leaned toward the Reformation anyhow, as Bucer never tired of repeating. And he felt that prince-bishops would be easily won over when given assurances that they could keep ecclesiastical property for themselves and continue ruling as secular princes. At the same time, Protestants had to accept the fact that not all church ordinances and ceremonies introduced in the first centuries of the church's existence could simply be dismissed as flawed. Bucer therefore wished to take advantage of the current situation by winning over well-disposed members of the opposing camp with a sympathetic approach and concessions in marginal issues—thus isolating the pope politically and theologically.

The conversations took place in utmost secrecy from December 15 to 31, 1540, in Gropper's quarters in Worms, and consisted essentially of an exchange between him and Bucer. The twenty-three articles that emerged from these discussions were based on a draft by Gropper. Bucer's part in formulating them cannot be determined exactly. The closing articles do state that an agreement could not be reached on the issues of private masses, the veneration of saints, and obligatory yearly confession. Bucer professed himself to be in agreement with the remaining statements, which dealt with the Bible, tradition and ecclesiastical offices, original sin, justification and good works, the church, sacraments, and ceremonies, even though these declarations went a long way toward placating the Catholic side, at least in their wording. According to the original plan, two respected princes, each from a different side of the confessional divide, namely, Philip of Hesse and Elector Joachim II of Brandenburg, were to be informed confidentially of the contents of the "Worms Book." Granvelle insisted, however, that Philip be required to approve it in advance. The Landgrave, in a precarious position on account of his bigamy and therefore intent on remaining in the emperor's good graces, gave his consent, after Bucer briefed him on the document's contents and goals on January 7, 1541, in Giessen. Philip, though, was quick to add that he perceived the book solely "as the beginning" of conversations, and that he had no intention of allowing himself to become isolated from his fellow Protestants.[29]

On January 9, Bucer was back in Worms. Granvelle had obtained what he wanted. Bucer's goals, however, were much broader and, on the whole, considerably more complicated. To undermine the cohesion of the Catholic princes gradually, as he hoped, a minimum degree of unity had to be present among Protestants. This was far from being the case, however. Electoral Saxony was particularly adamant in its rejection of Bucer's way of proceeding. Not only Luther but Melanchthon as well was strictly opposed to his course of action. Elector John Frederick summed up the mood dominant in Saxony when he declared: "Whoever wants to accommodate should accommodate to God and his Word and accept his doctrine."[30] Conditions were thus all but favorable for the imperial diet that was to meet in Regensburg in the spring of 1541.

Regensburg

The imperial estates—that is, the prince electors and the imperial princes or their representatives—as well as the delegates of the cities represented in the Diet, began arriving in the months of February and March. Emperor Charles V arrived on February 23 and Bucer on March 10. The leading political figure was Chancellor Granvelle. But the papal legate, Cardinal Gasparo Contarini, soon proved to be the decisive religious and ecclesiastical personage in the Catholic camp. He had experienced faith in Christ in younger years as a release from fear and doubt, in a way similar to Luther's, but he deliberately integrated this experience into traditional church theology and piety.[31] In this respect, Contarini was better acquainted with the religious roots of the Reformation than were most other Catholic theologians.

When the imperial diet opened on April 5, Charles V informed the estates that he wished to have the religious issue discussed by a relatively small committee. On April 21 he appointed Eck, Julius Pflug, and Gropper to represent the Catholic side, and Melanchthon, Bucer, and Johannes Pistorius to be spokesmen for the Protestants. Under no circumstances could the emperor have avoided naming Eck; after all, he had been Luther's opponent from the very beginning and had fought against the Reformation untiringly for the past two decades. As the spokesman of the Saxon Reformation, Melanchthon was an equally indispensable candidate. The fact that Charles also chose Pflug and Pistorius in addition to Bucer and Gropper shows how much importance he attached to coming to an agreement. The bishop-elect of Naumburg-Zeitz as well as the superintendent of Alsfeld and confidant of Landgrave Philip were both resolute supporters of a politics of peaceful rapprochement, as a matter of principle and for practical reasons.

Expectations and hopes on both sides—Bucer's too, of course—were enormously high when conversations began on April 27 under the chairmanship of Granvelle and of Count Palatine Frederick. Just how willing each side was to accommodate to the other is demonstrated by the fact that both Eck and Melanchthon finally declared themselves ready to accept the text placed before them—sealed by Granvelle and lacking a title page—as the basis for discussions. This "Regensburg Book"[32] was essentially Gropper's and Bucer's "Worms Book," only slightly revised by Contarini and a group of Catholic theologians. Melanchthon no longer persevered in the electoral Saxon demand that the Augsburg Confession be the sole point of departure for negotiations. Furthermore, Eck's gruff excoriation of this new "Regensburg Book" found no majority backing within the Catholic camp.

Both sides were able to agree on the first four articles, which dealt with the fall of humankind and original sin, by April 27 without any major difficulties. The issue of justification by faith proved to be more problematic. Eck and Melanchthon soon were at loggerheads on this issue. In spite of this, both sides were able to agree on a newly drafted text by May 2. Contarini and Bucer had played key roles in conceiving it.

Conference participants were exhilarated at this success, for the crucial stumbling block preventing reconciliation between the two confessions had apparently been removed. Their disillusionment was renewed, however, as early as the following day, when ecclesiology was discussed. Which took precedence: the Bible or the *magisterium*, the teaching authority of the church? The Roman and the Protestant camps clashed irreconcilably on this question. The Protestants had no other choice but to put their differing views on record and let the colloquy continue its sessions with this issue unresolved. But the same collision of views repeated itself in discussions on the sacraments and their significance. To be sure, some agreements were reached on May 4, when articles 10–13, dealing with baptism and confirmation, were debated. Negotiations broke down completely, however, on May 5, when the Mass and the Lord's Supper were the order of business. Contarini had inserted the concept of "transubstantiation" into the fourteenth article, referring to the dogma proclaimed at the Fourth Lateran Council in Rome in 1215, according to which bread and wine became the actual substance of Christ's body and blood in the Mass. With this position, the Venetian cardinal stood up unconditionally for Roman Catholic teaching. Even more crucial was the fact that he obtained the support of the entire Catholic camp for his position. Under absolutely no circumstances could the Protestants accommodate to this position—even though Bucer did undertake a weak effort on May 8. Expectations of uniting and renewing Christendom in Germany, so high on the eve of the colloquy, thus ran aground because of conflicting understandings of the church and of its teaching authority. Bucer's hopes of effortlessly neutralizing the pope and his supporters from a theological and political standpoint turned out to be an illusion. The exact opposite was taking place: his opponents were beginning to regain lost ground. This renewal of Catholic energy was one of the most significant results of the Regensburg colloquy.

In spite of these setbacks, the colloquy continued. The six theologians discussed the remaining articles from May 14 to 22. Of course, by now they were hardly listening to one another but rather doing their best to accentuate the differences between their respective positions. Charles V and Granvelle redoubled efforts to conclude the colloquy with some kind of a settlement. For this reason, on June 8 they presented the imperial estates with copies of the "Regensburg Book" along with the Protestant counterarticles (there were nine of them by now),[33] in order for them to express their views. But in the meantime, both the papal court and Luther had rejected the agreement reached on justification by faith. This state of affairs made the imperial estates all the more reluctant to come out in favor of the "Regensburg Book." On July 5, the Catholic camp demanded a text more reflective of its own position, whereas the Protestants announced on July 12 that they were going to interpret all joint statements in the light of the Augsburg Confession and its *Apologia*. Mutual tolerance was the last thing each side was interested in now. Bucer passionately beseeched his fellow Protestants not to fall back on pure doctrine but rather to take the offensive and, making this unique situation work in their favor, have the imperial diet officially endorse the articles that had been agreed upon. His pleas were not heard.

Accordingly, on July 29, 1541, the Regensburg diet issued a closing decree (*Reichstagsabschied*) quite hostile to Protestant concerns. It did at least call on prince-prelates to carry out reforms in their territories. It also extended the legal protection of the empire to the Protestant estates for another eighteen months. Finally, Charles V gave his—alas, merely oral—promise as emperor that he would continue to try to bring about a national church council; in case he should fail in this, the confessional issue would once again be on the agenda of the next imperial diet. Yet what was to be made of this promise? Was there any reason to believe such negotiations would succeed in the future, after they had failed so miserably under such favorable conditions?

Charles V was deeply disappointed over the outcome of the colloquy. His attempt to reach a peaceful settlement of the confessional issue had unmistakably failed. It is hardly probable, however, that he steered directly toward a religious war from this point on. A more reasonable goal for him for the time being was to weaken the Schmalkaldic League, which had recently gained more strength and self-assurance than Charles felt comfortable with. He had two opportunities to do so in Regensburg, and he made use of them skillfully. The first concerned Philip of Hesse. Charles pardoned him for his bigamy, but in exchange Philip committed himself in a secret deal with the emperor on June 13, 1541, to prevent the duke of Cleves from joining the Schmalkaldic League and to hinder an alliance between the League and France from coming about. Furthermore, he had to promise to support the Habsburg claims on Gelderland and Zutphen. Charles V also entered into a similar treaty with Joachim II of Brandenburg. This prince-elector refrained from joining the Schmalkaldic League, obtaining permission in return to introduce his new church ordinance. Two influential princes from the Protestant camp had thus been neutralized.

The outcome of the Regensburg colloquy was also a major setback for Bucer, and this failure weighed heavily on him. It did not, however, make him waver in his goals or in his strategy. He especially entreated Philip of Hesse to do everything in his power to ensure that the religious colloquies not become a past episode but rather continue to be an element of imperial politics. "Since God has shed so much grace upon us," wrote Bucer to Philip, "that we are called his Protestants, our governments and we all therefore have the right and the duty to place ourselves like a wall in front of God's house in this issue and not to budge until the church has been helped. This is something we could achieve at the next Imperial Diet if we would only insist upon it in a truly Christian way. We will be helpless in confronting the Turks and have no peace among ourselves as long as we persevere in religious discord and thus remain under God's severest wrath."[34]

Principles, not pragmatism, guided Bucer when he wrote these words. He did not let it rest at that, however. For one thing, he continued to count on widespread dissatisfaction in Germany with the ecclesiastical estates' aversion to reform, and he tried to foster this dissatisfaction with his publications. In addition, he pinned his hopes on the Reformation's continued and apparently relentless expansion in various German territories. On July 14, before the Regensburg diet adjourned, Bucer handed over a memorandum to the emperor with concrete recommendations for overcoming the downfall of the church.[35] Proceeding from the proposals made previously for solving the issue of church property, Bucer now drew the following conclusions. He suggested that the articles agreed upon in Regensburg should serve as the point of departure for a rapprochement between both sides. Each side should be allowed to administer the sacraments in the form it saw most fitting; each side should also be guaranteed the free election of pastors, the right for pastors to marry, and the use of church property to support pastors adequately. One needs only to place this text alongside the text that Melanchthon wrote on this subject at the same time to realize the extent to which Bucer had become the decisive figure of Protestantism during these years. Whereas Melanchthon pontificated and expressed his views on the church and society on the basis of his pedagogical model—that is, of the school—Bucer took legal and social circumstances and obligations into account and wrote extensively on the need for change and the possibilities for bringing about change—while articulating the very same theological views as Melanchthon.

Since subsequent developments, as we have seen, ran entirely counter to the limited mutual tolerance that Bucer demanded of both sides, the Strasbourg reformer now concentrated his literary efforts on repeating the call of the closing decree of the Regensburg diet to prince-bishops to carry out ecclesiastical reforms in their territories. One could do the church a big favor quite quickly, he wrote in the summer of 1541, in a small booklet on corruption in the church (*Abusum ecclesiasticorum indicatio*) that was reprinted many times, if one would simply renew the clergy by imposing the standards of the Bible and the rules of the early church upon it.[36] Bucer still counted on the spontaneous, relentless expansion of the Reformation in the Holy Roman Empire. He intended to help this process along through his theological and ecclesiastical negotiations, but he also wanted to encourage the Protestant imperial estates to make use of their actual political power. For this reason, in a letter to Landgrave Philip on August 28, 1541, he emphasized what he saw as being most important: "I do hope that something happens in Cologne, Münster, the Palatinate and in Cleves because of the articles we agreed upon [in Regensburg]."[37] In fact, something did happen. But once again, the ecclesiastical and political developments that followed were not necessarily the ones Bucer's bold plans called for.

The "Cologne Reformation"

The Electorate

The spiritual jurisdiction of the archbishop of Cologne may have been far-reaching—his diocese included the archdiaconates of Bonn, Cologne, Xanten, and Soest, and the bishoprics of Liège, Utrecht, Münster, Osnabrück, and Minden were directly subordinate to him—but the territory he headed as a prince-bishop, the Cologne Electorate, was hemmed in from all sides, to an almost extreme extent.[38] Located on the west bank of the Rhine River, it comprised a narrow strip of land rarely wider than six miles and extending some forty-five miles, all the way from Kempen in the north to Godesberg in the south. The Electorate had several exclaves in addition, for instance, Rheinberg in the north and the districts of Altenahr and Nürburg in the south, as well as Linz and Altenwied on the right bank of the Rhine. This situation was typical for the empire at the end of the Middle Ages. Typical as well was the sprinkling of extraneous enclaves found within the territory of the Electorate. Even more significant was the fact that the important free imperial cities of Aachen and Cologne did not belong to the Electorate. They were subject to the spiritual jurisdiction of the archbishop but not subordinate to him politically.

Actual political power in this region of Germany lay not with the elector of Cologne but with the duke of Jülich-Cleves-Berg. His territory surrounded that of the Electorate from all sides. The Duchy stretched as far as the Meuse River and the city of Aachen to the west, included the territory of Berg (*Bergisches Land*) toward the east as far as Soest, and extended north as far as Cleves (*Kleve*), and later, after the takeover of Gelderland and Zutphen, even as far as the Ijsselmeer. Traditionally, the dukes of Jülich-Cleves-Berg had always been quite assertive when it came to organizing and reforming the church in their territory—as the contemporary saying *Dux Cliviae papa est in terris suis* ("the Duke of Cleves is pope in his territories") testified.[39] This pro-active stance lessened even more the influence that the archbishop of Cologne had on his own diocese.

But even the political sway he held over the territory of his Electorate was subject to limitations. Every new archbishop was forced to swear an oath upon an agreement of 1453, the "hereditary territorial agreement" (*Erblandesvereinigung*), which relinquished a significant portion of his power to the estates and particularly to the cathedral chapter. The chapter was the sole representative of the clergy in the territorial diet (*Landtag*), which also included representatives of the three temporal estates of the counts, the knights, and the cities. The cathedral chapter also had the right to convoke the diet without the consent of the archbishop. Finally, the latter was obliged to appoint two members of the diet to be part of his standing committee of councillors. The archbishop could not raise taxes or incur debts without the consent of the territorial diet. He also needed its approval to pawn a territory or begin a war. We can easily see the extent to which all these arrangements strictly limited the power of the prince-archbishop of Cologne if we also take the manifold connections between the cathedral chapter and the university, as well as the city council of Cologne, into account. Cologne was a free imperial city and thus not subject to the elector's jurisdiction. He had to rule together with a chapter that included not only sixteen prelates from the highest nobility of the empire but also eight university professors, most of them theologians or experts in canon law. If we also consider that some of them held the pastorate of a church in town, it is clear that in Cologne the cathedral chapter, significant sectors of the citizenry, and the university and the city council were all inextricably connected. The extremely conservative and strictly orthodox theological faculty of the university set the religious tone for the city. There was little breathing space for other views in Cologne.

Hermann von Wied, born in 1477, became the archbishop of Cologne in 1515. In the initial years of his term he gave little indication of being any different from the other prince-prelates of the empire, although he did show some interest in stabilizing the traditional church. Later, however, he attached increasing importance to the issue of church reform. The first actual steps he took in this direction were probably due to his close adviser Johannes Gropper. They consisted of a provincial chapter of the Cologne diocese, which convened in the cathedral of the city in March 1536, as well as the publication in 1538 of the reform statutes promulgated by this chapter. The failure of these sweeping efforts led Hermann von Wied to place his hopes on the religious colloquies that soon followed. As already mentioned, Hermann was personally present in Hagenau. The urgent appeal made on all prelates in the closing decree of the Regensburg diet, to carry out reforms in the church, was one that the archbishop took very much to heart. It may be true that he was not exactly a learned man. But he was a sincere Christian, took his faith seriously, and was determined to assume his responsibility before God in improving the state of the church. He assembled a small circle of advisers to help him in this task, mostly humanists with Reformation leanings. But it was ultimately Bucer and Gropper whom Hermann was counting on to pull off the Reformation in the prince-archbishopric of Cologne. Both had gotten along well in Worms and Regensburg and had since kept closely in touch.

The Reformation Attempt

Bucer and Gropper met with Hermann von Wied on February 5, 1542, at the castle of Buschhoven, his hunting retreat in the Kottenforst area some eight miles west of Bonn.[40] They discussed the introduction of church reform measures in the prince-archbishopric. One month later

Bucer urged the archbishop once again to carry out a "truly Christian Reformation" in his territory, in order to set a shining example for the other imperial estates, especially the prince-bishops.[41] Hermann von Wied submitted his reformation proposals to the territorial diet in the middle of March. All four estates of the diet—including the cathedral chapter that would later oppose him so doggedly—gave the archbishop a free hand to carry out the reforms seen as so necessary by all sides.

This spirit of harmony dissipated immediately when it became known whom Hermann von Wied intended to appoint for this task. The secretary recording the proceedings of the theological faculty of the University of Cologne on July 26 excitedly took note of rumors that "the Archbishop is planning to invite Bucer over to Cologne from Strasbourg to let him win converts for Lutheranism."[42] This note was, of course, a crude oversimplification. But a grain of truth was present, inasmuch as Bucer was naturally no neutral figure interested in mediating impartially between two opposing sides but quite the contrary, a prominent church official and theologian bent on carrying through his vision for the reform of the church. And this vision was precisely what the clergy of Cologne intended to resist with all their available means.

Bucer and Gropper's friendship did not survive this polarization. At the beginning of August, the latter was still assuring his Strasbourg colleague that enduring personal and theological ties united them. With time, however, Gropper became weary of the hostility he had to endure within his own camp—rumors refused to abate that he was ultimately responsible for Bucer's coming to the Electorate of Cologne. Furthermore, Bucer's strong sense of calling began to frighten even Gropper, leading him eventually to retreat to the safety of his traditional Catholic circles. Regardless of the prerequisites and conditions for his appointment to Bonn, wrote Bucer to Gropper on January 2, 1543, "Here I am and I intend to remain within the Lord's calling."[43] To this he added, "I belong to the party of the Protestants," which, however, did not mean reckless addiction to innovation but rather the readiness to allow everything to prevail that fit in, and agreed, with the rule of Christ.

At the end of the month Bucer tried anew to regain Gropper's sympathy by writing him a lengthy letter of a fundamental nature.[44] Once again Bucer asserted his conviction of being on Christ's side and of experiencing Christ's very own persecution in the adverse circumstances he was going through. Gropper also belonged more properly on Christ's side, the side of truth, admonished Bucer. Of course, this allegiance would mean changing his life conduct—among other things, by no longer persisting in the accumulation of ecclesiastical benefices! Bucer waited in vain for a personal response to this letter. By now Gropper had become firmly entrenched in the Catholic camp, which was undertaking everything in its might to rid the prince-bishopric of Bucer.[45]

Bucer had been living in Bonn since December 14, 1542. The city had about two thousand inhabitants at the time.[46] Most of them were artisans and small merchants, with some fishermen and ferrymen. The town was only thinly populated, with extensive vegetable gardens, orchards, and vineyards lying within city walls. What distinguished Bonn from comparable towns was neither the market for the surrounding villages nor the Rhine tariff it charged, but rather the fact that it housed the headquarters of the electoral administration and the residence of the prince-bishop. This had a noticeable effect on the city: its population included a significant minority of court officials and servants; the civic constitution permitted citizens only very limited self-administration under the supervision of electoral officials. A conspicuous feature of the city was the so-called *Stiftsstadt* in the northern part of Bonn: it included the stately cathedral (*Münster*), the parish church of St. Remigius south of it, and the castle-like electoral palace. The latter, where Bucer probably had his lodging, was located approximately where the buildings of the University of Bonn stand today. On December 23, 1542, Bucer wrote to Strasbourg reporting that his accommodations were very comfortable and that the electoral administrator was providing him with a magnificent diet of fish and meats.

Bucer preached in Bonn cathedral on December 17 for the first time. Soon afterward, he began preaching there three times a week. On December 18 he also started a series of lectures in Latin on 1 Corinthians in the local Franciscan monastery, providing an exegesis of the biblical text for his listeners three times a week. These tasks constituted only a small portion of Bucer's daily workload, which also included negotiations, traveling, drafting memoranda and expert opinions of all sorts, as well as quite a bit of writing. It is therefore understandable that he complained to Landgrave Philip at the end of April 1543: "Since I am almost alone, I am consuming and exhausting myself."[47]

On December 19, 1542, the Cologne cathedral chapter and university had filed a formal complaint with the archbishop, protesting against Bucer's appointment. Hermann von Wied summoned Bucer to his quarters in Brühl, where the Strasbourg reformer remained from December 24 until the close of the year. With the new year, however, Bucer returned to Bonn. On January 9, Gropper presented the archbishop with a hastily drafted Catholic reform proposal, which both Hermann von Wied and Bucer rejected. It is probably no coincidence that its text has not survived.

A territorial diet (*Landtag*) convened in Bonn from March 12 to 16. Bucer, by now a controversial figure, was conspicuously absent, as he had deliberately not been invited. The territorial estates did authorize Hermann von Wied once more to conduct church reforms within his prince-archbishopric and to appoint the appropriate persons for this task—just as long as Bucer was not among them. When the archbishop resolutely asserted that he would stick by Bucer, the representatives of the three temporal estates gave in—but not the cathedral chapter. An open struggle was now beginning.

Bucer was somewhat at a disadvantage in this situation, because neither the cathedral chapter nor the theological faculty agreed to participate in a disputation with him. Bucer's tremendous skills as a public speaker and his ready wit were thus put out of commission. All he could do now was to express himself in written form—and it was in writing that his verbal gifts became handicaps. He had always lacked an ability to formulate things briefly, to simplify his written trains of thought, and especially to bring matters to a point. Things were complicated by the fact that a plethora of popular and learned writers joined in the literary fray, publishing some 140 writings in the course of this controversy, from December 1542 to the spring of 1547. Just as important was the fact that the Catholics now succeeded for the first time in making broad use of the printing press to their advantage.

It was in this setting that Bucer, in March 1543, published the first of his writings of defense against the Cologne cathedral chapter under the title *What Is Presently Being Taught and Preached in the Name of the Holy Gospel of Our Lord Jesus Christ in Bonn, in the Bishopric of Cologne* (*Was im Namen des Heiligen Evangeliums unseres Herrn Jesus Christus jetzt zu Bonn im Stift Köln gelehrt und predigt wird*).[48] The fact that the book was reprinted twice within a very short time speaks for itself. In this work, Bucer began by expounding his theological principles in very simple, almost popular language, writing among other things on justification by faith, monastic life, marriage, and the duties of civil authority. He then prudently defended his activity at Bonn, particularly by referring to the closing decree of the Regensburg diet. He concluded his treatise with the admonition to rejoice, after all, that the gospel was being preached and abuses in the church were being eliminated, and with a call to his readers to do all they could to help crown these efforts with success.

Considerably less convincing than this work—which Bucer, still hoping to bring about a public disputation, dedicated to the city council and the University of Cologne—was his second book of defense, published at the end of July 1543.[49] It was directly motivated by a malicious *Judgment* (*Iudicium*) issued by the prior provincial of the Carmelites, Eberhard Billick, and from which even the cathedral chapter distanced itself. Melanchthon's reply appeared in June.[50] In this renewed defense, Bucer fought against the *Iudicium*'s attempt to slander the Reformation, the city of Strasbourg, and his own person. He defended the Reformation understanding of sin and of the new life of discipleship of those justified by faith, in addition to discussing the veneration of saints, confirmation, and particularly the Mass and the Lord's Supper, as well as confession and absolution. Bucer echoed one central tenet again and again: "God wants us to turn to him and to surrender to him completely and with all our hearts. That is the honor we are to give him. But this can only occur if we find comfort solely in his grace and mercy."[51] On the whole, however, this second defense turned out to be rather too long and much too involved and detailed in its argumentation to attract major attention or have any lasting effect on Reformation efforts. At about the same time, Bucer and Melanchthon drafted their *Christian and True Justification* (*Christliche und wahre Verantwortung*).[52] It was a brief memorandum addressed to the archbishop of Cologne in which the two reformers rejected the allegations and calumnies that the university in particular, but also the city council, had uttered against them. The work that soon attracted major attention, however, was Hermann von Wied's *Simple Consideration Concerning the Establishment of a Christian Reformation Founded upon God's Word* (*Einfältiges Bedenken, worauf eine christliche, im Worte Gottes gegründete Reformation . . . anzurichten sei*),[53] which laid out the guidelines for reforming the church in the Electorate of Cologne.

Bucer had already begun working on this major text in January 1543. Melanchthon came to Bonn at the beginning of May and assisted him in drafting the ordinance. Caspar Hedio, coming from Strasbourg, joined them a month later. By then, however, the *Simple Consideration* was essentially complete. Melanchthon and Bucer are thus to be considered the rightful authors. Determining exactly how much each one wrote, though, is extraordinarily difficult. We can be certain that Melanchthon drafted the sections on the Trinity, creation, and original sin. But this does not mean that he did not also write other chapters or have a say in their formulation. A further, entirely different question is establishing which texts served as models. It is clear that one very important source was the Brandenburg-Nuremberg church ordinance of 1533, but it was certainly not the only one.

In spite of this variety of authors and models, anyone picking up and reading the *Simple Consideration* would have had the impression of holding a rather uniform document in his hands. In his foreword, Hermann von Wied admitted that the ordinance was far from perfect and represented only a first step in putting the closing decree of the Regensburg diet into practice. He considered improvements possible in some sections and encouraged a debate over the draft. After this preface came an introduction that clearly reflected Bucer's thought and summarized the central ideas of the entire ordinance: taking the Bible as our point of departure, humans are called to proclaim God's truth; this is the church's primary duty; and all our preaching, teaching, faith, and action must center on Jesus Christ. Bucer presented the goals of the *Simple Consideration* even more concisely to Bullinger some weeks later when he wrote: "Everything has been ordered in accordance with evangelical simplicity, so that regardless of what the church does with words or signs, it is always preaching and communicating Christ alone, and this clearly and effectively, as well as proclaiming and strengthening people in the conviction that forgiveness of sins and certainty of grace can only be found in him."[54]

Alas, the clarity and succinctness manifested above is not to be found in the *Simple Consideration* itself. In more than three hundred pages divided into sixty chapters, both authors present readers with a curious combination of theological principles, devotional meditations, church law statutes, and liturgical instructions. This work is proof once again that Bucer could not reduce himself simply to presenting and discussing the right dogmatic tenets. Critics were not at a loss to find enough to criticize about Bucer's publications—the Swiss[55] as well as Luther, who said of the *Consideration*: "The whole thing is too long and nothing but eyewash; I could tell right away that Bucer, the chatterbox, was at work here."[56] This plan for reformation was indeed anything but brief and concise. On the contrary, it deliberately attempted to be broad and thus all the more inclusive. Bucer was convinced that both the congregation as a whole and the individual Christian participated in Christ's presence, and that a new way of living and thinking arose from this participation. He therefore rejected any attempts to cramp Christian teaching into a narrow doctrinal norm.

Instead, Bucer's goal was to coax Catholics to change their orientation gradually, step by step, and he wanted to do this by preaching Christ; such preaching included the message of sinners being justified alone through faith, as well as the two sacraments of baptism and the Lord's Supper. Furthermore, he wanted worship services to be held in the vernacular, priests to be permitted to marry, and the cup to be given to the laity in the Lord's Supper. Finally, not only were traditional church ceremonies to be scrutinized critically, but also the legal statutes of the church. Bucer's method of proceeding earned him much criticism. In a letter to Philip of Hesse on April 29, 1543, he made the following allusion to Luther: "Many in Wittenberg grunt against me without my having deserved it. They should rather discern from my activity whether I am conducting God's affairs in a pure or impure fashion. How easy it is, behind a glass of beer or wine in a cozy tavern, to tear to shreds the humble servants involved in struggle and conflict! But then again, if this were not happening to us, then our service would not be tested in the right way."[57]

This draft for the Cologne reformation was discussed with Hermann von Wied at the beginning of July. The archbishop studied the text five hours a day for five days, concentrating particularly on the quotations from the Bible. On July 23 he submitted the *Consideration* to the territorial diet. The three temporal estates expressed their consent with the plan; the cathedral chapter rejected it flatly, referring instead to the statutes of the provincial synod of 1536 and insisting that they be put into action. The diet's closing decree on July 26, 1543, took note that the archiepiscopal reform program had been accepted and expressed the hope that the cathedral chapter would agree to it, after all, sometime within the next three weeks. It appeared as if the decisive step for introducing the Reformation in the prince-bishopric of Cologne had been taken.

As in the case of the previous territorial diet, Bucer was not present at this one. Nevertheless, he remained the life and soul of these efforts at reformation. He unceasingly called on Philip of Hesse to provide Hermann von Wied with moral and political support. Evangelical preaching and the administration of the Lord's Supper in both kinds was, in fact, already taking place in a number of cities—among them, Kempen, Linz, and Andernach. The center of the Reformation movement, however, was clearly the electoral residence in Bonn. The Franciscan monastery in Bonn emptied itself, some of its former members began preaching in the surrounding villages, and priests started marrying. At the same time, following the example of Strasbourg's new Latin school of 1539, a Protestant academy of sorts began developing in Bonn to serve as a counteruniversity to that of Cologne. It cannot be denied that these were only rudimentary beginnings. And yet they were significant, for Duke William IV of Jülich-Cleves-Berg was beginning to show interest for the Reformation, and the bishop of Münster, Franz von Waldeck, was waiting for Hermann von

Wied to have success in order to follow his example. The initial accomplishments of the Reformation in electoral Cologne, as modest as they were, carried enormous weight.

Setbacks

Ultimately, it was not internal or external difficulties that brought about the collapse of the "Cologne reformation" but rather Emperor Charles V's victorious military campaign against Duke William IV of Jülich-Cleves-Berg. William had gained control over Gelderland and Zutphen by succession—a takeover that was legally far from incontestable. The Duchy now represented a threat to the Habsburg Low Countries, especially since Duke William sought an alliance with France in order to shore up his power and consolidate his political independence. In addition, he was gradually introducing the Reformation into his Duchy, hoping in this way for a religious and military rapprochement with the Schmalkaldic League. A decisive factor in preventing this approximation to the Protestants from ultimately succeeding was the secret agreement (mentioned above) that Landgrave Philip, because of his bigamy, had been forced to make with Charles V. This being the case, the Habsburg emperor was able to conquer the small fortress of Düren, without encountering any opposition, with a brutal attack in August 1543 that provoked horror and dismay in the entire Duchy. On September 7, Charles imposed his demands on Duke William in the town of Venlo: Gelderland and Zutphen were to fall to the emperor; all religious innovations were to be annulled; the alliance with the French king was to be replaced with a treaty that committed the duke to unconditional allegiance to the emperor.

The significance of these events can hardly be overestimated. For one thing, Emperor Charles V had demonstrated unmistakably to all that he was powerful enough to suppress by sheer force any attempt at religious or political change. At the same time, by giving ample proof of its internal disunity and its political ineffectiveness, the Schmalkaldic League had made it clear to Charles V that he would have an easy time routing the Protestants.

Few people in the evangelical camp, though, fully realized the significance of these events or understood their consequences. Among them was Martin Bucer. He had witnessed the triumphant entry of Charles V and his troops into Bonn on August 17, 1543. He had seen for himself how the imperial army looted this "Lutheran" territory and deliberately caused havoc in it, vandalizing acres and acres of vineyards.[58] Bucer was forced to leave Bonn ten days later. He returned to Strasbourg by way of Hesse, taking time in Frankfurt to admonish Landgrave Philip once again in a stern letter: the terrible events currently besetting the Protestants were God's just punishment for their contempt of God's revealed truth and their failure to take discipleship seriously, as one could clearly see from the fact that they were not introducing church discipline! Everybody had some share in the blame, asserted Bucer, but the civil authorities were particularly responsible, for they wielded the greatest authority and influence. Bucer expressly included Philip in his criticism because the Landgrave—together with the elector of Saxony—enjoyed "the highest reputation among the princes who profess the Holy Gospel"—and enjoyed this reputation just as much "among enemies as among friends."[59]

Bucer entreated Philip countless times in the coming weeks to devote himself less to eating well and drinking liberally, and especially admonished him not to spend so much time hunting but rather to attend to his governmental duties more faithfully and to put particular effort into increasing the religious discipline and devotion of his court and territory. The Landgrave lent Bucer's critique a willing ear but disagreed wholeheartedly with the Strasbourg reformer's conviction that an amended piety and the resulting greater cohesion among Protestants would automatically solve the crisis of the Reformation. Bucer repeated his demands in a memorandum he sent to Philip in October 1543.[60] Replying on November 11, the Landgrave claimed that little of what Bucer was calling for could be put into practice. He did not shrink from drastic examples to support his case.[61] The archbishop of Cologne, he wrote, essentially had no idea of what was occurring. The Schmalkaldic League found itself at the point of collapse. Most important, the situation had changed completely with respect to the Catholics: they "now smell a rat, wondering why you consented to an agreement in Regensburg, considering what resulted from it, what you did in the Archbishopric of Cologne, and what happened as a consequence in the Bishoprics of Münster and Osnabrück, and that with the passage of time their affairs came to naught. Especially because Gropper, Julius Pflug and others, who originally were on your side, from now on will clearly be against you."[62]

Bucer knew this all too well. Not naïveté but the refusal to succumb to his own feelings of discouragement and hopelessness made Bucer try to mobilize the Landgrave in this way. Bucer was indeed capable of appraising the Protestant situation in extraordinarily somber terms, as a lengthy letter to Heinrich Bullinger of December 28, 1543, shows.[63] After briefly describing the situation in the prince-bishopric of Cologne, he bitterly lamented Luther's recent crude invectives against the Swiss regarding the Lord's Supper. Indefensible as the Wittenberg Reformer's behavior was, however, Bucer could still insist on not forgetting that Luther remained "an admirable instrument of God for the salvation of His people." Besides, Bucer continued, it was inadmissible for Christians to accuse and inveigh against one another. Their duty was to tolerate and amend one another in love and patience—only by acting in this spirit would they be capable of achieving anything for their cause.

The same conclusions were true for high-level politics, Bucer felt. He saw quite clearly that Charles V was now the dominant political figure in Germany. He fittingly described the emperor, whom he had observed at close quarters in Bonn, as a gruff man who "pursues his goals with extreme doggedness, if indeed sometimes secretively and in an impenetrable way." Absolutely no doubt could remain that Charles V was going to impose his will upon Germany, if not through negotiations then by force of arms. Bucer continued his description in unwitting admiration: "Everything about him was imperial: his words, his actions, his countenance, his bearing—and his gifts. Even those who have already known him for a long time were utterly amazed at his agility, resoluteness, enthusiasm, earnestness and majesty." Later on in his letter Bucer wrote: "The Emperor could achieve so much if he would only strive to be the Emperor of Germany and Christ's servant."

What was the situation in the Protestant camp? Bucer only saw quarrel, discord, selfishness, and the greatest imaginable disunity. "So these are our pillars," he mused in conclusion. Only Philip of Hesse was exempted from his criticism. The Landgrave, wrote Bucer, could think in a long-term fashion and felt a responsibility for the whole. But what was an individual capable of achieving, particularly if the cities went their own way anyhow, without second thoughts? "Mercury, the God of merchants, has corrupted most of them anyway." And as far as the foreign powers were concerned, the French king had squandered his credit by forming a military alliance with the Ottomans, the English king stood silently on the sidelines, and the Danish king had withdrawn. "Just contemplate the ruins of Europe!"

Bucer concluded: "Hence I see that men are completely at a loss when it comes to saving Germany from its downfall." He finished his letter with the plea: "May the Lord Jesus grant that we consecrate ourselves to him with our entire hearts. Only in this way will we escape God's wrath, which is already blazing up against us. The hour of the prophets has arrived. The Lord grant that we may call people to repent with the same prophetic spirit."

Admittedly, Bullinger was not impressed with this letter. He continued to make derogatory remarks about Bucer and used every available opportunity to distance himself from the Strasbourg reformer in the rudest way possible.

Perseverance

Fighting with the Written Word

Bucer's long-term goal was that the Reformation take hold in the entire Holy Roman Empire—and far beyond. Particularly from the beginning of the 1540s, Bucer had become convinced that this objective could be reached only if the Protestant camp were willing to make concessions to those temporal and ecclesiastical princes who did, in fact, wish to reform their territories but did not want to introduce the Lutheran confession. Bucer's plan was two-pronged: on the one hand, he sought to initiate conversations between open-minded leading figures in both camps; on the other, he hoped the imperial estates would officially endorse this project. His ultimate aim remained the convocation of a national council: the renewal of the church in Germany was to arise from the cooperation between the imperial representatives and Protestant theologians, together with any other theologians who strove for a true reform of the church. This plan could be carried out only if one succeeded in convincing as many rulers as possible, or at least their advisers, of its necessity. Furthermore, where reforms had gained a foothold as a consequence of the closing decree of the Regensburg diet, these at the very least had to be defended, if not expanded. This need for defense and expansion was now primarily the case in the Electorate of Cologne. Finally, Bucer's plan was crucially dependent on the ability of Protestants to neutralize the growing self-confidence of the pope's supporters among the Catholics and their growing influence on ecclesiastical politics.

Bucer made a heroic effort to achieve as much as possible in all the areas mentioned above. He was seriously hampered, however, by the almost complete absence of any opportunities to confront his opponents personally. He thus had to limit himself to the written and printed word, a means he used to the maximum. His enormous, almost frantic literary output barely manages to conceal the series of setbacks he had to endure. At no point did he succeed in achieving a major breakthrough. In spite of all the trouble he went to and toil he performed, despite all his efforts, Bucer essentially ended up treading water.

Already in 1542 he drafted a lengthy treatise addressed to the Dutch theologian Albert Pighius, a resolute adherent of the pope. In it he set forth the essence of true church unity and outlined a path he believed would lead to this unity.[64] Not by insisting on the primacy of the pope but rather by comprehending more clearly and completely Christ's pure teaching, as well as its ethical consequences for the individual and society, could one recover church unity, wrote Bucer, once again presenting Erasmus, the church fathers, the statements of the Bible, as well as the teachings of the great theologians of the Middle Ages, particularly Thomas Aquinas, as being in perfect agreement with one another.

Soon after, the Strasbourg preachers placed high expectations on the new bishop of their region, Erasmus of Limburg.[65] A learned person, Limburg had a sincere interest in renewing the church and was under pressure from many, including Hermann von Wied, to introduce reforms at long last. Much effort and trouble was put into arranging a meeting between the new bishop and the Strasbourg pastors, a meeting that finally came about under Bucer's leadership in Molsheim on October 18, 1542, but that unfortunately ended without any results. Even more disappointing for Bucer were his attempts to come to an understanding with Bartholomaeus Latomus, an adviser at the court of the archbishop of Trier. Bucer and Latomus had gradually begun to win each other's confidence, even though the Reformation attempt in Cologne was seriously straining relationships between both archbishoprics. The archbishop of Trier was particularly appalled at the fact that evangelical sermons were being preached and the newfangled evangelical Lord's Supper was being distributed in Andernach and Linz, towns that were politically part of the Electorate of Cologne but fell under the spiritual jurisdiction of the diocese of Trier. When Bucer went a step further and tried to convince Latomus to introduce the Reformation into the territory of Trier, their budding friendship fell apart. A bitter literary battle[66] ensued, particularly over the matter of the marks of the true church and the meaning of church traditions. Bucer vigorously rejected the charge that "we oppose the entire ancient and proven church, and that everything about us is new or was thought up recently."[67] In fact, it was the evangelicals that had authentic church tradition on their side, affirmed Bucer; they, and not the papists, preserved the pure, unadulterated church of Jesus Christ. Bucer then went on to expound his understanding of the church as a republic. As far as its head—Christ—is concerned, the church is a monarchy, asserted Bucer; but as a community of the faithful it is a republic. In it, all Christians are equal and fundamentally capable of filling any church office. All of them are called to show one another the way to God, serve their fellow human beings, and attend their bodily and spiritual needs, each one with his or her own gifts. Politically, Bucer was a resolute supporter of the estates' rights, as we have seen above, and decidedly antimonarchical. These tendencies were even more pronounced when it came to his understanding of the church. Was it not absurd, Bucer asked Latomus, to assume that one person—the pope—was more capable of caring for the church's welfare than was the entire fellowship of believers?

At the same time that Bucer was suffering these individual reversals, Protestantism also endured serious political setbacks. Bucer had drafted his response to Latomus in March 1544, during the diet of Speyer. This assembly, which lasted from February to July of that year, was entirely dominated by Charles V, who stirred up emotions against the French because of their alliance with the Ottomans. The emperor did make a significant concession to the Protestants by treating them de facto like a confession in their own right, at the same level with the Catholics. He did, however, always qualify these concessions by refusing to extend them beyond an upcoming council or the next imperial diet. He also gave supporters of the traditional church the impression that he was not going to keep his promises to the evangelicals. Prepared in this way, the imperial troops launched a war against France and won it swiftly. But Charles's real victory was a diplomatic one: the peace treaty signed on September 18, 1544, in Crépy, a village near Laon, included a secret supplementary agreement committing Francis I to rescind his alliance with the Ottomans, send delegates to the pope's council, and help Charles V coerce the Protestants into returning to the Catholic fold.

On October 9, 1544, the cathedral chapter, the clergy, and the University of Cologne all appealed to the emperor and to the pope, formally requesting protection from their archbishop. At about the same time, Elector Palatine Frederick II began approaching the Protestant camp cautiously. During these months, Bucer worked with great self-sacrifice on his *Steadfast Defense (Beständige Verantwortung)*, which aimed to refute the *Christian and Catholic Counter-Report* Gropper had written against Hermann von Wied's Reformation plan.[68] But even potential readers favorably inclined to Bucer were probably intimidated by the resulting behemoth of a volume—over six hundred printed folio-size pages! Bucer was unable to resist the temptation of assembling every single theological and ecclesiastical objection of his opponents and then proceeding to rebut each of them, one after another. The outcome was a tediously long and exhaustively comprehensive collection of information lacking the slightest persuasive quality and leaving no doubt as to the insurmountable nature of doctrinal differences separating both camps. It is no surprise that the announced publication of the Latin translation of the work was not carried out until much, much later (1613 and 1618).

As the date for the coming imperial diet in Worms—the spring of 1545—approached, Bucer once again summoned up all his energy to help bring about a free national council in place of the council that Pope Paul III had convoked at Trent. Accordingly, he tried to furnish the memorandum prepared by the Wittenberg theologians on the Reformation of the empire with a considerably sharper edge. He deemed it necessary to give much more prominence to the numerous failures and grievous faults of the German bishops, as he wrote in a letter to Philip of Hesse. On the whole, he felt the Protestants should put much more pressure on their opponents. If indeed the emperor would not be won over for this cause, Bucer remained convinced that some imperial estates could probably be persuaded. "For when truth and justice are brought to light and driven into people's hearts well," he wrote, "then they are a miraculous power. This primarily among the children of truth, of course; but they also are capable of achieving much by destroying the defiance of God's enemies."[69]

Bucer therefore concentrated most of his attention on the imperial estates and their activities. He drafted a number of pamphlets aimed at statesmen, whom he tried to convince to convene a national council. In the first of them, the *Christian Reminder* (*Christliche Erinnerung*), Bucer picked up, once again after twenty-five years, the theme of Luther's *Address to the Christian Nobility*:[70] the pope, claimed Bucer, lacks the desire and the ability to reform the church, for he stands in the antichrist's camp. God will overturn him, however. In fact, he has already begun to do so. And if only the emperor, the princes, and the imperial estates, and the court advisers and jurists as well, would finally assume their Christian responsibility to amend abuses in the church, then "we will all see and experience gradually how Christ our Lord will execute and get rid of this enemy of his, without hands or a sword, but only through the spirit of his mouth."[71]

In a second work, Bucer discussed "how easily and fittingly" (*Wie leicht und füglich*) Christians should be able to get along with one another and without the pope.[72] Let us submit ourselves to Christ, Bucer admonished his readers; let us obey and trust him alone, on the basis of Holy Scripture, and let us love our fellow humans as ourselves—then we will have met all the prerequisites for the unity of the church. All further disagreements and differences can be settled from this starting point. Bucer was by no means unaware of the political, social, moral, and religious obstacles blocking the way to such a settlement. The pope doubtless wanted to continue his rule; bishops and prelates were worried about maintaining their prestige and their income; the Protestant princes were hungry for political power and ecclesiastical property; and finally, would it not threaten the unity of Christendom if Germany went its own way? Bucer refused to accept these as legitimate excuses. He remained convinced that only if God's clear demands were met would peace and tranquillity reign within the empire and at its borders.

Bucer published a third booklet[73] repeating these thoughts in the summer of 1545. Finally, he tried once again to bring into play the agreement he had reached with Georg Witzel in 1539.[74] All these endeavors, though, were ultimately futile. Emperor Charles V made it clear to the pope that he was about to wage a war against the Protestants. Paul III promised him a handsome financial subsidy. While the diet of Worms was still in session, Charles V accepted the appeal of the Cologne chapter, clergy, and university, thus clearly taking sides in their conflict with Hermann von Wied. A request for help that the temporal estates of the Electorate of Cologne addressed to the Schmalkaldic League in December 1544 remained unanswered. Equally ineffectual was Hermann von Wied's appeal in July 1545 to a free German national council. Was there anything left for Bucer to try—particularly considering that everything pointed to the fact that the pope's council in Trent was about to become reality? On September 26, 1545, Bucer wrote to Landgrave Philip: "We see and grasp quite well what times we are living in, and whose coins alone are valid, and that all promises only hold good as long they are advantageous." Strasbourg and Hesse contemplated conducting a preventive war.[75] Doing so would protect the incipient Cologne reformation and pave the way for a national church council. According to the plan, Philip of Hesse would assume the role of the classical Roman "dictator," and Luther would legitimate this action with a memorandum drafted in Latin and in German. Alliances would then be sought with England, Denmark, and Switzerland. The mere order in which Bucer listed these ideas shows how unrealistic they were. This was no sober, clear-eyed plan based on political reality—it was an expression of despair and powerlessness.

Bucer was left with only his pen as a weapon. He used it to combat the "papists" and their council in Trent fiercely, while continuing to work in Germany for the convocation of a national council. The theologians of Louvain, complained Bucer, shrugged off the Bible, equated the church of Jesus Christ with the pope, and proclaimed a "new faith" with such grotesque matter-of-factness![76] The Lord was granting the antichrist so much power! "That is why it is urgent that we turn to the Lord in all earnestness and pray to him and beseech him incessantly to destroy this utter Anti-Christendom with the spirit of his mouth, as he has already begun to do gloriously."[77] Were not the council fathers at Trent aware, asked Bucer in a pamphlet in August 1545, that the pope and his supporters had, from a theological, legal, and especially moral standpoint, long ago forfeited the right to hold church offices?[78] The evangelicals, in contrast, wanted nothing other than "the pure and simple restoration of Christ's lordship."[79] Admittedly, Bucer was not able to influence the course of events with these arguments.

This inability to influence matters also became obvious in the Electorate of Cologne. The temporal estates still stood by the archbishop, who was determined to carry out his program of reform. But the optimistic feeling of being on the verge of bringing about something new was definitely gone. Bucer now needed to restore the confidence of Reformation supporters and was also forced to refute the trenchant theological and personal accusations that Anton Engelbrecht had launched against him in an anonymous booklet. The former suffragan bishop of Speyer and later evangelical preacher had returned to the Catholic Church and had old accounts to settle with Bucer. Bucer responded with a brief commentary on the 120th Psalm.[80] In it he made the following point: "All of us whom Christ has chosen out of the world should stick to Christ, our only savior and peacemaker. And in the midst of all the persecution that the world and all anti-Christians are inflicting upon us through their lies and wars, we find comfort in the fact that he, our peace, has overcome the world with its prince and its god, so that they can no longer harm us."[81]

About eighteen months later, in the fall of 1547, Bucer once again tried to comfort the small congregation in Bonn.[82] By then its situation had worsened dramatically: the Schmalkaldic League had been defeated; its leaders, the Saxon elector and Philip of Hesse, were prisoners of the emperor. In January 1547, the Cologne territorial estates, meeting in the choir of the cathedral of Cologne, confirmed Adolf von Schaumburg as the new archbishop of Cologne. Hermann von Wied, who had been excommunicated by Rome on April 16, 1546, formally relinquished his electoral and archiepiscopal titles and rights on February 25, 1547. "Did things really have to end in this way?" asked Bonn's stunned evangelicals in a letter to Bucer. How could God have allowed this to happen? After all, had they not submitted to his will and, led by his Spirit, purified and renewed the teaching and the life of the church? Bucer returned to theological basics in his response, asserting that, when facing God, Christian individuals and fellowships are entitled to only one thing: to confess their guilt. Only then, when men diminish and humble themselves, can God's power come into effect. "The more our physical arm declines and disintegrates, all the more powerfully and gloriously shall he, our Good Shepherd—to whom alone God has granted all power in heaven and on earth—uncover and stretch forth his divine arm to protect and to save us before the eyes of all the heathen, so that the whole world may see how our God helps us just as he has promised."[83] Bucer's theology once again took on a fundamentally eschatological outlook, as pronounced as at the time of his evangelical beginnings.

Life in Strasbourg

The early 1540s brought deep changes in Bucer's private life. On August 28, 1541, he informed Philip of Hesse that he was in the midst of reclaiming the endowment his wife had brought with her when entering the convent of Lobenfeld more than twenty years ago. Bucer needed the money to provide his adult daughters with dowries appropriate to his social standing. When he wrote to Philip once again less than three months later to thank him for his contribution of 100 *Taler*, he also disclosed the sad news that his wife and three of his children had died in the meantime.[84] As Bucer wrote to friends in Bohemia on March 29, 1542, the plague had already begun to rage in Strasbourg at the beginning of August 1541, when he returned from the diet of Regensburg.[85] The epidemic killed over three thousand people in Strasbourg in less than a year, reported Bucer; hardly a home in the city had not lost a family member. At least nine people died in Bucer's own house: two servants; a foreign boarding student; his wife, Elisabeth, on November 16; three children; and, at the turn of the year, two more infant daughters. It probably strikes us today as somewhat odd that Bucer could interpret such a tremendous personal calamity as divine punishment for his sins and the sins of his family, and that in appraising his deceased wife he dryly noted that she "relieved me, for the past twenty years, entirely of all household duties and child-care, and looked after everything in an honest and circumspect fashion."[86] Bucer was also incapable of casually recalling exactly how many children had issued from his marriage.[87] To understand this apparent lack of concern, we must consider the immense infant mortality of this period and also take into account that the notion of a mutual romantic bond between marriage partners and heightened emotional sensitivity, particularly toward infants, played less of a role at the end of the Middle Ages than in our own time. "Affective ties between husband and wife and between parents and children were not essential to the existence and stability of a marriage. All the better of course, when they ensued additionally."[88] A wife expected her husband to provide her with economic sustenance and legal protection, while a husband wanted a wife who was dependable and hardworking. It is understandable that a couple initially regarded its numerous newborns with a certain stoic aloofness, since the chances of an infant's survival were much smaller than the probability that it would perish. Relatively prompt remarriage after the death of a spouse was similarly taken for granted. In fact, Bucer did marry again, on April 16, 1542. His new wife was Wibrandis, née Rosenblatt, the widow of his colleague Wolfgang Capito, who had died on November 4, 1541, also a victim of the plague. It was Wibrandis's fourth marriage. She had survived all her previous husbands: the Basel scholar Ludwig Keller (Cellarius); the reformer of the same city, Johannes Oecolampadius; and, as mentioned, Wolfgang Capito. She would outlive Bucer as well. She died in Basel on November 1, 1564, at the age of sixty.

In 1542, Bucer moved into a new house just across the street from St. Thomas Church (today at no. 15 on the Rue St. Thomas). He had been elected dean of the collegiate chapter of St. Thomas in the course of its reorganization, which entitled him to an official residence in the deanery. It was a stately building, but not too large for Bucer's large family and his many long-term guests: Wibrandis brought four children from her previous marriages and her mother into her new marriage; she and Martin later also had a daughter of their own, Elisabeth. Of Bucer's own children, it is clear that his mentally and physically handicapped son Nathanael (1529–82) lived in the house at least part of the time. In addition, domestic servants and especially many refugees who had been forced to flee their mother countries on account of their evangelical faith were present as well. Supporting a household of this size was understandably no easy task. Still, Bucer often had to respond to accusations that joining the Reformation had benefited him financially, indeed, had turned him into a wealthy man. In 1546, Bucer declared that, on the average, his income as dean of the collegiate chapter amounted to slightly less than 80 Rhenish guldens a year, depending on the harvest.[89] In addition, he received about 17 guldens for his lectures in theology and possibly 70 guldens from boarders. This would mean that Bucer's annual income was about three times that of a former monk, who received a gulden a week from the confiscated property of the monastery—enough to set up house and support a family. But then again, the city of Strasbourg paid Jean Sturm, the rector of the local academy, 150 guldens a year for his work, and rewarded the lawyer and civic attorney Ludwig Gremp as much as 340 guldens a year for his toils. Bucer's income may have been clearly above average,[90] but it certainly was not enough to qualify his standard of living as opulent, particularly given the size of his household and the large number of guests frequenting his house.

At the same time, Bucer worked untiringly, often until late at night. The Italian humanist, theologian, and refugee from the Inquisition Peter Martyr Vermigli (1499–1562), who lived in Strasbourg for several years, wrote in 1542: "I have never seen Bucer inactive. He spends his time either preaching or looking after the order and leadership of the church. . . . After having done this kind of work all day, he devotes his nights to study and prayer. Seldom did I wake up and not find him awake as well."[91] As a result of such overwork, Bucer suffered ever increasingly from chronic bronchitis, severe indigestion, and recurring ulcers. More than anything, however, he began to age rapidly.

This waning of his physical strength and well-being was accompanied by feelings of extreme gloom. The dissonance, inner strife, and bitter divisions within the Protestant camp had depressed Bucer for quite some time already. Now fear of God's wrath weighed him down as well, wrath he believed was provoked by unsatisfactory moral conduct among the Reformation's supporters, especially in Strasbourg. "Truly, if we do not acknowledge, accept, keep and deepen God's blessed covenant better than we are doing it now, God will answer in kind and break it; he will no longer be our God and Savior but will—as he already did with his ancient people—abandon us to our enemies miserably, bringing about our temporal and eternal ruin."

These sentences can be found in Bucer's catechism of 1543.[92] At the same time, Bucer continued to promote the inner autonomy of congregations. For instance, in order to give congregational singing as central as possible a place in worship, he had a very attractive hymnal printed in 1541. But he put his greatest effort as tenaciously and unwaveringly as ever before into the enforcement of church discipline within the city. Like its predecessors, this catechism also called on the youth to submit voluntarily to the disciplinary measures of the church. Yet people in Strasbourg took offense at the fact that church discipline was apparently applied more strictly at St. Thomas—the congregation in which Bucer was a pastor, and his assistant Conrad Hubert and city council member Claus Kniebis were active as church wardens—than in the other Strasbourg parishes.[93]

What hurt Bucer more was the persistent rumor, already mentioned previously, that he was the actual author of the *Dialogus Neobuli*—in other words, an advocate of polygamy and thus a moral hypocrite of the worst sort. A satirical poem against the "scribes" that circulated clandestinely contained the following statement about Bucer:

> By character a Jew, a false Christian,
> Never at a loss for cunning artifices, a sophist,
> He's the author of this booklet.
> A hypocrite and an insincere scribe
> Who perverted God's words and works. . . .[94]

By this time, Bucer evidently had powerful enemies in Strasbourg. He himself considered the civic secretary Michael Han to be one of his most ardent opponents, who, to make matters worse, had a whole network of personal and family connections.[95] Never had the petitions and complaints that Bucer and the pastors filed with the city council to protest religious and moral abuses in Strasbourg been as ineffective as they were at this time.[96] Realizing this, Bucer urged the creation of an autonomous church "convent" made up of representatives of the pastors, their helpers, and the teachers, whose foremost function would be to deliberate over theological, ecclesiastical, and moral issues without the interference of the civil authorities. This convent was founded in June 1544. Bucer and Hedio were elected president and vice president, respectively, for life. It is not known how the city council reacted.

Not even at this time was Bucer ready to exempt the authorities from the ecclesiastical responsibilities that they bore, in his opinion. He emphasized this several times in his correspondence with the Bohemian Brethren (Unitas Fratrum) between 1540 and 1542. This small, moderate group that had issued from the Hussite movement of the fifteenth century sought contact with the Strasbourg pastors. They were impressed with Bucer as an exegete, but they admired him even more as the author of *On True Pastoral Care*, for this book contained in condensed form all that seemed necessary to them for the inward and outward edification of the church. It was only Bucer's enlistment of the services of government for carrying out church discipline that drew criticism—indeed, sharp and detailed criticism—from these Czech Christians. Did Bucer not realize, they asked, that these views glaringly contradicted the life and teachings of Jesus? And on whom would Bucer ground his conviction that "a reform and a re-edification of the Christian church could be expected by means of the sword of civil authority" especially now, in these end times?[97]

Bucer did not find it hard to correct this distortion of his theology. He praised the Bohemian Brethren for their practice of church discipline, criticized what he found to be an exaggerated regard among them for celibacy, and concluded that a government that wished to obey Christ's commandments should certainly not be prevented from "punishing those who openly harm the Christian religion and encouraging the rest to shun all evildoing."[98] Bucer remained convinced that God had instituted the representatives of political authority as watchmen over the entire Ten Commandments and therefore also over the first three, which concern religious conduct. But considerably more far-reaching in their consequences for the religious role of government were Bucer's theological understanding of divine law, the thrust of which was love for one's fellow human beings, and, closely connected with the latter, his conviction that the Holy Spirit developed and activated the order God had implanted into the fabric of all creation. This formed the background for Bucer's claim "But civic institutions and governments are no less the work of the very same Holy Spirit that rules in all ecclesiastical institutions and offices."[99] It is impossible to summarize more concisely the essence of Bucer's theology, with its double emphasis on law and Holy Spirit.

Just as intrinsic to his theological profile, however, was the fact that Bucer did not consider this view of the religious role of government to apply necessarily to all churches. He expressly allowed the Bohemian Brethren to drop the offending sections of *On True Pastoral Care* in the Czech translation that was printed in a splendid edition in 1545. Once again, Bucer gave more importance to agreement in principle than unity in issues even important to his theology. "It is manifestly evident," he wrote from Regensburg to Johannes Augusta and "all brethren in Bohemia and Moravia who preach Christ," on August 11, 1541, "that we do not agree in everything—we do agree, however, in all things elementary, fundamental and necessary to piety."[100]

Chapter Seven

Defeat

The Schmalkaldic War

Antagonisms Get Worse

The long-awaited council was solemnly inaugurated in the Tirolean city of Trent in the southernmost tip of the Holy Roman Empire on December 13, 1545. Pope Paul III had called the council, and he also kept close control over it by means of his legates Giovanni del Monte, Marcello Cervini, and Reginald Pole. No Protestants were present. Only after solving difficult preliminary problems could actual theological discussions begin on February 7, 1546—mostly discussions over the significance of the Bible and church tradition as well as over their relationship to one another. Ten days later, on February 18, 1546, Luther passed away in Eisleben, the city of his birth.

Seen together, both events symbolize the end of an era. Protestantism was no longer the decisive theological and religious power; the Catholic Church assumed a new vigor, self-assertiveness, and clear contours of its own. The antagonism between both camps grew accordingly. The theological and political altercations between them became more uncompromising, ruder, and harsher. Reconciliation and the settlement of differences counted less and less. The new priorities were to confront opponents, to persevere doggedly in the struggle against them, and, if possible, to defeat them.

Upon hearing of Luther's death, Bucer wrote the following to Albert Hardenberg, his former companion-in-arms during the failed Cologne reformation attempt: "I know how many people hate Luther. And yet the fact remains: God loved him very much and never gave us a holier and more effective instrument of the Gospel. Luther had shortcomings, in fact serious ones. But God bore them and put up with them, never granting another mortal a mightier spirit and such divine power to proclaim His Son and strike down the Antichrist. If God so accepted him and drew him near to Himself in spite of his being a sinner—a sinner, of course, who abhorred evil like no other—who am I, a wretched servant and miserable sinner who shows so little zeal in pursuing justice, to reject him and turn him down on account of his failings, which we, of course, should not condone? Do we not often ask others to tolerate even greater failings in ourselves?"[1] Few obituaries written in the immediate aftermath of Luther's death approach this conciseness and profundity. The nobility of feeling manifest in this appraisal is all the more noteworthy considering how harsh and unjust Luther had often been to Bucer.

The incipient Council of Trent elicited an entirely different response from Bucer, namely, one of sharp condemnation. In his two books *On the True and False Administration of the Lord's Supper* (*De vera et falsa caenae dominicae*),[2] he asked the theologians assembled in Trent whether they were not aware that self-righteousness, immorality, and crude ignorance of the fundamentals of Christian doctrine reigned in their midst—and not the Holy Spirit to which they laid claim. How could the true church of Jesus Christ be in Trent if the council simply disregarded Jesus' and the Bible's clear teachings on the cup for the laity in the Lord's Supper and refused to correct the false understanding of this sacrament as a sacrifice— with no other argument than the supposed right of the church and the pope to do so? This attitude on the part of the council outraged Bucer. The actual course of deliberations in Trent confirmed his worst fears. In the early summer of 1546 he edited *Two Decrees of the Council of Trent* (*Zwei Decret des Trientischen Concili*)[3] with an accompanying commentary. These were the decrees of April 8, 1546, that promulgated dogmas on the authentic canon and the significance of the Bible, the tradition of the church, and their relationship to one another. Bucer wrote: "There you have it, my dear Christians: the lovely, free, Christian Council of Trent and its fruits—namely, that from now on you may neither read the Holy Scriptures in the original nor in translations; that no one may present it and explain it to you in a way that does not ratify the Pope's most abominable abominations, these being his assumption that he is a lord over divine Scripture, over the laws, peoples and goods of the entire world, that he has all rights in the shrine of his heart, that his entire idolatry constitutes the only true worship of God as well as a means—that, additionally, must be bought from him—to get to heaven; thus are souls surrendered to the depths of hell, and bodies and goods are given to infamy and the persecution of God. Lord Jesus, resist and ward off your enemy! And preserve us in your saving kingdom! Amen."[4]

Bucer was already back in Strasbourg by the time he had written the lines above. He had spent the three-month period from December 1545 to the middle of March 1546 in Regensburg, taking part in one last religious colloquium convoked by the emperor prior to the imperial diet that would begin on June 5.[5] It was clear from the very beginning that no settlement would be reached. Accordingly, the Catholic representatives refused to go beyond the agreement already reached in the same city five years before. Bucer's antagonist at Regensburg, the imperial court theologian Pedro Malvenda from Spain, went one step further and asserted that it was only up to the council meeting in Trent to take decisions on points of doctrinal disagreement. The Protestant representatives, on their part, demanded written records, certified by notaries, of the statements of all parties, since it was clear they were dealing not with people of goodwill but rather with outright adversaries. The debate soon centered on the topic of justification. Bucer later published the documents that emerged from this discussion.[6] Bucer appraised the situation quite soberly: "We may be able to have a disputation with these opponents and defend Christ's truth against their fallacies. However, we cannot have a Christian and friendly conversation with them, because they are neither friends nor Christians, and besides they condemn us publicly as their worst enemies and as unchristians."[7]

These being the circumstances, was one even justified in taking part in such a colloquy in the first place? Bucer certainly thought so. Once again, he contemplated the laborious and often unnerving negotiations in Regensburg in February 1546 from a European perspective. The pope's supporters were looking for arguments that would justify their going ahead in Trent without—and against—the Protestants, and the emperor was eager for public evidence that the Protestants were unwilling to come to any real agreement. Bucer worked against these interests loudly and resolutely, not only through personal letters but also by means of a small treatise in which he described the course of this Regensburg colloquy. In all of these he asserted unmistakably that the evangelicals had done all they could to reach an accord, but the Catholics had been unwilling. Bucer's success is demonstrated by the fact that his *Report* (*Bericht*) went through six printings in the course of one year.[8]

The hostility with which both confessional camps now confronted each other was made gruesomely evident when Alfonso Díaz arranged for the murder of his brother Juan, a convert to Protestantism, in Neuburg on the Danube. Bucer had last spoken with Juan Díaz on March 25. Two days later the Spanish evangelical was killed by an assassin's hatchet. Juan's brother, traveling at the time in the entourage of Emperor Charles V, had hired the murderer. Understandably, Bucer perceived this as further proof for the unfathomable depravity and wickedness of the papists, as well as an admonition on fellow evangelicals to follow the suffering Christ and carry his cross.[9]

Resort to Arms

The Regensburg diet began its sessions on June 5, 1546, as we mentioned above. There were no members of the Schmalkaldic League present. The atmosphere at the diet was eerie, almost unreal. Parties were being celebrated, royal weddings held, and yet almost everybody knew that a war was imminent—a terrible and merciless war that would pit the emperor and his allies against the Protestants. At the same time, Emperor Charles V was scoring one victory after another on the diplomatic front. He concluded a treaty with Bavaria on June 7 and reached an agreement with Duke Moritz of Albertine Saxony on June 18, promising him the affluent bishoprics of Magdeburg and Halberstadt as protectorates in exchange for military assistance in attacking Elector John Frederick of Ernestine Saxony, Moritz's own cousin. An auxiliary army formed by the pope set out for Germany on July 4, richly endowed with letters of indulgence and apostolic blessings. The Schmalkaldic League mobilized its own troops on the very same day.

The Protestants proved incapable of exploiting their initial victories. Schertlin von Burtenbach managed to conquer the southern city of Füssen on July 10. Soon after, he occupied the Ehrenberg mountain pass, the gateway to Tirol. Instead of pushing forward to fend off the approaching papal forces and break up the council in nearby Trent, the army retreated at the request of the southern German cities, Ulm in particular, who demanded protection against Charles V. He, however, had practically no troops at his disposal and was sojourning in Regensburg, where he signed the decree placing the Saxon elector and the Hessian Landgrave under the imperial ban on account of breach of the peace and rebellion against the emperor.

The coming weeks were taken up with large-scale army movements on both sides of the Danube. But while the number of the emperor's troops increased continually, first through reinforcements from Italy, then from the Spanish Low Countries, the number of Schmalkaldic troops remained unchanged. What proved ultimately decisive, though, was Duke Moritz's attack on his cousin's territory on October 30. He had demanded—and obtained—from Charles V the title "Saxon Elector" as well as the electoral domains including Wittenberg in exchange for this action. Now, in the middle of November, Elector John Frederick set out with the greater part of the Schmalkaldic army to defend his terrritory. The remaining Protestant army fell apart in the coming months. This enabled Charles V to move effortlessly through southern Germany as a victor in the spring of 1547. Strasbourg surrendered on March 21. Jacob Sturm rendered homage to the emperor in Nördlingen, falling prostrate at his feet in symbolic submission. The once proud Alsatian imperial city officially broke its ties with the Schmalkaldic League and gave Charles V renewed assurances of its loyalty. As a penalty, Strasbourg had to hand over all its cannon and pay the stately sum of 30,000 Rhenish guldens.

This first defeat of the Schmalkaldic League was soon followed by the second and definitive one. On the morning of April 24, 1547, the troops of the emperor crossed the Elbe at Mühlberg, hardly encountering any resistance. Fully concentrated on his worship service, and equally preoccupied with the sumptuous meal that would follow it, Elector John Frederick had given little attention to protecting his encampment. As a consequence, his army was soundly defeated at the Lochau heath, and by the end of the day he had become Charles V's prisoner. During all of this, Philip of Hesse brooded in Kassel, crippled by indecision. He finally surrendered to Charles V on June 19 in Halle on the river Saale and was promptly arrested. For all appearances, the Habsburg emperor had become the uncontested ruler of Germany.

Christian Fellowship

Two theological convictions began crystallizing in Bucer's reflections and statements already during the Schmalkaldic war, and assumed concrete forms especially after the League's disastrous defeat. The first view amounted to a theological interpretation of recent events. It explained the Protestants' failures and defeats as a punishment that God had inflicted on them because of their ingratitude toward God's revealed truth, their absence of faith, and, in particular, their lacking the ethical fruits of faith, that is to say, a new life of austere discipline and moral integrity.[10] Bucer asserted that God would continue to smite and humiliate the Protestants— and this also meant the city of Strasbourg and its citizens—if they did not repent, turn to God, and truly mend their ways. Bucer thus passionately and devotedly championed a point of view one encounters in large portions of the Old Testament and that is usually described as the Deuteronomic theology of history: Whenever Israel did not obey God, God punished it with domestic and international crises. But if Israel repented, turned once again to God's commandments and ordinances, and did its utmost to obey these, it was blessed accordingly with internal and external fortune and success. Bucer was convinced of the truth of this last statement. For if the Protestants, especially in Strasbourg, would constitute a true Christian fellowship in terms of their faith, and particularly in terms of the life they were leading, then they could expect the biblical promise to hold true that God "would turn away his harsh wrath from the entire people and instead impart his grace and his blessings in a wonderful way."[11]

The second viewpoint that gained an increasingly strong foothold in Bucer's mind concerned the responsibility of individual Christians. Convincing the people to repent and to convert was neither the sole responsibility of government nor the exclusive duty of the pastors. It was rather the task of the entire Christian fellowship, and for Bucer this included the laity in particular. Of course, this was no new emphasis on Bucer's part. He had already been fighting for this for some twenty years, as he wrote in November 1547.[12] But the vehemence with which Bucer made this demand and, more important, the actual steps he took to see it fulfilled increased immensely in the previous months.

At the beginning of April 1547, Bucer, along with his colleagues Matthew Zell, Paul Fagius, and Johannes Marbach, submitted the major treatise *Regarding the Abolishment of Crude Vices and the Establishment of Good Order and Discipline* (*Wegen Abschaffung grober Laster und Aufrichtung guter Ordnung und Disziplin*)[13] to the city council. This work proves how obviously necessary it was for the Strasbourg reformer to take a two-pronged approach: civil authorities were to issue public mandates enforcing discipline and morality on the one hand, and individual congregations were to carry out practical systems of penance and church discipline on the other.[14] Some steps were taken even before all this began. For example, with the onset of the Schmalkaldic War, the pastors began holding "days of repentance" once a month; soon after, they introduced weekly "repentance sermons," which were preached every Tuesday in the cathedral. But there were also setbacks: on January 6, 1546, the city council rejected the pastors' formal request that they be allowed to convoke or summon their parishioners in order to question them on their faith and their moral conduct. That is the task of church wardens, replied the council—even though it was an open secret that this institution simply did not function, among other reasons because of the councilmen's own misgivings! To justify his and his colleagues' measures, Bucer then called attention to the danger of Anabaptists and other sectarians infiltrating the congregations.[15] By the time the Strasbourg city council debated this topic once again, about a year later, small groups had arisen in the parishes of St. Thomas and Young St. Peter, consisting of church members who discussed their faith with one another and taught, admonished, and comforted one another. They also submitted to a voluntary church discipline and spoke of themselves as a *christliche Gemeinschaft*, a Christian fellowship.[16]

The treatise *Regarding the Abolishment of Crude Vices* presented its arguments against this backdrop. It primarily emphasized the duties and responsibilities of civil authorities in the light of the requirements God makes on his people, and it mercilessly condemned the resounding failure of the city's inhabitants to fulfill the Ten Commandments. It was not a matter of proclaiming lofty aims and issuing new, stricter ordinances, wrote Bucer. Much more important was to finally enforce the laws already existing. That would amount to "a true Christian Reformation!"[17] At the same time, the pastors enlisted the council's support in allowing congregations the freedom to organize themselves independently and establish their own structures. For how could one be Christian other than by a personal decision and commitment? It was an established fact that the latter were necessary in order to become the citizen of a city: "The right to become a member in an artisan guild is one that one must desire personally; one can only receive it personally and it requires promising obedience to the guild; the names of all the members are recorded individually; and at appointed times, the guild members come together to hear their articles and ordinances and to swear an oath by them. They also have their own courts and their own penalties."[18] A life in covenant with God could not possibly be had for less! It was not enough for the civil authorities to enforce morality on the entire population under threat of punishment. Convinced Christians had to begin setting up their own autonomous congregational structures as well, including a system of voluntary church discipline. The fact that this had not happened yet constituted in Bucer's opinion "the worst flaw and defect" of the Strasbourg church. Because of this, pastoral care—which in Bucer's opinion also represented an effort to educate the entire people—was prevented from "bringing all the baptized, young as well as old, to true communion with, and obedience to Jesus Christ."[19]

The council responded positively to the requests that the authorities impose harsher punishments. The council members were also apparently influenced by the traditional view that misfortune and military defeat were divine punishments that one could alleviate or even avert through contrition and penitence. Old disciplinary mandates were once again enforced, and soon after the city even issued a new disciplinary ordinance. On January 25, 1548, after many postponements and interruptions, it was finally approved by the council, printed thereafter, and read out loud in the assembly halls of the guilds.

The council, however, responded negatively to the pastors' insistence that the church be granted more autonomy and the congregations especially have the freedom to organize themselves anew. Initially, the council simply refused to give its consent to these plans. Then, on October 31, 1547, it forbade the pastors to take any measures leading to the establishment of a congregational church discipline. But the parishes of St. Thomas and Young St. Peter, and later St. William and St. Nicholas as well, had already come a long way in developing such disciplinary structures and organizing "Christian fellowships." A document of August 1547 illustrates well how these groups understood themselves.[20] This text describes the life of the Christian as one in which everyone must assume individual responsibility for learning the teachings of the church and following Christ in discipleship. Christians need help, admonishment, discernment, and warning in both areas—they thus need a fellowship of like-minded, equally committed fellow Christians. At the same time, the text dispels notions that this fellowship is a particularly "pious" affair. It is not a matter of religious top performance but of living a Christian life in accordance with the Ten Commandments and enforcing church discipline upon this foundation—and of committing oneself voluntarily to this form of life by entering one's name into a book and notifying the ecclesiastical and political representatives of the respective parish. The central role of civil government was therefore to be left untouched. But Bucer certainly wanted to deal the moral and religious abuses in the city a mighty blow by means of these *christliche Gemeinschaften*. They were to function as crystallization points, aiming at winning over no less than the entire population—including the city's rulers.

Strasbourg's ruling class, however, was certainly not going to tolerate an encroachment on its political authority, which, after all, also extended over the church. The council therefore issued a renewed order on November 7, 1547, for the *christliche Gemeinschaften* to cease their activities. This measure unleashed a flurry of oral and written negotiations on the part of Bucer, Fagius, and their associates during the rest of the month of November, attempting, on the one hand, to win over the council after all for this project and seeking, on the other, to heal the division that this issue had caused among the city's pastors.

Bucer played an important role, but not the decisive one, in all of this. Paul Fagius, pastor of Young St. Peter and professor of Hebrew and Old Testament at the Strasbourg academy, became the leading figure of this initiative.[21] He had already invested much effort into the organization of a system of church discipline during his ministry in the southern German city of Isny from 1537 to 1542.[22] In Strasbourg, Fagius continued advocating the same cause with unfading enthusiasm. It is a sign of Bucer's nobility of character and pliancy of disposition that he was willing to learn from and get swept away by his younger colleague, and later even placed his own name and disputational ability at Fagius's disposal, thus assuming the risk for the latter's resoluteness and intrepid rush forward.

On November 9, 1547, Bucer, Fagius, and their colleagues Johannes Lenglin and Johannes Marbach submitted a *Short Report* (*Kurzer Bericht*) to the council dealing with the essence and purpose of a Christian fellowship in a fundamental and exhaustive way.[23] Every Christian, they asserted, lives in communion with Christ and therefore also in communion with other Christians, for whose salvation and welfare each Christian should care and provide. Hence, a sense of personal responsibility and the possibility of fulfilling this responsibility in the sphere of the fellowship are essential marks of the church. Or, stated more precisely, they are the ecclesiastical offices through whose service the church lives. They went on to place extraordinary emphasis on the necessary diversity of these church offices. Preachers and carers of souls cannot do everything; they need people to assist them in teaching, admonishing, and disciplining. Only in passing is it mentioned that these "ministers of pastoral care" (*Seelsorgediener*) are to be elected from among the members of the Christian fellowship. The authors of the memorandum go into greater detail when describing the work of these ministers, which is to teach and admonish according to the Ten Commandments. They also explained the procedure for receiving new voluntary members into these fellowships, a procedure that even included a special ceremony for women. Greatest importance was attached to determining how church discipline as described in Matthew 18 should be exercised concretely. Much tact and sensitivity are necessary in all of this, asserted the authors: "At all times and in all things we must consider how we can win over people's hearts and awaken true acknowledgment of, and repentance for sins."[24]

There can be no doubt that this statement was aimed at assuaging governmental mistrust over an autonomous ecclesiastical order of discipline. In fact, the submitted memorandum can be characterized on the whole as an attempt to enlist the authorities' sympathy and support. The authors reassured the council that neither it nor its organs would be excluded or passed over. Altogether, "the honorable council" would "consistently retain the upper hand. It can also readily oppose whatever damages or is detrimental to its rule."[25] Could the civil authorities ultimately oppose efforts to improve piety? Did not government have a special interest in supporting people who shared this concern? And as far as the accusation that this church discipline erected a new papacy was concerned, it was manifestly evident to all that the pope and antichrist "had little by little expelled and driven out laypeople from all church tasks and institutions."[26]

Strasbourg's rulers, however, did not allow themselves to be convinced. Worse yet: some pastoral colleagues began expressing their criticism. Bucer and his friends did their very best to convince Zell, Hedio, Nigri, and Steinlin of the need to proceed in this way. Interestingly enough, it was the companions of long standing who proved to be particularly hesitant. This was probably due not only to disagreement over the issues themselves but to personal disillusionment as well. Theobald Nigri, for instance, wrote: "If only 'the Pillars' had spent more time in the past with actual church work than with so many other things!"[27] Others disliked the way in which these fellowships were being created: by inviting all the citizens of a certain neighborhood to their respective parish church "in the name of our Lord Jesus Christ—and of the church wardens" (as it was expressed in some parishes, in the hope of getting the wardens to finally cooperate).[28]

Finally, many considered it too risky to take action without the approval, perhaps even against the will, of the civil authorities. This is what Caspar Hedio felt when he concluded: "The ship may sail more slowly if one proceeds in consonance with the authorities as well as with the knowledge, the agreement, and the counsel of the church wardens appointed by the authorities, but at least it sails more safely. Besides, those who have an aversion to certain pastors are then less likely to thwart the work that needs to get done."[29]

These tensions did not lead to an open quarrel between the Strasbourg pastors. One of the main reasons for this was that all of them, especially Bucer, were strictly opposed to any plans to establish an autonomous church disciplinary ordinance that included ban and excommunication by the city council. Bucer's reflections on this issue reached a mature form in his work *On the Church's Defects and Failings* (*Von der kirchen mengel vnd fähl*), which was probably written at this time.[30] Bucer begins by differentiating between temporal and spiritual rule, that is, state and church power. It was not his intention to separate them in an absolute way, but rather to ensure "that temporal authority limits itself to its sphere and does not arrogate to itself more power than God granted and entrusted to it, in other words, that it does not seek to interfere with the matters of the church."[31] After drawing this clear boundary, Bucer closely examined the activities of the church such as preaching, administering the sacraments, granting absolution, banning and excommunicating, as well as the church's external ordinances and ceremonies. To be sure, much had been reached and significant improvements had taken place everywhere since the introduction of the Reformation; however, there had been no authentic building of congregations in Strasbourg. And now it was a matter of carrying through with this.

Bucer developed a model that called for the voluntary coming together of those who took their Christian faith seriously and aimed toward winning over the entire city population little by little. The members of each "Christian fellowship" (*christliche Gemeinschaft*) were to select representatives from each parish who would work together with the pastors and the church wardens, helping them counsel, teach, and supervise. In this way, Bucer was apparently hoping to prevent the smaller fellowship circles from becoming estranged and drifting away from the larger, more impersonal congregations to which they belonged. There was no doubt for Bucer, however, that it was the small groups that bore the greatest importance; it was they who would ultimately set the tone of and determine the greater church. In practical terms, this implied that all church work boiled down to two things: first of all, inviting people to join these fellowships; second, and as a consequence of the first, neglecting those Christians who were simply not willing "to commit themselves to the right, true obedience of the church."[32] Bucer recognized this as a problem, but he considered it an insignificant one. And he certainly did not give credence to the dire claims of those who warned that these plans represented the victory of a new popery or of Anabaptist ideas. "We are far from excommunicating and banning. All we want is to fulfill our duty and obligation as ministers of the church so that all those who want to be true Christians can finally commit themselves to true church obedience, openly and voluntarily confessing what they think of the Gospel that we have been preaching to them for such a long time by the grace of Christ."[33]

Bucer's plans for Strasbourg did not come true. Things took an even crueler turn for him: on December 24, 1547, the council refused definitively to allow him to publish his book *On the Fellowship of Churches (Von gemeinschaft der kirchen)*. The fight over the Interim was approaching its climax and drowning out all other matters, including the conflict over the Christian fellowships. This latter issue was far from resolved, however.

The Interim

The Political Situation

Parallel to these events, the imperial diet of Augsburg solemnly initiated its sessions on September 1, 1547. It was clearly dominated by the victorious Charles V, who for the very first time not only had carte blanche to do whatever he wished in Germany but also was not pressed by any political problems in the broader European arena.[34] Henry VIII of England had died on January 28, 1547, and Charles's other major enemy, Francis I of France, had passed away on March 31. In June of the same year, Charles concluded a five-year armistice with the Ottoman sultan Suleiman the Magnificent.

Charles V was eager finally to fulfill his political goals of reorganizing the German empire and settling the religious schism. He was sober enough regarding his first objective not to aim toward a centralized government of the kind he exercised in Spain. Yet his proposal to rule the empire by means of a robust federation subject to his command was foiled by the strong resistance put up especially by Bavaria. Charles had to content himself with curtailing a few rights of the imperial estates: from now on, the imperial chamber court would be directly subordinate to the emperor, and only he would be entitled to impose the imperial ban.

The second issue to be resolved, the confessional division of the empire, was significantly more complicated. Paradoxically, the more Charles V triumphed over the Schmalkaldic League, the more he became estranged from the pope. Among other reasons, it was fear of becoming too dependent on the German emperor that led the Council of Trent to push on with its proclamation of the Roman Catholic teachings on original sin and on justification as dogmas in June 1546 and January 1547, respectively. At the same time, the pope withdrew his supporting army from Germany. On March 3, 1547, the council issued the decree on the sacraments, thus dogmatizing traditional Roman Catholic teaching that retained all seven sacraments. On March 11, the council relocated from Trent to Bologna in the Church States, thus shifting from imperial to papal territory. Charles V was now deprived of any possibility of directly influencing the settlement of the religious question.

But Charles was forced to undertake something in this issue if he entertained any hopes of settling the confessional division of the German empire. It was more than improbable that the Protestants would voluntarily submit to the decrees of Trent. He therefore needed to find a theological formula that did justice to evangelical concerns without distancing itself too much from normative Catholic doctrine as defined so narrowly in Trent. It remains to be seen whether Charles V actually intended to make his "provisional settlement" (thus the name Interim) binding for both Protestants and Catholics. In any case, he would soon learn that the inmost core of Catholic supporters, who by now had become extremely vigorous and self-confident, flatly rejected the emperor's procedure.

Charles was incapable of reaching a political deal with this extreme group that demanded an unconditional re-Catholicization of the German empire. There were two other options at his disposal. Strasbourg's magistrate and senior statesman Jacob Sturm not only formulated the first of these options but also represented it with incredible skill, obstinacy, and flexibility, successfully combining unwavering resoluteness with supple evasiveness. In the course of only a few months, the militarily defeated Sturm proved himself to be an opponent almost equal to the victorious emperor, and certainly more influential than his fellow citizen and old comrade-in-arms Martin Bucer. Sturm called for letting theological differences simply be for the time being, entrusting their settlement to a future German national council in which both parties could debate with one another openly and on equal footing. What the two confessions needed to do first was find a means of peaceful political coexistence in the empire.

The emperor, though, was not willing to go down the path outlined by Sturm. Instead, he opted for the concept of Michael Helding, suffragan bishop of Mainz, who believed that a religious and theological settlement should take precedence. Many details of the Interim text that Helding coauthored are no longer accessible. The other author was the impressive humanist, scholar, and bishop Julius Pflug. The text was revised a number of times, and the Protestant theologian Johannes Agricola from Brandenburg went over it as well. The final document, completed by the end of February 1548, essentially represented a traditional Catholic response to the controversial theological questions of the day in the form of twenty-six articles. While much of it was kept deliberately vague, it was all the more evident in the discussion of rites and ceremonies that the text was fundamentally oriented toward the Catholic side. It would therefore require cunning and force to impose the Interim on Germany. The force would be provided by Spanish troops lingering in Germany, especially in its southern regions, which were now completely vulnerable to the emperor's attacks. It was more opportunism than cunning that led the electors of Brandenburg and the Palatinate to comply with Charles V's wishes: after already having secretly agreed to the Interim on March 15, 1548, they now submitted this text to the emperor as a Protestant proposal. To maintain credibility, they needed the consent of a convincing public figure. And that person was Martin Bucer—who also happened to have connections with the Brandenburg elector.[35]

In Augsburg

Bucer departed from Strasbourg on January 27, 1548—not before having made his last will and testament[36]—and headed for Ulm. It had been Sturm's wish that he stand ready to come to Augsburg, some fifty miles away, in case he was needed for consultations. Bucer remained in Ulm for seven weeks, staying in close touch with Bernhard Besserer, the grand old man of this imperial city who provided Bucer with the latest news and much more. On March 30, Bucer arrived in Augsburg. He had come on his own initiative, without any political guarantees. The elector of Brandenburg accommodated him in his quarters—and immediately took measures preventing Bucer from getting in touch with anybody else, hoping obviously to wring an endorsement of the Interim from the Strasbourg reformer. At the same time, Bucer was told to imagine the tremendous ascendancy the gospel would gain, not only in the Catholic territories of the empire but in France, Italy, England, Denmark, Hungary, and Poland as well, should the Interim be ratified. Much emphasis was placed on the claim that the Interim text was a formula for religious unity to which all parties could consent.

Initially, Bucer felt fairly positive about the Interim.[37] He read its theological statements against the background of the religious colloquies of recent years in which he had invested so much time and energy. Of course, he saw the need for making big changes and improvements in the text. There were, however, sections that could be interpreted in a Protestant way. One thing that Bucer did find troubling was the fact that the Interim called for all Catholic rites and ceremonies to be reintroduced. He knew how much power such external patterns could exert on people, and not just on the simple-minded. Yet he was willing to give his consent to the project in order to finally make some progress along the long path toward church unity. Bucer therefore declared on April 2 that he was willing to ratify the text of the Interim, but could do so only with significant reservations. Furthermore, this was only his personal opinion. And the important thing anyhow was to get as many experts as possible from both sides together to discuss this draft. Bucer stuck to essentially this position during the entire month of April 1548. Unlike Sturm, he had not yet realized that the time for religious colloquies had passed.

The electors of the Palatinate and of Brandenburg both heard what they wanted to hear and informed the emperor accordingly. This made them all the more disappointed and angry when Bucer began to expound his fundamental misgivings and his criticism in greater detail. The emperor was absolutely insistent on obtaining Bucer's signature under the Interim. On April 10, however, Bucer refused to sign his name under the official minutes of the previous day's discussions. He would do his utmost to attain church union, wrote Bucer to the electors, but signing this document could only damage that greater project. "For there is very much I am able to tolerate and to do with a good conscience in these matters that I would not dare advise others to tolerate or to do who do not feel the same way."[38] And what good would it have been to sign the document if once again, as in 1541 during—and especially after—the Regensburg colloquy, his fellow Protestants would pounce upon him? For the time being, Bucer could not offer more than his express readiness to work intensely toward church unity. "And if I were to give more, I would only make my own efforts to help the church towards unity entirely useless."[39]

Bucer was firmly convinced of this. But questions remained. After all, the kind of church unity that Bucer had in mind had long ceased to be an option. On April 13 he was placed under house arrest in the quarters of the elector of Brandenburg, and on April 17, at the orders of the emperor, he was put in close confinement.[40] Finally, on April 20, Bucer signed the Interim. He was freed, and he left Augsburg the very same day. By April 25 he was back in Strasbourg.

Resistance

The Interim was published on May 15, 1548, going into effect only for Protestants, as had been explicitly noted. Accordingly, the disappointment within the Protestant camp was great. On May 26, 1548, the text, which had become known in Strasbourg only a day earlier, was read to the imperial diet. The Strasbourg city representatives, Jacob Sturm and Hans von Odratzheim, who were still in Augsburg, immediately requested that a formal theological opinion against the Interim be drafted.[41] Bucer, the statement's main author, found himself now in a completely new situation. It was no longer a matter of two parties working together to reestablish church unity but rather to oppose the dictate of a single camp that, to make matters worse, was dominated by the papists. The only possible response was to unashamedly confess one's allegiance to evangelical truth. Bucer also took the opportunity once again to attack the reestablishment of Catholic ceremonies and rites sharply.

A shorter version of Bucer's statement, boiled down to a call to conversion and repentance as well as to perseverance in the central articles of the Christian faith, which Bucer went on to list, was proclaimed out loud from all Strasbourg pulpits on June 3. It did not take long, however, for an anonymous counterstatement, *Consideration and Reminder of the Sermons* (*Bedenken und Erinnerung auf die Predigten*), to begin circulating, probably in handwritten form. It was well received, particularly among the ruling elite. The stage was thus set for a conflict that would become virulent in the following weeks.

The anonymous author of the *Consideration*—Bucer labeled him an Epicurean—accused the Strasbourg preachers of being animated by the same irresponsible spirit as the Münster Anabaptists of yore. Just like those radicals, the Strasbourg pastors were teaching fanatical and absolute obedience to the Word of God alone, even if it meant noncompliance with the government's commands. The pastors were also leading the people to believe that God would certainly not let them down if they only trusted in God. Such reasoning would lead the city to ruin, argued the *Consideration*. Bucer hastened to demonstrate the fundamental theological difference between what the local pastors and what the Münster Anabaptists had preached. He did so in a *Concise Summary of Christian Doctrine and Religion* (*Ein Summarischer vergriff der Christlichen Lehre und Religion*), published on July 2, 1548, which included a shortened version of his admonition of June 3 as well an exposition of evangelical teaching in twenty-nine articles. Emperor Charles V ordered all copies of the book to be destroyed.[42] Bucer may have defended and pled the cause of the Protestant faith with unrivaled courage in this vernacular treatise, but he was essentially unable to convince his opponents that he was not a religious fanatic about to plunge the city into a disaster.

This was partly because Bucer insisted on making statements that could be misinterpreted in this way, gruffly claiming that the people of Strasbourg had sinned and had therefore been punished by God with military defeat. Help and salvation could result only from repentance and conversion. Any form of acquiescence to the Interim meant continuing to forsake God and would consequently bring about even more punishment and calamities. Over and over again Bucer demanded of the people of Strasbourg that they place their trust in no one but God and God's Word. "Why worry about what may befall us externally? One cannot fare badly when obeying God, for all misfortune arises from placing our own human thoughts and interests before God's Word and counsel or from our mixing the two."[43] That was the epitome of Bucer's theological memorandum for the council; he and Fagius said much the same in the sermons they preached during these months.

A climate of unrest and growing tension ensued, exploding into an open civic crisis in August 1548, as not only wealthy merchants but even members of the council began renouncing their citizenship and leaving town in wagons jam-packed with their entire possessions. The situation had become, in fact, quite threatening. The incorporation of the Interim into the closing decree of the imperial diet of June 30 had given it the status of imperial law. On August 6, Charles V "outlawed" Constance, imposing the imperial ban on it after it had refused to implement the law. Three days later he rejected making any concessions to Strasbourg, allowing the city only one more month to decide. He approached the city once again, however, as early as August 24, since nothing had taken place. In desperation, the magistrates asked the *Schöffen* (leading guild officials) whether the council should not begin negotations with the bishop over the appropriate way of introducing the Interim. On August 27, while 132 *Schöffen* gave their consent, 134 of them wished to allow the entire citizenry to vote on this issue. Doubtless such an action would have split the city irreparably—and caused the downfall of the ruling council. The magistrates tried frantically to assuage boiling tempers and, reminding the *Schöffen* that there was no legal basis for submitting the question to a general referendum, called on these three hundred guild representatives to vote once again on August 30, 1548. This time 204 *Schöffen* voted in favor of the council's policy, only four against. This was a decisive defeat for Bucer— and a major success for the politics of Jacob Sturm.

Bucer's unceasing insistence on an autonomous system of church discipline had long earned him the dislike of the magistrates; his reputation in the council was demolished even more thoroughly by his efforts to set up "Christian fellowships," as we saw previously. It did not help Bucer's popularity in merchant circles when he insulted the one hundred or so traders fleeing Strasbourg to save their goods and commercial relationships from imperial outlawry, calling them shirkers of social duty and unpatriotic servants of mammon. To be sure, they were in favor of peace and conciliation. But that is also what, besides the *Schöffen*, countless other craftsmen and simple people also wished. Perhaps the term *honorable peace* describes most accurately what rich and poor alike sought at this point. They wanted to rescue the city's liberties and rights—which certainly included those of their own social class—and preserve religion, in other words, the faith of the Reformation. The more areas of life the city of Strasbourg covered in every respect, that is, the more civic community and ecclesiastical community became co-extensive, the more sense the sermons calling for only penance and military resistance made. These were also the circles in which the Christian fellowships had their roots. And we hear an echo of this piety when, during the consultation of the *Schöffen*, the "Gardener" and former member of the Council of Fifteen, Lorenz Graff, proclaims: "Each must transform his own life and the sins must be punished, just as in Nineveh— otherwise all is in vain."[44]

But even these groups must have begun getting their doubts when they heard Bucer declare after October 15, 1548—when Constance surren- dered to the emperor, losing all its rights and privileges as an imperial free city—that all this could and should not lead Strasbourg to waver in its unconditional rejection of the Interim. "And even if the entire world would abandon Christ, not a single person abandons Him without being eternally damned."[45] Bucer stuck to this position stubbornly and uncompromisingly in the coming months. Under no circumstances would he give his consent to the plan negotiated mainly by Jacob Sturm, calling for the cathedral and the churches of Old St. Peter and Young St. Peter to be handed over to the Catholics, with Protestant worship services continuing to be held in the remaining parish churches. Negotiations were wrong, asserted Bucer, call- ing instead for days of penance and prayer to be imposed on the entire city. In this way, Strasbourg would finally give God due glory and rightly do away with all misled efforts at reaching a compromise. Bucer could still count on a small core of preachers, among them Fagius and Marbach, who supported his position courageously and resolutely. They even refused to tone down their bitter attacks on the Interim after the city began discus- sions with the bishop in January 1549 on the possible terms under which a compromise could be reached. Bucer flatly rejected the arguments that the council was now wielding and that Sturm had probably formulated, such as that one would never run out of areas in which one could morally improve the people of Strasbourg, so that ecclesiastical politics (as pursued by Bucer) could be laid aside, for the time being at least; or that congrega- tions were more than well informed about the imperfections of the papacy and the errors of the Interim. Bucer replied by arguing that the compro- mise proposed by the magistrates constituted a theologically and therefore politically extremely questionable means of safeguarding the civic and reli- gious liberties of the city. "On the other hand, we do know from all of Holy Scripture that the means I just mentioned—collective penance, conversion and prayer—serve those goals with certainty."[46]

Later, in a letter written from his English exile, Bucer would bitterly accuse his one-time companion and now successful antagonist of having led the church of Strasbourg to its ruin.[47] Several personal, even affec- tionate remarks notwithstanding, Bucer gravely censured Sturm as a statesman for not having placed his unconditional trust in the Word of God. Bucer failed once again to differentiate carefully between his own decision of conscience and the decisions taken by magistrates in fulfillment of their governmental duties—in spite of the fact that he had occasionally made such distinctions in his last Strasbourg statements. It is difficult to understand and do justice fully to the claims to absolute theological and political truth that Bucer makes in this letter. His earlier flexibility and dexterity, his instinctive feel for power structures and political necessities, are completely absent here. But then again, never before had Bucer found himself in such an extreme situation. Is it enough to assume that, after having suffered so many defeats and disappointments, all Bucer wished to do now was to stand up for God's manifest truth? Was he reacting to the failure of April 20, 1548, in Augsburg? Or had he simply become old, unyielding, and rigid in his views?

In February 1549, Bucer drafted one last memorandum that was eventually signed by the majority of the Strasbourg pastors.[48] It addressed the question of how the Protestant faith could be preserved in the city in spite of the Interim. After passing bitter theological judgment, once again, on the whole chain of developments that had led to the introduction of the Interim, he submitted a number of very interesting suggestions: the reduced groups of confessing Christians were to be encouraged and strengthened by means of public morning prayers, congregational singing, catechetical instruction, and, not least, house visits by the pastors. We thus once again encounter central elements of Bucer's original plan for establishing Christian fellowships.

The rapprochement between city council and bishop led to Bucer's and Fagius's dismissal on March 1, 1549. Whether the decisive factor was the council, the bishop, or even the emperor is a moot issue.[49] In any case, Bucer no longer had any number of supporters worth mention in Strasbourg. Jacob Sturm, of all people, was charged with informing Bucer of his dismissal. Bucer and Fagius held brief farewell sermons on March 3. They gave lessons in the Strasbourg academy for the last time on March 23. They went in hiding for a brief period in the house of the indomitable Katharina Zell, widow of their comrade-in-arms Matthew Zell, in order to shake off pursuers. Finally, on the night of April 5/6, 1549, Bucer, along with Fagius and some companions, left Strasbourg as he had arrived some twenty-five years previously—as a refugee.

In his final weeks in Strasbourg, Bucer vigorously attacked the city council for succumbing to military pressure to re-Catholicize and called instead for the unflinching proclamation of the Word of God, for "whom every knee should bend and whom every tongue should confess as Lord over all things with the highest freedom and fervor." The photographed sample of Bucer's handwriting (Archives Municipales de Strasbourg, AST 39, no. 15, p. 355) corresponds to the passage edited in BDS 17, pp. 589,23–590,4.

Chapter Eight

Exile and Final Days

England

Arrival

Bucer remained one of the most prominent and highly esteemed figures of the Protestant camp. This was evident not least from the countless invitations that he started receiving from 1547 on, among others from Melanchthon in Wittenberg and Calvin in Geneva, offering him sanctuary. He ended up choosing England, however, essentially because he was convinced that it was in this country in which the Reformation was apparently advancing so successfully that his special gifts and unique experiences could be put to use in the most meaningful and fruitful way and had the greatest chance of making a lasting impact.

Bucer had already cultivated many, if somewhat casual, ties with England and with its people previously. Not to be overrated but certainly worth mention is his acquisition of Thomas More's *Utopia* while a monk. More significant is the fact that he drafted an opinion on Henry VIII's marital difficulties,[1] met with Bishop Stephen Gardiner—soon becoming involved in an acrimonious literary altercation with him—and corresponded with other English bishops, even dedicating some of his books to them, particularly to Thomas Cranmer, the archbishop of Canterbury. All of these connections, however, were little more than incidental and probably also perceived as such by Bucer. In the measure, however, that his position in Strasbourg became more vulnerable and the invitations from England more insistent, Bucer made increasingly concrete plans to emigrate to the British Isles. The financier and statesman John Hales, a personal friend of Cranmer and of the duke of Somerset and one of the most powerful men of England, established the decisive connections that created the necessary conditions and paved the way for Bucer's emigration to England.[2]

Bucer and Fagius left Strasbourg under cover of night by boat on the River Ill. On April 7, 1549, in Raon, on the western foothills of the Vosges, some fifty miles west of Strasbourg, they were joined by their traveling companion Valérand Poullain, who would serve them as guide and interpreter. Poullain had pastored the French refugee congregation in Strasbourg from 1542 on and had also spent some time in Canterbury in 1547, setting up an expatriate congregation. One of Fagius's students of Hebrew, the twenty-seven-year-old Matthias Negelin of Württemberg, as well as a servant by the name Peter, responsible for the horses, completed the traveling party.

The trip took place without any major hitches, except for an incident in Amiens on April 15, when the group was temporarily arrested under the suspicion of being on a secret mission to smuggle money and secret documents to England. The precious little cash they actually had on them and Poullain's persuasiveness quickly convinced their captors otherwise, and they were set free. By April 18 they were in Calais, at the time an English outpost. There they rested for five days and sold their horses—in Negelin's opinion, much too cheaply.

On April 23 they crossed the English Channel to Dover by calm weather. The passage took five hours. From there they traveled on to Canterbury, where Fagius's son, who would also help them as an interpreter, was expecting them. Bucer and his company finally arrived in London on April 25, where Thomas Cranmer received them with full honors in Lambeth, at the time a small town on the opposite bank of the Thames. Peter Martyr Vermigli and many other religious refugees from the Continent also welcomed them there as part of Cranmer's entourage. Bucer spent the following months in Croydon, where Cranmer had his summer residence, some twenty miles south of London. A few days after his arrival, Bucer and Fagius were introduced to King Edward VI and the entire court. Bucer described this encounter enthusiastically in a letter to Jacob Sturm.[3] In glowing terms he praised the scholarship and piety holding sway at the court, referring not only to the duke of Somerset but particularly to the king himself. He also retold Sturm, with great satisfaction and a certain measure of implicit reproach, how he, Bucer, had explained to the twelve-year-old king that the negligence of church discipline lay at the root of the German Protestants' downfall, and how the king responded, with tears in his eyes, that God may have punished his people for their ungratefulness and disobedience, but that God would certainly receive it mercifully once again, if it repented and did penance.

Everything thus seemed to start off quite promisingly for Bucer. Even before his arrival, his publications had made him a renowned man in England, not least because he had dedicated two of his most important books, his commentaries on the Gospels and on Romans, to leading church figures of this country. Bucer was obviously esteemed by and could count on the warm support of those wielding power in England. He was aware of the challenging tasks and great opportunities awaiting him, and he was determined to make use of them. Yet, how much did Bucer really know about the country in which he was now living? And what means did he have at his disposal to influence events effectively?

The Kingdom

The political, economic, and social reality of England had little to do with Bucer's deludingly pleasant first impressions at the royal court.[4] In fact, a full-scale uprising, especially of peasants, had been underway since April 1549 in a whole range of counties, beginning in the southwest, in Cornwall, but then spreading also to the east, to Norfolk, and elsewhere. A motley combination of factors—social, economic, as well as religious—had led to this mass rebellion. Enclosures of common land, new land-lease contracts, and, as a result, the loss of traditional social security structures played just as much a role as inflation and the dismantling of traditional religious life with its saints' days, images, and familiar Latin liturgy. The protest thus had a markedly conservative character; farmers demanded the reestablishment of "old law." This did not prevent their opponents from perceiving this revolt as a radical attempt, inspired by the devil, to overthrow the entire established order. Archbishop Cranmer asked in outrage: "Will you now have the subjects to govern their King, the villains to rule the gentlemen, and the servants their masters? If men would suffer this, God will not; but will take vengeance on them that break his order, like Dathan and Abiram."[5] Bucer agreed wholeheartedly.

By midsummer of 1549, the insufficiently armed and poorly led bands of insurgents had suffered a monumental defeat. The crucial problems remained, however. Bucer had arrived in England at the very climax of a grave and all-encompassing crisis. Unrest and insecurity were widespread, along with feelings of fear and mistrust—the kingdom was clearly in the throes of profound social and economic upheaval. In rural areas, where 95 percent of the English people lived, farms were increasing in size and land previously cultivated was now turned into pasturage. It was the middle and smaller tenant farmers who bore the brunt of these changes: their leases were shortened, the levies and duties they had to pay increased, and soon they were unable to support their families. Whoever did not wish to become a day laborer was forced to emigrate to the cities.

The results were a rural exodus, unemployment, and an explosive increase in poverty. Further causes for this development were the rapidly increasing prices of foodstuffs as well as of wool and, correspondingly, cloth. The wealthy tried to take advantage of this situation, either by enlarging their farms or by fencing in or "enclosing" as much pasture land as possible for their sheep. This being an extremely conspicuous measure, it soon stood at the center of all the political, economic, and religious and ethical confrontations, diverse as they were. Doubtless the enclosure of common land was being overrated in its actual consequences. In a sense, the sheep became an excuse for all the difficulties, problems, and calamities that common people were having to endure. It is, of course, undeniable that at a local and maybe even regional level the common people did experience the process of enclosure as the destruction of the very foundations of village life. However, these enclosures never reached the dimensions their opponents claimed in their statements. Additionally, they were not the cause of the inflation that was weighing upon the entire population.

The common people remained convinced, however, that the enclosures diminished the amount of land available for farming and thus forced prices up. In light of these assumptions, it is hard to explain, however, why prices rose sharply in 1548/49 after a very good harvest—only to fall considerably in 1551/52, when yields were particularly poor. Today we are aware of the central significance of two factors that led to this extreme crisis in the late 1540s in England: rapid population growth and the disastrous effects of England's war against Scotland and France.

Some two million people lived in England and Wales around the year 1540. By 1547 that number had increased to almost three million. This population explosion caused a shortage of food and an increase in prices. Many poor people, particularly those living in the country, had to resort to additional sources of income. They therefore spun wool or wove cloth for master manufacturers who supplied them with raw material and bought the finished products from them. This contributed considerably to the burgeoning export of English wool and coarse cloth to the Spanish Netherlands and especially to Antwerp. But since the Crown continually reduced the proportion of fine metal in gold coins from 1544 onward, and nearly doubled the number of coins circulating by the year 1551, increased exports kindled inflation. Not until after Bucer's death did the economic tide show signs of turning.

It had long been clear to all involved that something needed to be done. Yet few realized that it was especially the unremitting wars against France and Scotland that were ruining the country. These conflicts tied up much of the energy of government and devoured enormous resources. They led Henry VIII to forfeit the financial independence of the Crown in the final years of his rule. After his death the fighting continued, first against Scotland and, from August 8, 1549, against France again. And since the new king, Edward VI, was a child, not only were social and economic security sorely wanted, but confidence in leadership as well. The sense of crisis grew. The country became increasingly difficult to govern.

Besides, Edward Seymour, the duke of Somerset, had awakened great expectations upon becoming the "Protector of the Realm" and thus the leading political figure in England after the death of Henry VIII. These hopes found a concrete expression in a series of writings demanding a comprehensive solution to the deplorable state of affairs. The authors of these works—among them John Hales, Hugh Latimer, William Turner, Thomas Becon, and John Hooper—were socially conservative, made reform proposals expressive of a certain evangelical paternalism, and believed that profound changes could be brought about through legislation. They were later given the common title "Men of the Commonwealth," although in reality they never constituted a monolithic group, nor did they ever submit a joint program for reform. They had much to say about moral decay, divine wrath, and the responsibility of the Christian but were at a loss when it came to proposing concrete political and social measures.

Protector Somerset's reforms also remained unclear, irresolute, and ineffective because he always subordinated them to the political and financial requirements of war-making. Therefore, his struggle against enclosures, his attempts to fix the prices of basic foodstuffs, and his efforts at establishing poor relief and reforming the universities all failed. To make matters worse, Somerset made many enemies because of his self-conceit and stubbornness (and even more because of similar qualities in his wife), so that he soon lost all credibility and authority. On November 11, 1549, he was overthrown and imprisoned in the Tower.

John Dudley, the earl of Warwick and, since the fall of 1551, duke of Northumberland, was England's new strong man. His political goals started to become apparent in the spring of 1550. Initially, he obtained the support of the Catholic opposition in his endeavor to overthrow Somerset. Later, however, he turned against the Catholics in order to stabilize his own power base. He urgently needed the support of all forces of reform in the country—from the king, an avid Reformation supporter, to the

great landowners and noblemen, whose interest in change was more pragmatic—in order to make up for the ruinous policies of the past decades,
as well as to consolidate his own position. An attempt at monetary reform
was among the measures he took. Peace was made with France on March
29, 1550, and finally with Scotland as well on July 19, 1551. At the same
time, the Church of England began to open itself increasingly to the influence of Protestantism.

The State of the Church

Among the tremendous hopes pinned upon the Protector after the death
of Henry VIII were important religious expectations.[6] It was manifest that
the former king's strategy had failed, but the course to be adopted in its
place was far from obvious.

Henry VIII had made himself the supreme head on earth of the Church
of England in the Supremacy Act of 1534. The aversion to Rome widespread in the kingdom had paved the way for this decision. Yet, beyond
this measure, Henry wished to leave the church as it was, refraining from
introducing any changes, particularly in the church's doctrine. He met
with only limited success, for new evangelical ideas were being washed
ashore from the Continent, and incompletely suppressed local traditions
such as John Wycliffe's legacy and the popular Lollard movement began
making themselves felt once again. Besides, Henry's supremacy over the
church had the consequence of relativizing canon law. Finally, the dissolution and expropriation of monasteries by Henry and his leading statesman Thomas Cromwell represented a significant encroachment on the
financial foundations of the church.

For things not to slip out of hand, Henry issued a law in 1539 fixing the
central tenets of church doctrine in six articles that were in agreement with
traditional Roman Catholic teaching. These articles concerned transubstantiation in the Mass, auricular confession, the prohibition of clerical
marriage, as well as withholding the communion cup from the laity. Any
deviation from this norm was persecuted brutally. Henry stuck to these six
articles until his death. By 1547 not only the new young king but also Somerset, Archbishop Cranmer, and many more agreed that this course should
not be continued. At the same time, they realized the need to proceed very
cautiously in order to stir as little outrage as possible among the common
people. In any case, Somerset deemed Charles V's neutrality essential. The
Protector deliberately pursued a religious policy that could be interpreted
as reform Catholicism, in order not to give the emperor any excuses to

forestall English trade with Antwerp or, more alarmingly, to enter the war on Scotland's side. The result—like most of Somerset's politics—was an unclear compromise that left everybody dissatisfied.

Initially, before the end of July 1547, the *Book of Homilies*, an official volume of sermons to be read and expounded every Sunday, was published in the name of the king. These sermons were a clear expression of Reformation ideas: they proclaimed the justification of men by God through faith in Jesus Christ alone, the administration of both bread and wine to all communicants in the Lord's Supper, the abolition of auricular confession and of all images and ceremonies conducive to "superstition," and, finally, the permission of clerical marriage and the use of the vernacular in worship services. However, the *Book of Common Prayer* published in June 1549 not only discontinued this course toward Reformation but actually went back on steps already taken. Many elements of the Roman Catholic teaching on the Mass reappeared, and liturgical vestments, candles, hallowed anointing oil, and prayers for the dead were all once again mentioned. It was now evident that what was being sought was only the modification of existing structures, not the definitive establishment of the Reformation. This latter and quite decisive step did not follow until 1550, under Warwick. In the spring of that year, a new *Ordinal* for the ordination of clergymen was presented; soon afterward, Bishop Ridley began replacing altars with tables in his London diocese. Of considerable more import was the fundamentally revised version of the *Book of Common Prayer* that appeared in 1552. Even though it retained many ceremonies and rites of the medieval church, it purported to exclude all Roman Catholic doctrines. Finally, in June 1553, the "Forty-two Articles" appeared, formulating the teachings of the Church of England in an evangelical sense, partly under the influence of Heinrich Bullinger but of John Calvin as well. Bucer was able to contribute only indirectly to these developments.

Projects and Conflicts

During their first months in England, Bucer and Fagius spent most of their time in Croydon.[7] There they were charged with the daunting task of preparing a new Latin translation of the Bible, accompanied with a brief commentary. This ambitious enterprise did not get very far, however. Only the draft of Bucer's commentary on the first eight chapters of the Gospel of Matthew has survived. Probably about this same time, Bucer produced a small treatise on the appropriate selection, training, and ordination of clergymen.[8]

It had been intended that Bucer and Fagius take up teaching positions at the University of Cambridge, with Bucer assuming the Regius Professorship of Divinity created by Henry VIII with funds obtained from the confiscation of church property. Bucer's salary amounted to 100 pounds a year, a sum sufficient to allow him a comfortable life in spite of inflation. Bucer would have time—until September 29, 1549, when Michaelmas Term (as the semester beginning in the autumn was called) began—to become accustomed to his new environment, engage his new colleagues in conversation, and appraise the situation in England. His first actual visit to Cambridge took place around the middle of June, when he came for several weeks, looking for living accommodations for himself and his family. Bucer gained not only new acquaintances during these months but many new friends as well. By this time he perceived conditions in the English kingdom much more realistically—and, in fact, gloomily—than he had in the previous months.

During these weeks in June, Bucer was dragged entirely against his will into a controversy raging between Peter Martyr and his Oxford colleagues over the Lord's Supper. Catholicism was still firmly entrenched at the University of Oxford. To change this situation, Peter Martyr, who was Regius Professor of Divinity at Oxford from 1547, initiated a debate over the Mass and the Lord's Supper. Now he was asking Bucer to support him. Both men had become better acquainted with one another in recent years; they did not, however, see entirely eye to eye on the Lord's Supper. Martyr's wish that Bucer speak out publicly on this issue was certainly understandable but not without its perils, for it threatened to expose significant differences in the theological views of the two friends and thus was hardly conducive to increasing their impact upon the Reformation in England. Furthermore, Bullinger—whose understanding of the Lord's Supper deeply influenced Martyr—was mistrustfully keeping tabs on Bucer from his vantage point in Zurich, and a good many of Bullinger's supporters not only openly opposed Bucer but even felt unmitigated hatred toward him.[9] Bucer could therefore only lose by entering into this debate and issuing the requested statement. He thus vigorously entreated Martyr to temper the flames of conflict. The devastating consequences of the eucharistic controversy in Germany, as well as the bitter memories of his concord efforts—"when I rolled a Sisyphean stone up a hill, as it were"—were still painfully fresh in his mind. Bucer wanted nothing more than to prevent a similar conflict from repeating itself in England. He wished to follow neither the papists nor the Lutherans, asserted Bucer, nor Zwingli and his supporters, but rather to adhere simply to the mystery of the real presence of Christ in the Supper, where the Lord gives himself to believers. Bucer concluded with an appeal that neatly summarizes what he felt on other issues as well: "We must aspire with the utmost zeal to edify as many people as we possibly can in faith and in the love of Christ—and to offend no one."[10] Martyr allowed himself to be won over to this view.

Bucer was seriously ill by the time the semester was supposed to begin. He was not able to come to Cambridge until the beginning of November.[11] His friend and companion of Strasbourg days, Paul Fagius, died there on November 13, 1549, barely forty-five years old. His death dealt Bucer a tremendous blow. From now on he felt completely isolated in England. His many acquaintances and even friends could do little to change this— not even the conferral, with much pomp and ceremony, of an honorary doctorate in theology, probably after December 4, the official date of Bucer's appointment as a professor. Never before had the University of Cambridge bestowed such a degree. In his thank-you speech, Bucer under-scored the need for state and church, for their own mutual benefit, to work in close cooperation training and teaching young people.[12]

In the same speech, Bucer described himself as a sick, old, and thor-oughly decrepit man. This harsh depiction did justice to reality. Bucer was not able to begin his lectures until shortly before Christmas. He began by expounding Psalm 119 to his students at his own home. Then, on Janu-ary 14, 1550,[13] he began giving public lectures on the letter to the Eph-esians.[14] Ecclesiology thus stood clearly at the center of his interests and his efforts. Bucer also began presiding over academic disputations and preached repeatedly on John 6. But in March 1550 his health once again suffered a serious setback, from which he recovered only gradually. It was not until May that he was able to set foot in the lecture hall again, over-whelmed by feelings of restlessness and impatience with himself—so much lay waiting to be done for the reform of the church!

During the holiday month of July, Bucer spent some time in the coun-try at the residence of the duchess of Suffolk. After that, he spent eleven days in Oxford, visiting Peter Martyr. While Bucer was slowly regaining his strength, a most unpleasant conflict was brewing behind his back in Cambridge. One of his colleagues, John Young, derided Bucer's under-standing of justification in a lecture. Young particularly took offense at Bucer's assertion that the good works of unbelievers were sinful. Two con-cerns collided here: an overriding emphasis on ethics and the evangelical and biblical conviction that any human action not inspired by faith dis-pleased God. But there apparently was more to the conflict than this. Fol-lowing a public disputation on August 8, Bucer sent a written record of the altercation—which dealt with the Bible as a sufficient foundation for the church, the latter's fallibility, and the justification of man by faith alone and not works—to his opponents Young, Thomas Sedgwick, and Andrew Perne, asking them for their comments and corrections. The three refused to even look at the text.[15] At the same time, all three, and Young in particular, continued to stir up emotions against Bucer with all available means, both written and oral, in public and in private. These Cambridge scholars perceived him as an outsider who was obviously being given preferential treatment and now was even assuming the airs of a teacher and daring to place constraints on and introduce foreign innovations into the English church. He had clearly become a thorn in their sides. The whole affair aroused a great deal of attention. Young must have met with substantial support, for he eventually submitted a formal denunciation against Bucer to the vice chancellor Walter Haddon, accusing the Strasbourg reformer of false teachings that contradicted the Bible and the church fathers.

Bucer was outraged and deeply hurt. He immediately drafted five theses and convoked a day-long public disputation on these theses to take place in June. Following this, after being allowed to see Young's statement, he drafted a lengthy confutation of his opponent.[16] He sent this counter-statement to his friend Edmund Grindal on August 31, asking him to forward it to John Cheke as well as to the bishop of London.[17] This time around, Bucer turned heavy guns on his opponents: appealing to the authority of the *Book of Homilies*, he accused Young of bringing the errors of Pelagius, already condemned by the early church, back to life, and then proceeded to charge Young with sins against God, the Bible, the church, and the king. Cheke then came from London to prevent matters from getting out of hand. He attempted to settle the controversy in Bucer's favor—and ultimately succeeded.

An intriguing subordinate issue in this heated debate was the question as to whether Christians are allowed to lend money in exchange for interest. Young embraced church tradition wholeheartedly by answering negatively, whereas Bucer gave a positive answer, thus assuming a more modern standpoint.[18] The question was of current relevance, since many were dependent on interest income for financing their university studies. Bucer began by distinguishing between interest and usury and then developed the principle of his theology, that every Christian should live for his fellow man, connecting it to the notion of equity (*Billigkeit*) and Jesus' Golden Rule: "In everything do to others as you would have them do to you" (Matthew 7:12). Therefore, those who only possessed money or their salaries—as examples Bucer mentioned widows, children, students, clergymen, and state officials—should lend their money for interest to peasants, craftsmen, or merchants, in case these need it for their work. "For money is also God's gift, and God demands that we use it rightly."[19]

Shortly thereafter, the controversy over the Lord's Supper threatened to flare up one more time. In September, Jan Laski (John à Lasco), the pastor of the London refugee congregation ("Stranger Church") since 1549, visited Bucer in Cambridge, hoping to reach a doctrinally sound agreement over the Lord's Supper among the émigrés. Bucer initially suggested to the distinguished Polish exile that they exchange views confidentially. He then sent Laski a *Confession*[20] consisting of fifty-four articles steering a cautious course between Zwinglians and Lutherans. Bucer wished for the real presence of Christ in the Lord's Supper to be understood in a "symbolic" way, as a "metaphor" to be resolved neither rationally nor magically. One cannot fail to notice the proximity to Calvin's understanding of the Lord's Supper. Bucer's death, however, would cut the conversations short.

Bucer was much more involved in the vestments controversy that took place at the same time. At issue was whether clergymen were required to continue wearing their traditional habits. The conflict was triggered by the refusal of John Hooper, the new bishop of Gloucester, to don the time-honored episcopal garments on the occasion of his ordination. Hooper was influenced by Bullinger, who—in the wake of Zwingli—rejected all traditional rites and ceremonies as superstitions detrimental to the purity of Reformation doctrine. Laski, Martyr, and Hooper as well now began trying to obtain Bucer's support for their position. After all, it was no secret that he had carried out similar reforms in Strasbourg. On the other hand, Archbishop Cranmer found it unacceptable for the new episcopal *Ordinal* to be overruled so soon after it had been published, with his very own authorization, in March 1550. As soon as he was informed about the controversy, Cranmer sent a formal inquiry to Bucer, asking him whether it was permissible to wear the prescribed liturgical vestments without offending God. He also asked inversely whether anyone refusing to wear the prescribed garments did not sin against God and the authorities.[21] As seriously as Bucer took these inquiries and opinions, he still managed to stay above the fray and raise the debate to a level somewhat more sublime.[22] Of course he had attempted to recover the simplicity of the early church his entire life, and this in many aspects, including the outward form of worship services, Bucer admitted to Hooper. But he still could not see— and this was directed as much against Cranmer as it was against Hooper— how the indeed very crucial question of obedience to God could be reduced to a controversy over vestments. Did Paul not write extensively and compellingly about Christian freedom? Who could doubt that the church was, and is, entitled to find pragmatic solutions to countless controversies over external matters?

A further aspect was just as important to Bucer. Were there not questions much more important than the issue of clerical garments? It is a known fact, he wrote to Hooper, that we do not have enough pastors; we do not have Christian congregations worth the name; we neither administer the sacraments in the right way, nor do we impart true pastoral care; we give no catechismal instruction, not to mention the absence of any church discipline. Most Christians in this country do not know what the word *church* really means; they know nothing of living congregations or of the fellowship of saints, and even less about the kingdom of Christ. That is where we should begin if the church is to be reformed—not with squabbles over vestments! Hooper was not swayed by Bucer's arguments. Only after Bucer's death did he submit to Cranmer, following a prolonged imprisonment in the Tower.

Among Bucer's last theological treatises is a major memorandum, completed on January 5, 1551, on the 1549 *Book of Common Prayer.*[23] Cranmer had requested an opinion as to how this prayer book should be revised. Whether Bucer's statement had any influence at all on the revision, and, if so, the degree to which Cranmer actually followed Bucer's recommendations—these remain matters of conjecture.[24] The leitmotiv of this memorandum, as of so many other of Bucer's works, was that faith and love among people be furthered. This was the norm for deciding what to do and what to refrain from doing in the church. Bucer deemed as unnecessary and superfluous the overabundance of holidays, the frequent ringing of church bells, genuflections in worship, crossing oneself, blessing and consecrating all kinds of objects, liturgical vestments, private masses, extreme unction, prayers for the dead, and other ceremonies. Instead, he considered it crucial for the congregation to know and understand what the worship service, church life, and especially faith were all about. He therefore called for a summary of Christian doctrine to be drawn up. A catechism should be written according to which the people could be taught. He also demanded a major overhaul of the administrative structures of the church.

Bucer was thus once more pressing for a comprehensive and radical reform of the English church, the state of which he appraised increasingly pessimistically.[25] For example, on May 25, 1550, he wrote Calvin that seemingly everything was wrong here: the clergymen were uneducated papists responsible for several churches at one time, to which they ministered only superficially. There were many congregations that had not heard a sermon for years. The university professors were either papists or

Epicureans "who, as far as they are able, entice young people to come to their lectures and imbue them with hatred for sound Christian teaching and discipline." Influential people at the royal court and elsewhere in England appeared to be entirely oblivious to religious issues, saying that it was the business of the bishops to attend to these. The bishops, on their part, claimed they could do nothing without the support of government! At the same time, the noblemen were enriching themselves shamelessly with the church's property. Therefore, "it is greatly to be feared that the dreadful wrath of God will very shortly blaze forth against this kingdom also."[26] Bucer was not painting an exaggeratedly dismal picture of reality. Other sources confirm his assessment. For instance, an inspection of the diocese of Gloucester in 1551 revealed that 168 priests out of a total of 311 were unable to recite the Ten Commandments; 34 did not know who had formulated the Lord's Prayer, and 10 did not know it by heart.[27] What could be done about this? Bucer remained convinced of the utter necessity of training a new generation of pastors. It was for this reason that he began teaching a course on "the significance and practice of the sacred ministry."[28] In it, Bucer presented a pastoral theology of sorts that concentrated on the person of the minister. This made it possible for him to discuss the intellectual and moral requirements as well as deal with fundamental theological topics—such as church and congregation, the essence and variety of ministries, and church offices. The further development of this theme was also interrupted by Bucer's death.

The Rule of Christ

Bucer certainly did not come to England to live the quiet, secluded life of a small-town professor. Neither was it enough for him to formulate expert opinions every once in a while. On the contrary, his writings show that he aspired to nothing less than the radical, comprehensive renewal of England that was to begin with religious reform and would be followed by a reshaping of social and moral conditions, as well as a recasting of the economic and administrative structures of the country. This is what Bucer meant when he spoke or wrote about spreading and consolidating the rule of Christ in England.

In other words, he wished to establish the Reformation in the broadest sense and have all areas of life subjected to the lordship of Christ—and not merely organize a church. And Bucer was convinced that he knew the right ways and means of achieving this goal. He was thus disappointed, even embittered, that those in power hardly consulted him. He then found out about the custom of presenting a memoir to the king at the beginning of a new year. On October 21, 1550, he sent his friend John Cheke a manuscript version of his major treatise *On the Kingdom of Christ* (*De Regno Christi*) in order that Cheke pass it on to King Edward VI. The book was not printed until 1557 in Basel.[29] In this work, Bucer developed his program for a sweeping Reformation. He presented the king with the principles and rules he should follow in order to establish new church structures in England with lasting success. This treatise condensed Bucer's long years of experience and activity as a practical Christian, a church leader, and an ecclesiastical organizer in Strasbourg and many other German cities and territories. But it also was an epitome of Bucer's theology as developed from 1523 onward. *De Regno Christi* thus constitutes a summary of Bucer's thought and his practical visions, a compendium that he himself described as his legacy.[30]

In terms of its linguistic style and compositional structure, the work was admittedly far from being a masterpiece. Bucer remained too true to his writing habits for things to be otherwise. The treatise consists of two parts. The first one addresses the essence of the kingdom of Christ and, departing from there, discusses the duties and tasks of the church, including its assumed close cooperation with the civil authorities. The second part of the book lists the practical measures the king should take, presenting them in the form of fourteen lengthy laws, including detailed instructions on their implementation. Two familiar elements of Bucer's theology thus reappear: his great confidence in legal measures and—closely related to the first—his demand that church and state act in unison.

All of this was also somewhat related to the conviction, dating back to classical antiquity and also developed by the theology and philosophy of later periods, that religion is the most secure foundation of any state and thus the most reliable guarantee for the well-being of the individual and of entire society. This theme had always occupied Bucer's thought under the aspect of the common good, or *bonum commune*. His reflections on this topic, however, had always been considerably more sophisticated—and this was particularly the case in *De Regno Christi*. For in this work Bucer described the relationship between temporal rule and the rule of Christ as one of mutual submission: just as the person who is subject to Christ's rule—the Christian, in other words—obeys government and therefore finds a place for himself within the existing political and social orders, in the same way do those who govern, wherever their place in government may be, submit themselves and their political power to the rule of Christ. "Thus, as the kingdom of Christ subjects itself to the kingdoms and powers of the world, so in turn every true kingdom of the world (I say kingdom, not tyranny) subjects itself to the kingdom of Christ, and the kings themselves are among the first to do this, for they are eager to develop piety not for themselves alone, but they also seek to lead their subjects to it."[31] Put in simpler terms: the king who is a Christian bears his responsibilities as a Christian in his place in society—in the same way as peasants, craftsmen, or noblemen who are Christians do—and must fulfill the duty imposed on all Christians to work for the establishment of Christ's rule in this world.

This goal only made sense for Bucer because he at the same time called for changes, if not in the structures, at least in numerous regulations and customs of society. This aspect had also occupied his thought from the very beginning of his Strasbourg ministry, as we have seen. Bucer was not concerned with doing away with "upper" and "lower," and he was not working toward making social equals out of kings, peasants, patricians, artisans, and day laborers. What he rather wanted was that the needs of one's fellow man be attended to within these social structures; or to put it in theological terms, that the love of fellow man be realized. And precisely this had always been for Bucer, and thus was also in *De Regno Christi*, not just a matter of principles, convictions, or faith but always one of rules and regulations—and therefore of law.

The tension between God's law governing all of life and the freedom bestowed by the Holy Spirit, a tension that pervades Bucer's entire thought and ministry, also dominates this work. The fundamental order of creation and hence the law according to which all of creation exists, the self-evident commitment of all creatures to their fellow creatures, had been destroyed by sin. Believers, in whom the Holy Spirit reigns—Bucer usually designates them as "the elect" and "the predestined" in order to preclude any notion of meritorious human works as radically as possible—will naturally and self-evidently behave in congruence with how God originally disposed his creation: they will love their fellow human beings; they will live for others and not for themselves. But such people were exceptionally few. In order for them not to end up being a negligible minority, not only in the world but in the church as well, church discipline was necessary. This second aspect had become increasingly important for Bucer in the recent past. For this reason he vigorously emphasized discipline as the third note or defining characteristic of the church besides the right preaching of God's Word and the proper administration of the sacraments. At the same time, Christ's kingdom could by no means be limited to the church. Setting up Christ's rule therefore meant promulgating ordinances, enacting laws, and taking concrete measures that affected and permeated all of society.

We can understand this way of thinking that runs through and characterizes all of *De Regno Christi* only if we grasp it as the reestablishment of a humaneness that finds its truest expression in the love of man for his fellow man. This was at least the goal, in Bucer's view, of all the legal measures taken by the Christian king, who bore special responsibility and power: these measures aimed at amending the disruption by sin of God's order of existence—an order that essentially boiled down to love of one's neighbor.

A problematic aspect of Bucer's concept was that he identified the order implanted by God in creation of love for one's fellow creatures specifically with the laws and norms of the Old Testament. The criterion for interpreting and applying God's law, which aimed at loving one's fellow man, was not so much the imperative of love but ended up consisting of specific biblical rules. It is thus not exaggerated to claim that the inflexible biblicism that Bucer also manifested in this work at least hindered, if not foreclosed, important theological insights. For all of a sudden love of one's fellow man was no longer the standard for interpreting the Bible; instead, biblical formulations and wordings threatened to ossify into rigid laws. And whenever the letter of the Bible flatly and glaringly contradicted the ontological principle of commitment to one's fellow creatures, Bucer emphasized and repeated unremittingly that God—who was goodness, mercy, and loving-kindness personified—could not do other than to aim toward social humaneness and love in all his ordinances and laws. Often enough, this was not a train of thought one could reasonably follow. But Bucer would respond to his critics by asking how man could presume to know better than God what is good and salutary.

As a matter of principle, Bucer also understood law in metaphysical, and therefore timeless, terms. Unlike man, God does not change, stressed Bucer. Therefore, biblical laws, especially those of the Old Testament, remained normative inasmuch as Christ had not expressly abolished them. In addition, the Holy Spirit did not relativize God's law in the slightest; on the contrary, it allowed Christians to understand the meaning of the law and conferred on them the will and the capacity to fulfill its requirements. In doing what the law demanded, they provided the following generations with examples and precedents. For Bucer it went without asking that these models were to be found primarily in the Bible. But they could also be found among the church fathers and in the legislation of the Christian emperors of late Roman antiquity.

The comments made above provide the background for the fourteen laws of reform that Bucer wished to see enacted in England. They also shed light on the content of those fourteen laws. Before going on to present these laws in detail, Bucer embarked on a preliminary discussion of the fundamental characteristics of the church, beginning with the preaching of the gospel, the good news of the sinner's justification by God's mercy alone. He then set forth the essence of church offices, which are necessary for serving the congregation, and wrote at some length on the proper administration of the two sacraments of baptism and the Lord's Supper. He concluded this first section with a detailed exposition of church discipline, which Bucer interpreted as care, companionship, and custody, as the coordination of the penance process, and as a ceremony. As much as Bucer allowed temporal authority to intervene in church matters, he made it clear beyond all doubt that the state was not free to do as it pleased but rather bore the responsibility of helping the church become once again an independent institution. Bucer therefore vigorously upheld the autonomy of the church in *De Regno Christi*.

This did not prevent him from strongly urging the king to take the reform of the church into his own hands. After all, the Bible was full of reports of great political rulers devoting their attention to religious issues and working to renew the faith of their subjects. The king had to be ready to die, if necessary, for this cause—a side-swipe at Jacob Sturm's and the Strasbourg city council's pusillanimity toward the Interim. Of course, Bucer did not expect that Edward VI would be able to carry through all of the legal measures envisioned. Bucer's plans called first for itinerant evangelists to wander through England preaching the gospel. Equipped with a great deal of patience and good arguments, they would attempt to win over as many people as possible. Bucer was convinced beyond the shadow of doubt that their endeavor would succeed. Afterward, the Parliament would approve the introduction of the Reformation. Finally, the entire people would endorse this process; Bucer believed a national council should be convoked that would include ecclesiastical and secular representatives from all counties of the kingdom. The fourteen laws of reform, drafted by Bucer and thereafter to be enacted by the king, would constitute the summary, the confirmation, and, not least, the charter of the thus-renewed covenant between God and the English people.

The first seven of the fourteen laws dealt with church topics in the narrow sense of the term. Beginning with catechetical instruction, the hallowing of Sundays and holidays, and the reverence due to church buildings, Bucer went on to set up principles for reorganizing church offices, dealing with church property, establishing a comprehensive system of poor relief, and, finally, overhauling matrimonial law. The chapter on marriage turned out inordinately long, since Bucer incorporated his hitherto unpublished matrimonial treatises into this section. Once again he presented, extensively and in great detail, his surprisingly modern ideas on divorce and on women's rights.[32]

The next seven laws dealt with social and economic issues, questions of general education, administration, as well as with civil and criminal law in the broadest sense. Bucer attempted to address conditions in England much more specifically in this section than in the one dedicated to purely ecclesiastical matters. He had remarkable success in this respect. Bucer knowledgeably expounds the need to reform the existing administrative structures as well as criminal law; he speaks of the need to protect farmers and check enclosures; he demands that women be taught to weave so that England be able to export cloth besides raw wool; on the whole, he calls for the governmental control of trade and for wages and prices to be fixed by law. These were essentially the same demands that English critics had been making for quite some time already. Like them, Bucer wished to improve the well-being of the general population in England. In his proposals, however, Bucer did more than echo the complaints of the past and supplement them with calls for a higher morality. Absolutely crucial for any reform endeavor, stressed Bucer, was a comprehensive religious renewal that included the formation of new, different human beings who dared to live radically changed lives based on faith and love. To be sure, he was counting on the close cooperation of the civil authorities, who were to promulgate the laws and enforce them. If there was one point at which Bucer's deepest convictions were fundamentally and self-evidently coterminous with those already holding sway in England, it was certainly this one: the belief that the king should have dominant influence on the church. When Archbishop Cranmer stated the view that government, through its laws, should reestablish God's order and in this way create the outward conditions that would enable the Holy Spirit to bring about inward changes in people,[33] he was expressing exactly what Bucer believed.

Bucer's ideal society, it should not be denied, bore distinctively authoritarian features. Bucer not only considered psychological and social compulsion to be necessary and, in fact, perfectly admissible, but even physical coercion as well. He was similarly enthusiastic in advocating a surveillance state in which everybody would have his own—private *and* public— "watchman, inspector and observer."[34] Bucer obviously did not have our hindsight over the totalitarian nightmares of the twentieth century to learn from. We must also be fair in recognizing that the vision of an intimate, close-knit Christian fellowship was guiding him. Yet a tendency toward legalism in Bucer's theology cannot be denied.

Bucer wanted living congregations: Christians living in close fellowship with one another but who also, because of their faith, assumed responsibility for the social and economic spheres of the surrounding world. One distinctive feature characterized Bucer's theology from its very inception up to this grand design: the conviction that faith permeated all areas of life and that Christians therefore bore responsibility for them. This went fundamentally beyond the moralizing laments and reproaches of many of his English contemporaries, as well as their calls for improved ethical and religious attitudes. Bucer wanted to create something new; he wanted to reshape the kingdom of England in congruence with the kingdom of Christ, comprehensively and down to the last detail. To be sure, many of his proposals were very traditional. Others, like the attempt to stop enclosures, were economically and politically obsolete. However, among them were many modern features that pointed to the future. There are certainly traces of the happy balance between self-interest and commonweal, properly described as the central progressive element in the literature of the period and manifested most clearly in Sir Thomas Smith's *Discourse of the Commonweal of this Realm of England*,[35] present in Bucer's *De Regno Christi*, for instance, if one considers his statements on interest revenue and especially on divorce. To be sure, as thematically rich and stimulating as Bucer's work "on the kingdom of Christ" was, it did not become the charter of the Reformation in England, as Bucer had wished and hoped.

Life in Cambridge and Death

Day-to-Day Life

Bucer would never feel at home in England. His remaining time was too brief to allow him even to begin acclimatizing himself to life in Cambridge. Everything here was unfamiliar, he complained in a letter to William Farel in January 1550: "the weather, the language, the food, the customs, the housing, and just about everything else."[36] The open fireplaces did not provide him with the accustomed warmth, making him feel as if he was freezing constantly. The wine he was used to drinking was unaffordably expensive. Furthermore, worries over political and ecclesiastical developments in Germany as well as over his family, which had stayed behind in Strasbourg, weighed down his spirits. A letter Bucer wrote to Calvin in August 1549 poignantly expresses how imprisoned and forlorn he felt in England: "I am spending my old age in exile, far away from my native country, banished from my church I loved so dearly, my school, and my city—where I was able to accomplish a few things by God's grace—separated from my beloved friends and brethren: all of this in order to live now in a country that may be kind and gracious to me, but whose language I do not know, whose food I cannot get used to, whose way of life is unfamiliar—and, finally, a country in which I see no clear perspective of achieving something for the Lord through my efforts."[37]

Of course, Bucer had friends and patrons in Cambridge and elsewhere. Walter Haddon, professor of Roman Law and vice chancellor of the university, was among them, as were John Cheke, the Greek scholar Nicholas Carr, the theologians Matthew Parker and Edmund Grindal, who later would become successive archbishops of Canterbury. These men were the vehicles by which at least some of Bucer's convictions and goals made their way into the further development of the Anglican Church. Women of noble rank also supported Bucer, for instance, Lady Jane Grey and especially the duchess of Suffolk. The numerous attentions and favors showered so lavishly upon Bucer could not obscure the fact that he was no longer an influential churchman, as he had been in Strasbourg and in Germany, but was now only a small-town professor, far from the centers of power.

Cambridge had about twenty-five hundred inhabitants at this time. Almost all aspects of town life were influenced in some way or another by the university. Admittedly, its scholarly and religious reputation had declined considerably in recent years. In spite of an official endorsement by the university, it was clear that getting the Reformation firmly established—in Cambridge as elsewhere—was going to be much more difficult than merely ridding Great St. Mary's and the college chapels of side altars and images or whitewashing religious murals in churches. In addition, Bucer's altercation with Young and other fellow professors had repercussions on students' attitudes. The new professor from Germany, so rigorous and lacking in charm, could hardly lay claim to popularity. The fact that Bucer began his morning lectures one hour earlier than was the norm[38] also did little to ingratiate him with students. As one student wrote to a friend in May 1550, "Doctor Bucer cries incessantly, now in daily lectures, now in frequent sermons, that we should practice penitence, discard the depraved customs of hypocritical religion, correct the abuses of feasts, be more frequent in hearing and having sermons, constrain ourselves by some sort of discipline. Many things of this kind he impresses on us even ad nauseam."[39]

During his stay in Cambridge, Bucer lived in housing owned by Trinity College, of which he was a member by virtue of his Regius Professorship. The house in which he quite probably lived, Physwick Hostel, no longer stands, having disappeared in the course of the expansion of the Great Court at Trinity College in later years.[40] Bucer was joined in September 1549 by his wife Wibrandis Rosenblatt and his stepdaughter Agnes Capito. In March 1550, an Alsatian tiled stove, made possible through a gift of 20 pounds by the king, was built in Bucer's study on the second floor of the family residence. A second one on the ground floor was built some time later. This greatly appreciated convenience was no luxury but rather a bitter necessity for Bucer's ill and aged body.[41] Life in such close proximity to the predominantly Catholic Trinity College, outraged at the conspicuous presence of a married former priest, must certainly not have been easy for Bucer and his family.[42]

Wibrandis returned to Strasbourg in May 1550 in order to settle household affairs. By the close of the summer she was back in Cambridge with the furniture and their personal effects, accompanied this time by her own children and her elderly mother Magdalena Strub. Since Bucer's salary was apparently paid only irregularly, the whole family often had to do without basics. Unlike some of his colleagues, he lacked the necessary means for carrying out a little farming or animal husbandry on the side— although the duchess of Suffolk did give him a cow and a calf. On the other hand, it would be exaggerated to claim the family suffered actual privation. After Bucer's death, Wibrandis still would be in possession of the stately sum of 380 pounds after settling the family's Cambridge household and selling her deceased husband's books.

A set of rules for daily life (*Formula vivendi*) that Bucer probably drafted in the fall of 1550 gives us a fascinating glimpse into day-to-day existence in the Bucer household.[43] Quite likely Bucer had already established similar sets of rules during his life in Strasbourg. The same guiding principles that he had formulated once again in his magnum opus on the kingdom of Christ were also to become reality in the household and the family: moral and religious discipline, love of God and of one's fellow human beings. Only those persons willing to submit themselves to these rules were welcome to live under his roof. This also implied their assuming quite precise duties that were monitored quite strictly by the head of household. Especially the two students living with the family, Martin Brem and a certain Wilhelm, were expected to follow these rules. This meant they had to get up every morning at four. After prayer they had to light up the house and get the fires going in the stoves. The main work of the students consisted of copying Bucer's manuscripts—no easy task in view of the Strasbourg reformer's almost illegible handwriting. They also were to keep careful record of all incoming and outgoing mail, as well as give private lessons to Bucer's infant daughters. They were to wait on the family during meals as well as take care of and wash Bucer's clothing. One of the students was always expected to accompany Bucer wherever he went. There is no doubt that these strict rules, based on the assumption that the household head bore supreme authority, were in line with the presuppositions and convictions of the times. Yet the thoroughness with which Bucer regulated even the smallest details gives ample reason to assume that life under his roof was not necessarily simple—especially if one considers that his wife Wibrandis was hardly less domineering.

The End

As we saw previously, Bucer was already old, feeble, and physically almost completely exhausted by the time he arrived in England. Illnesses without end bound him time and again to his bed, among them chronic coughing, rheumatism, lithiasis, intestinal ailments, and leg ulcers. In the final months of his life he was additionally plagued by fits of persistent vomiting, shivering, and sweating. For a time he even suffered under a partial paralysis of the right side that particularly hampered the use of his arm and hand—a situation that he had difficulty accepting, considering how much work he was hoping to carry out yet. All these symptoms point quite probably toward a severe case of tuberculosis, which eventually cost him his life.

After every one of these recurrent attacks, Bucer managed to muster enough strength to continue his work. However, when his health broke down once again on February 13, 1551, it soon became clear that his weakened body had no more reserves to fall back on. Bucer's condition became increasingly worse in spite of continuous, devoted care. On February 22, 1551, he dictated an addition to his last will. In it he named Walter Haddon and Matthew Parker as executors of his testament, commended his loved ones to Thomas Cranmer, thanked his stepdaughter Agnes Capito for her loving care, and closed with the words: "May the Lord rule everything else. He is the protector of widows and the father of orphans."[44]

The situation of the church in Germany tormented and anguished Bucer until his very death. Did not the very same fate threaten England, should it respond with the same indifference to God's Word now revealed so openly and clearly? On the afternoon of February 28, 1551, Bucer urged those surrounding his deathbed to do all they could to make his grand design for the kingdom of Christ come true. That very same night he died, at only fifty-nine years of age.

He was solemnly laid to rest in the choir of Great St. Mary's in the presence of a large crowd of university professors and students, as well as of local townspeople. Haddon held a Latin funeral oration, whereas Parker gave a eulogy in English.[45] This impressive event had a gruesome sequel some years later. On February 6, 1556, in the midst of her campaign of militant re-Catholicization, Queen Mary had Bucer and Fagius posthumously tried as heretics. Their caskets were disinterred and chained to the stake at the Cambridge marketplace, and later burned along with all the available books of both theologians. On July 22, 1560, Elizabeth I rehabilitated Bucer and Fagius in a formal act. A brass plaque on the floor of the choir in Great St. Mary's reminds visitors today of the earlier location of Bucer's grave.

Chapter Nine

Conclusion

B ucer's work and ministry did not end with his death—neither in England nor on the Continent. His personality and his ideas had impressed
and inspired too many people for his influence to cease abruptly. Bucer's
books as well had a life of their own: copies continued to exist in private
libraries and continued to be read. His writings were also reprinted and
translated into many different vernacular languages, often transporting
his thought under a fictitious name or even anonymously. This dissemination of his ideas and its historical and theological consequences have yet
to be sufficiently studied.

We should nevertheless be cautious of overestimating the impact of
Bucer's theology in subsequent years, however extensive it may have been.
Bucer's name did indeed come up frequently in the second half of the sixteenth century in many places: in England, in the German Empire, in
Strasbourg, of course, but also in other imperial cities and territories, as
well as in the Netherlands, in Switzerland, and in many other European
countries. But it often turned out to be only select statements from his letters and books that were being quoted out of context and used by people
in entirely different situations in order to shore up their own positions with
Bucer's enduring theological and ecclesiastical authority. Bucer was thus
turned into a spokesman for views of which he had never been the sole or
even the leading espouser. For instance, the Anglicans as well as the Puri-
tans laid claim to him in England, and on the Continent the Lutherans as
well as the Reformed saw him as one of their own. The Dutch Remon-
strants, influenced by humanism, rallied around Bucer and his writings at
the beginning of the seventeenth century in their struggle against the
narrow-minded and strict Calvinism of their times.

Thus tremendously diverse groups became convinced of the congeniality between their own and Bucer's theology—certainly a sign of the Strasbourg reformer's lasting impact, albeit at the price of both over- and underestimating him in the process. Put another way, his ideas were domesticated and adapted to the views and needs of the confessional age. In consequence, soon the image ensued of Bucer as a spineless and accommodating theologian, more interested in the effectiveness of his conciliatory formulations than in God's revealed truth. Bucer, of course, never founded an independent school of theological thought. Neither did a "Buceran" denomination emerge from his ministry. There were several reasons for this, including the simple political fact that only the princely territories, and not the imperial cities, would prove to have a future in the German Empire. In addition, Bucer's time in England was too brief to allow him to leave a durable imprint on the church there. A further essential reason was Bucer's inability and unwillingness to cast his theology into a clearly and firmly structured mold and thus turn it into a readily teachable and learnable dogmatic system, as Calvin and Melanchthon had succeeded in doing. In view of stiffening confessional fronts on both the Catholic and the Protestant side, unequivocal theological, ecclesiastical, and religious positions were called for and needed in the second half of the sixteenth century. In such a context, Bucer's answers were often found wanting and outdated.

Yet the same things that apparently limit the efficacy of his theology can also be seen as an asset. Bucer's theology was unique in that it could not be easily brought to a point or readily fixed doctrinally. It was not only Bucer's restless, unremitting, and persistent individual personality that transcended boundaries during his lifetime. The theological and ecclesiastical effects of his work and ministry as well continued to overcome boundaries after his death. We thus can fully grasp Bucer only if we view him squarely in the center of the impassioned controversies and bitter rifts of the Reformation era. From his perspective, they presented him with ever new and awesome challenges that he was only too glad to take on. He was not ready to shy away from wide-ranging responsibilities, often fully aware that by assuming them he was getting himself entangled in extremely complicated and sometimes even distressing problems.

In a rapidly and thoroughly changing world, Bucer was bent on understanding others and coming to an agreement with them. This was hardly a craving for harmony and appeasement at any, or almost any, price. It is perhaps most fitting to describe Bucer as a theologian of dialogue. This does not mean he was not sure of what he believed. On the contrary, his own theological standpoint was quite clear and firm. But he did not use it primarily to contrast his own position over against that of his opponents, but rather as a point of departure for embarking in an exchange with them. Bucer remained sensitive to elements of truth in the arguments of his antagonists, and even more to elements of truth in their lives and actions. This allowed him to associate quite freely with Luther and Zwingli and their respective supporters, always open to learning from them but at the same time intent on maintaining his independence. He entered into conversations with Anabaptists and supporters of the Catholic Church with the same self-assurance. This is probably the aspect of Bucer's personality and theology that seems most current and modern.

It is worth emphasizing once again, however, that Bucer was never guided by mere considerations of utility or glib accommodation. His conduct was inextricably connected to the fabric of his theology, in which competing strands intersected and intermingled. Traditions of the High and Late Middle Ages and crucial Reformation insights were closely interwoven in his thought. We have already seen how Bucer was fascinated by the vision of a thoroughly Christian society brought about by the close-knit cooperation of church and state; yet his model was not merely a replica of the received concept of the *corpus christianum* but rather presupposed a fully new ecclesiology based on the individual responsibility of every single Christian. While Bucer promoted with all available means the establishment of state church structures and the enforcement of obligatory doctrinal norms, he also sought simultaneously to safeguard liberty of conscience and even to make practical allowances for the possibility of diverging views. He incessantly proclaimed God's law to be eternally and inalterably valid, even to the point of sounding crudely legalistic; yet at the same time he subordinated God's law to the work of the Holy Spirit, who creates people anew, bestows on them the gift of faith in God, and sows in them love for their fellow human beings and the desire to seek the welfare of both the civic community and the Christian fellowship.

These differing strains vied with one another in Bucer's thought and actions, influencing and imbuing one another. Every statement he made implied a counterstatement. And affirming a position meant for Bucer also seeking to win over those who rejected that position. For him, entering into conversation with Christians who held views on faith different from his own was not a choice but a necessity. The ultimate foundation for this attitude was, and this was no coincidence, the Reformation doctrine of justification by grace through faith. The conviction that God unconditionally loves human beings as they are stood at the center of Bucer's theology and his entire church work. This conviction also gave him the capacity to deal with and endure differing views and even positions diametrically opposed to his own. The doctrine of justification also put limits on his theology's innate tendency toward absoluteness and totality. This, of course, did not lead to tolerance in the modern sense of the term, but rather to a recognition of the incompleteness and transience of all human attempts to understand the mysteries of God.

What relevance, if any, does this have for us?

Of course, we are not called to continue or repeat anything of what Bucer did. Yet by remembering this past, we learn of convictions, experiences, and aims still worth pondering. Among these are, to begin with, Bucer's realization over four centuries ago of what we now call "theological pluralism," taking it for granted today. Next, we are challenged by Bucer's ecclesiastical perspective that was oblivious to national boundaries: his view focused not only on the situation of the church in Germany but extended all the way to Christians in the Low Countries, France, England, as well as in Italy, Denmark, Poland, Hungary, Bohemia, and Moravia. This supranational vantage point assumed that Christians must be willing to listen to one another and learn from one another, thus creating a common ground that allows differing parties to unite without smothering their uniqueness and particularity.

Further, we have to take note of Bucer's compelling urge to see the gospel and a living Christian faith encompass all of society, including its structures and institutions. As we saw, he was particularly energetic in demanding that Christians assume responsibility for shaping the world they live in, a point amply illustrated in previous sections.

A final point worth reflecting on is Bucer's lifelong struggle to build a church that was generous in including as many people as possible—and yet that vigorously upheld discipline and moral standards; a church that respected the individuality and responsibility of each single member and had its foundation in grass-roots congregational life—yet at the same time was not afraid to get involved in surrounding society and was even willing to cooperate with the politically powerful.

There are certainly countless questions that Bucer left unanswered. But his intense and unconditional devotion to the problems and challenges of his times has left us a legacy of such immensity that we have barely begun doing it justice. Of course, nothing of this legacy can be blindly imitated, as we already noted above. Yet remembering Bucer and his work can perhaps help future generations grapple with issues that remain fundamental.

Chapter Ten

New Insights

Fortunately, Bucer scholarship has not stood still since the appearance of the German original of this book in 1990. On the contrary, it has advanced remarkably. This is true for critical editions of the Strasbourg reformer's works and letters just as it is for research on his life and work. The *Bucer-Forschungsstelle* in Heidelberg, which edits the Strasbourg reformer's German-language works, is also in the process of completing a new bibliography of his works. A detailed inventory of secondary literature on Bucer was published in 1999.[1] In 1997, Gottfried Seebass, the director of the *Forschungsstelle*, published a very illuminating review of Bucer research since 1991.[2] The above publications provide the basis for the following remarks in which I present new and controversial scholarly viewpoints, respond to critiques of my own views, and discuss areas of research full of promise.

The Years until Bucer's Arrival in Strasbourg

To my knowledge, there have been no new works on the reformer's family and his early surroundings in Sélestat. Two interesting essays, however, deal with Bucer's report on Luther's Heidelberg disputation of 1518 (see chapter 2).[3] Both essentially arrive at the same conclusions: Bucer did not by any means "misunderstand" Luther on account of an Erasmian background supposedly blinkering his perception of the Wittenberg reformer. In fact, he probably grasped exactly what Luther said and was equally accurate in reporting it. The two authors interpret apparent inaccuracies in Bucer's report within the framework of Luther's theology at the time. Their conclusion is thus not surprising: "Incontestable evidence of Bucer's own theological emphases cannot be found in a single passage of his report."[4] I do not wish to insist on all the details of my original interpretation of Bucer's account of the disputation, according to which the young Dominican heard and understood Luther's comments in harmony with his Erasmian and Thomistic presuppositions.[5] I would, however, continue to plead for the continuing validity of a fundamental hermeneutic principle: that none of the men upon whom Luther made a deep and lasting impression—indeed an impression that left some of them, such as Bucer, fundamentally changed for the rest of their lives—were intellectual and theological *tabulae rasae* on the eve of their encounter with the Wittenberg reformer. Consequently, they—especially the creative and restless spirits among them—played a role more significant than that of constituting mere receptacles of Luther's theology. I thus consider it methodologically important not to lose sight of the preconditions and presuppositions that future supporters of the Reformation brought with them when encountering Luther. Both studies fail to take this dimension into account. As a result, while justifiably rejecting the simplistic attribution of everything to Erasmus's influence, they come dangerously close to the opposite extreme of turning Luther into an overwhelmingly dominant figure.

Taking issue with my claim that linguistic style and particularly theological content preclude Bucer's authorship of the anonymous pamphlets *A Beautiful Dialogue* (*Ain schöner Dialogus*) and *Neu-Karsthans* (see chapter 2), Siegfried Bräuer argues in an incisive and well-thought-out article for attributing at least *Neu-Karsthans* to Bucer, for it is "certainly imaginable" that he could have written such a work.[5] Thomas Kaufmann makes similar points, while ultimately placing greatest emphasis on the impossibility of determining authorship.[6] I think we can all agree that analysis, however thorough, of only the text of *Neu-Karsthans* will never provide a sufficiently solid foundation for demonstrating that Bucer was its author. One question requiring definite clarification is why the author who proves to be such an involved and committed theologian in his writings of the years 1518 to 1523 does not show even a sign of it in *Neu-Karsthans*. I do not find explanations very convincing that appeal to the new historical context and the different literary genre. But since this issue cannot be solved with final certainty, it probably makes most sense to conclude with a *non liquet* verdict.

Little is known about Elisabeth Silbereisen and her marriage with Bucer (chapter 2). Herman J. Selderhuis has recently gathered the scattered information available.[7] While Doris Ebert provides us with a much more detailed account, she relies to a great extent on speculation and quite a bit of imagination. She does succeed in arguing with some probability that Bucer's son Nathanael was born not in 1529 but rather in 1539 or 1540 (chapter 6).[8]

A Preacher in Strasbourg

Recent scholarship has paid heightened attention to Bucer's early writings. By carefully studying what the reformer said about civil authority in his programmatic work *That No One Should Live for Himself* (*Das ym selbs niemant . . . leben soll*), Matthieu Arnold establishes the extent to which Bucer either relied on Luther or maintained an independent stance.[9] Gustave Koch discusses what concrete changes a layperson in Wissembourg would have experienced in her or his day-to-day life as a result of embracing the message Bucer preached in Wissembourg.[10] Already the second volume of Bucer's correspondence (letters of the years 1524 to 1526) had provided us with ample evidence of the growing, and soon exclusive, importance of the conflict over the Lord's Supper. This topic also plays a central role in volume 3, which contains the correspondence of the years 1527 to 1529.[11] Yet Bucer's letters of these years also show that a multitude of religious and social problems plagued him and his colleagues in Strasbourg. Anabaptists posed an increasingly important challenge during this time. Bucer's participation in the Bern disputation of 1528 not only widened his horizon but also increased the number of people corresponding with him. These experiences strengthened him in the conviction that evangelicals divided over the eucharistic controversy had to forget their differences and present a common front, at least when dealing with opponents of the Reformation. Finally, these letters shed some light on Bucer's private life, including his taking on the important pastorship of St. Thomas Church in the heart of the city in April 1529.

A burning issue at the time Bucer began his ministry in Strasbourg was the growing theoretical and later practical opposition of many priests to clerical celibacy (see chapter 3). Using Bucer's letter to Otilia von Berckheim of April 1524 as a point of departure, Bernd Moeller expounds the far-reaching consequences that clerical marriage had on the development of the new "social class" of Protestant pastors.[12] At about this same time, evangelical preachers started pronouncing judicial rulings in marital matters, deliberately disregarding hitherto valid canon law. They decreed divorces and allowed divorced people to remarry. At least the first four memoranda in the tenth volume of *Martin Bucers Deutsche Schriften* reflect this unique historical phenomenon.[13] Important motifs in Bucer's marriage and divorce memoranda are his understanding of marriage as an intimate, close fellowship in which each partner helps and serves the other unconditionally and both help and serve the rest of society.[14]

As we have seen, Bucer was only one among many important figures during these early years (see chapter 3). Michel Weyer succeeds in giving us a vivid portrayal of the popular preacher Matthew Zell's thoughts and actions, as well as of the personality of his remarkable wife, Katharina Schütz.[15] Reinhard Bodenmann achieves the same for Caspar Hedio.[16] Yet the central theme remains the Lord's Supper (chapter 3). The works of Thomas Kaufmann represent a significant scholarly contribution to our understanding of this controversy from the perspective of the Strasbourg preachers.

To begin with, Kaufmann persuasively identifies Capito and Bucer as the authors of two anonymous pamphlets printed in the fall of 1525.[17] Both imprints constitute direct and indirect attacks on Luther's interpretation of the Lord's Supper. Whether or not Bucer actually wrote one of them (it purports to have been authored by a certain Cunrat Ryss zu Ofen) must remain an open issue. We are well advised to remain cautious, given the clear conformity of this text with arguments typical for Andreas Karlstadt, and the fact, pointed out by Marc Lienhard,[18] that a citizen by the name of Conrad Ryff zu Ofen is known to have lived in Strasbourg in 1528.

More significant for our purposes is Kaufmann's composition, on the basis of these sources, of an argumentative line that runs as follows: the Strasbourg reformers, and Bucer foremost among them, were always accommodating and conciliatory in public, especially when confronting the Wittenberg theologians. Secretly, however, they polemicized and stirred up emotions against them. They therefore acted disingenuously and certainly not irenically. Kaufmann develops this thesis in greater detail in his dissertation.[19]

I want to make it clear from the outset that I have no doubts about the quality of Kaufmann's book. It represents an excellent and compellingly argued piece of scholarship. This is true for its demonstration of Luther's dominating influence in the early years of the Reformation. Bucer's own position is rightly placed in the context of his colleagues and not studied in isolation. Kaufmann also coherently describes the Strasbourg preachers' estrangement from Luther's understanding of the Lord's Supper and their gradual espousal of Zwingli's and Oecolampadius's views. He shows that Bucer was clearly convinced of the rightness of his own interpretation of the Bible passages that deal with the Lord's Supper and therefore undertook everything at his disposal to disseminate and enforce his views. There can be no doubt that Bucer was intent on pushing back Luther's influence in this area. It is equally indisputable that in pursuit of this goal he resorted to decidedly questionable means. It remains to be seen, however, if justice is done to Bucer by portraying him as a conspiratorial figure drawing strings behind the scenes and plotting sinister schemes against the Wittenberg Reformers. I also would hesitate to characterize Bucer's addition of annotations—plainly identified by the Strasbourg reformer as his own differing opinion—to his Latin translation of the fourth volume of Luther's *Postils* as an "outrage."[20] Kaufmann is entirely right in rejecting, on the basis of historical fact, the flawed perspective that Bucer was obsessed with reconciling opposing views and reaching an agreement at any cost. Yet Kaufmann never finds himself at a loss when it comes to calling attention to statements by Bucer that confirm just this stereotype. This results in the repetition, scarcely concealed, of the timeworn accusation that the Strasbourg reformer was equivocal and dishonest.

This aspect of Bucer's conduct should certainly not be glibly dismissed. But is there a single scholar who adhered or adheres to the simplistic view, so vigorously attacked by Kaufmann, that Bucer was a thoroughgoing irenicist? Certainly not Walther Köhler; nor, for that matter, Jacques Pollet. Are we thus left with accusing an imaginary "Stupperich school"?[21] I would find it more helpful to propose that Bucer's behavior was guided by two criteria: on the one hand, Bucer sincerely believed he was theologically right in his understanding of the Lord's Supper, since he was convinced of having the statements of the Bible—the very foundation of the Reformation—on his side; he therefore felt he had not only the right but also the obligation to stand up for his own position. On the other hand, though, he also believed that this disagreement among Protestants over the Lord's Supper should not be allowed to jeopardize evangelical unity when confronting supporters of the Roman Church in Strasbourg, the German Empire, and beyond. This second conviction was of a pragmatic and political nature, and it presented Bucer with several tactical options. He felt he had these options precisely because he strongly believed—on the basis of his understanding of the Lord's Supper—that the points of disagreement did not pertain to the very core of the gospel and of evangelical faith. In a letter he wrote to Jakob Otter in September 1525, resolutely defending Zwingli's interpretation of the words of consecration, Bucer concludes by pointing out that the controversy fortunately concerns an issue "of not so much importance" (*non adeo magni momenti*).[22] I believe this statement sincerely expresses Bucer's views. Of course, this is not enough to make an irenicist of him. But neither does it provide sufficient grounds for turning him into a dishonest tactician. Only after some time did Bucer finally realize that Luther—precisely because of his *own* understanding of the Lord's Supper—could not treat this disagreement as a trifling one.

A number of recent publications deal with Bucer as a biblical exegete (see chapter 3). Bernard Roussel places Bucer within a "Rhenish school of biblical exegesis" at home in southwestern Germany and identifies the philological, rhetorical, and theological features typical for his exegetical works.[23] Using her superbly meticulous critical edition of Bucer's commentary on the Gospel of John as a point of departure, Irena Backus summarizes the central thoughts of this work throughout the 1527, 1530, and 1536 editions of this work.[24] She demonstrates how Bucer develops his concept of the church in this commentary against the backdrop of the introduction of the Reformation in Bern and in opposition to Catholics and Lutherans. She also expounds the *Retractationes* that Bucer added to this work after the 1536 Wittenberg Concord. Bucer's commentary on Ephesians of 1527 dealt with very similar topics, as Peter Stephens shows in his comparison with the posthumous edition of 1550–51.[25] In the first edition, Bucer highlights Christ's relationship to the church as his body in order to give prominence to the unity of the church and the fellowship of Christians among one another. The later version attached greater importance to the church offices, doctrines, and sacraments, thus emphasizing the church as an institution. This is certainly due to the fact that Bucer found himself in a completely different situation in England. Besides, he now unmistakably possessed a deeper appreciation for the historical continuity of the church and the reality of its existence as an organization. In an informative article, Gerald Hobbs analyzes the direct and indirect impact that Bucer's major commentary on the Psalms had through its translation into the English vernacular.[26] All the interesting studies mentioned above make the lack of critical editions of Bucer's biblical commentaries painfully apparent.

Spokesman of the Strasbourg Reformation

The volume of Bucer's correspondence that appeared most recently offers a wealth of information, not only on Bucer's personal life (e.g., his having to bathe in mineral springs because of scabies), but especially on the different theological confrontations in which he was involved.[27] Of greatest importance during this period, of course, were Bucer's efforts to put an end to the eucharistic controversy during the negotiations surrounding the diet of Augsburg (see chapter 4). This is a theme that Wilhelm H. Neuser also addresses in an article on Bucer's activity as a mediator during the same period.[28] By carefully analyzing thirty-one documents that issued from Bucer's pen from July 1530 to April 1531, Neuser demonstrates how the Strasbourg reformer cautiously and gradually drew near to Luther's position. Bucer always proceeded in the following way: first, he rejected the sharpest formulations from both sides as being too radical; then he sought wordings that expressed the theological intentions of the Swiss as well as of the theologians in Wittenberg. His firm conviction that both sides essentially saw eye to eye gave him the freedom and self-assurance to follow this path. To be sure, at the same time he adhered to the view that the Lutherans were the "weak in faith" in this issue, and because of this, they had to be tolerated with love and patience. Finally, Neuser emphatically rejects the insinuation that Bucer behaved deceitfully or even untruthfully in these discussions. The Lord's Supper is only one of the topics dealt with in Bucer's written defense against the attacks of the bishop of Avranches, Robert Céneau (see chapter 4). Ian P. Hazlett has prepared a painstaking and richly commented edition of this work, which has appeared as volume 5 in the *Opera latina* series.[29] When Bucer wrote the *Defensio adversus axioma catholicum*, he did not know that Céneau was a theologian who may have been willing to carry out reforms, but who was ultimately a resolute supporter of the Roman Catholic Church, and who also had excellent contacts to similar-minded and politically influential circles in the court of the French queen mother. Neither did Bucer know that the French chancellor to whom he had dedicated his book, Cardinal Antoine Duprat, also belonged to this group. In his onslaught against Bucer, Céneau was probably not intending to single out a solitary heretic but rather wishing to attack all humanistic and evangelical-minded persons in his Norman diocese, in addition to certain associates of King Francis I, who at the time was speaking out for rapprochement with German Protestants and reforming the French national church. The fact that Céneau chose Bucer, of all people, as the object of his attack exemplifies how renowned the Strasbourg reformer had become in France.

Bucer defended not only his own but also the common Protestant understanding of the Lord's Supper by appealing to both Oecolampadius and Luther in his arguments and thus rebuffing the claim that the evangelical camp was plagued by dissension and disunity. Céneau had asserted that the latter were the unfailing signs of a heresy. But Bucer did not leave it at that. He went on to expound the fundamentals of Reformation theology and practice in a conciliatory, winning fashion. His guiding principle was the affirmation that all Christians agreed on the essentials of the faith and that abuses in the church could be done away with on the basis of the Bible, the church fathers, and even early scholastics. Never before had he come comparably close in approaching Catholic positions in this way. This was indeed a new chapter in his efforts at achieving union.

According to Hazlett's compelling conjecture, Bucer based the first part of his defense against Céneau on the *Counsel* (*Consilium*) he had written for the French envoy whom King Francis I had sent to Germany in 1534 in order to gain support for discussions over necessary church reforms between like-minded people of both confessions. From this point onward, Bucer was certainly ready to embark on such negotiations.

With the *Defensio* we reach the theme of Bucer's Europe-wide engagement (see chapter 4). More than any other reformer, Bucer included the Christendom of all of Europe in his field of view. A number of recent studies analyze Bucer's contacts and relations with Reformation-minded groups of varying dimensions in different European countries.[30] In an informative article, Marc Lienhard offers a clarifying explanation of this phenomenon from a broad perspective.[31] In an essay of my own, I discuss the theological presuppositions of Bucer's model, which aimed at dialogue and cooperation between the churches of Europe.[32] This did not mean that there was no such thing as absolute truth for Bucer, nor that he was willing to postpone theological efforts at attaining this truth. But since he made a fundamental distinction between essential and secondary articles of the Christian faith, unsettled dogmatic issues did not have to impede the religious and moral endeavors to bring about a closer cooperation between the churches of Europe, a cooperation that would be characterized by mutual giving and taking.

Using Bucer's relations to France as an example, Ian P. Hazlett demonstrates how rationally and pragmatically the Strasbourg reformer pursued his European goals.[33] In view of the centralized government of the country, Bucer focused his entire attention on winning over the leading personalities at the court, and even the king himself. He tried to establish an evangelical foothold in a French-speaking city from where he could attempt to raise support for his cause by means of pamphlets, letters, and sermons. This did not succeed in the case of Metz, but it did in Geneva, as we know from Calvin's experience after returning from Strasbourg.

Bucer's innovative ideas in marriage law have already been discussed above. He developed his thought on this matter in a particularly detailed and precise way while helping the city council of Ulm with the introduction of the Reformation (see chapter 4). Volume 10 of *Martin Bucers Deutsche*

Schriften, which we mentioned previously, contains at least four marriage memoranda addressed to the Ulm city council, among them the voluminous treatise *On Marriage and Divorce according to Divine and Roman Law* (*Von der Ehe und Ehescheidung aus göttlichem und kaiserlichem Recht*). These texts understandably play a central role in the book by Herman J. Selderhuis, mentioned previously.[34] In it, Selderhuis engages in a meticulous compilation of Bucer's statements on marriage, which he then analyzes systematically. He makes a convincing case for Bucer's positive valuation of marriage as a moral fellowship, as well as for the improvement of the status of women that went along with this. For Bucer, ending a disrupted marriage by means of divorce and allowing the divorcées to remarry was nothing other than the dissolution of a marriage that had already ceased existing *de facto.* Selderhuis does charge Bucer with not having carried out the forthright exposition of the clear sense of Scripture—contrary to his expressed intentions. This critique is not to be dismissed easily. Yet in arguing in this way, Selderhuis does not make sufficient allowances for the peculiarity of Bucer's theological hermeneutics. Bucer's point of departure was the order of existence expressed in Genesis 2:28 and instituted by God since creation. First Corinthians 7:2 bore witness to the fact that this order remained valid under the new covenant. This was the fundamental presupposition upon which Bucer based his exegesis, carried by the conviction that no biblical statement could contradict the order of existence that God had built into the very fabric of creation. According to Bucer, the Holy Spirit elucidates the meaning of the statements of the Old and New Testaments, as well as of the decrees of Roman law, thus making possible the well-being of individuals as well as of entire communities, as wished by God.

The Synod of 1533 (chapter 4) dealt with the doctrinal, social, and ethical reorganization of church structures in Strasbourg. Stephen E. Buckwalter has presented a detailed study of Bucer's and Capito's attitudes toward Anabaptists in Strasbourg until 1528.[35] A further study by Matthieu Arnold underscores Bucer's failure to convince the city council to take a tougher stance against Anabaptism.[36]

John S. Oyer offers a comprehensive view of Bucer's position toward Anabaptism.[37] Contrary to Bullinger or Melanchthon, Bucer was sincerely concerned with winning back Anabaptists to the Protestant fold. This did not prevent him from attacking them head on whenever he felt that the established church was in danger. But he took them very seriously on a theological level, especially when they criticized the church for its absent discipline. Amy Nelson Burnett has shown how the Anabaptist emphasis on commitment to Christ influenced Bucer's understanding of confirmation.[38] When church structures in Strasbourg became firmer, Bucer's approach to the Anabaptists became more characterized by pastoral concern.

I have outlined how Bucer's theological understanding of the cooperation between church and state is manifested in the sixteen articles discussed in the Synod of 1533.[39] Since Christ rules over the whole world and not just over the church, all Christians must also strive to carry out his will in their respective professions and estates. In this way, they serve and benefit one another and promote the spiritual and earthly welfare of the ecclesiastical and civil community. Church and state make use of different means in this process. However, since they ultimately pursue the same goal, the spiritual fellowship and the civic community are practically coterminous, constituting a single pious and morally upright society.

The spiritualists, particularly Schwenckfeld and his supporters, rejected this far-reaching influence of the civil authorities over questions of faith and religious fellowship. R. Emmet McLaughlin shows that one of the main reasons why Bucer opposed spiritualists so vigorously was precisely the sympathy and approval they received from Strasbourg's ruling elite.[40] This social group was less than enthusiastic about enforcing a new church ordinance. Accordingly, these powerful citizens, influenced by the spirit of Schwenckfeld, distanced themselves from the preachers' efforts to set up compulsary doctrinal norms. The same phenomenon can be observed in Esslingen, Ulm, Augsburg, Württemberg, and elsewhere, leading Bucer to resist the Silesian spiritualist and his supporters untiringly in the following months and years. His success, however, was minimal, for these spiritualist circles were often closely intertwined with the respective political leadership of a city. On the whole, Sebastian Franck was less influential, although the criticism he leveled at Bucer was similar to that of Schwenckfeld. Two recent articles deal with this topic.[41] Like other spiritualists, Franck advocated a markedly inward form of piety and vigorously attacked Bucer's *Dialogi oder Gesprech* (*Dialogues or Discussion*) of 1535 (see chapter 4) in a work with the paradoxical title *War Booklet of Peace* (*Kriegbüchlin des Friedes*). Franck gruffly rejected Bucer's view that the laws of the Old Testament retained their normative validity, arguing instead for an allegorical interpretation of the Bible under the guidance of Christ's Spirit.

A further work that appeared in the wake of the Synod of 1533 is Bucer's catechism of the year 1534 (chapter 4). In a stimulating article, Michèle Monteil compares it to Luther's *Small Catechism* of 1529.[42] Although the two works have much in common on account of the joint catechetical tradition they draw on, they also show marked pedagogical differences:

whereas Luther imparts knowledge mostly by means of brief summaries and frequent repetitions, Bucer's preferred method is the dialogue, developing theological statements step by step, gradually casting them in more concrete forms, developing them further and then presenting them one last time succinctly. This procedure is obviously more intellectually demanding on catechumens, for it requires that they follow and join in the process of grappling with the questions of faith. Whereas Luther's catechism concentrates on soteriology and thus on the individual, Bucer consistently focuses on life in the ecclesiastical and civic community. Because of his distinction between law and gospel, Luther replaced the received catechetical pattern of faith-law-prayer with one of law-faith-prayer. Bucer, by contrast, was able to express his emphasis on ethics precisely within the traditional pattern, interpreting law in accordance with Old Testament Torah as God's loving, salvation-bringing instruction.

A Champion of Protestant Unity and the Reformation of the Empire

It has been often observed that legal issues, and especially the recourse to Roman civil law, played an increasingly important role in Bucer's thought during these years. An international symposium devoted to this theme was held in Emden, Germany, in March 2001. Among the many interesting papers presented, the observations of Cornel A. Zwierlein merit special attention.[43] He demonstrates that Bucer concerned himself with Roman as well as with early canon law quite intensely from the late 1520s onward. During the 1530s, as Bucer himself began to participate in the promulgation of laws, he made extensive use of these two legal sources. The Strasbourg reformer subsumed all things conducive to truth and goodness under "God's law" (*lex Dei*). The norm on which he based this was, of course, the Bible. But the actual details for carrying out the intended reform of society were provided by Roman law, which Bucer, along with other humanists, understood as the substantial concretion of the "Golden Rule." Therefore, we can almost describe the Reformation, in Zwierlein's fitting terms, as having made its appearance in the form of a major legal reform. I believe this is an idea worth pursuing.

Many of the studies mentioned in my survey up to this point deal with the late 1530s and early 1540s; but a number of them also include Bucer's early years in their scope. This is particularly true for the topic of Bucer's efforts to establish a system of church discipline. Several stages can be identified in this process, as his disciplinary endeavors became increasingly concrete and intense beginning in the late 1520s, throughout the 1530s, and culminating in the 1540s. His goals, however, always remained the same. Amy Nelson Burnett has made several contributions in this field (see chapter 5).[44] They make evident that Bucer was not merely concerned with church discipline in a narrow sense but was committed to establishing a Christian social order that included strict religious and moral norms, as well as actual day-to-day conduct according to these norms. Education played a crucial role for Bucer in this process. Pastors were to be the primary educating agents, but ultimately all of society was to be involved. Bucer's goal was that every individual Christian internalize evangelical values. The path leading to this consisted of instructing, informing, teaching, and educating people. This process was to begin by providing children and servants with catechetical instruction. Bucer wished that adults be subject to an examination before participating in the Lord's Supper, that they also be given the possibility of confessing privately, and that the entire congregation confess its faith publicly with some regularity. None of this became true in Strasbourg. Neither were Bucer's efforts to introduce confirmation crowned with success. The late Jean Rott has given us a detailed presentation of the problems facing the church wardens (*Kirchenpfleger*) in this respect.[45] As late as 1541, the patrician Jacob Wetzel publicly denied such an office the right to exist: after all, the civil authorities and not the pastors were responsible for questions of public morality. In a further rout, the authorities turned down Bucer's 1546 request to be allowed, on account of the inaction of the church wardens, to summon parishioners himself in order to admonish and discipline them. Christian Meyer's essay on the Strasbourg Hymnal of 1541 deserves mention at this point.[46] The preface to this splendid edition is the only place in which Bucer speaks in great detail about his understanding of music. He perceived music as an expression of God's order. Music was capable, more than words, of moving and stirring the soul—which of course opened the possibility of it being misused. For this reason, Bucer demanded that trivial and light music be discarded for the benefit of music devoted to the worship and praise of God, especially in catechetical instruction. Willem van 't Spijker summarizes the state of research on the relationship between Bucer and Calvin (see chapter 4).[47] The two men were united not only by friendship ties but also by a common theology. Crucial in forming Calvin's thought were his Strasbourg years, which Spijker describes in great detail.[48] He thus sees Calvin's later views on theology and social ethics as the presentation of Bucer's thoughts "in a precise and brief form."[49] In my opinion, the lines of continuity drawn here are somewhat too direct.

Two smaller contributions to this much-discussed topic deserve our attention. Cornelis Augustijn discusses the circumstances surrounding Calvin's sharp criticism of Bucer in a letter written in 1538.[50] One of the reasons for Calvin's accusations was his worry that Bucer was making far too many concessions to the Catholics, even to the point of being willing to abandon justification by faith, as we saw in the *Defensio* against Robert Céneau. A second reason was Calvin's irritation over the fact that Bucer had reached a theological settlement with the Bernese, whose political power extended to the very gates of Geneva, and that this agreement was achieved at the expense of the Zwinglians, or more precisely of Bullinger in Zurich. Calvin's and Bucer's fundamentally different assessments of the papal church can seen as a reflection of their varying tactics. Whereas Calvin could see only ghastly blasphemy in the Catholic Church, and particularly in its Mass, for Bucer it continued to be a church in spite of all of its abuses, which absolutely needed to be done away with—a church in which Christians could and should remain as long as they stood up for reforming it. Francis Higman makes a similar point in an instructive article on "Bucer and the Nicodemites." He shows that even though Bucer resolutely clung to unequivocal theological norms and regarded church reforms as absolutely necessary,[51] he still considered the patient path of slow inward and outward reforms to be much more effective and promising than the one of direct confrontation with the traditional church.

Bucer dwelled on this theme during the 1540s, particularly during the religious colloquies with the Catholics (see chapter 6). Cornelis Augustijn is entirely correct in pointing out that Bucer's activities during this period are far from having been adequately researched.[52] Augustijn himself, however, has contributed enormously to Bucer research with his work on these colloquies, as volume 9/1 of *Martin Bucers Deutsche Schriften*, which he edited, amply proves.[53] We are now able to see how Bucer not only sent his Leipzig reformation draft to the members of the Schmalkaldic League but also made it available to resolutely Catholic circles, in order to create a common basis for conversations. We are also shown how Bucer, in the same way, not only took part in the sessions of the Schmalkaldeners but also through his two propaganda writings *Vom Tag zu Hagenaw* (*On the Hagenau Meeting*)[54] assiduously sought to win support for a religious colloquy free from the pope's influence. Augustijn's volume centers on the "Worms Book" (*Wormser Buch*) in both its Latin and German versions (the latter probably prepared by Bucer).[55] Gropper and Bucer were the main authors of this work, which concentrates on dogmatic and ecclesiastical issues that remained the matter of controversy between Protestants and

Catholics and offers solutions for overcoming differences. Although the "Worms Book" has a lot in common with Bucer's Leipzig draft, altogether it argues from a more theological perspective.

In arriving at a comprehensive assessment of the work, Augustijn places much importance on the fact that Bucer chose justification by faith as his point of departure, instead of ecclesiology, as Gropper would have preferred. Volkmar Ortmann gives a differing view in his thorough and well-thought-out study on Bucer's efforts to achieve church unity through these religious colloquies.[56] Bucer did in fact argue on the basis of ecclesiology, following Gropper's *Enchiridion* for the most part. But the formulations chosen by Bucer did not intend to be a record of unchangeable results; rather, they were the departure point for conversations, the outcome of which remained open. Under these conditions, it was certainly an official, even legal victory for Bucer that Protestant views were not excluded anywhere in the document. Ortmann argues just as convincingly that the concept championed by Bucer did not have its roots in the political situation around 1540 but can be traced back to his *Defensio* against Robert Céneau of 1534, as we saw above. The moment had apparently come for carrying out what Bucer had hoped and planned for, for so long: creating a united church in the German Empire, delivered of superstition and obvious abuses by incorporating the insights of Reformation theology. As Ortmann fittingly summarizes: "The Worms Book is an expression of Bucer's wish to present Protestant doctrine in such a manner that Catholics can recognize it as true, thus paving the way for an Evangelical Reformation."[57] A necessary preparatory step toward this goal would be a national council in which the opposing parties come to an agreement based on the Bible and—only in second place—the church fathers and the decisions of the early church councils. This implied retaining the received institutional structure of the church. We need not mention that Bucer's readiness to go along with this stood in diametrical opposition to many of his earlier statements and endeavors and met with bitter criticism from fellow Protestants. Yet I disagree with Augustijn when he, on the basis of these facts, infers that Bucer developed two quite separate ecclesiological conceptions, the second of which prevailed during this period of his life. Augustijn[58] does not take sufficiently into consideration Bucer's consistent and unswerving rejection of the pope as the enemy of all church reforms and his repeated attacks on the papal church. Bucer certrainly may have been willing to allow the reintroduction of some elements of Catholic ritual and custom that the Protestants had done away with. The same was true, albeit to a considerably less extent, for the theological substantiation of certain doctrinal articles such as the veneration of saints.

Bucer nevertheless remained convinced that the Reformation would achieve a decisive breakthrough if the church would accept the authority of the Bible in questions of doctrine and, by implication, the Reformation view of justification by faith. This would lead to the isolation of the opponents of the Reformation and would bring about, with God's help, the gradual transformation of the church. That is at least how the leading figures in the Cologne cathedral chapter and theological faculty interpeted Bucer's intents—and accordingly, they refused to cooperate with him. Therefore, Bucer can only to a limited extent be described as an ecumenically minded irenicist.[59] Of course, his views changed with time; yet he did not undergo a radical change of mind. How much research is still waiting to be done in this area, however, is made evident once again by Cornelis Augustijn, who with good reason claims that not Calvin but Bucer was the author of the anonymous pamphlet *Consilium admodum paternum Pauli III* of March 1541.[60] Nick Thompson calls our attention to the fact that Bucer was willing to tolerate the *canon missae* in exchange for the concession of the cup to laypeople in the Lord's Supper and the discontinuation of private masses.[61]

Jochen Remy retraces the path leading from the religious colloquies to the "Cologne reformation" (see chapter 6).[62] In doing so, he demonstrates that the latter endeavor can be perceived as a continuation of the effort to reach a consensus by means of colloquies. A portion of these sources—Bucer's first writing of defense, his and Melanchthon's *Christian and True Justification* (*Christliche und wahre Verantwortung*), and the Strasbourg reformer's *Simple Consideration* (*Einfältiges Bedenken*)—are now available in a solid, if somewhat scantily commented, critical edition in volume 11/1 of *Martin Bucers Deutsche Schriften*.[63] We can expect the continued edition of Bucer's Cologne writings to shed more light on this area.[64] Christoph Strohm has pointed out that for Bucer "legal arguments played a key role for substantiating his own position and refuting that of his opponents" in the Cologne reformation attempt.[65] The authority of tradition was also a hotly contested issue in Cologne. Amy Nelson Burnett has described how Bucer used the church fathers to defend the *Simple Consideration* against charges that it deviated from early church practice.[66]

Final Years

Gottfried Hammann provides a number of helpful summaries[67] of the major study[68] that he wrote on Bucer's ecclesiology, concentrating especially on the Strasbourg reformer's "Christian fellowships" (*christliche Gemeinschaften*) (see chapter 7). Hammann shows how Bucer, basing himself on the early Christian model, aimed at building a church that was open to everyone and yet remained a fellowship in which pure doctrine and a life of holiness prevailed. The crisis brought about by the emperor's war against the Schmalkaldic League—in Bucer's view, God's punishment for Protestants' moral laxness—led the Strasbourg reformer to the theoretical and practical solution of setting up fellowships of committed Christians within the different Strasbourg parishes. Thomas A. Brady sees this as a renewed effort on the part of Bucer to bring back to life the very clerical authority he had rejected earlier.[69] Brady's polemical account of the discord between Bucer and Jacob Sturm over the Interim (see chapter 7) is one-sided and does not muster the slightest empathy for Bucer. Disregarding the sources and most recent scholarship, Brady tends to caricature Bucer as a war hawk, an opportunist, a crusader, and even a cynic.[70]

Much recent literature deals with Bucer's final years in England.[71] They coincide in warning against overestimating Bucer's influence in shaping the Anglican Church. Diarmaid MacCulloch's standard work on Thomas Cranmer—with whom Bucer had remained in touch since 1530—clearly indicates how limited Bucer's scope of activity in England indeed was.[72] It is probably in the 1552 revision of the Book of Common Prayer that Bucer exercised the greatest influence. However, Jochen Remy goes too far in assuming, on the basis of evidence that is much too general, that English translations of Bucer's Cologne writings had a tangible influence already on the first edition of the Book of Common Prayer of 1549.[73] In spite of her thorough comparison of Bucer's *Censura* with the 1552 Book of Common Prayer, Christine Klingenspor is able only to allude to possible influences.[74]

Scott Amos has, in a number of recent essays, shed additional light on aspects of Bucer's stay in England, including his critical stance toward aspects of the conduct of the English Reformation,[75] his involvement in the revision of the 1549 Book of Common Prayer,[76] his epistolary relationship with Peter Martyr Vermigli,[77] and his sojourn in Cambridge.[78] Amos has also contributed an essay on Bucer's understanding of the relationship between civil and canon law and biblical law as it is seen in *De Regno Christi*.[79] Furthermore, Amos's recent Ph.D. dissertation has focused attention on Bucer's lectures on Ephesians, given during his tenure as Regius Professor of Divinity at the University of Cambridge between January 1550 and early 1551.[80] While the thesis is more concerned with the lectures as an exercise in the teaching and practice of theology in the light of biblical humanism, it has also further extended our knowledge of Bucer's tenure as Regius Professor.

Going beyond the studies previously mentioned, Andreas Gäumann has attempted a "comprehensive survey of Bucer's Reformation thought and action and his relationship to civil authority."[81] In his view, all theological convictions of the Strasbourg reformer converge in the concept of *regnum Christi*, which is capable of subsuming his understandings of Christology, ecclesiology, law, justification, sanctification, ethics, as well as his assessment of temporal authority. We are informed that cooperation with the civil authorities—for Bucer, a clear theological necessity—succeeded for the most part in establishing the Reformation in Strasbourg, but not when it came to persecuting "dissidents" and setting up an autonomous system of church discipline. Bucer's activities outside of Strasbourg are also interpreted as efforts to extend the *regnum Christi*.

Gäumann manages to draw up systematically sharp, vivid, and convincing theses, yet he does this at the cost of historical simplification. His assessment of Bucer is strangely contradictory: Was the Strasbourg reformer "fanatical"[82] or exceedingly "accommodating and conciliatory"?[83] The two are hardly compatible. Gäumann's systematic and theoretical approach to his topic allows little room for the nuances made necessary by attention to technical details. This is particularly obvious regarding the topic of church discipline. As much as Bucer emphasized the church's independence from temporal authorities in exercising ecclesiastical discipline, he was also capable of claiming with the same vehemence that church discipline was the responsibility of government and could be carried out in only cooperation with the authorities. Indeed, Bucer's thought and action can hardly be subsumed under one concept, even if it is one as central to his theology as that of *regnum Christi*.

Finally, Willem van 't Spijker offers some reflections on Bucer's theological legacy on the basis of his last wills and testaments of the years 1541, 1548, and 1551 (see chapter 8).[84]

As we have seen throughout this book, Martin Bucer's personality was too intricate and dynamic for us to be able to reduce it to a simple, clear-cut common denominator. Continuing research of his theology and work shows that the two were characterized not just by tension but by open contradictions. Bucer undeniably underwent changes of many different kinds in the course of his lifetime. Yet there are also essential features of his thought and action that remained unchanged. One reality does not exclude the other. In Bucer, in fact, the two are intricately intertwined. Perhaps the intensity of such contrasts is precisely the hallmark of great spirits. In any case, it fosters unremitting interest in the life and work of this reformer.

Notes

Chapter 1

1. Quoted in Lebeau and Valentin, *L'Alsace*, p. 306; see also Ammann, "Wirtschaftsgeltung"; Barth, *Rebbau*; Gény, *Reichsstadt*. The German name of Sélestat is Schlettstadt.
2. Gény, *Reichsstadt*, esp. pp. 84–86.
3. Ibid., p. 17; see also Adam, *Histoire*.
4. Adam, *L'humanisme*; Knepper, *Schul- und Unterrichtswesen*; Kohls, *Schule*, pp. 23–28.
5. Gebwiler, *Schlettstädter Chronik*, p. 29.
6. Adam, *L'humanisme*, p. 538.
7. Modern German edition by O. Herding, Munich 1965.
8. As a foreword to Lefèvre's edition of Aristotle's *Physics*, printed in 1514. See Knepper, *Schul- und Unterrichtswesen*, pp. 319ff.
9. Gebwiler, *Schlettstädter Chronik*, p. 28.
10. This is how Bucer spelled his family name, especially when writing in German. Modern scholarship has opted for the latinized form used simultaneously by Bucer himself. One also encounters the forms Bucerus, Bucaerus, Buczer, and even the grecized form Boukeros.
11. Gény, *Schlettstadter Stadtrechte*, p. 683.
12. *Zinsbuch der Stadt Schlettstadt*, Strasbourg, Archives de l'Hôpital, H 2, fol. 16^v.
13. *Bürgerbuch* (citizenship registry) *der Stadt Schlettstadt*, Archives de Sélestat, BB 45, 217.
14. Ibid., BB 45, 222.
15. Martin Bucer, *Der CXX. Psalm* (Strasbourg, 1546), fol. F 4^r (BDS 17, p. 61,7–11).
16. Ammann, "Wirtschaftsgeltung," p. 99.
17. Since his name was not entered into the Sélestat *Bürgerbuch* (citizenship registry) until 1480, it is probable that he lived in another city previously.
18. *Bürgerbuch* (citizenship registry) *der Stadt Schlettstadt*, Archives de Sélestat, BB 45, 229.
19. *Livre de bourgeoisie*, vol. 2, no. 5846.
20. Strasbourg, Archives de l'Hôpital, 591, fol. 91^v, 93^v–94^r.
21. See BDS 1, p. 281,14–15.
22. See note 20, above, and the diary of Dr. J. von Gottesheim, p. 278.

273

23. This is what Conrad Hubert, Bucer's lifelong secretary, reports in his foreword to Bucer's *Scripta anglicana fere omnia* (Basel, 1577), fol. A 2ᵛ.
24. Bucer owned Latin books at the time of entry into the order (see BDS 1, p.160,24–25). Knowledge of Latin was a prerequisite for admission into a Dominican monastery. See also Greschat, "Dominikanermönch," pp. 34–35, n. 23.
25. Adam, *L'humanisme*, p. 36.
26. Knepper, *Schul- und Unterrichtswesen*, p. 281.
27. For this and the following, see my article in note 24, above, and the abundant literature mentioned there.
28. See Greschat, "Dominikanermönch," pp. 30–31, n. 2.
29. Gény, *Reichsstadt*, pp. 171ff.; Gebwiler, *Schlettstädter Chronik*, pp. 15–16; Löhr, "Akten," pp. 250ff. and 265.
30. I believe that this information gives me good reason to date Bucer's entry into the monastery somewhat more precisely than Jean Rott does, who cautiously dates it somewhere between 1506 and 1507 (BCor 1, pp. 155–56, n. 6).
31. BDS 1, p. 161,19–20.
32. Gény, *Reichsstadt*, p. 171.
33. Jacobus de Voragine, *Golden Legend*, vol. 4, pp. 178–80; Jacobus de Voragine, *Legenda aurea*, vol. 1, pp. 707–8.
34. BCor 1, no. 2, pp. 42–58. See also Greschat, "Bücherverzeichnis."
35. BDS 1, p. 160,28ff.
36. For the details, see my article mentioned in note 24, above.
37. Bebel, *Opusculum*.
38. See my article mentioned in note 24, above.
39. Ritter, *Histoire de l'imprimerie alsacienne*, p. 168; Schmidt, *Histoire littéraire de l'Alsace*; Rott, "Note sur l'imprimerie alsacienne"; Chrisman, *Lay Culture*.

Chapter 2

1. A wealth of information on Heidelberg and its university are provided by Doerr, ed., *Semper Apertus*; Musall and Scheuerbrandt, "Bild und Struktur"; Ritter, *Heidelberger Universität*.
2. On the details, see Greschat, "Dominikanermönch," as well as the references in BCor 1, esp. no. 2.
3. Doerr, ed., *Semper Apertus*, vol. 5, pp. 336–37; Lossen, "Dominikanerkloster Heidelberg."
4. Edited in BCor 1, no. 2. The edition of Bucer's correspondence has outdated several items edited in BDS 1 and 2. See also Greschat, "Bücherverzeichnis."
5. BCor 1, no. 11 (March 19, 1520), p. 104,49–50.
6. Regarding this topic, also see Augustijn, *Erasmus von Rotterdam*, who offers ample bibliographical information.
7. Bucer, *De vera ecclesiarum in doctrina, ceremoniis et disciplina reconciliatione et compositione*, [Strasbourg] 1542, bb 4ʳ.
8. BCor 1, no. 4, September 14, 1518, p. 74, ll. 42ff. See also no. 5, March 10, 1519, p. 78, ll. 26–27.
9. BCor 1, no. 7, January 15, 1520, pp. 89–90, ll. 145–46; no. 9, January 23, 1520, p. 100, ll. 100ff.
10. Luther's theses are edited in WA 1, pp. 353–74; StA 1, pp. 186–218; English translation: *Luther's Works*, trans. J. Pelikan and H. Lehmann, vol. 31, pp. 39–70; Bucer's report is

in BCor 1, no. 3, May 1, 1518. See also Scheible, "Universität Heidelberg"; Greschat, "Anfänge"; Greschat, "Ansatz."

11. StA 1, pp. 210,21–211,4; WA 1, p. 364,4–16.
12. BCor 1, p. 62, l. 97.
13. BCor 1, p. 61, ll. 54ff.
14. BCor 1, no. 6, July 30, 1519, p. 81, ll. 43ff.; no. 8, January 23, 1520, p. 93, ll. 35ff.
15. Erasmus of Rotterdam, *Collected Works*, vol. 66, pp. 93–94; *Erasmus von Rotterdam: Ausgewählte Schriften*, vol. 1, pp. 268–70.
16. Geiger, *Reuchlin*, esp. pp. 203ff.
17. BCor 1, p. 78, ll. 26ff.
18. BCor 1, no. 22, pp. 131–32, note 6.
19. BCor 1, no. 6, July 30, 1519, p. 82, ll. 61–62.
20. BCor 1, no. 14.
21. BCor 1, no. 17, September 19, 1520, p. 118, ll. 22ff.
22. BCor 1, no. 18.
23. BCor 1, no. 31, p. 148, note 14.
24. BCor 1, no. 33.
25. Otto Brunfels, in a letter to Beatus Rhenanus, March 18, 1520, BCor 1, no. 11, p. 104, note 19. Papal Nuncio Girolamo Aleander portrays Bucer in similar terms ("giovine, di un capo terribile brongino"), BCor 1, no. 31, p. 148, note 14.
26. On Sickingen, see Ulmann, *Sickingen*; Press, "Adel, Reich und Reformation"; Hitchcock, *Background of the Knight's Revolt*; Schauder, "Martin Bucer und Franz Sickingen."
27. Holborn, *Hutten*, provides a general treatment of this subject; see also Rott, "Ulrich de Hutten"; Greschat, "Bucer und Hutten."
28. Edited in BDS 1, pp. 379–495. Bucer is presented there as the author of both these pamphlets.
29. Bucer's report of this meeting and Aleander's account of it are offered in BCor 1, no. 32. See also Reuter, ed., *Reichstag zu Worms.*
30. On this point, see the *Deutsche Reichstagsakten, Jüngere Reihe. Deutsche Reichstagsakten unter Kaiser Karl V.*, vol. 2: *Der Reichstag zu Worms 1521*, ed. Adolf Wrede (Gotha: F. A. Perthes, 1896; reprint, Göttingen: Vandenhoeck & Ruprecht, 1962).
31. After Ludwig V's death in March 1544, Frederick would become Elector Palatine as Frederick II until 1556.
32. BDS 1, p. 180, 11f.
33. BCor 1, no. 36 (May 27, 1521).
34. BCor 1, no. 37 (August 27, 1521), p. 172,55f.
35. See BCor 1, no. 42 (July 7, 1522); Rott, "Réforme a Nuremberg"; Pollet I, pp. 12–16.
36. BDS 1, p. 173,21ff. A document of April 14, 1518, in the *Landesarchiv Speyer* (C 49/34) informs of Sickingen's patronage rights. I am grateful to Theodor Knocke of Immenstadt for this information.
37. On Wissembourg (German name: Weissenburg), see Landsmann, *Wissembourg*; Schweer, *Weissenburg im Elsass.*
38. This settlement does not appear to have been permanent. The Schlettenbach contract (see below) restored the earlier status quo. On this, see BCor 1, pp. 89–90, note 27; p. 192, note 5.
39. On this see Rott, "Bauernkrieg und Stadt Weissenburg."
40. BDS 1, pp. 69–147.

41. BDS 1, p. 90,3–6.
42. BDS 1, p. 117,7–12.
43. BDS 1, p. 86,27–87,4.
44. On this and the following, see BCor 1, no. 43 (January 19, 1523).
45. Diary of the Wissembourg canon Beatus Dietrich, City Archives, Sélestat, ms. 188: *Weißenburger Stiftsherren 1513–1622*, fol. 3ʳ.
46. BCor 1, no. 43, p. 190, ll. 29ff.

Chapter 3

1. On this, see Andreas, "Strassburg an der Wende"; Chrisman, *Strasbourg and the Reform*; Rapp, *Réformes et Réformation*; Brady, *Ruling Class*; Livet and Rapp, eds., *Histoire de Strasbourg*, vol. 2. All these works offer helpful bibliographies.
2. On this matter, see a helpful summary in Brady, *Politics of the Reformation*, pp. 42–46.
3. See Brady, *Ruling Class*, p. 165.
4. Ibid., p. 51.
5. Fundamental for this issue is Rott's study "Artisanat et mouvements sociaux."
6. On this, see, besides the literature mentioned in note 1, above, Lienhard, "Réforme à Strasbourg."
7. See Edwards, *Printing, Propaganda and Martin Luther*, esp. chaps. 2, 4, and 6.
8. Winckelmann, *Fürsorgewesen*, remains unsurpassed on this topic.
9. Lienhard, "Mentalité populaire," p. 58, note 44.
10. Rott, "Radikale und gemäßigte Evangelische."
11. Moeller, "L'édit Strasbourgeois," pp. 57–58, presents the text of the edict.
12. The following observations are based primarily on BCor 1 and 2, as well as BDS 1 and 2.
13. BCor 1, no. 45, p. 196, ll. 65ff.
14. BDS 1, p. 297,29ff.
15. BDS 1, p. 347,4ff.
16. BDS 1, pp. 29–67.
17. BDS 1, p. 51,34ff.
18. BDS 1, p. 63,16ff.
19. BDS 1, pp. 149–84.
20. Edited in Schottenloher, ed., *Flugschriften zur Ritterschaftsbewegung*, pp. 52–71.
21. BDS 1, p. 183,22ff.
22. On this, see Stephen E. Buckwalter, *Die Priesterehe in Flugschriften der frühen Reformation* (Gütersloh: Gütersloher Verlagshaus, 1998), pp. 230–31.
23. On Katharina Zell, see McKee, *Katharina Schütz Zell*.
24. I base my observations on the fundamental research of Jean Rott, the results of which are summarized in BCor 1, pp. 21–26.
25. BCor 1, p. 242,161–62.
26. It is edited in BOL 1, pp. 3–58.
27. BDS 1, p. 375,21ff.
28. BCor 1, nos. 77 and 78; see also BDS 1, pp. 310–44.
29. On this and the following, see BDS 2, pp. 15–173.
30. BDS 2, p. 93,15ff.
31. BCor 1, nos. 80–84. On this, see Bornert, *La Réforme protestante*.
32. BDS 1, pp. 185–278.

33. BDS 1, p. 248,15ff.
34. On this, see Rott, "Guerre des Paysans"; Conrad, *Reformation*; Blickle, *Revolution.*
35. On this and the following, see BCor 2, nos. 92–94.
36. Rott, "Recueil," pp. 280–81.
37. BCor 2, no. 100.
38. On this, see, besides the literature already mentioned: TAE, vol. 1; Rott and Nelson, "Straßburg—Täuferstadt" (English translation: "Strasbourg: The Anabaptist City"); Deppermann, *Melchior Hoffman*, esp. pp. 139ff.; Peter, "Le maraîcher Clément Ziegler."
39. Rott, "Après sept années de prédication." The following quotation is taken from p. 532, ll. 151–62.
40. TAE, vol. 1, nos. 68 and 92.
41. BDS 2, pp. 225–58.
42. On Capito's relationship to Cellarius, see Seifert's definitive study, "Reformation und Chiliasmus."
43. On this, see especially Köhler, *Zwingli und Luther,* vol. 1; Bizer, *Studien zur Geschichte des Abendmahlsstreits*; Pollet I and II; Rott, "Bucer et les débuts"; Hazlett, "Development of Bucer's Thinking."
44. On the following, see Bucer's letter to Germanus, BCor 2, no. 109.
45. On Zwingli concerning this topic, see Pollet, *Huldrych Zwingli*; Locher, *Zwinglische Reformation*; Stephens, *Theology of Zwingli.*
46. For Luther, see Bizer, *Studien*; and Lienhard, *Luther, témoin de Jésus-Christ* (German translation: *Martin Luthers christologisches Zeugnis*).
47. BDS 4, p. 82,20ff.; p. 83,6ff.
48. On this, see BDS 2, pp. 173–223 and 259–75.
49. ZW 8, pp. 724–25.
50. WA 26, pp. 261–509; English translation in *Luther's Works*, vol. 37, pp. 151–372.
51. *Vergleichung D. Luthers vnnd seins gegentheyls vom Abentmal Christi*, edited in BDS 2, pp. 305–83. The title "Vergleichung" in today's German usage suggests a "comparison"; however, in the early sixteenth century this word carried predominant connotations of "conciliation" or "agreement"—a translation that also fits in better with Bucer's intentions.
52. BDS 2, p. 358,14ff.
53. Besides the literature mentioned in note 45, see also Köhler, "Zwingli und Straßburg."
54. On the following, see Pfister, *Kirchengeschichte der Schweiz*, vol. 2, pp. 70–79; Pollet II, pp. 401–36; BDS 2, pp. 277–94; BDS 4, pp. 15–160.
55. BCor 1, no. 63, p. 233, ll. 230–31.
56. BDS 1, p. 376,12ff. A basic study on this topic is Kohls, *Schule.*
57. On this, see BDS 2, pp. 410–14.
58. On Bucer as an exegete, see Lang, *Evangelienkommentar*; Müller, *Bucers Hermeneutik*; Roussel, "Bucer exegète"; Hobbs, "How Firm a Foundation."
59. "Atqui in Ecclesiis nihil nisi certa Dei verba loqui oportebat, quibus citra ullam dubitationem mens niti queat" (folio 6^r of the 1527 edition of the commentary).
60. Quoted by Peter, "Strasbourg et la Réforme française," p. 276.
61. On this, see BDS 2, pp. 423–558 (taking into account the corrections made later in BCor 2), as well as the study based on a broader array of sources by Chrisman, *Strasbourg and the Reform*, esp. pp. 155–76.
62. BDS 2, p. 498,16–17.

63. Brady, "'Sind also zu beiden theilen Christen'"; Brady, *Protestant Politics*, p. 60.
64. BDS 2, p. 473,24ff.
65. BDS 2, p. 514,15ff.
66. Quoted by Rott, "Recueil," p. 282.

Chapter 4

1. For a general treatment of this subject, see Brandi, *Deutsche Geschichte*; Elton, *Reformation Europe*; Lutz, *Reformation*; Moeller, *Deutschland*; Romano and Tenenti, eds., *Grundlegung*.
2. An exemplary study of this phenomenon can be found in Maschke, "'Obrigkeit' im spät-mittelalterlichen Speyer."
3. "... ein jeder [solle] sich halten, wie er das gegen Gott, auch kaiserliche Majestät und das Reich getraue zu verantworten." Quoted by Brandi, *Deutsche Geschichte*, p. 167.
4. *Deutsche Reichstagsakten, Jüngere Reihe. Deutsche Reichstagsakten unter Kaiser Karl V.*, vol. 7, ed. Johannes Kühn. (Gotha: F. A. Perthes, 1935; reprint, Göttingen: Vandenhoeck & Ruprecht, 1963), p. 1277.
5. On this and the following, see BDS 4, pp. 323–64; Köhler, *Zwingli und Luther*, vol. 2; Schubert, *Bekenntnisbildung und Religionspolitik*; Bizer, *Studien*; Pollet I; Hazlett, "Development"; Brecht, "Luthers Beziehungen."
6. BDS 4, p. 355,12ff.
7. BDS 3, pp. 442–71.
8. *Enarrationes perpetuae in sacra quatuor Evangelia*, Strasbourg 1530, fol. A2ᵛ; BCor 4, p. 40,7–11.
9. BDS 3, pp. 321–38.
10. BDS 3, pp. 13–185.
11. On this, see Rott, *Investigationes historicae*, vol. 1, pp. 283–95; also see Rott, "Martin Bucer und die Schweiz."
12. WA Br 6, pp. 24–26.
13. ZW 11, pp. 339–43 (known as the *epistola irata*).
14. ZW 11, pp. 345,11–12: "te posthac nihil de concordia solicitabo, oroque veniam, quod tantis meorum impendiis meoque labore et periculo te adeo fatigarim."
15. On this and the following, see BDS 4, pp. 409–48.
16. BDS 8, pp. 41–54; Pollet I, pp. 67–79.
17. BDS 8, pp. 45,13–17; Pollet I, 72,6ff.
18. BDS 4, p. 447,29ff.
19. BDS 4, pp. 307–19. On the following, see also pp. 465–514 in the same volume.
20. BDS 4, p. 503,20ff.
21. Schiess, *Briefwechsel*, vol. 2, p. 797.
22. On this, see CR II, p. 641, as well as col. 675.
23. BDS 5, pp. 109–258. The introduction to this important text (pp. 111–18) unfortunately misses essential points.
24. "Die sacramenten sind göttliche handlungen der kirchen, vom Herren darzu verordnet, das in denselbigen, die gaben Gottes und unser erlösung, volbracht durch unseren Herren Jesum Christum, auß götlichen zusagungen, mit worten und sichtbaren zeichen denen, welche die kirch sölcher erlösung auß Gottes zusage fähig erkennet, dargereicht und ubergeben werden." BDS 5, p. 160,5–9.
25. BDS 5, p. 202,9ff.
26. BDS 5, p. 254,27ff.

27. *Martini Buceri Opera Latina*, vol. 5: *Defensio adversus Axioma Catholicum, hoc est criminationem R. P. Roberti Episcopi Abrincensis* (1534), ed. Hazlett.
28. BDS 5, pp. 259–360.
29. Schiess, *Briefwechsel*, vol. 1, p. 742.
30. BDS 5, p. 277,21ff.
31. On this, see the list in Rott, *Correspondance de Martin Bucer.*
32. Pollet II, pp. 439–61; see also Bucer's memorandum on Henry's marriage, BDS 10, pp. 103–19.
33. On this, see Pollet II, pp. 488–533; see also Seidel, *Frankreich,* esp. pp. 88–122.
34. This letter has yet to be published. It is available in the Archives Municipales de Strasbourg, AST 42, no. 8; a transcript is available in the Bibliothèque Nationale et Universitaire de Strasbourg, Thesaurus Baumianus, vol. 8, fol. 53–60.
35. Schiess, *Briefwechsel*, vol. 2, pp. 813–14.
36. On the following, see Endriss, *Reformationsjahr*; Pollet II, pp. 163–220; BDS 4, pp. 183–305 and 365–98; unfortunately, the latter does not mention the very important altercation with Osswald.
37. On this, see Burnett, *Yoke of Christ.*
38. See ibid., pp. 58–60.
39. BDS 10, pp. 163–404. A further fundamental treatise by Bucer, closely related to the first, is the *Scriptum maius vom Ehegericht*, BDS 10, pp. 427–76. On the issue of marriage as viewed by Bucer, see Selderhuis, *Marriage and Divorce* (Dutch original: *Huwelijk en Echtscheiding*); and Wendel, *Le mariage.*
40. BDS 10, p. 270,11–14. Bucer would present very similar ideas on marriage and divorce in his major treatise *On the Kingdom of Christ* (*De regno Christi*), written shortly before his death in England. The writer John Milton translated and published this controversial section of *De regno Christi* into English in the seventeenth century. See Martin Bucer, *Common Places*, trans. and ed. David E. Wright, pp. 468–69; *Complete Prose Works of John Milton*, vol. 2, ed. Sirluck, pp. 416–79.
41. On this and the following, see Roth, *Reformationsgeschichte*; Wolfart, *Augsburger Reformation*; Pollet II, particularly pp. 221–74; Seebass, "Martin Bucer und die Reichsstadt Augsburg."
42. BDS 4, pp. 399–408.
43. Quoted by Pollet II, p. 248, footnote 1.
44. BDS 6/1, pp. 77–82.
45. Thus Wolfart, *Augsburger Reformation*, p. 116; on this, see also Seebass, "Die Augsburger Kirchenordnung von 1537"; and de Kroon, *Studien.*
46. Augustine's *Letter 185*, also known as *The Correction of the Donatists.*
47. BDS 6/2, pp. 17–38.
48. BDS 6/2, pp. 39–188.
49. BDS 6/2, p. 127,10ff.
50. BDS 6/2, p. 151,22ff.
51. On this, see Lienhard, "Réforme"; and Chrisman, *Strasbourg;* as well as the still relevant work by Köhler, *Züricher Ehegericht*, vol. 2, pp. 349ff.
52. BDS 2, pp. 538–45.
53. BDS 4, pp. 161–81. It bore the title *That No Images Are to Be Tolerated among Believers—A Clear Demonstration on the Basis of Divine Scripture* (*Das einigerlei Bild bei den Gotgläubigen . . . nit mögen geduldet werden, helle anzeyg auß göttlicher Schrifft*).

54. *Letter of Defense (Epistola Apologetica)*, BOL 1, pp. 59–225.
55. BDS 4, pp. 449–62.
56. BDS 4, p. 453,22ff.
57. BDS 5, pp. 366–77.
58. BDS 5, p. 367, 3ff.
59. On this topic, see TAE, vols. 1 and 2; Deppermann, *Melchior Hoffman;* Rott and Verhuis, eds., *Anabaptistes.*
60. Schiess, *Briefwechsel,* vol. 1, p. 369: "Ora pro nostra ecclesia, quam haeretici incredibiliter vastant; nam nostra praepostera indulgentia sic invaluerunt, ut nec malum hoc nec remedium eius ferri prope possit."
61. TAE I, no. 292a.
62. TAE I, nos. 277, 302, and 303.
63. TAE I, no. 303, p. 526,27ff.
64. TAE I, no. 266, p. 345,10ff.
65. The sources on this and the following can be found in TAE II; the fundamental book on this topic continues to be Wendel, *L'église de Strasbourg.* The edition provided in BDS 5 unfortunately does not measure up to the standards set by the aforementioned works. See also the literature mentioned in note 51, as well as Lienhard, ed., *Croyants et sceptiques.*
66. BDS 5, pp. 383–401.
67. BDS 5, pp. 402–21.
68. TAE II, no. 475.
69. TAE II, no. 492.
70. BDS 5, pp. 502–11.
71. Quoted by Wendel, *L'église de Strasbourg,* p. 95.
72. TAE II, no. 405, p. 118,10ff.
73. TAE II, no. 523.
74. See, besides the literature already mentioned, especially Lienhard, ed., *Croyants et sceptiques.*
75. BDS 5, pp. 432–501.
76. BDS 5, p. 458,35ff.
77. BDS 5, pp. 43–107.
78. "What Should Be Believed Concerning the Baptism of Infants." Partially edited in Stupperich, *Schriften von evangelischer Seite gegen die Täufer* (Münster, 1983), pp. 8–35.
79. BDS 6/3, pp. 19–173.
80. BDS 5, pp. 15–41.
81. On this, see especially TAE II, nos. 373 and 393; Schiess, *Briefwechsel,* vol. 1, pp. 400–401.

Chapter 5

1. Pol. Cor. I, p. 285.
2. On this, see the instructive itinerary compiled by Rott, *Correspondance de Martin Bucer,* pp. 97–100.
3. BDS 4, pp. 358–59. Fundamental for understanding the following is BDS 6/1, besides the literature cited previously. See also Leppin, "Theologischer Streit," esp. pp. 163–66.
4. On this, see Neuser, *Die Abendmahlslehre Melanchthons.*
5. BDS 6/1, p. 71,25ff.

6. BDS 6/1, p. 108,20ff.
7. Edition of the German original in *Bekenntnisschriften der reformierten Kirche*, ed. Müller, pp. 101–9; English translation in *Reformed Confessions of the 16th Century*, ed. Cochrane, pp. 100–111. See also Bucer, *Common Places*, trans. and ed. David E. Wright, p. 372, n. 6.
8. The following chronological facts are based on de Kroon, "Syllogismus," pp. 182–84. For the following, see also Bucer, *Common Places*, trans. and ed. David E. Wright, pp. 355–79.
9. BDS 6/1, p. 154,1ff.
10. BDS 6/1, p. 170,14ff.
11. M. Greschat, "Bucers Anteil."
12. BDS 6/1, p. 233,12.
13. WA Br 8, no. 3128.
14. BDS 6/1, p. 311,17f. Bucer makes a similar statement in the dedication of the third edition of his commentary on the Gospels (1536) to Edward Fox, bishop of Hereford: "Quid inconstantiae sit, proficere in scientia salutis?" (fol. 7 ^{r}).
15. Letter of October 23, 1537; cf. Pollet II, p. 399.
16. Quoted in Strasser, "Letzten Anstrengungen," p. 15.
17. Köhler, *Zürcher Ehegericht*, vol. 2, pp. 418–19 and 441–42.
18. TAE III. See also Gerber, "Anabaptistes."
19. On this, see BDS 6/2, pp. 191–249; as well as TAE III, no. 920, pp. 330–37.
20. The *Enarratio in Evangelion Iohannis* is now available as BOL II in an exemplary critical edition; fundamental for the Romans commentary are Roussel, "Lecteur," and de Kroon, *Studien*.
21. Introduction, fol. 4^v.
22. Introduction, fol. 5^r.
23. On this, see BDS 7, pp. 505–75; as well as Kohls, *Schule*; and particularly Schindling, *Humanistische Hochschule*.
24. On this, see esp. Pannier, *Calvin*; Courvoisier, "Bucer et Calvin"; Wendel, *Calvin*; Wiedeburg, "Freundschaft"; Spijker, "Invloed."
25. "vir ille . . . praeter reconditam eruditionem, copiosamque multarum rerum scientiam, praeter ingenii perspicaciam, multam lectionem, aliasque multas ac varias virtutes, quibus a nemine fere hodie vincitur, cum paucis est conferendus, plurimos antecellit." Letter to Simon Grynaeus, October 18, 1539. See Herminjard, vol. 6, no. 828, p. 76.
26. Schiess, *Briefwechsel*, vol. 1, p. 873.
27. BDS 6/3, pp. 175–223.
28. BDS 6/3, p. 199,30ff.; for a similar passage, see also 194,24ff. See also Burnett, *Yoke of Christ*, pp. 104–5.
29. BDS 6/2, pp. 203–12.
30. BDS 7, pp. 67–245. The introduction to this edition unfortunately does not address decisive theological and church organizational issues.
31. BDS 7, pp. 146,36ff.
32. BDS 7, p. 193,28–29.
33. Besides the studies of Demandt, *Hessen*; and W. Heinemeyer, *Werden Hessens*; the fundamental work on this topic remains Sohm, *Territorium*.
34. On the following, see Steitz, *Geschichte*; as well as the literature mentioned in note 33.
35. Lenz, *Briefwechsel*, vol. 1, p. 322. See also pp. 317–26, as well as Franz, *Wiedertäuferakten*.
36. For a detailed analysis, see Franz, *Wiedertäuferakten*, vol. 4, pp. 98–146.

37. On this, see BDS 7, pp. 247–318.
38. Franz, *Wiedertäuferakten*, vol. 4, p. 270.
39. On this, see BDS 7, pp. 319–94; as well as Salfeld, "Judenpolitik"; Maurer, "Judenfrage"; Battenberg, "Judenordnungen."
40. On this, see BDS 6/2, pp. 149–50; 153,32ff.; 168,24ff.; on obstinate Anabaptists, see TAE II, no. 673, p. 462,15ff.
41. BDS 7, p. 356,5ff.
42. BDS 7, p. 388,25ff.
43. On this, see BDS 7, p. 358,20ff. and 393,17ff.
44. For the following, the sources in Lenz, *Briefwechsel*, vols. 1 and 2; and the discussion in Eells, *Attitude*, remain fundamental.
45. BDS 10, pp. 486–539.

Chapter 6

1. Turmair, "Ursachen des Türkenkrieges." *Gesammelte Werke*, vol. 1. Quotation from pp. 240–42.
2. Besides the literature mentioned in note 1 of chapter 4, see also Stupperich, *Humanismus*; Jedin, *Trient* I; Brandi, *Kaiser Karl*; Skalweit, *Reformation*.
3. Still current on this is Pollet III, esp. pp. 406–71; Fraenkel, *Einigungsbestrebungen*; Augustijn, *Godsdienstgesprekken*. See also Ortmann, *Reformation und Einheit der Kirche*.
4. Witzel, "Warer Bericht," 17.
5. Lenz, *Briefwechsel*, vol. 1, no. 17, p. 48.
6. Bucer published them in 1545 under the title *Ein Christlich ongefährlich bedencken*. See note 74, below.
7. On this, see, for instance, CR III, no. 1796, col. 688–92.
8. BDS 7, p. 439,33ff.
9. BDS 7, pp. 395–502.
10. *Von Kirchengütern*, 1540. See BB, no. 65.
11. On this, see Pollet III, pp. 248–52.
12. *Von Kirchengütern*, fol. F 3ʳ.
13. Ibid., fol. b 1ʳ.
14. *An statui et dignitate;* BB, no. 67. A German translation of it also circulated widely.
15. BB, no. 67a, fol. B 1ʳ.
16. The Latin original had the title *Per quos steterit*; a German translation entitled *Vom tag zu Hagenaw* appeared soon after. Both are edited in BDS 9/1, pp. 146–321.
17. *Vom tag zu Hagenaw*, fol. O 1ʳ, BDS 9/1, p. 314,22–23.
18. Lenz, *Briefwechsel*, vol. 1, no. 28, p. 94 (August 2, 1539).
19. Ibid., vol. 1, no. 27, p. 93 (July 7, 1539).
20. On this, see WA Br 9, no. 3436, pp. 19–35 (January 18, 1540), as well as CR III, no. 1948, col. 989–1003 (April 11, 1540).
21. See note 19, above.
22. Lenz, *Briefwechsel*, vol 1, no. 28, p. 96.
23. On the details of these conversations, which later became the matter of great controversy, see Gropper, *Briefwechsel*, vol. 1, esp. no. 139, pp. 351–58.
24. As previously, I base this information on the exact chronology provided by Rott, *Correspondance de Martin Bucer*, p. 99.

25. Besides the literature already mentioned above in note 3, see Lenz, *Briefwechsel*, vol. 3, pp. 31–72, Augustijn, "Gesprekken"; Braunisch, "Artikell"; Braunisch, *Theologie*.

26. On him, see Pollet III, pp. 35–49.

27. Lenz, *Briefwechsel*, vol. 1, no. 89, p. 238.

28. Ibid., vol. 1, no. 101, p. 278.

29. Ibid., vol. 1, no. 112 (January 7, 1541).

30. CR IV, no. 2252, col. 346.

31. Rückert, *Theologische Entwicklung Contarinis*; Jedin, "Turmerlebnis."

32. Augustijn presents a critical edition of Gropper's and Bucer's "Worms Book" along with the additions made in the "Regensburg Book" in BDS 9/1, pp. 323–483. Pfeilschifter presents another historical-critical edition of the "Regensburg Book" in *Acta Reformationis Catholicae*, vol. 6/3.2, pp. 21–88. See also Augustijn, "Quest of Reformatio."

33. The Protestant counterarticles are reprinted in CR IV, col. 349–76. In 1541, Bucer edited both texts as well as the documents mentioned in the following context. See BB, no. 69, as well as 69a–69f.

34. Lenz, *Briefwechsel*, vol. 2, no. 129, p. 37.

35. Reprinted in the *Acta Colloqui* (forthcoming in BDS 9/2), fol. 48^v–59^r. The Melanchthon text quoted in the following passage can also be found in the *Acta*, fol. 59^v–65^r.

36. BB, no. 68; a critical edition of this work is forthcoming in BDS 9/2.

37. Lenz, *Briefwechsel*, vol. 2, no. 127, 31.

38. See the helpful summary of research, with extensive references to further literature, in Petri and Droege, eds., *Rheinische Geschichte*, vol. 2, esp. pp. 9–60.

39. See Varrentrap, *Hermann von Wied*, p. 27.

40. On the Cologne reformation attempt, see Varrentrap, *Hermann von Wied*; Schlüter, *Publizistik*; Köhn, *Bucers Entwurf*; most recently Pollet III, esp. pp. 96–234; and Pollet IV, pp. 33–162; as well as Burnett, *Yoke of Christ*, pp. 143–62.

41. March 5, 1542, Pollet IV, pp. 60–62, esp. p. 62,90ff.

42. Pollet IV, p. 46,29ff.

43. Gropper, *Briefwechsel*, no. 107, pp. 283–84.

44. Ibid., no. 111, pp. 294–300.

45. Schlüter, *Publizistik*, pp. 124–28, reports on the written controversy between Bucer and Gropper. One of the most important sources on this is Bucer's booklet *On the Only Right Way* (*Von den einigen rechten Wegen*) of 1545 (edited in BDS 11/2, pp. 253–349). *How Easily and Fittingly* (*Wie leicht und füglich*) of the same year also deserves consultation (edited in BDS 11/2, pp. 355–434).

46. On the details, see Philippson, *Stadt*; Dietz, *Topographie*; Niessen, *Geschichte*. On Bucer's living quarters, see document AST 133, no. 20, in the Archives Municipales de Strasbourg (partially edited in Schiess, *Briefwechsel*, vol. 2, no. 987, pp. 167–70).

47. Lenz, *Briefwechsel*, vol. 2, p. 145.

48. BDS 11/1, pp. 19–130.

49. *Die ander verteydigung vnd erklerung der Christlichen Lehr* (BB, no. 76), BDS 11/2, pp. 31–247.

50. *Responsio ad scriptum quorundam delectorum a clero secundario Coloniae Agrippinae*. Melanchthon, *Werke in Auswahl*, vol. 6, pp. 381–421.

51. BDS 11/2, p. 99,10–13.

52. BDS 11/1, pp. 133–44.

53. BDS 11/1, pp. 147–429.
54. Letter of September 26, 1543, quoted in Pollet III, p. 155, n. 2.
55. Pollet III, p. 159–60.
56. WA Br 10, p. 618,11ff.
57. Lenz, *Briefwechsel*, vol. 2, no. 166, p. 147.
58. Pollet IV, p. 92,140ff: Bucer's letter to Count Palatine Ottheinrich, August 6, 1544.
59. Lenz, *Briefwechsel*, vol. 2, no. 172 (September 13, 1543).
60. Ibid., vol. 2, no. 175, pp. 173–87.
61. Ibid., vol. 2, no. 178, pp. 191–97.
62. Ibid., vol. 2, no. 178, pp. 196.
63. Ibid., vol. 2, pp. 225–31.
64. *De vera ecclesiarum in doctrina, ceremoniis et reconciliatione et compositione*, 1542 (BB, no. 73).
65. See Lenz, *Briefwechsel*, vol. 2, p. 36, n. 5 (November 30, 1541).
66. See Schlüter, *Publizistik*, pp. 121–23. For Bucer's remarks, see *Scripta duo adversaria*; BB, no. 78.
67. *Scripta duo adversaria*, p. 4.
68. *Bestendige Verantwortung auß der heiligen Schrift*, Bonn 1545; BB, no. 86. An edition of this work will appear in BDS 11/3.
69. Lenz, *Briefwechsel*, vol. 2, no. 203, pp. 292–305; quotation from p. 299.
70. *Eine Christliche Erinnerung*; BB, no. 83.
71. Ibid., p. 144–45.
72. *Wie leicht und füglich* (*How Easily and Fittingly*); BB, no. 84; edited in BDS 11/2, pp. 355–454.
73. *Von den einigen rechten Wegen* (*On the Only Right Way*); BB, no. 80; edited in BDS 11/2, pp. 253–349.
74. *Ein christlich ongefährlich bedencken* (*An Upright Christian Consideration*); BB, no. 79; edited in BDS 9/1, pp. 13–51.
75. Lenz, *Briefwechsel*, vol. 2, pp. 362ff (quotation from p. 376).
76. *Der newe glaub, von den Doctoren zu Löwen* (*The New Faith, as Presented by the Doctors of Louvain*); BB, no. 82. Three editions of this work appeared in 1545. For a general treatment, see Jedin, *Trient*, vol. 1, pp. 325ff.
77. *Der newe glaub*, fol. K 3^v–4^r.
78. *De concilio*, 1545; BB, no. 85.
79. *De concilio*, fol. m 2^r.
80. *Der CXX. Psalm*, BDS 17, pp. 17–80. Engelbrecht's pamphlet was entitled *Abconterfeytung Martin Butzers* (ed. Werner Bellardi, 1974).
81. *Der CXX. Psalm*, BDS 17, p. 42,13ff.
82. *Ein Sendbrieve Martini Buceri* (*An Open Letter of Martin Bucer*), BDS 17, pp. 81–109.
83. BDS 17, p. 106,26ff.
84. Lenz, *Briefwechsel*, vol. 2, pp. 32–38.
85. Molnár, "Correspondance," pp. 151–53.
86. Lenz, *Briefwechsel*, vol. 2, p. 38.
87. Some details, if not entirely accurate, are provided by Mieg, "Note"; and Eells, *Martin Bucer*, p. 517.
88. Ariès, *Geschichte der Kindheit*, p. 47. This passage only appears in Ariès's preface to the German translation of his *L'enfant et la vie familiale sous l'ancien régime*, and not in the English translation, *Centuries of Childhood*.

89. BDS 17, p. 67,24ff.
90. I owe this data to Jean Rott, who compiled detailed information (letter of June 17, 1989). More generally, see Hanauer, *Études économiques.*
91. Quoted in Lienhard and Willer, *Straßburg,* p. 57.
92. BDS 6/3, pp. 225–65. The quotation is from p. 263,24ff.
93. City council sessions on this topic on February 12, 1543. See TAE IV, no. 1260. See also BDS 6/2, p. 198, n. 44.
94. TAE III, appendix to no. 1178, pp. 516–19 (April 15, 1542); the quotation is from p. 518,4ff.
95. Ibid.
96. For instance, see TAE IV, no. 1421 (February 4, 1545).
97. Molnár, "Correspondance," p. 133.
98. Ibid., p. 144.
99. Ibid., p. 145.
100. Ibid.

Chapter 7

1. Pollet I, pp. 214–15 (April 10, 1546).
2. BB, no. 88.
3. BB, no. 91.
4. Quoted from Hortleder, *Der römischen keyser,* p. 636.
5. On this, see Lenz, *Briefwechsel,* vol. 2, esp. nos. 227–31.
6. *Disputatio Ratisbonae, in altero colloquio,* 1548; BB, no. 99.
7. Lenz, *Briefwechsel,* vol. 2, no. 231 (April 5, 1546).
8. *Ein wahrhafftiger Bericht vom Colloquio zu Regensburg (A True Report on the Colloquy in Regensburg);* BB, no. 90; regarding the reprints, see BB, no. 90a–90b, 90d–90f.
9. Preface to *Historia vera de morte Ioannis Diazii;* BB, no. 92.
10. The passages in Bucer's writings exemplifying this are countless. See, e.g., BDS 17, pp. 122,19ff.; 174,24ff.; 180,35ff.; 198,5ff.; 211,1ff.; 221,28ff.; 230,24ff.; 237,15ff.; 487,4ff.; 492,15ff.; 557,31ff.; 558,24ff.; 560,7ff.; 571,22ff.; 584,24ff., 588,2ff.; 618,14ff.
11. BDS 17, p. 237,18–19. This is a passage from the work *Wegen Abschaffung grober Laster* (*Regarding the Abolishment of Gross Vices*) of April 1547.
12. *Mehrung götlicher gnaden vnd geists* (*Increase of Divine Grace and Spirit*), BDS 17, p. 329,18ff.
13. BDS 17, pp. 207–44.
14. On this, see BDS 17, pp. 153–345; as well as Burnett, *Yoke of Christ,* passim, esp. pp. 180–207; see also Bellardi, *Geschichte;* Hammann, "Vision de l'église." Bellardi obstructs his own and the reader's accurate appraisal of this phenomenon by wrongly dating the work *On the Church's Defects and Failings* (*Von der kirchen mengel vnd fähl*) around the end of 1545 and the beginning of 1546 (see TAE IV, no. 1526; there Jean Rott expresses the very illuminating conjecture that Bucer was probably referring to his unpublished book *On the Fellowship of Churches* [*Von gemeinschaft der kirchen*], particularly since the time reference "inerthalb vier vnd zwentzig jaren" [p. 165,3] is more readily applicable to 1547 than it is to 1546). Bellardi has an unfortunate tendency to interpret these events from within the framework of seventeenth- and eighteenth-century Lutheran Pietism.
15. TAE IV, no. 1510, e.g., from the first half of the year 1546.

16. TAE IV, no. 1542 (February 21, 1547).
17. BDS 17, p. 235,24ff.; he repeats this emphatically at p. 228,26ff. and throughout the treatise.
18. BDS 17, p. 218,17ff.
19. BDS 17, p. 220,7ff.
20. BDS 17, p. 245–55.
21. On Fagius, see the monograph by P. Raubenheimer.
22. Very instructive is Fagius's undated treatise *Ecclesiasticae disciplinae instituendae ratio*, a manuscript copy of which is stored in the Strasbourg municipal archives (AST 165, fol. 223–26).
23. BDS 17, pp. 256–90.
24. BDS 17, p. 272,12ff.
25. BDS 17, p. 285,21ff.
26. BDS 17, p. 284,16ff.
27. BDS 17, p. 314, n. 28.
28. BDS 17, p. 296,12ff. See also 338,9ff.
29. Quoted in Bellardi, "Bedacht Hedios," p. 128.
30. BDS 17, pp. 156–95. See also note 14, above.
31. BDS 17, p. 164,9ff.
32. BDS 17, p. 188,5ff
33. BDS 17, p. 192,31ff.
34. On this and the following, see Mehlhausen, *Interim*; Jedin, *Trient*, vol. 2; Rabe, *Reichsbund*; Pflug, *Correspondance*, vol. 3.
35. See the preface to the *Disputatio Ratisbonae, in altero colloquio*; BB, no. 99.
36. Baum, *Capito und Butzer*, pp. 569–72.
37. On this, see BDS 17, pp. 346–38; Augustijn, "Strasbourg, Bucer, et la politique de Colloques"; Bellardi, "Bucer und das Interim."
38. "Ego enim pro mea conscientia valde multa subire et facere possem in his rebus, quae aliis non habentibus idem de his rebus iudicium subeunda et facienda suadere non ausim." Bucer's letter to the Electors, April 10, 1548, in BDS 17, pp. 416–21. The quote is taken from p. 420,37ff.
39. "Et si plura darem, me facerem plane inutilem ad concordiam Ecclesiarum adiuvandam." BDS 17, p. 421,16ff.
40. Pol. Cor. IV, p. 919–20, n. 7.
41. On the following, see BDS 17, pp. 111–50 and 439–620; Weyrauch, *Krise*; Brady, *Protestant Politics*, pp. 337–47; Brady, *Politics of the Reformation*, pp. 221–30; Brady, *Ruling Class*, esp. pp. 259ff.
42. Pol. Cor. IV/2, p. 1078. Regarding the *Concise Summary* (*Summarischer vergriff*), see BDS 17, pp. 111–50.
43. BDS 17, p. 486,17ff.
44. Quoted in Brady, *Ruling Class*, p. 270.
45. BDS 17, p. 547,18–19.
46. BDS 17, p. 579,2ff.
47. Rott, "Un Recueil," pp. 814–18.
48. *Advice: The Company of Pastors' Further Clarification (Rhatschlag: Des Kirchen Conuents fernere Erclärung)*, BDS 17, pp. 593–620. Bucer also issued a vigorous condemnation of

the council's acquiesence to the Interim in a Response (*Responsio ad Senatum*, BDS 17, pp. 574–592; see p. 226 above) submitted several weeks previously.

49. Concerning Charles V's satisfaction upon hearing of Bucer's dismissal, see Pol. Cor. IV, p. 1173.

Chapter 8

1. Edited in BDS 10, pp. 103–19.
2. Janelle, "Voyage"; Wendel, introduction to *De regno Christi*, BOL 15.
3. Rott, "Un Recueil," esp. pp. 814–18 (letter of May 17, 1549).
4. The following studies are helpful: Bush, *Government Policy*; Jones, *Mid-Tudor Crisis*; Palliser, *Age of Elizabeth*; Youings, *Sixteenth-Century England*.
5. Quoted in Loades, *Oxford Martyrs*, p. 91.
6. Besides the literature mentioned in note 4, see Dickens, *English Reformation*; Elton, *Reform and Reformation*; Loades, *Oxford Martyrs*.
7. For the following section, see, besides the literature mentioned above, Bucer's *Scripta anglicana*; Harvey, *Bucer in England*; Hopf, *Bucer and the English Reformation*; Hall, "Angleterre"; Pollet I, pp. 257–96.
8. *De ordinatione legitima ministrorum ecclesiae* (*On Restoring Lawful Ordination*). In *Scripta anglicana*, pp. 238–59.
9. E.g., John Burcher wrote to Bullinger on April 20, 1550: "Bucerus in veterem morbum periculosissime reincidit. Nullam, aut exiguam plane, spem vitae esse scripsit Ricardus Hilles. Si moriatur, felix et beatior omnibus terris Anglia, quae uno anno liberabitur a duobus perniciosissimis ingeniis, Paulino et Bucerano." Quoted by Wendel, BOL 15, p. xxviii, n. 104 ("Bucer has had a most dangerous relapse into his old disease. Richard Hilles writes word that there is little or no hope of his recovery. In case of his death, England will be happy and more favoured than all other countries in having been delivered in the same year from two most pernicious talents, that of Paul [Fagius] and of Bucer." Translation based on *Original Letters*, vol. 2, pp. 662–63). See also Amos, "Alsatian," p. 108.
10. Letter to Peter Martyr on April 20, 1549, in Pollet I, pp. 265–72. Quotation: p. 266,27ff.
11. He must have been in Cambridge at the beginning of November, as he traveled up to London on November 5 in the company of Francis Dryander (Francisco de Enzinas) to attend Parliament (see MacCulloch, *Thomas Cranmer*, p. 449; citing Dryander to Bullinger, *Epistolae tigurinae*, p. 234).
12. *Scripta Anglicana*, pp. 184–90.
13. The date of January 13, 1550, which often shows up in the literature, can hardly be accurate. On January 12, a Saturday, Bucer wrote to Farel that he was hoping to begin his lectures on the following Monday (quoted in Hopf, *Bucer and the English Reformation*, p. 254). It is puzzling, however, that Isaac Cellarius apparently writes to Dryander on January 25, 1550 (quoted in Harvey, *Bucer in England*, p. 47, footnote), that Bucer began his lectures on January 10.
14. On the significance of these lectures, see Amos, "Exegete as Theologian."
15. *Disputatio docta in Comitiis Academiae Cantabrig. Publice habita*. In *Scripta Anglicana*, pp. 711–88.
16. Bucer gathered this material in August and prefaced it with a letter dated "3 Id. Augusti (i.e., August 11) 1550." See Amos, "Alsatian," pp. 113–14, n. 81.

17. *Controversia inter Joh. Jvngvm et Mart. Bucerum.* In *Scripta Anglicana*, pp. 797–862.
18. *Tractatus de Vsuris.* In *Scripta Anglicana*, pp. 789–96.
19. *Tractatus de Vsuris*, p. 791.
20. *Exomologesis sive Confessio de Sacra Eucharistia.* In *Scripta Anglicana*, pp. 538–45. English translation with helpful detailed commentary and notes by Wright, trans. and ed., *Common Places*, pp. 381–400.
21. *Scripta Anglicana*, pp. 681–84.
22. The *Tomus Anglicanus* offers only a fragmentary documentation of this event. A clearer depiction can be found in Hopf, *Bucer and the English Reformation*, pp. 131–70.
23. *Scripta Anglicana*, pp. 456–503. The title *Censura super libro sacrorum* was not formulated until after Bucer's death.
24. On this, see most recently Amos, "Bucer and the Revision," pp. 107–26.
25. See also Amos, "'It Is Fallow Ground Here,'" pp. 41–52.
26. Calvin, *Opera quae supersunt omnia*, vol. 13, pp. 574–77; English translation in *Original Letters*, vol. 2, pp. 545–48 (quotations taken from *Opera*, pp. 574–75; translation of quotes based on *Original Letters*, vol. 2, pp. 546–47).
27. Palliser, *Age of Elizabeth*, p. 331.
28. *De vi et usu sacri Ministerii.* In *Scripta Anglicana*, pp. 553–610.
29. The fundamental study on this work remains Wendel, BOL 15. Most of *De Regno Christi* has been translated into English by Wilhelm Pauck, with Paul Larkin, in *Melanchthon and Bucer*, pp. 153–394. The English writer John Milton translated extracts of *De Regno Christi* dealing with marriage and divorce into English in the seventeenth century (these are therefore omitted by Pauck and Larkin); see *Complete Prose Works of John Milton*, vol. 2, pp. 416–79.
30. See, most recently, Amos, "Use of Canon and Civil Law," pp. 147–65.
31. *De Regno Christi*, BOL 15, p. 14; English translation based on Pauck, *Melanchthon and Bucer*, pp. 186–87.
32. See note 29, above.
33. On this, see Loades, *Oxford Martyrs*, pp. 37ff.
34. *De Regno Christi*, BOL 15, p. 276; English translation: Pauck, *Melanchthon and Bucer*, p. 368.
35. On this work of 1549, see Elton, *Reform and Reformation*, esp. pp. 323ff.
36. January 12, 1550; quoted in Hopf, *Bucer and the English Reformation*, p. 255.
37. Calvin, *Opera quae supersunt omnia*, vol. 13, p. 355. An alternative translation is available in Hall, "Martin Bucer in England," p. 152, who quotes from G. C. Gorham, *Gleanings of a Few Scattered Ears during the Period of the Reformation in England*, London, 1857, pp. 106–7.
38. The Edwardian Statutes for Cambridge called for theology lectures to begin at nine in the morning; see *Collection of Statutes for the University and the Colleges of Cambridge*, ed. J. Heywood (Cambridge, 1840), pp. 6–7.
39. Letter of Thomas Horton to Francis Dryander (Francisco de Enzinas), May 15, 1550. Quoted by C. H. Smyth, *Cranmer and the Reformation under Edward VI* (Cambridge, 1926), p. 163; see also Hall, "Angleterre," p. 423, n. 62.
40. On this, see Hopf, *Bucer and the English Reformation*, p. 15; and esp. the detailed information in Amos, "Alsatian," p. 111, n. 75.
41. BOL 15, p. 2. Concerning the stove, also see Amos, "Alsatian," p. 111, n. 75.

42. Amos, "Alsatian," p. 112.
43. On this, see Wendel, "Un document inédit."
44. E. Staehelin, *Briefe und Akten*, vol. 2, pp. 827–29.
45. These and other laudatory statements by contemporaries of Bucer can be found in *Scripta Anglicana*, pp. 864–959. See also Amos, "Alsatian," p. 100, n. 29, and p. 103, n. 48.

Chapter 10

1. *Bucer—Bibliographie/ Bibliographie Bucer 1975–1998*, ed. Thomas Wilhelmi, Bernd Paul, Michael Herrmann, and Danièle Fischer, preface by Matthieu Arnold and Gottfried Seebass (Strasbourg: Association des Publications de la Faculté de Théologie Protestante, 1999). An update of current secondary literature is being prepared by the *Bucer-Forschungsstelle* along with the bibliography of Bucer's works.
2. Gottfried Seebass, "Bucer—Forschung seit dem Jubiläumsjahr 1991," *Theologische Rundschau* 62 (1997): 271–300.
3. Martin Brecht, "Martin Bucer und die Heidelberger Disputation," in Willem van 't Spijker, ed., *Calvin—Erbe und Auftrag. Festschrift für Wilhelm Heinrich Neuser zum 65. Geburtstag* (Kampen, 1991), pp. 214–28; Thomas Kaufmann, "Bucers Bericht von der Heidelberger Disputation," *Archiv für Reformationsgeschichte* 82 (1991): 147–70.
4. Kaufmann, "Bucers Bericht," p. 169.
5. Siegfried Bräuer, "Bucer und der Neukarsthans," in Christian Krieger and Marc Lienhard, eds., *Martin Bucer and Sixteenth Century Europe. Actes du Colloque de Strasbourg 28–31 août 1991* (Leiden: E. J. Brill, 1993), pp. 103–27 (henceforth quoted as *M.B. and Europe*).
6. Thomas Kaufmann, *Die Abendmahlstheologie der Straßburger Reformatoren bis 1528* (Tübingen: J. C. B. Mohr [Paul Siebeck], 1992), pp. 85–86.
7. Herman Johan Selderhuis, *Marriage and Divorce in the Thought of Martin Bucer* (Kirksville, Mo.: Thomas Jefferson University Press at Truman State University, 1999), pp. 116–23 (English translation of *Huwelijk en Echtscheiding bij Martin Bucer* [Leiden: Uitgeverij J. J. Groen BV, 1994], pp. 139–46).
8. Doris Ebert, *Elisabeth Silbereisen. Familie und Lebensstationen.* [Eppingen:] Heimatverein Kraichgau, 2001, esp. pp. 91–93 and 149–50.
9. Matthieu Arnold, "'Dass niemand ihm selbst, sondern anderen leben soll.' Das theologische Programm Martin Bucers von 1523 im Vergleich mit Luther," *Theologische Beiträge* 32 (2001): 237–48.
10. Gustave Koch, "The Christian Life in the Light of the 'Summary' of Martin Bucer of 1523," *Reformation and Renaissance Review* 3 (2001): 140–51. In her study "Le nom et l'être de Dieu—Exode 3,14—selon Thomas d'Aquin et Martin Bucer," *Revue d'histoire et de philosophie religieuses* 81 (2001): 425–47, Annie Noblesse-Rocher presents only scant evidence of Thomas Aquinas's influence upon Bucer.
11. *Correspondance de Martin Bucer,* vol. 3 (1527–1529), ed. Christian Krieger and Jean Rott (Leiden: Brill, 1995).
12. Bernd Moeller, "Die Brautwerbung Martin Bucers für Wolfgang Capito. Zur Sozialgeschichte des evangelischen Pfarrerstandes," in *Philologie als Kulturwissenschaft*, ed. L. Grenzmann et al. (Göttingen: Vandenhoeck & Ruprecht, 1987), pp. 306–25. I failed to mention this article in the original German version of my book.
13. *Martin Bucers Deutsche Schriften*, vol. 10: *Schriften zu Ehe und Eherecht*, ed. Stephen E. Buckwalter and Hans Schulz (Gütersloh: Gütersloher Verlagshaus, 2001).

14. See note 7, above. I will discuss Selderhuis's study in greater detail below.

15. Michel Weyer, "Martin Bucer et les Zell—une solidarité critique," in *M.B. and Europe*, pp. 275–95. On Katharina Zell, see also the impressive biography and critical edition of her writings by Elsie McKee.

16. Reinhard Bodenmann, "Martin Bucer et Gaspard Hedion. Vicissitudes des relations entre deux collègues, 1523–1549," in *M.B. and Europe*, pp. 297–315.

17. Thomas Kaufmann, "Zwei unerkannte Schriften Bucers und Capitos zur Abendmahlsfrage aus dem Herbst 1525," *Archiv für Reformationsgeschichte* 81 (1990): 158–88.

18. Marc Lienhard, review of Thomas Kaufmann, *Die Abendmahlstheologie der Straßburger Reformatoren bis 1528* (Tübingen 1992), *Revue d'histoire et de philosophie religieuses* 74 (1994): 265–72.

19. See note 6, above. Kaufmann summarizes his theses in his essay "Streittheologie und Friedensdiplomatie. Die Rolle Martin Bucers im frühen Abendmahlsstreit," in *M.B. and Europe*, pp. 239–56.

20. "Ungeheuerlichkeit" (Kaufmann, *Abendmahlstheologie*, p. 370).

21. Thus Kaufmann in his article "Streittheologie," p. 239.

22. An excerpt of the Latin version has been critically edited and amply commented by Jacques V. Pollet, *Martin Bucer. Etudes sur la Correspondance*, vol. 2 (Paris: Presses Universitaires de France, 1962), pp. 71–82.

23. Bernard Roussel, "Bucer exégète," in *M.B. and Europe*, pp. 39–54.

24. Irena Backus, "Church, Communion and Community in Bucer's Commentary on the Gospel of John," in David F. Wright, ed., *Martin Bucer: Reforming Church and Community* (Cambridge: Cambridge University Press, 1994), pp. 61–71.

25. Peter Stephens, "The Church in Bucer's Commentaries on the Epistle to the Ephesians," in Wright, ed., *Bucer*, pp. 45–60.

26. Gerald Hobbs, "Martin Bucer and the Englishing of the Psalms," in Wright, ed., *Bucer*, pp. 161–75. Hobbs also offers some observations on the dissemination of Bucer's early interpretation of the Psalms in his article "Connaissances bibliques, réligion populaire—les premiers psaumes versifiés de la Réforme à Strasbourg 1524–1527," *Revue d'histoire et de philosophie religieuses* 78 (1998): 415–33.

27. *Martin Bucer: Briefwechsel / Correspondance*, vol. 4: *January–September 1530*, ed. Reinhold Friedrich, Berndt Hamm and Andreas Puchta (Leiden: Brill, 2000). Vol. 5 (*September 1530–May 1531*) is due to appear in the course of 2004.

28. Wilhelm H. Neuser, "Martin Bucer als Mittler im Abendmahlsstreit (1530/31)," in Athina Lexutt and Vicco von Bülow, eds., *Kaum zu glauben. Von der Häresie und dem Umgang mit ihr* (Rheinbach, 1998), pp. 140–61.

29. *Martini Buceri opera latina*, vol. 5: *Defensio adversus axioma catholicum, hoc est criminationem R. P. Roberti Episcopi Abrincensis* (1534), ed. William Ian P. Hazlett (Leiden: Brill, 2000).

30. On this, see the articles in *M.B. and Europe*, pp. 471–575.

31. Marc Lienhard, "Martin Bucer, le réformateur européen," *Bulletin de la société de l'histoire du protestantisme français* 138 (1992): 161–80.

32. Martin Greschat, "Martin Bucers Konzept der Erneuerung der Kirche in Europa," in Martin Greschat, ed., *Die christliche Mitgift Europas—Traditionen der Zukunft* (Stuttgart, 2000), pp. 46–62.

33. Ian P. Hazlett, "A Pilot-Study of Martin Bucer's Relations with France 1524–1548," in *M.B. and Europe*, pp. 513–21.

34. See note 7 above.
35. Stephen E. Buckwalter, "Die Stellung der Straßburger Reformatoren zu den Täufern bis 1528," *Mennonitische Geschichtsblätter* 52 (1995): 52–84.
36. Matthieu Arnold, "Le rôle des autorités civiles dans la lutte contre les anabaptistes. La conception du magistrat de Strasbourg et celle de Martin Bucer," in A. Doering-Manteuffel and K. Nowak, eds., *Religionspolitik in Deutschland* (Stuttgart, 1999), pp. 11–28.
37. John S. Oyer, "Bucer Opposes the Anabaptists," *Mennonite Quarterly Review* 68 (1994): 24–50.
38. Amy Nelson Burnett, "Martin Bucer and the Anabaptist Context of Evangelical Confirmation," *Mennonite Quarterly Review* 68 (1994): 95–122.
39. Martin Greschat, "The Relation between Church and Civil Community in Bucer's Reforming Work," in Wright, ed., *Bucer*, pp. 17–31. On this, see also below, the discussion on chapter 8.
40. R. Emmet McLaughlin, "Martin Bucer and the Schwenckfelders," in *M.B. and Europe*, pp. 615–26.
41. André Séguenny, "Pourquoi Bucer détestait les spirituels. Quelques réflexions après la lecture des dialogues de Bucer de 1535," in *M.B. and Europe*, pp. 627–34 (English translation in *Mennonite Quarterly Review* 68 [1994]: 51–58); Stephan Waldhof, "Der Evangelist des gewappneten Moses. Sebastian Francks Auseinandersetzung mit Martin Bucers Obrigkeitsverständnis," *Zeitschrift für Kirchengeschichte* 107 (1996): 327–54.
42. Michèle Monteil, "Le petit catechisme (1529) de Luther et la brève explication écrite (1534) de Bucer—deux modèles d'instruction catéchétique," *Etudes germaniques* 50 (1995): 447–66.
43. Cornel A. Zwierlein, "Reformation als Rechtsreform. Bucers Hermeneutik der lex Dei und sein humanistischer Zugriff auf das römische Recht," in Christoph Strohm, ed., *Martin Bucer und das Recht. Beiträge zum internationalen Symposium vom 1. bis 3. März in der Johannes a Lasco Bibilothek Emden* (Geneva: Librairie Droz, 2002), pp. 29–81. Irena Backus ("Roman and Canon Law"), David F. Wright ("Decretum Gratiani"), Cornelis Augustijn ("Regensburger Reichstag"), Matthieu Arnold ("L'équité chez Bucer") and Willem van 't Spijker ("Recht und Kirchenzucht") present further important ideas on this topic. Gottfried Seebass ("Kirchengüter") considers Bucer's contribution to the discussion on the use of ecclesiastical property.
44. Amy Nelson Burnett, *The Yoke of Christ—Martin Bucer and Christian Discipline* (Kirksville, Mo.: Sixteenth Century Journal Publishers, 1994); Burnett has also written "Church Discipline and Moral Reformation in the Thought of Martin Bucer," *Sixteenth Century Journal* 22 (1991): 439–56; "Confirmation and Christian Fellowship—Martin Bucer on Commitment to the Church," *Church History* 64 (1995): 202–17.
45. Jean Rott, "The Strasbourg Kirchenpfleger and Parish Discipline—Theory and Practice," in Wright, ed., *Bucer*, pp. 122–28.
46. Christian Meyer, "Gesangbuch, darin begriffen . . . Martin Bucer et le chant liturgique," in *M.B. and Europe*, pp. 215–25.
47. Willem van 't Spijker, *Calvin. Biographie und Theologie* (Göttingen: Vandenhoeck & Ruprecht, 2001). The same author provides a more detailed analysis of this topic in "Calvin's Friendship with Martin Bucer: Did It Make Calvin a Calvinist?" in *Calvin and Spirituality*, ed. David Foxgrover (Grand Rapids, Mich.: Calvin Studies Society, 1998), pp. 169–86.

48. Discussed in van 't Spijker, *Calvin*, pp. 142–55.
49. Ibid., p. 208.
50. Cornelis Augustijn, "Bern and France: The Background to Calvin's Letter to Bucer dated January 12, 1538," in W. H. Neuser and H. J. Selderhuis, eds., *Ordenlich und fruchtbar. Festschrift für Willem van 't Spijker* (Leiden: Groen en Zoon, 1997), pp. 155–69.
51. Francis Higman, "Bucer et les Nicodémites," in *M.B. and Europe*, pp. 645–58. Related to this is a point made by Barbara Pitkin, "Seeing and Believing in the Commentaries on John by Martin Bucer and John Calvin," *Church History* 68 (1999): 865–85. She observes that Bucer attached greater importance for the faith to signs and wonders than Calvin did.
52. Cornelis Augustijn, "Bucer und die Religionsgespräche von 1540/41," in *M.B. and Europe*, pp. 671–80; see also, by the same author, "Bucer's Ecclesiology in the Colloquies with the Catholics, 1540–41," in Wright, ed., *Bucer*, pp. 107–21.
53. *Martin Bucers Deutsche Schriften*, vol. 9/1: *Religionsgespräche (1539–1541)*, ed. Cornelis Augustijn (Gütersloh: Gütersloher Verlagshaus, 1995).
54. These are edited in BDS 9/1 (as in n. 53), pp. 93–145 and pp. 149–321, respectively.
55. This is Cornelis Augustijn's thesis in his article "Das Wormser Buch," *Blätter für Pfälzische Kirchengeschichte* 62 (1995): 7–46.
56. Volkmar Ortmann, *Reformation und Einheit der Kirche. Martin Bucers Einigungsbemühungen bei den Religionsgesprächen in Leipzig, Hagenau, Worms und Regensburg 1539/41* (Mainz: Verlag Philipp von Zabern, 2001).
57. "Das Wormser Buch ist Ausdruck von Bucers Anliegen, die protestantische Lehre so darzulegen, dass sie von der altgläubigen Seite in ihrer Wahrheit anerkannt und der evangelischen Reformation der Weg bereitet wird" (Ortmann, *Reformation und Einheit der Kirche*, p. 227).
58. See his "Bucer's Ecclesiology in the Colloquies with the Catholics, 1540–41," in Wright, ed., *Bucer*, pp. 107–21.
59. An example for this view is provided by Willem van 't Spijker, "De kerk in Bucers oecumenisch streven," in Frank van der Pol, ed., *Bucer en de kerk* (Kampen, 1991), pp. 10–54.
60. Cornelis Augustijn, "Die Autorschaft des Consilium admodum paternum," in van 't Spijker, ed., *Calvin—Erbe und Auftrag*, pp. 255–69.
61. Nick Thompson, "Martin Bucer's Assessment of the Canon of the Mass in the Era of Religious Colloquies," *Reformation and Renaissance Review* 3 (2001): 51–77.
62. Jochen Remy, "Die Religionsgespräche von Hagenau, Worms und Regensburg (1540/41) als Ausgangspunkt für die Kölner Reformation," *Monatshefte für Evangelische Kirchengeschichte des Rheinlands* 43 (1994): 29–49.
63. *Martin Bucers Deutsche Schriften*, vol. 11/1: *Schriften zur Kölner Reformation*, ed. Christoph Strohm and Thomas Wilhelmi (Gütersloh: Gütersloher Verlagshaus, 1999).
64. In fact, the following volume has appeared since the conclusion of this chapter: *Martin Bucers Deutsche Schriften*, vol. 11/2: *Schriften zur Kölner Reformation*, ed. Thomas Wilhelmi (Gütersloh: Gütersloher Verlagshaus, 2003).
65. Christoph Strohm, "Die Berufung auf kanonisches Recht, römisches Recht und Reichsrecht in der Auseinandersetzung um die Kölner Reformation 1543–1546," in Strohm, ed., *Martin Bucer und das Recht*, pp. 123–45; the quote is taken from p. 125.
66. Amy Nelson Burnett, "Martin Bucer and the Church Fathers in the Cologne Reformation," *Reformation and Renaissance Review* 3 (2001): 108–24.

67. Gottfried Hammann, "Ecclesiological Motives behind the Creation of the 'Christliche Gemeinschaften,'" in Wright, ed., *Bucer*, pp. 129–43; Gottfried Hammann, "Die ekklesiologischen Hintergründe zur Bildung von Bucers 'Christlichen Gemeinschaften' in Straßburg (1546–1548)," *Zeitschrift für Kirchengeschichte* 105 (1994): 344–60.

68. Gottfried Hammann, *Entre la secte et la cité. Le projet d'église du réformateur Martin Bucer (1491–1551)* (Geneva: Labor et Fides, 1984). The German translation bears the title *Martin Bucer 1491–1551. Zwischen Volkskirche und Bekenntnisgemeinschaft* (Stuttgart: Franz Steiner Verlag, 1989).

69. Thomas Brady, *Protestant Politics: Jacob Sturm (1489–1553) and the German Reformation* (Atlantic Highlands, N.J.: Humanities Press, 1995), p. 278. German translation: *Zwischen Gott und Mammon. Protestantische Politik und deutsche Reformation* (Berlin: Siedler, 1996), p. 234.

70. Admittedly, many of these drastic formulations are present only in the German translation of Brady's work (*Zwischen Gott und Mammon*, p. 218: "überzeugter Kriegsfalke"; cf. *Protestant Politics*, p. 264. *Zwischen Gott und Mammon*, p. 220: "Bucers Zweckzynismus"; cf. *Protestant Politics*, p. 267. *Zwischen Gott und Mammon*, p. 233: "Kreuzritter"; cf. *Protestant Politics*, p. 277).

71. See, among others, Howard Dellar, "The Influence of Martin Bucer on the English Reformation," *Cahiers d'histoire mondiale* 106 (1992): 351–56; David F. Wright, "Martin Bucer (1491–1551) in England," *Anvil* 9 (1992): 249–59; David F. Wright, "Martin Bucer in England—and Scotland," in *M.B. and Europe*, pp. 523–32; Basil Hall, "Martin Bucer in England," in Wright, ed., *Bucer*, pp. 144–160. J. William Black observes Bucer's influence in Richard Baxter's conception of church discipline centered on the parish congregation: "From Martin Bucer to Richard Baxter: 'Discipline' and Reformation in 16th and 17th Century England," *Church History* 70 (2001): 644–73.

72. Diarmaid MacCulloch, *Thomas Cranmer: A Life* (New Haven, Conn.: Yale University Press, 1996).

73. Jochen Remy, "Die 'Kölner Reformation' und ihre Bedeutung für die englische Kirchengeschichte. Anmerkungen zu einer Verhältnisbestimmung zwischen dem 'Einfältigen Bedenken' und dem 'Book of Common Prayer,'" *Veröffentlichungen des Kölnischen Geschichtsvereins* 67 (1993): 119–40.

74. Christine Klingenspor, "Martin Bucer als europäischer Reformator. Sein Einfluß auf das englische Book of Common Prayer von 1552 (Censura von 1551)," *Blätter für Pfälzische Kirchengeschichte* 59 (1992): 5–36.

75. N. Scott Amos, "'It Is Fallow Ground Here': Martin Bucer as Critic of the English Reformation," *Westminster Theological Journal* 61 (1999): 41–52.

76. N. Scott Amos, "Martin Bucer and the Revision of the 1549 Book of Common Prayer: Reform of Ceremonies and the Didactic Use of Ritual," *Reformation and Renaissance Review* 2 (1999): 107–26.

77. N. Scott Amos, "Strangers in a Strange Land: The English Correspondence of Martin Bucer and Peter Martyr Vermigli," in *Peter Martyr Vermigli and the European Reformations*, ed. Frank James III (Leiden, forthcoming).

78. N. Scott Amos, "The Alsatian among the Athenians: Martin Bucer, Mid-Tudor Cambridge and the Edwardian Reformation," *Reformation and Renaissance Review* 4,1 (June 2002): 94–124.

79. N. Scott Amos, "The Use of Canon and Civil Law and Their Relationship to Biblical Law in *De Regno Christi*," in Strohm, ed., *Martin Bucer und das Recht*, pp. 147–65.

80. N. Scott Amos, "The Exegete as Theologian: Martin Bucer's 1550 Cambridge Lectures on Ephesians and Biblical Humanist Method in Theology" (Ph.D. diss., University of St Andrews, June 2003).

81. Andreas Gäumann, *Reich Christi und Obrigkeit. Eine Studie zum reformatorischen Denken und Handeln Martin Bucers* (Bern: Peter Lang, 2001). The bibliography unfortunately contains numerous errors.

82. Ibid., p. 416 ("fanatisch").

83. Ibid., pp. 503 and 528 ("harmoniebedürftig").

84. Willem van 't Spijker, "Bucer's Doctrinal Legacy as Formulated in His Last Three Wills and Testaments," *Reformation and Renaissance Review* 3 (2001): 152–66.

Bibliography

The works preceded by an asterisk are discussed in chapter 10, "New Insights."

I. Reference Works

Bucer-Bibliographie / Bibliographie Bucer 1975–1998. Edited by Thomas Wilhelmi, Bernd Paul, Michael Herrmann, and Danièle Fischer. Preface by Matthieu Arnold and Gottfried Seebass. Strasbourg: Association des Publications de la Faculté de Théologie Protestante, 1999.

Hartweg, Frédéric, and Klaus-Peter Wegera. *Frühneuhochdeutsch. Eine Einführung in die deutsche Sprache des Spätmittttelalters und der frühen Neuzeit.* Tübingen: Niemeyer, 1989.

Köhn, Mechtild. "Bucer-Bibliographie 1951–1974." In de Kroon and Krüger, eds., *Bucer und seine Zeit,* pp. 133–65.

Rott, Jean. *Correspondance de Martin Bucer. Liste alphabétique des correspondants.* Strasbourg, 1977.

Seebass, Gottfried. "Bucer-Forschung seit dem Jubiläumsjahr 1991." *Theologische Rundschau* 62 (1997): 271–300.

Stupperich, Robert ed. "Bibliographia Bucerana." In *Schriften des Vereins für Reformationsgeschichte* 169. Gütersloh: C. Bertelsmann, 1952, pp. 37–96 (referred to as BB).

II. Primary Sources

A. Martin Bucer

Correspondance.
  Volume 1 (until 1524). Edited by Jean Rott. Leiden: E. J. Brill, 1979.
  Volume 2 (1524–1526). Edited by Jean Rott, with the cooperation of Reinhold Friedrich. Leiden: E. J. Brill, 1989.
  * Volume 3 (1527–1529). Edited by Jean Rott and Christian Krieger, in cooperation with Matthieu Arnold and Reinhold Friedrich. Leiden: E. J. Brill, 1995.
  * Volume 4 (January–September 1530). Edited by Reinhold Friedrich, Berndt Hamm, and Andreas Puchta, in cooperation with Matthieu Arnold and Christian Krieger. Leiden: E. J. Brill, 2000.

Volume 5 (September 1530–May 1531). Edited by Reinhold Friedrich, Berndt Hamm, Roland Liebenberg, and Andreas Puchta, in cooperation with Matthieu Arnold and Christian Krieger. Leiden: E. J. Brill, 2004.

Deutsche Schriften.
  Volume 1: *Frühschriften 1520–1524.* Edited by Robert Stupperich. Gütersloh and Paris: Gütersloher Verlagshaus, 1960.
  Volume 2: *Schriften der Jahre 1524–1528.* Edited by Robert Stupperich. Gütersloh and Paris: Gütersloher Verlagshaus and Presses Universitaires de France, 1962.
  Volume 3: *Confessio Tetrapolitana und die Schriften des Jahres 1531.* Edited by Robert Stupperich. Gütersloh and Paris: Gütersloher Verlagshaus and Presses Universitaires de France, 1969.
  Volume 4: *Zur auswärtigen Wirksamkeit 1528–1533.* Edited by Robert Stupperich. Gütersloh and Paris: Gütersloher Verlagshaus and Presses Universitaires de France, 1975.
  Volume 5: *Strassburg und Münster im Kampf um den rechten Glauben 1532–1534.* Edited by Robert Stupperich. Gütersloh: Gütersloher Verlagshaus, 1978.
  Volume 6, 1: *Wittenberger Konkordie (1536). Schriften zur Wittenberger Konkordie (1534–1537).* Edited by Robert Stupperich, Marijn de Kroon, and Hartmut Rudolph. Gütersloh: Gütersloher Verlagshaus, 1988.
  Volume 6, 2: *Zum Ius Reformationis: Obrigkeitsschriften aus dem Jahre 1535. Dokumente zur 2. Strassburger Synode von 1539.* Edited by Robert Stupperich. Gütersloh: Gütersloher Verlagshaus, 1984.
  Volume 6, 3: *Martin Bucers Katechismen aus den Jahren 1534, 1537, 1543.* Edited by Robert Stupperich. Gütersloh: Gütersloher Verlagshaus, 1987.
  Volume 7: *Schriften der Jahre 1538–1539.* Edited by Robert Stupperich. Gütersloh and Paris: Gütersloher Verlagshaus and Presses Universitaires de France, 1964.
  Volume 8: *Abendmahlsschriften 1529–1541.* Edited by Stephen E. Buckwalter. Gütersloh: Gütersloher Verlagshaus, 2004.
* Volume 9, 1: *Religionsgespräche (1539–1541).* Edited by Cornelis Augustijn, with the cooperation of Marijn de Kroon. Gütersloh: Gütersloher Verlagshaus, 1995.
  * Volume 10: *Schriften zu Ehe und Eherecht.* Edited by Stephen E. Buckwalter and Hans Schulz. Gütersloh: Gütersloher Verlagshaus, 2001.
  * Volume 11, 1: *Schriften zur Kölner Reformation.* Edited by Christoph Strohm and Thomas Wilhelmi. Gütersloh: Gütersloher Verlagshaus, 1999.
  Volume 11, 2: *Schriften zur Kölner Reformation.* Edited by Thomas Wilhelmi. Gütersloh: Gütersloher Verlagshaus, 2003.
  Volume 17: *Die letzten Strassburger Jahre 1546–1549. Schriften zur Gemeindereformation und zum Augsburger Interim.* Edited by Robert Stupperich. Gütersloh: Gütersloher Verlagshaus, 1981.

Opera latina.
  Volume 1: *De Caena Dominica. Epistola Apologetica. Refutatio Locorum Eckii.* Edited by Cornelis Augustijn, Pierre Fraenkel, and Marc Lienhard. Leiden: E. J. Brill, 1982.
  Volume 2: *Enarratio in Evangelion Iohannis (1528, 1530, 1536).* Edited by Irena Backus. Leiden: E. J. Brill, 1988.
  Volume 3 (Martin Bucer and Matthew Parker): *Florilegium patristicum.* Edited by Pierre Fraenkel. Leiden: E. J. Brill, 1988.

Volume 4: *Consilium theologicum privatim conscriptum*. Edited by Pierre Fraenkel. Leiden: E. J. Brill, 1988.
* Volume 5: *Defensio adversus Axioma Catholicum, hoc est criminationem R. P. Roberti Episcopi Abrincensis (1534)*. Edited by William Ian P. Hazlett. Leiden: E. J. Brill, 2000.
Volume 15: *De regno Christi (1551)*. Edited by François Wendel. Paris: Presses Universitaires de France, 1954.
Volume 15 bis: *Du Royaume de Jésus-Christ (1558)*. Edited by François Wendel. Paris: Presses Universitaires de France, 1954.
Scripta anglicana fere omnia. Edited by Conrad Hubert. Basel: Petrus Perna, 1577.

Works of Bucer in English Translation

Common Places of Martin Bucer. Translated and edited by David F. Wright. Abingdon, England: Sutton Courtenay Press, 1972.
Melanchthon and Bucer. Edited by Wilhelm Pauck. Library of Christian Classics 19. Philadelphia: Westminster Press, 1969. (Pp. 153–394 contain Martin Bucer's *De Regno Christi*.)

B. Other Authors

Beatus Rhenanus. *Briefwechsel*. Edited by Adalbert Horawitz and Karl Hartfelder. Reprint, Hildesheim, 1966.
Bebel, Heinrich. *Opusculum Henrici Bebelii, Iustingensis de institutione puerorum*. Strasbourg: Matthias Schürer, 1513.
Bekenntnisschriften der reformierten Kirche. Edited by Karl Müller. Leipzig, 1903. Reprint, Zurich, 1987.
Calvin, John. *Opera quae supersunt omnia*. Edited by Wilhelm Baum et al. 44 vols. Braunschweig, 1863–1900.
Complete Prose Works of John Milton. Vol. 2. Edited by E. Sirluck. New Haven, Conn.: Yale University Press, 1959.
Correspondance des réformateurs dans les pays de langue française. Edited by A. L. Herminjard. Geneva: H. Georg; Paris: Michel Levy, 1866–1897. Reprint, Nieuwkoop: De Graaf, 1965.
Deutsche Reichstagsakten, Jüngere Reihe. Deutsche Reichstagsakten unter Kaiser Karl V. 8 vols. Gotha: F. A. Perthes, 1893–1935. Reprint, Göttingen: Vandenhoeck & Ruprecht, 1970–1971.
Engelbrecht, Antonius. *Abconterfeytung Martin Butzers (1546)*. Edited by Werner Bellardi. Münster: Aschendorff, 1974.
Erasmus of Rotterdam. *Erasmus von Rotterdam: Ausgewählte Schriften*. Edited by Werner Welzig. 8 vols. Darmstadt: Wissenschaftliche Buchgesellschaft, 1968–1980.
———. *Collected Works of Erasmus*. Vol. 66: *Spiritualia. Enchiridion. De contemptu mundi. De vidua christiana*. Edited by John W. O'Malley. Toronto: University of Toronto Press, 1988.
Franz, Günther, ed. *Wiedertäuferakten 1527–1626. Urkundliche Quellen zur hessischen Reformationsgeschichte*. Vol. 4. Marburg a. d. Lahn: Elwert, 1951.
Gebwiler, Jerome. *Schlettstädter Chronik*. Edited by Joseph Gény. Sélestat, 1890.
Gottesheim, Jacques de. "Les éphémérides de Jacques de Gottesheim (1524–1543)." Edited by Rodolphe Reuss. *Bulletin de la société pour la conservation des monuments historiques d'Alsace* 19 (1899): 261–81.
Gropper, Johannes. *Briefwechsel*. Vol. 1: *1529–1547*. Edited by Reinhard Braunisch. Münster: Aschendorff, 1977.

Hortleder, Friedrich. *Der römischen keyser . . . Handlungen und Auschreiben.* Frankfurt, 1618.

Jacobus de Voragine. *Golden Legend or Lives of the Saints, as Englished by William Caxton.* New York: AMS Press, 1973.

———. *Legenda Aurea.* Translated into German and edited by Richard Benz. Jena: Diederichs, 1925.

Lenz, Max. *Briefwechsel Landgraf Philipp's des Grossmübthigen von Hessen mit Bucer.* 3 vols. Leipzig, 1880–1891.

Luther, Martin. *Luthers Werke in Auswahl.* Edited by Otto Clemen et al. 8 vols. Berlin: Walter de Gruyter, 1912–1930. Reprint, 1962–1966.

———. *Luther's Works.* Edited by Jaroslav Pelikan and Helmut T. Lehmann. 55 vols. St. Louis: Concordia Publishing House and Philadelphia: Fortress Press, 1955–1986.

———. *Studienausgabe.* Edited by Hans-Ulrich Delius et al. 6 vols. Berlin: Evangelische Verlagsanstalt, 1979– .

Melanchthon, Philipp. *Corpus Reformatorum: Philippi Melanthonis opera quae supersunt omnia.* Edited by Karl Bretschneider and Heinrich Bindseil. 28 vols. Halle a. d. Saale: A. Schwetschke & Sons, 1834–1860.

———. *Werke in Auswahl.* Edited by Robert Stupperich. 9 vols. Gütersloh: G. Mohn, 1951– .

Original Letters Relative to the English Reformation. Translated and edited by Hastings Robinson. 2 vols. Cambridge: University Press, 1846–1847.

Pflug, Julius. *Correspondance.* Edited by Jacques Vincent Pollet. Vols. 2 and 3. Leiden: E. J. Brill, 1973 and 1977.

Politische Correspondenz der Stadt Strassburg im Zeitalter der Reformation. Edited by Hans Virck, Otto Winckelmann, Harry Gerber, and Walter Friedensburg. 5 vols. Strasbourg: Trübner, 1882–1898; Heidelberg: Carl Winter, 1928–1933.

Reformed Confessions of the 16th Century. Edited by A. C. Cochrane. London, 1966.

Regensburger Buch (1540/41). In G. Pfeilschifter, ed., *Acta Reformationis Catholicae,* vol. 6/3.2. Regensburg: Friedrich Pustet, 1974, pp. 21–88.

Schiess, Traugott, ed. *Briefwechsel der Brüder Ambrosius und Thomas Blaurer, 1509–1548.* 3 vols. Freiburg im Breisgau: Fehsenfeld, 1908–1912.

Schottenloher, Karl, ed. *Flugschriften zur Ritterschaftsbewegung des Jahres 1523.* Münster: Aschendorff, 1929.

Schriften von evangelischer Seite gegen die Täufer. Edited by Robert Stupperich. Münster: Aschendorff, 1983.

Staehelin, Ernst, ed. *Briefe und Akten zum Leben Oekolampads.* Vol. 2. Leipzig: Heinsius, 1934. Reprint, New York and London: Johnson, 1971.

TAE = *Täuferakten Elsass.* Edited by Manfred Krebs, Jean Rott, et al. 4 vols. Gütersloh: G. Mohn, 1959–1988 (= *Quellen zur Geschichte der Täufer,* vols. 7, 8, 15, and 16).

Turmair, Johannes (Aventinus). *Gesammelte Werke.* Vol. 1: *Kleinere Historische und Philologische Schriften.* Munich, 1881.

Wittmer, Charles, and Jean Charles Meyer, eds. *Le livre de bourgeoisie de la ville de Strasbourg 1440–1530.* 3 vols. Strasbourg: Heitz, 1948–1961.

Witzel, Georg. "Warer Bericht von den Acten der Leipsischen und Speirischen Collocution zwischen Mar. Bucern und Georg. Wicelien [Witzel]" (Cologne, 1562). In G. Pfeilschifter, ed., *Acta Reformationis Catholicae,* vol. 6/3.2. Regensburg: Friedrich Pustet, 1974, pp. 17–20.

Zwingli, Huldreich. *Sämtliche Werke.* Leipzig: Heinsius; Zurich: Verl. Berichtshaus, Theologischer Verlag, 1905– .

III. Secondary Works

Adam, Johann. *Evangelische Kirchengeschichte der Stadt Strassburg bis zur franzoesischen Revolution.* Strasbourg: J. H. E. Heitz, 1922.

Adam, Paul. *Histoire religieuse de Sélestat.* 2 vols. Sélestat: Alsatia, 1967 and 1971.

———. *L'humanisme à Sélestat. L'école, les humanistes, la bibliothèque.* 3d ed. Sélestat: Alsatia, 1973. German translation: *Der Humanismus zu Schlettstadt: Die Schule, die Humanisten, die Bibliothek.* Sélestat: Amis de la Bibliothèque Humaniste, 1995.

Ammann, Hektor. "Von der Wirtschaftsgeltung des Elsass im Mittelater." *Alemannisches Jahrbuch* (1955): 95–202.

* Amos, N. Scott. "The Alsatian among the Athenians: Martin Bucer, Mid-Tudor Cambridge and the Edwardian Reformation." *Reformation and Renaissance Review* 4,1 (June 2002): 94–124.

* ———. "The Exegete as Theologian: Martin Bucer's 1550 Cambridge Lectures on Ephesians and Biblical Humanist Method in Theology and Exegesis." Diss., University of St. Andrews, 2003.

* ———. "'It Is Fallow Ground Here': Martin Bucer as Critic of the English Reformation." *Westminster Theological Journal* 61,1 (1999): 41–52.

* ———. "Martin Bucer and the Revision of the 1549 Book of Common Prayer: Reform of Ceremonies and the Didactic Use of Ritual." *Reformation and Renaissance Review*, 2 (December 1999): 107–126.

* ———. "Strangers in a Strange Land: The English Correspondence of Martin Bucer and Peter Martyr Vermigli." In *Peter Martyr Vermigli and the European Reformations*, ed. Frank James III. Leiden, forthcoming.

* ———. "The Use of Canon and Civil Law and Their Relationship to Biblical Law in *De Regno Christi*." In Strohm, ed., *Martin Bucer und das Recht*, pp. 147–65.

Andreas, Willy. "Strassburg an der Wende vom Mittelalter zur Neuzeit," *Elsass-Lothringisches Jahrbuch* 13 (1934): 27–67.

Anrich, Gustav. *Martin Bucer.* Strasbourg: Karl J. Trübner, 1914.

Ariès, Philippe. *L'enfant et la vie familiale sous l'ancien régime.* Paris: Plon, 1960. English translation: *Centuries of Childhood: A Social History of Family Life.* New York: Vintage Books, 1962. German translation: *Geschichte der Kindheit.* 5th ed. Munich: Deutscher Taschenbuch-Verlag, 1982.

* Arnold, Matthieu. "'Dass niemand ihm selbst, sondern anderen leben soll.' Das theologische Programm Martin Bucers von 1523 im Vergleich mit Luther." *Theologische Beiträge* 32 (2001): 237–48.

* ———. "L'équité chez Martin Bucer." In Strohm, ed., *Martin Bucer und das Recht*, pp. 201–214.

* ———. "Le rôle des autorités civiles dans la lutte contre les anabaptistes. La conception du Magistrat de Strasbourg et celle de Martin Bucer." In Anselm Doering-Manteuffel and Kurt Nowak, eds., *Religionspolitik in Deutschland. Von der frühen Neuzeit bis zur Gegenwart. Martin Greschat zum 65. Geburtstag.* Stuttgart: Kohlhammer, 1999, pp. 11–28.

Augustijn, Cornelis. "Allein das heilig Evangelium. Het mandaat van het Reichsregiment 6 maert 1523." *Nederlands Archief voor Kerkgeschiedenis* 48 (1967/68): 150–65.

* ———. "Die Autorschaft des Consilium admodum paternum." In Willem van 't Spijker, ed., *Calvin—Erbe und Auftrag. Festschrift für Wilhelm Heinrich Neuser zum 65. Geburtstag.* Kampen: Kok, 1991, pp. 255–69.

* ———. "Bern and France. The Background to Calvin's Letter to Bucer Dated January 12, 1538." In Wilhelm Neuser and Herman J. Selderhuis, eds., *Ordenlich und fruchtbar. Festschrift für Willem van 't Spijker.* Leiden: Groen en Zoon, 1997, pp. 155–69.

* ———. "Die Berufung auf kanonisches und römisches Recht auf dem Regensburger Reichstag 1541: Die *Abusuum Indicatio.*" In Strohm, ed., *Martin Bucer und das Recht*, pp. 113–121.

* ———. "Bucer und die Religionsgespräche von 1540/41." In Krieger and Lienhard, eds., *Martin Bucer and Sixteenth Century Europe*, pp. 671–80.

* ———. "Bucer's Ecclesiology in the Colloquies with the Catholics, 1540–41." In Wright, ed., *Martin Bucer: Reforming Church and Community*, pp. 107–21.

———. *Erasmus von Rotterdam. Leben-Werk-Wirkung.* Munich: C. H. Beck, 1986.

———. "De Gesprekken tussen Bucer en Gropper tijdens het Godsdienstgesprek te Worms in December 1540." *Nederlands Archief voor Kerkgeschiedenis* 47 (1965/66): 208–30.

———. *De Godsdienstgesprekken tussen Rooms-Katholieken en Protestanten van 1538 tot 1541.* Haarlem: Bohn, 1967.

———. "The Quest of Reformatio." In *The Reformation in Germany and Europe: Interpretations and Issues*, ed. Hans R. Guggisberg and Gottfried G. Krodel. Gütersloh: Gütersloher Verlagshaus, 1993, pp. 64–80.

———. "Strasbourg, Bucer et la politique des colloques." In Georges Livet and Francis Rapp, eds., *Strasbourg au coeur religieux du XVIe siècle.* Strasbourg, 1977, pp. 197–206.

* ———. "Das Wormser Buch." *Blätter für Pfälzische Kirchengeschichte* 62 (1995): 7–46.

* Backus, Irena. "Bucer's View of Roman and Canon Law in His Exegetical Writings and in His Patristic Florilegium." In Strohm, ed., *Martin Bucer und das Recht*, pp. 83–99.

* ———. "Church, Communion and Community in Bucer's Commentary on the Gospel of John." In Wright, ed., *Martin Bucer: Reforming Church and Community*, pp. 61–71.

Bainton, Roland H. *Women of the Reformation in Germany and Italy.* Boston: Beacon Press, 1974.

Baron, Hans. "Religion and Politics in the German Imperial Cities during the Reformation." *English Historical Review* 52 (1937): 405–27; 614–33.

Barth, Médard. *Der Rebbau im Elsass und die Absatzgebiete seiner Weine. Ein geschichtlicher Durchblick.* 2 vols. Strasbourg and Paris: Le Roux, 1958.

Barthelmé, Annette. *La réforme dominicaine au XVe siècle en Alsace et dans l'ensemble de la province de Teutonie.* Strasbourg: Heitz, 1931.

Battenberg, Friedrich. "Judenordnungen der frühen Neuzeit in Hessen." In *Neunhundert Jahre Geschichte der Juden in Hessen: Beiträge zum politischen, wirtschaftlichen und kulturellen Leben.* Wiesbaden: Komm. für die Geschichte der Juden in Hessen, 1983, pp. 83–122.

———. "Des Kaisers Kammerknechte. Gedanken zur rechtlich-sozialen Situation der Juden in Spätmittelalter und früher Neuzeit." *Historische Zeitschrift* 245 (1987): 545–99.

Baum, Adolf. *Magistrat und Reformation in Strassburg bis 1529.* Strasbourg: J. H. E. Heitz, 1887.

Baum, Johann Wilhelm. *Capito und Butzer. Strassburgs Reformatoren.* Elberfeld: R. L. Friderichs, 1860.

Bellardi, Werner. "Ein Bedacht Hedios zur Kirchenzucht in Strassburg aus dem Jahre 1547." In de Kroon and Krüger, eds., *Bucer und seine Zeit*, pp. 117–32.

———. "Bucer und das Interim." In de Kroon and Lienhard, eds., *Horizons européens*, pp. 267–94.

————. *Die Geschichte der "Christlichen Gemeinschaften" in Straßburg (1546/1550). Der Versuch einer "zweiten Reformation."* Leipzig: Heinsius, 1934.

Berg, Cornelis W. van den. "Anton Engelbrecht—un 'épicurien' strasbourgeois." In Marc Lienhard, ed., *Croyants et sceptiques au XVIe siècle.* Strasbourg, 1981, pp. 111–20.

Bizer, Ernst. *Studien zur Geschichte des Abendmahlsstreits im 16. Jahrhundert.* Gütersloh: C. Bertelsmann, 1940.

* Black, J. William. "From Martin Bucer to Richard Baxter. 'Discipline' and Reformation in 16th and 17th Century England." *Church History* 70 (2001): 644–73.

Blickle, Peter. *Gemeindereformation. Die Menschen des 16. Jahrhunderts auf dem Weg zum Heil.* Munich: Oldenbourg, 1985. English translation: *Communal Reformation: The Quest for Salvation in Sixteenth-Century Germany.* Atlantic Highlands, N.J.: Humanities Press, 1992.

————. *Die Revolution von 1525.* 3d ed. Munich: R. Oldenbourg, 1993. English translation: *The Revolution of 1525: The German Peasants' War from a New Perspective.* Baltimore: Johns Hopkins University Press, 1981.

* Bodenmann, Reinhard. "Martin Bucer et Gaspard Hedion. Vicissitudes des relations entre deux collègues." In Krieger and Lienhard, eds., *Martin Bucer and Sixteenth Century Europe,* 297–315.

Bornert, René. *La Réforme protestante du culte à Strasbourg au XVIe siècle (1523–1598).* Leiden: E. J. Brill, 1981.

Bornkamm, Heinrich. "Martin Bucer. Der dritte deutsche Reformator." In *Das Jahrhundert der Reformation. Gestalten und Kräfte.* Göttingen: Vandenhoeck & Ruprecht, 1961, pp. 88–112.

Brady, Thomas A. Jr. *The Politics of the Reformation in Germany: Jacob Sturm (1489–1553) of Strasbourg.* Atlantic Highlands, N.J.: Humanities Press, 1997.

————. *Protestant Politics. Jacob Sturm (1489–1553) and the German Reformation.* Atlantic Highlands, N.J.: Humanities Press, 1995. German translation: *Zwischen Gott und Mammon. Protestantische Politik und deutsche Reformation.* Berlin: Siedler, 1996.

————. *Ruling Class, Regime and Reformation at Strasbourg, 1520–1555.* Leiden: E. J. Brill, 1978.

————. "'Sind also zu beiden theilen Christen des Gott erbarm.' Le mémoire de Jacques Sturm sur le culte public à Strasbourg (août 1525)." In de Kroon and Lienhard, eds., *Horizons européens,* pp. 69–79.

————. *Turning Swiss. Cities and Empire, 1450–1550.* Cambridge and New York: Cambridge University Press, 1985.

Brandi, Karl. *Deutsche Geschichte im Zeitalter der Reformation und Gegenreformation.* Darmstadt: Wissenschaftliche Buchgesellschaft, 1960.

————. *Kaiser Karl V. Werden und Schicksal einer Persönlichkeit und eines Weltreiches.* 5th ed. Darmstadt: Wissenschaftliche Buchgesellschaft, 1959.

* Bräuer, Siegfried. "Bucer und der Neukarsthans." In Krieger and Lienhard, eds., *Martin Bucer and Sixteenth Century Europe,* pp. 103–27.

Braunisch, Reinhard. "Die 'Artikell' der 'Warhafftigen Antwort' (1545) des Johannes Gropper. Zur Verfasserfrage des Worms-Regensburger Buches (1540/41)." In Remigius Bäumer, ed., *Von Konstanz nach Trient.* Paderborn: Schoeningh, 1972, pp. 519–45.

————. *Die Theologie der Rechtfertigung im "Enchiridion" (1539) des Johannes Gropper.* Münster: Aschendorff, 1974.

Brecht, Martin. "Die deutsche Ritterschaft und die Reformation." *Ebernburg-Hefte* 3 (1969): 27–37.

———. "Luthers Beziehungen zu den Oberdeutschen und Schweizern 1530/31 bis 1546." In Helmar Junghans, ed., *Leben und Werk Martin Luthers von 1526 bis 1546*. Berlin: Evangelische Verlagsanstalt, 1983, pp. 497–517 (vol. 1) and pp. 891–94 (vol. 2).

*———. "Martin Bucer und die Heidelberger Disputation." In Spijker, ed., *Calvin—Erbe und Auftrag*, pp. 214–28.

———. *Martin Luther*. 3 vols. Stuttgart: Calwer Verlag, 1981–87. English translation: *Martin Luther*. 3 vols. Philadelphia: Fortress Press, 1985–1993.

* Buckwalter, Stephen E. *Die Priesterehe in Flugschriften der frühen Reformation*. Gütersloh: Gütersloher Verlagshaus, 1998.

———. "Die Stellung der Straßburger Reformatoren zu den Täufern bis 1528." *Mennonitische Geschichtsblätter* 52 (1995): 52–84.

* Burnett, Amy Nelson. "Church Discipline and Moral Reformation in the Thought of Martin Bucer." *Sixteenth Century Journal* 22 (1991): 439–56.

* ———. "Confirmation and Christian Fellowship—Martin Bucer on Commitment to the Church." *Church History* 64 (1995): 202–17.

* ———. "Martin Bucer and the Anabaptist Context of Evangelical Confirmation." *Mennonite Quarterly Review* 68 (1994): 95–122.

* ———. "Martin Bucer and the Church Fathers in the Cologne Reformation." *Reformation and Renaissance Review* 3 (2001): 108–24.

* ———. *The Yoke of Christ—Martin Bucer and Christian Discipline*. Kirksville, Mo.: Sixteenth Century Journal Publishers, 1994.

Bush, M. L. *The Government Policy of Protector Somerset*. London: Edward Arnold; Montreal: McGill-Queen's University Press, 1975.

Buszello, Horst, Peter Blickle, and Rudolf Endres, eds. *Der deutsche Bauernkrieg*. Paderborn: Schoeningh, 1984.

Chrisman, Miriam Usher. *Lay Culture—Learned Culture. Books and Social Change in Strasbourg 1450–1599*. New Haven, Conn.: Yale University Press, 1982.

———. "La pensée et la main: Mathias Schürer, humaniste-imprimeur." In Francis Rapp and Georges Livet, eds., *Grandes figures de l'humanisme alsacien: courants, milieux, destins*. Strasbourg: Librairie Istra, 1978, pp. 159–72.

———. *Strasbourg and the Reform. A Study in the Process of Change*. New Haven, Conn.: Yale University Press, 1967.

Conrad, Franziska. *Reformation in der bäuerlichen Gesellschaft. Zur Rezeption reformatorischer Theologie in Elsaß*. Stuttgart: Franz Steiner, 1984.

Cooper, Charles H. *Annals of Cambridge*. Vol. 2. Cambridge, 1843.

Courvoisier, Jacques. "Bucer et Calvin." In *Calvin à Strasbourg 1538–1541. Quatre études publiées à l'occasion du 400e anniversaire de l'arrivée de Calvin à Strasbourg par le soins de la commission synodale de l'église réf. d'Alsace et de Lorraine*. Strasbourg: Fides, 1938, pp. 37–66.

* Dellar, Howard. "The Influence of Martin Bucer on the English Reformation." *Cahiers d'histoire mondiale* 106 (1992): 351–56.

Demandt, Karl E. *Geschichte des Landes Hessen*. Kassel: Bärenreiter, 1959.

Deppermann, Klaus. "Judenhaß und Judenfreundschaft im frühen Protestantismus." In B. Martin and E. Schulin, eds., *Die Juden als Minderheit in der Geschichte*. Munich: Deutscher Taschenbuch-Verlag, 1981, pp. 110–30.

————. *Melchior Hoffman. Soziale Unruhen und apokalyptische Visionen im Zeitalter der Reformation.* Göttingen: Vandenhoeck & Ruprecht, 1979.

————. "Die Straßburger Reformatoren und die Krise des oberdeutschen Täufertums im Jahre 1527." *Mennonitische Geschichtsblätter* 25 (1973): 24–52.

————. "Täufergruppen in Augsburg und Straßburg -ihre soziale Rekrutierung und Theologie." In B. Kirchgässner and F. Reuter, eds., *Städtische Randgruppen und Minderheiten.* Sigmaringen: Thorbecke, 1986, pp. 161–82.

Dickens, Arthur Geoffrey. *The English Reformation.* University Park: Pennsylvania State University Press, 1996.

Diehl, Wilhelm. *Martin Butzers Bedeutung für das kirchliche Leben in Hessen.* Halle a. d. Saale: Verein für Reformationsgeschichte, 1904.

Dietz, Josef. *Topographie der Stadt Bonn vom Mittelater bis zum Ende der kurfürstlichen Zeit.* Vol. 1. Bonn: Röhrscheid, 1962.

Doerr, Wilhelm, ed. *Semper Apertus. Sechshundert Jahre Ruprecht-Karls-Universität Heidelberg 1366–1986.* Berlin and Heidelberg: Springer, 1985.

Dorlan, Alexandre. *Histoire architecturale et anecdotique de Schlestadt.* 2 vols. Paris, 1912.

Dotzauer, Winfried. "Der 'Warliche Bericht' des Reichsherolds Caspar Sturm über den Kriegszug der drei Verbündeten gegen Franz von Sickingen im Jahre 1523." *Ebernburg-Hefte* 3 (1969): 73–97.

Ebert, Doris. *Elisabeth Silbereisen. Familie und Lebensstationen.* [Eppingen:] Heimatverein Kraichgau, 2001.

Edwards, Mark U. Jr. *Printing, Propaganda, and Martin Luther.* Berkeley, Los Angeles, and London: University of California Press, 1994.

Eells, Hastings. *The Attitude of Martin Bucer toward the Bigamy of Philip of Hesse.* New Haven, Conn.: Yale University Press, 1924.

————. *Martin Bucer.* New Haven, Conn.: Yale University Press, 1931. Reprint, New York: Russell & Russell, 1971.

Elton, Geoffrey R. "England und die oberdeutsche Reform." *Zeitschrift für Kirchengeschichte* 89 (1978): 3–11.

————. *Reformation Europe, 1517–1559.* New York: Harper & Row, 1966. German translation: *Europa im Zeitalter der Reformation 1517–1559.* 2d ed. Munich: C. H. Beck, 1982.

————. "Reform and the 'Commonwealth-Men' of Edward VI's Reign." In *Studies in Tudor and Stuart Politics and Government.* Vol. 3. Cambridge, 1983, pp. 234–53.

————. *Reform and Reformation. England 1509–1558.* London, 1977.

Endriss, Julius. *Das Ulmer Reformationsjahr 1531 in seinen entscheidenden Vorgängen.* Ulm: K. Höhn, 1931.

Erbes, Jean. *Martin Bucer, le Réformateur alsacien inconnu et méconnu.* Grasse: Librairies Protestantes, 1966.

Fabian, Ekkehart. *Die Entstehung des Schmalkaldischen Bundes und seiner Verfassung 1524/29– 1531/35.* 2d ed. Tübingen: Osiander, 1962.

Ficker, Johannes. "Das größte Prachtwerk des Straßburger Buchdrucks. Zur Geschichte und Gestaltung des großen Straßburger Gesangbuchs 1541." *Archiv für Reformationsgeschichte* 38 (1941): 198–230.

Fraenkel, Pierre. *Einigungsbestrebungen in der Reformationszeit. Zwei Wege, zwei Motive.* Wiesbaden: Franz Steiner, 1965.

Fuchs, François J. "Les marchands strasbourgeois étaient-ils des épicuriens?" In Lienhard, ed., *Croyants et sceptiques,* pp. 93–100.

Gäbler, Ulrich. *Huldrych Zwingli. Eine Einführung in sein Leben und sein Werk.* Munich: Beck, 1983.

———. "Luthers Beziehungen zu den Schweizern und Oberdeutschen von 1526 bis 1530/31." In Junghans, ed., *Leben und Werk Martin Luthers,* vol. 1, pp. 481–96; vol. 2, pp. 885–91.

Gäumann, Andreas. *Reich Christi und Obrigkeit. Eine Studie zum reformatorischen Denken und Handeln Martin Bucers.* Bern: Peter Lang, 2001.

Geiger, Ludwig. *Johann Reuchlin. Sein Leben und seine Werke.* Leipzig: Duncker & Humblot, 1871. Reprint, Nieuwkoop: B. de Graaf, 1964.

Gény, Joseph. *Die Reichsstadt Schlettstadt und ihr Anteil an den socialpolitischen und religiösen Bewegungen der Jahre 1490–1536.* Freiburg im Breisgau and St. Louis: Herder, 1900.

———. *Schlettstadter Stadtrechte.* 2 vols. Heidelberg: Winter, 1902.

Gerber, René. "Les anabaptistes à Strasbourg entre 1536 et 1552." In Jean Rott and Simon L. Verhuis, eds., *Anabaptistes et dissidents au XVIe siècle.* Baden-Baden: Koerner, 1987, pp. 311–22.

Goertz, Hans-Jürgen. *Umstrittenes Täufertum, 1525–1975. Neue Forschungen.* Göttingen: Vandenhoeck & Ruprecht, 1975.

Green, V. H. H. *Religion at Oxford and Cambridge.* London, 1964.

Greschat, Martin. "Die Anfänge der reformatorischen Theologie Martin Bucers." In M. Greschat and J. F. G. Goeters, eds., *Reformation und Humanismus.* Witten: Luther-Verlag, 1969, pp. 124–40.

———. "Der Ansatz der Theologie Martin Bucers." *Theologische Literaturzeitung* 103 (1978): 81–96.

———. "Bucers Anteil am Bericht der oberländischen Prediger über den Abschluß der Wittenberger Konkordie." *Archiv für Reformationsgeschichte* 76 (1985): 296–98.

———. "Martin Bucer als Dominikanermönch." In de Kroon amd Krüger, eds., *Bucer und seine Zeit,* pp. 30–53.

———. "Martin Bucers Bücherverzeichnis von 1518." *Archiv für Kulturgeschichte* 57 (1975): 162–85.

* ———. "Martin Bucers Konzept der Erneuerung der Kirche in Europa." In *Die christliche Mitgift Europas—Traditionen der Zukunft.* Stuttgart: Kohlhammer, 2000, pp. 46–62.

———. "Martin Bucer und Ulrich Hutten." In de Kroon and Lienhard, eds., *Horizons européens,* pp. 177–93.

* ———. "The Relation between Church and Civil Community in Bucer's Reforming Work." In Wright, ed., *Martin Bucer: Reforming Church and Community,* pp. 17–31.

Hall, Basil. "Bucer et l'Angleterre." In Livet and Rapp, eds., *Strasbourg au coeur religieux,* pp. 401–29.

* ———. "Martin Bucer in England." In Wright, ed., *Martin Bucer: Reforming Church and Community,* pp. 144–60.

* Hammann, Gottfried. "Ecclesiological Motives behind the Creation of the 'Christliche Gemeinschaften.'" In Wright, ed., *Martin Bucer: Reforming Church and Community,* pp. 129–43.

———. "Die ekklesiologischen Hintergründe zur Bildung von Bucers 'Christlichen Gemeinschaften' in Straßburg (1546–1548)." *Zeitschrift für Kirchengeschichte* 105 (1994): 344–60.

———. *Entre la secte et la cité. Le projet d'église du Réformateur Martin Bucer (1491–1551).* Geneva: Labor et Fides, 1984. German translation: *Martin Bucer 1491–1551. Zwischen Volkskirche und Bekenntnisgemeinschaft.* Stuttgart: Franz Steiner, 1989.

———. "Martin Bucer—Sa vision de l'église selon le traité 'Von der waren Seelsorge.'" In Lienhard, ed., *Croyants et sceptiques*, pp. 73–89.

Harvey, A. Edward. *Martin Bucer in England*. Marburg a. d. Lahn: H. Bauer, 1906.

Hanauer, C. A. *Études économiques sur l'Alsace ancienne et moderne*. 2 vols. Paris and Strasbourg, 1876.

Hassinger, Erich. *Das Werden des neuzeitlichen Europa 1300–1600*. 2d ed. Braunschweig: G. Westermann, 1966.

Hauswirth, René. *Landgraf Philipp von Hessen und Zwingli*. Tübingen: Osiander (Kommissionsverlag), 1968.

Hazlett, Ian. "The Development of Martin Bucer's Thinking on the Sacrament of the Lord's Supper in Its Historical and Theological Context 1523–1534." Diss., Münster, 1975.

———. "Les entretiens entre Melanchthon and Bucer en 1534; réalités politiques et clarification théologique." In de Kroon and Lienhard, eds., *Horizons européens*, pp. 207–25.

* ———. "A Pilot-Study of Martin Bucer's Relations with France 1524–1528." In Krieger and Lienhard, eds., *Martin Bucer and Sixteenth Century Europe*, pp. 513–21.

Heinemeyer, Walter, ed. *Das Werden Hessens*. Marburg a. d. Lahn: Elwert, 1986.

* Higman, Francis. "Bucer et les Nicodémites." In Krieger and Lienhard, eds., *Martin Bucer and Sixteenth Century Europe*, pp. 645–58.

Hitchcock, William R. *The Background of the Knights' Revolt, 1522–1523*. Berkeley, 1958.

* Hobbs, Gerald R. "Connaissances bibliques, réligion populaire. Les premiers psaumes versifiés de la Réforme à Strasbourg 1524–1527." *Revue d'histoire et de philosophie religieuses* 78 (1998): 415–33.

———. "How Firm a Foundation: Martin Bucer's Historical Exegesis of the Psalms." *Church History* 53 (1984): 477–91.

* ———. "Martin Bucer and the Englishing of the Psalms." In Wright, ed., *Martin Bucer: Reforming Church and Community*, pp. 161–75.

Holborn, Hajo. *Ulrich von Hutten*. Göttingen, 1968.

Hopf, Constantin. *Martin Bucer and the English Reformation*. Oxford: Basil Blackwell, 1946.

Husser, Daniel. "Caspar Schwenckfeld et ses adeptes entre l'église et les sectes à Strasbourg." In Livet and Rapp, eds., *Strasbourg au coeur religieux*, pp. 511–35.

Jahns, Sigrid. *Reformation und Schmalkaldischer Bund. Die Reformations-, Reichs- und Bündnispolitik der Reichsstadt Frankfurt am Main 1525–1536*. Frankfurt: Kramer, 1976.

Janelle, Pierre. "Le voyage de Martin Bucer et Paul Fagius de Strasbourg en Angleterre en 1549." *Revue d'histoire et de philosophie religieuses* 8 (1928): 162–77.

Jedin, Hubert. *Geschichte des Konzils von Trient*. Vols. 1 and 2. Freiburg im Breisgau: Herder, 1949 and 1957. English translation: *A History of the Council of Trent*. 2 vols. London: Thomas Nelson, 1957 and 1961.

———. "Ein 'Turmerlebnis' des jungen Contarini." *Historisches Jahrbuch* 70 (1951): 115–30.

Jones, Whitney R. *The Mid-Tudor Crisis, 1539–1563*. London: Macmillan, 1973.

Kantzenbach, Friedrich Wihelm. *Das Ringen um die Einheit der Kirche im Jahrhundert der Reformation*. Stuttgart: Evangelisches Verlagswerk, 1957.

* Kaufmann, Thomas. *Die Abendmahlstheologie der Straßburger Reformatoren bis 1528*. Tübingen: J. C. B. Mohr (Paul Siebeck), 1992.

* ———. "Streittheologie und Friedensdiplomatie. Die Rolle Martin Bucers im frühen Abendmahlsstreit." In Krieger and Lienhard, eds., *Martin Bucer and Sixteenth Century Europe*, pp. 239–56.

* ———. "Zwei unbekannte Schriften Bucers und Capitos zur Abendmahlsfrage aus dem Herbst 1525." *Archiv für Reformationsgeschichte* 81 (1990): 158–88.

* ———. "Bucers Bericht von der Heidelberger Disputation." *Archiv für Reformationsgeschichte* 82 (1991): 147–70.

Keim, C. T. *Die Reformation der Reichsstadt Ulm. Ein Beitrag zur schwäbischen und deutschen Reformationsgeschichte.* Stuttgart, 1851.

Kittelson, James M. *Wolfgang Capito. From Humanist to Reformer.* Leiden: E. J. Brill, 1975.

* Klingenspor, Christine. "Martin Bucer als europäischer Reformator. Sein Einfluß auf das englische Book of Common Prayer von 1552 (Censura von 1551)." *Blätter für Pfälzische Kirchengeschichte* 59 (1992): 5–36.

Knepper, Joseph. *Jakob Wimpfeling (1450–1528). Sein Leben und seine Werke.* Freiburg im Breisgau, 1902.

———. *Das Schul- und Unterrichtswesen im Elsaß von den Anfängen bis gegen das Jahr 1530.* Strasbourg, 1905.

Koch, Ernst. "Johannes Bugenhagens Anteil am Abendmahlsstreit zwischen 1525 und 1532." *Theologische Literaturzeitung* 111 (1986): 705–30.

* Koch, Gustave. "The Christian Life in the Light of the 'Summary' of Martin Bucer of 1523." *Reformation and Renaissance Review* 3 (2001): 140–51.

Koch, Karl. *Studium Pietatis. Martin Bucer als Ethiker.* Neukirchen-Vluyn: Neukirchener Verlag, 1962.

Köhler, Walther. *Zürcher Ehegericht und Genfer Konsistorium.* 2 vols. Leipzig: Heinsius, 1932 and 1942.

———. *Zwingli und Luther. Ihr Streit über das Abendmahl nach seinen politischen und religiösen Beziehungen.* 2 vols. Leipzig and Gütersloh: C. Bertelsmann, 1924 and 1953.

———. "Zwingli und Straßburg." *Elsass-Lothringisches Jahrbuch* 20 (1942): 145–80.

Kohls, Ernst Wilhelm. "Blarer und Bucer." In *Der Konstanzer Reformator Ambrosius Blarer, 1492–1564.* Constance and Stuttgart, 1964, pp. 172–92.

———. "Martin Bucers Anteil und Anliegen bei der Abfassung der Ulmer Kirchenordnung im Jahre 1531." *Zeitschrift für evangelisches Kirchenrecht* 15 (1970): 333–60.

———. *Die Schule bei Martin Bucer in ihrem Verhältnis zu Kirche und Obrigkeit.* Heidelberg: Quelle & Meyer, 1963.

Köhn, Mechtild. *Martin Bucers Entwurf einer Reformation des Erzstiftes Köln. Untersuchungen der Entstehungsgeschichte und der Theologie des "Einfaltigen Bedenckens" von 1543.* Witten: Luther-Verlag, 1966.

Kottje, Raymund, and Bernd Moeller. *Ökumenische Kirchengeschichte.* Vol. 2. Munich: Chr. Kaiser Verlag; Mainz: Matthias-Grünewald Verlag, 1973.

Krahn, Henry G. "Martin Bucer's Strategy against Sectarian Dissent in Strasbourg." *Mennonite Quarterly Review* 50 (1976): 163–80.

Krieger, Christian, and Marc Lienhard, eds. *Martin Bucer and Sixteenth Century Europe. Actes du colloque de Strasbourg (28–31 août 1991).* 2 vols. Leiden: E. J. Brill, 1993.

Kroon, Marijn de. "Die Augsburger Reformation in der Korrespondenz des Straßburger Reformators Martin Bucer unter besonderer Berücksichtigung des Briefwechsels Gereon Sailers." In Reinhard Schwarz, ed., *Die Augsburger Kirchenordnung von 1537 und ihr Umfeld.* Gütersloh: G. Mohn, 1988, pp. 59–89.

———. "Bucer und Calvin. Das Obrigkeitsverständnis beider Reformatoren nach ihrer Auslegung von Römer 13." In Wilhelm Neuser, ed., *Calvinus Servus Christi.* Budapest: Presseabteilung des Ráday-Kollegiums, 1988, pp. 209–24.

———. "Bucer and the Problem of Tolerance." *Sixteenth Century Journal* 19 (1988): 157–68.

———. "Ein unbekannter 'Syllogismus' Martin Bucers zum Ius Reformationis aus der Zeit der Wittenberger Konkordie." *Archiv für Reformationsgeschichte* 77 (1986): 158–85.

———. *Studien zu Martin Bucers Obrigkeitsverständnis. Evangelisches Ethos und politisches Engagement.* Gütersloh: G. Mohn, 1984.

Kroon, Marijn de, and Friedhelm Krüger, eds. *Bucer und seine Zeit. Forschungsbeiträge und Bibliographie.* Wiesbaden: Franz Steiner, 1976.

Kroon, Marijn de, and Marc Lienhard, eds. *Horizons européens de la Réforme en Alsace. Das Elsass und die Reformation im Europa des XVI. Jahrhunderts. Mélanges offerts à Jean Rott pour son 65e anniversaire.* Strasbourg: Librairie Istra, 1980.

Krüger, Friedhelm. *Bucer und Erasmus. Eine Untersuchung zum Einfluß des Erasmus auf die Theologie Martin Bucers (bis zum Evangelien-Kommentar von 1530).* Wiesbaden: Franz Steiner, 1970.

Landsmann, O[ctave] R[abayoie]. *Wissembourg. Un siècle de son histoire, 1480–1580.* Rixheim, 1902.

Lang, August. *Der Evangelienkommentar Martin Butzers und die Grundzüge seiner Theologie.* Leipzig, 1900. Reprint, Aalen: Scientia, 1972.

———. *Puritanismus und Pietismus.* Neukirchen: Buchhandlung des Erziehungsvereins, 1941.

Lebeau, Jean, and Jean-Marie Valentin. *L'Alsace au siècle de la réforme, 1482–1621. Textes et documents.* Nancy: Presses Universitaires de Nancy, 1985.

Leder, Hans-Günter. *Johannes Bugenhagen. Leben und Wirkung.* Berlin, 1984.

Leijssen, Lambert. "Martin Bucer en Thomas van Aquino. De invloed van Thomas op het denkpatroon van Bucer in de Commentaar op de Romeinbrief (1536)." Diss., Louvain, 1978.

———. "Martin Bucer und Thomas von Aquin." *Ephemerides theologicae Lovanienses* 55 (1979): 266–96.

Lenz, Max. *Die Schlacht bei Mühlberg.* Gotha, 1879.

Leppin, Volker. "Theologischer Streit und politische Symbolik: Zu den Anfängen der württembergischen Reformation 1534–1538." *Archiv für Reformationsgeschichte* 90 (1999): 159–87.

Lienhard, Marc. "Les autorités civiles et les anabaptistes. Attitudes du magistrat de Strasbourg (1526–1532)." In Marc Lienhard, ed., *The Origins and Characteristics of Anabaptism. Proceedings of the Colloquium Organized by the Faculty of Protestant Theology of Strasbourg, 20–22 Feb. 1975.* The Hague: Nijhoff, 1977, pp. 196–215.

———. "Bucer et la Tetrapolitaine." *Bulletin de la société de l'histoire du protestantisme français* 126 (1980): 269–86.

———. *Luther, témoin de Jésus-Christ. Les étapes et les thèmes de la christologie du Réformateur.* Paris: Editions du Cerf, 1973. German translation: *Martin Luthers christologisches Zeugnis. Entwickung und Grundzüge seiner Theologie.* Göttingen: Vandenhoeck & Ruprecht, 1980.

* ———. "Martin Bucer, le réformateur européen." *Bulletin de la société de l'histoire du protestantisme français* 138 (1992): 161–80.

———. "Mentalité populaire, gens d'église et mouvement évangélique à Strasbourg en 1522–1523." In de Kroon and Lienhard, eds., *Horizons européens,* pp. 37–62.

———. "La percée du mouvement évangélique à Strasbourg. Le rôle et la figure de Matthieu Zell (1477–1548)." In Livet and Rapp, eds., *Strasbourg au coeur religieux,* pp. 85–98.

———. "La réforme à Strasbourg. Les événements et les hommes." In Livet and Rapp, eds., *Histoire de Strasbourg,* vol. 2, pp. 363–540.

————, ed. *Croyants et sceptiques au XVIe siècle. Le dossier des "epicuriens." Actes du colloque organisé par le GRENEP, Strasbourg, 9–10 juin 1978.* Strasbourg: Librairie Istra, 1981.

Lienhard, Marc, and Jakob Willer. *Straßburg und die Reformation.* Kehl: Morstadt, 1981.

Lipgens, Walter. *Kardinal Johannes Gropper (1503–1559) und die Anfänge der Katholischen Reform in Deutschland.* Münster: Aschendorff, 1951.

Livet, Georges. "Jacques Sturm, Stettmeister de Strasbourg. Formation et idées politiques 1489–1532." In Livet and Rapp, eds., *Strasbourg au coeur religieux,* pp. 207–41.

Livet, Georges, and Francis Rapp, eds. *Histoire de Strasbourg des origines à nos jours.* 4 vols. Strasbourg: Editions des Dernières Nouvelles de Strasbourg, 1980–1982.

————, eds. *Strasbourg au coeur religieux du XVIe siècle. Hommage a Lucien Febvre. Actes du colloque international de Strasbourg (25–29 mai 1975).* Strasbourg: Librairie Istra, 1977.

Loades, David M. *Oxford Martyrs.* 2d ed. Bangor: Headstart History, 1992.

Locher, Gottfried W. *Die Zwinglische Reformation im Rahmen der europäischen Kirchengeschichte.* Göttingen: Vandenhoeck & Ruprecht, 1979.

Löhr, Georg. "Die Akten der Provinzialkapitel der Teutonia von 1503 und 1520." *Archivum fratrum praedicatorum* 17 (1947): 250–84.

Looss, Sigrid. "Der frühe Martin Bucer: Ideologie und revolutionäre Wirklichkeit in der Zeit von Reformation und Bauernkrieg." *Jahrbuch für Geschichte* 10 (1974): 54–119.

Lossen, Richard. "Zur Geschichte des Dominikanerklosters Heidelberg 1476–1853." *Freiburger Diözesan-Archiv* 69 (1949): 167–85.

Luther und die Reformation in Deutschland. Ausstellung zum 500. Geburtstag Martin Luthers. Frankfurt: Insel, 1983.

Lutz, Heinrich. *Christianitas afflicta.* Göttingen: Vandenhoeck & Ruprecht, 1964.

————. *Reformation und Gegenreformation.* Munich and Vienna: Oldenbourg, 1979.

* MacCulloch, Diarmaid. *Thomas Cranmer: A Life.* New Haven, Conn.: Yale University Press, 1996.

* McKee, Elsie Anne. *Katharina Schütz Zell.* 2 vols. Leiden: E. J. Brill, 1999.

* McLaughlin, R. Emmet. "Martin Bucer and the Schwenckfelders." In Krieger and Lienhard, eds., *Martin Bucer and Sixteenth Century Europe,* pp. 615–26.

Martin Bucer zwischen Luther und Zwingli. Edited by Matthieu Arnold and Berndt Hamm. Tübingen: J. C. B. Mohr (Paul Siebeck), 2003.

Maschke, Erich. "'Obrigkeit' im spätmittelalterlichen Speyer und in anderen Städten." *Archiv für Reformationsgeschichte* 57 (1966): 7–23.

Maurer, Wilhelm. "Martin Butzer und die Judenfrage in Hessen." In Ernst Wilhelm Kohls and Gerhard Müller, eds., *Wilhelm Maurer, Kirche und Geschichte. Gesammelte Aufsätze.* Göttingen: Vandenhoeck & Ruprecht, 1970, vol. 2, pp. 347–65.

Mehlhausen, Joachim, ed. *Das Augsburger Interim von 1548.* Neukirchen-Vluyn: Neukirchener Verlag, 1970.

Mesnard, Pierre. *L'évangélisme politique de Martin Bucer.* Paris, 1956.

* Meyer, Christian. "Gesangbuch, darin begriffen . . . Martin Bucer et le chant liturgique." In Krieger and Lienhard, eds., *Martin Bucer and Sixteenth Century Europe,* pp. 215–25.

Mieg, Philippe. "Note sur la postérité de Martin Bucer." *Bulletin du cercle généalogique d'Alsace* 33 (1976): 21–23.

* Moeller, Bernd. "Die Brautwerbung Martin Bucers für Wolfgang Capito. Zur Sozialgeschichte des evangelischen Pfarrerstandes." In L. Grenzmann et al., eds., *Philologie als Kulturwissenschaft.* Göttingen: Vandenhoeck & Ruprecht, 1987, pp. 306–25.

Reprint, Bernd Moeller, *Die Reformation und das Mittelalter. Kirchenhistorische Aufsätze.* Göttingen: Vandenhoeck & Ruprecht, 1991.

———. *Deutschland im Zeitalter der Reformation.* 4th ed. Göttingen: Vandenhoeck & Ruprecht, 1999.

———. "L'édit strasbourgeois sur la prédication du 1ʳ décembre 1523 dans son contexte historique." In Livet and Rapp, eds., *Strasbourg au coeur religieux*, pp. 51–61.

———. "Frömmigkeit in Deutschland um 1500." *Archiv für Reformationsgeschichte* 56 (1965): 5–31.

———. *Johannes Zwick und die Reformation in Konstanz.* Gütersloh: Gütersloher Verlagshaus, 1961.

———. *Reichsstadt und Reformation.* Gütersloh: Gütersloher Verlagshaus, 1962. English translation: *Imperial Cities and the Reformation*, ed. and trans. H. C. Erik Midelfort and U. Mark Edwards Jr. Philadelphia: Fortress Press, 1972. Reprint, Durham, N.C.: Labyrinth, 1982.

———. "Was wurde in der Frühzeit der Reformation in den deutschen Städten gepredigt?" *Archiv für Reformationsgeschichte* 75 (1984): 176–93.

Molnár, Amedeo. "La correspondance entre les frères tchèques et Bucer de 1540 à 1542." *Revue d'histoire et de philosophie religieuses* 31 (1951): 102–56.

* Monteil, Michèle. "Le petit catéchisme (1529) de Luther et la brève explication écrite (1534) de Bucer: deux modèles d'instruction catéchétique." *Études germaniques* 50 (1995): 447–66.

Müller, Gerhard. "Landgraf Philipp von Hessen und das Regensburger Buch." In de Kroon and Krüger, eds., *Bucer und seine Zeit*, pp. 101–16.

Müller, Johannes. *Martin Bucers Hermeneutik.* Gütersloh: Gütersloher Verlagshaus, 1965.

Musall, H., and A. Scheuerbrandt. "Bild und Struktur der kurpfälzischen Residenzstadt Heidelberg an der Wende vom 16. zum 17. Jahrhundert." In W. Fricke and E. Gormsen, eds., *Heidelberg und der Rhein-Neckar-Raum.* Heidelberg: Geographical Institute, 1981, pp. 30–59.

Neuser, Wilhelm. *Die Abendmahlslehre Melanchthons in ihrer geschichtlichen Entwicklung (1519–1539).* Neukirchen-Vluyn: Neukirchener Verlag, 1968.

———. "Bucers Programm einer 'guten leidlichen Reformation' (1539–1541)." In de Kroon and Lienhard, eds., *Horizons européens*: pp. 227–39.

* Neuser, Wilhelm. "Martin Bucer als Mittler im Abendmahlsstreit (1530/31)." In Athina Lexutt and Vicco von Bülow, eds., *Kaum zu glauben. Von der Häresie und dem Umgang mit ihr.* Rheinbach-Merzbach: CMZ-Verlag, 1998, pp. 140–61.

Niessen, Josef. *Geschichte der Stadt Bonn. Teil 1.* Bonn: Dümmler, 1956.

Nijenhuis, Willem. *Ecclesia Reformata. Studies on the Reformation.* Leiden: E. J. Brill, 1972.

Noblesse-Rocher, Annie. "Le nom et l'être de Dieu—Exode 3,14—selon Thomas d'Aquin et Martin Bucer." *Revue d'histoire et de philosophie religieuses* 81 (2001): 425–47.

Oberman, Heiko A. *Die Reformation. Von Wittenberg nach Genf.* Göttingen: Vandenhoeck & Ruprecht, 1986. English translation: *The Reformation: Roots and Ramifications.* Grand Rapids: Wm. B. Eerdmans Publishing Co., 1994.

———. *Werden und Wertung der Reformation. Vom Wegstreit zum Glaubenskampf.* Tübingen: J. C. B. Mohr, 1977. Revised and abridged English version: *Masters of the Reformation: The Emergence of a New Intellectual Climate in Europe.* Cambridge: Cambridge University Press, 1981.

Oediger, F. W. *Über die Bildung der Geistlichen im Mittelalter.* Leiden, 1953.

* Ortmann, Volkmar. *Reformation und Einheit der Kirche. Martin Bucers Einigungsbemühungen bei den Religionsgesprächen in Leipzig, Hagenau, Worms und Regensburg 1539/41.* Mainz: Verlag Philipp von Zabern, 2001.

* Oyer, John S. "Bucer Opposes the Anabaptists." *Mennonite Quarterly Review* 68 (1994): 24–50.

Palliser, David. *The Age of Elizabeth: England under the Late Tudors 1547–1603.* London and New York, 1983.

Pannier, Jacques. *Calvin à Strasbourg.* Strasbourg, 1925.

Pariset, Jean-Daniel. "L'activité de Jacques Sturm, Stettmeister de Strasbourg, de 1532 à 1553." In Livet and Rapp, eds., *Strasbourg au coeur religieux,* pp. 253–66.

Pauck, Wilhelm. *Das Reich Gottes auf Erden. Utopie und Wirklichkeit. Eine Untersuchung zu Butzers "De regno Christi" und zur englischen Staatskirche des 16. Jahrhunderts.* Berlin: Walter de Gruyter, 1928.

Peremans, Nicole. *Érasme et Bucer d'après leur correspondance.* Paris: Les Belles Lettres, 1970.

Peter, Rodolphe. "Le maraîcher Clément Ziegler. L'homme et son oeuvre." *Revue d'histoire et de philosophie religieuses* 34 (1954): 255–82.

———. "Strasbourg et la Réforme française vers 1525." In Livet and Rapp, eds., *Strasbourg au coeur religieux,* pp. 269–83.

Petri, Franz, and Georg Droege, eds. *Rheinische Kirchengeschichte.* Vol. 2. Düsseldorf: Presseverband der Evangelischen Kirche im Rheinland, 1976.

Pfister, Rudolf. *Kirchengeschichte der Schweiz.* Vol. 2. Zurich: Zwingli-Verlag, 1974.

Philippson, Alfred. *Die Stadt Bonn. Ihre Lage und räumliche Entwicklung.* Bonn: Röhrscheid, 1947.

Pitkin, Barbara. "Seeing and Believing in the Commentaries on John by Martin Bucer and John Calvin." *Church History* 68 (1999): 865–85.

Pollet, Jacques Vincent. "Le couvent dominicain de Sélestat (XIIIe–XVIIIe siècles)." *Annuaire des Amis de la Bibliothèque Humaniste de Sélestat* (1983): 17–55.

———. *Huldrych Zwingli et la Réforme en Suisse.* Paris: Presses Universitaires de France, 1963.

———. *Martin Bucer. Études sur la correspondance avec de nombreux textes inédits.* 2 vols. Paris: Presses Universitaires de France, 1958 and 1962 (referred to as Pollet I and II).

———. *Martin Bucer. Études sur les relations de Bucer avec les Pays-bas, l'électorat de Cologne et l'Allemagne du nord.* 2 vols. Leiden: E. J. Brill, 1985 (referred to as Pollet III and IV).

Press, Volker. "Adel, Reich und Reformation." In W. J. Mommsen, ed., *Stadtbürgertum und Adel in der Reformation.* Stuttgart: Klett-Cotta, 1979, pp. 330–83.

Rabe, Horst. *Reichsbund und Interim. Die Verfassungs- und Religionspolitik Karls V. und der Reichstag von Augsburg 1547/48.* Cologne and Vienna: Böhlau, 1971.

Rapp, Francis. "L'évêque de Strasbourg Guillaume de Honstein et la Réformation." *Revue d'histoire et de philosophie religieuses* 54 (1974): 79–88.

———. *Réformes et Réformation à Strasbourg. Église et Société dans la Diocèse de Strasbourg (1450–1525).* Paris: Editions Ophrys, 1974.

Raubenheimer, Richard. "Martin Bucer und seine humanistischen Speyerer Freunde." *Blätter für pfälzische Kirchengeschichte* 32 (1965): 1–52.

———. *Paul Fagius aus Rheinzabern.* Grünstadt: Verein für Pfälzische Kirchengeschichte, 1957.

* Remy, Jochen. "Die Religionsgespräche von Hagenau, Worms und Regensburg (1540/41) als Ausgangspunkt für die Kölner Reformation." *Monatshefte für Evangelische Kirchengeschichte des Rheinlands* 43 (1994): 29–49.

* ———. "'Die Kölner Reformation' und ihre Bedeutung für die englische Kirchengeschichte. Anmerkungen zu einer Verhältnisbestimmung zwischen dem 'Einfältigen Bedenken' und dem 'Book of Common Prayer.'" *Veröffentlichungen des Kölnischen Geschichtsvereins* 67 (1993): 119–40.

Reuter, Fritz, ed. *Der Reichstag zu Worms von 1521. Reichspolitik und Luthersache.* Worms: Stadtarchiv Worms, 1971.

Ritter, François. *Histoire de l'imprimerie alsacienne aux XVe et XVIe siècles.* Strasbourg and Paris: Le Roux, 1955.

Ritter, Gerhard. *Die Heidelberger Universität. Ein Stück deutscher Geschichte.* Vol. 1. Heidelberg: Winter, 1936.

Romano, Ruggiero, and Alberto Tenenti, eds. *Die Grundlegung der modernen Welt. Spätmittelalter, Renaissance, Reformation.* 8th ed. Frankfurt am Main: Fischer, 1978.

Roth, Friedrich. *Augsburgs Reformationsgeschichte.* 4 vols. Munich: Ackermann, 1901–1911. Reprint, Munich, 1974.

Rott, Jean. "Après sept années de prédication évangélique, où en étaient les Strasbourgeois en 1528?" In *Investigationes historicae*, vol. 1, pp. 521–34.

———. "Artisanat et mouvements sociaux à Strasbourg autour de 1525." In *Investigationes historicae*, vol. 1, pp. 133–66.

———. "Der Bauernkrieg und die Stadt Weißenburg im Elsaß." In *Investigationes historicae*, vol. 1, pp. 210–25.

———. "Beatus Rhenanus et Martin Bucer: l'humaniste chrétien et le Réformateur." In *Investigationes historicae*, vol. 2, pp. 166–76.

———. "Bucer et les débuts de la querelle sacramentaire: l'instruction donnée à Grégoire Caselius pour sa mission auprès de Luther (octobre 1525)." In *Investigationes historicae*, vol. 2, pp. 182–202.

———. "Bucer, Martin—Réformateur strasbourgeois et européen." In *Investigationes historicae*, vol. 2, pp. 126–35.

———. "Le déroulement de la réforme à Strasbourg." In *Investigationes historicae*, vol. 1, pp. 368–78.

———. "Documents inédits sur le 'Bundschuh' et la Guerre des Paysans en Alsace." In *Investigationes historicae*, vol. 1, pp. 181–87.

———. "Documents strasbourgeois concernant Calvin." In *Investigationes historicae*, vol. 2, pp. 266–311.

———. *Investigationes historicae. Églises et société au XVIe siècle. Gesammelte Aufsätze.* Edited by Marijn de Kroon and Marc Lienhard. 2 vols. Strasbourg: Oberlin, 1986.

———. "Die 'Gärtner,' der Rat und das Thomaskapitel." In *Investigationes historicae*, vol. 2, pp. 177–80.

———. "La guerre des paysans et anabaptisme: le cas de boersch en Basse-Alsace." In *Investigationes historicae*, vol. 2, pp. 93–98.

———. "La guerre des paysans et la ville de Strasbourg." In *Investigationes historicae*, vol. 1, pp. 199–208.

———. "L'humaniste strasbourgeois Nicolas Gerbel et son diaire (1522–1529)." In *Investigationes historicae*, vol. 2, pp. 313–22.

———. "Jacques Sturm, scolarque de la haute-école (gymnase) de la ville de Strasbourg, 1526–1553." In *Investigationes historicae*, vol. 2, pp. 461–69.

———. "Magistrat et Réforme à Strasbourg: les Dirigeants municipaux de 1521 à 1525." In *Investigationes historicae*, vol. 1, pp. 379–90.

———. "Le magistrat face à l'épicurisme terre à terre des Strasbourgeois: Note sur les règlements disciplinaires municipaux de 1440 à 1599." In *Investigationes historicae*, vol. 1, pp. 535–49.

———. "Martin Bucer und die Schweiz: Drei unbekannte Briefe von Zwingli, Bucer und Vadian (1530, 1531, 1536)." In *Investigationes historicae*, vol. 2, pp. 203–34.

———. "Note sur l'imprimerie alsacienne aux XVe et XVIe siècles." In *Investigationes historicae*, vol. 1, pp. 110–22.

———. "Pfaffenfehden und Anfänge der Reformation in Straßburg." In *Investigationes historicae*, vol. 1, pp. 351–66.

———. "Radikale und gemäßigte Evangelische im Kampf um Straßburg: Das 'Judicium' des Pacatius von 1523." In *Investigationes historicae*, vol. 1, pp. 497–519.

———. "Un recueil de correspondances strasbourgeoises du XVIe siècle à la bibliothèque de Copenhague." In *Investigationes historicae*, vol. 1, pp. 243–312.

———. "La Réforme à Nuremberg et à Strasbourg: contacts et contrastes." In *Investigationes historicae*, vol. 1, pp. 391–442.

———. "Le sort des papiers et de la bibliothèque de Bucer en Angleterre." In *Investigationes historicae*, vol. 2, pp. 136–57.

* ———. "The Strasbourg Kirchenpfleger and Parish Discipline—Theory and Practice." In Wright, ed., *Martin Bucer: Reforming Church and Community*, pp. 122–28.

———. "Un traducteur et vulgarisateur: le réformateur strasbourgeois Gaspard Hédion (1494–1552)." In *Investigationes historicae*, vol. 2, pp. 323–25.

———. "Die Überlieferung des Briefwechsels von Bullinger und den Zürchern mit Martin Bucer und den Straßburgern." In *Investigationes historicae*, vol. 2, pp. 235–64.

———. "Ulrich de Hutten et les débuts de la Réforme à Strasbourg." In *Investigationes historicae*, vol. 1, pp. 465–96.

———. "Les visites pastorales strasbourgeoises aux XVIe et XVIIe siècles." In *Investigationes historicae*, vol. 1, pp. 551–63.

Rott, Jean, and Marc Lienhard. "Die Anfänge der evangelischen Predigt in Straßburg und ihr erstes Manifest: Der Aufruf des Karmeliterlesemeisters Tilman von Lyn (Anfang 1522)." In *Investigationes historicae*, vol. 1, pp. 444–63.

Rott, Jean, and Stephen Nelson. "Straßburg—Die Täuferstadt im 16. Jahrhundert." In *Investigationes historicae*, vol. 2, pp. 99–108. English translation: "Strasbourg: The Anabaptist City in the Sixteenth Century." *Mennonite Quarterly Review* 58 (1984): 230–40.

Rott, Jean, and Simon L. Verhuis, eds. *Anabaptistes et dissidents au XVIe siècle: Actes du Colloque International d'Histoire Anabaptiste du XVIe siècle tenu à l'occasion de la XIe Conférence Mennonite Mondiale à Strasbourg, juillet 1984.* Baden-Baden: Koerner, 1987.

* Roussel, Bernard. "Bucer exégète." In Krieger and Lienhard, eds., *Martin Bucer and Sixteenth Century Europe*, pp. 39–54.

———. "Martin Bucer Exégète." In Livet and Rapp, eds., *Strasbourg au coeur religieux*, pp. 153–66.

———. "Martin Bucer, lecteur de l'épître aux Romains." 2 vols. Diss., Strasbourg, 1970.

Rückert, Hanns. "Die Bedeutung der württembergischen Reformation für den Gang der deutschen Reformationsgeschichte." In *Vorträge und Aufsätze zur historischen Theologie.* Tübingen: J. C. B. Mohr (Paul Siebeck), 1972, pp. 239–51.

———. *Die Rechtfertigungslehre auf dem Tridentinischen Konzil.* Bonn, 1925.

———. *Die theologische Entwicklung Gasparo Contarinis.* Leipzig, 1926.

Salfeld, Siegmund. "Die Judenpolitik Philipp des Großmütigen." In *Philipp der Großmütige*. Marburg, 1904, pp. 519–44.

Schang, Pierre, and Georges Livet, eds. *Histoire du Gymnase Jean Sturm, berceau de l'Université de Strasbourg 1538–1988*. Strasbourg: Oberlin, 1988.

Schauder, Karlheinz. "Martin Bucer und Franz von Sickingen." *Blätter für pfälzische Kirchengeschichte* 49 (1982): 226–33.

Scheible, Heinz. "Die Universität Heidelberg und Luthers Disputation." *Zeitschrift für die Geschichte des Oberrheins* 131 (1983): 309–29.

Schindling, Anton. *Humanistische Hochschule und freie Reichstadt. Gymnasium und Akademie in Straßburg 1538–1621*. Wiesbaden: Franz Steiner, 1977.

Schlüter, Theodor. "Die Publizistik um den Reformationsversuch des Kölner Erzbischofs Hermann von Wied aus den Jahren 1542–1547." Diss., Bonn, 1957.

Schmidt, Charles. *Histoire littéraire de l'Alsace à la fin du XVe et au commencement du XVIe siècle*. 2 vols. Paris, 1879.

Scholl, Hans. "Wolfgangs Capitos reformatorische Eigenart." *Zwingliana* 16 (1983): 126–41.

Schubert, Hans von. *Die Anfänge der evangelischen Bekenntnisbildung*. Leipzig: Heinsius, 1928.

———. *Bekenntnisbildung und Religionspolitik 1529/30 (1524–1534). Untersuchungen und Texte*. Gotha: F. A. Perthes, 1910.

Schweer, Helga. *Weissenburg im Elsass. Eine Stadtgeographie*. Speyer: Pfälzische Gesellschaft zur Förderung der Wissenschaften, 1964.

Scribner, Robert W. "Why Was There No Reformation in Cologne?" *Bulletin of the Institute of Historical Research* 49 (1976): 217–41.

Seebass, Gottfried. "Die Augsburger Kirchenordnung von 1537 in ihrem historischen und theologischen Zusammenhang." In *Die Augsburger Kirchenordnung von 1537 und ihr Umfeld*, ed. Reinhard Schwarz. Gütersloh: Gütersloher Verlagshaus, 1988. Reprint, Gottfried Seebass, *Die Reformation und ihre Außenseiter. Gesammelte Aufsätze und Vorträge*, ed. Irene Dingel. Göttingen: Vandenhoeck & Ruprecht, 1997, pp. 125–48.

* ———. "Bucer-Forschung seit dem Jubiläumsjahr 1991." *Theologische Rundschau* 62 (1997): 271–300.

———. "Martin Bucer und die Reichsstadt Augsburg." In Krieger and Lienhard, eds., *Martin Bucer and Sixteenth Century Europe*, pp. 479–91. Reprint: Gottfried Seebass, *Die Reformation und ihre Außenseiter. Gesammelte Aufsätze und Vorträge*, ed. Irene Dingel. Göttingen: Vandenhoeck & Ruprecht, 1997, pp. 113–24.

———. "Martin Bucers Beitrag zu den Diskussionen über die Verwendung der Kirchengüter." In Strohm, ed., *Martin Bucer und das Recht*, pp. 167–183.

* Séguenny, André. "Pourquoi Bucer détestait les Spirituels. Quelques réflexions après la lecture des dialogues de Bucer en 1535." In Krieger and Lienhard, eds., *Martin Bucer and Sixteenth Century Europe*, pp. 627–34. English translation: "Why Bucer Detested the Spiritualists: Some Reflections on Reading Bucer's 'Dialogues' of 1535." *Mennonite Quarterly Review* 68 (1994): 51–58.

Seidel, Karl Josef. *Frankreich und die deutschen Protestanten. Die Bemühungen um eine religiöse Konkordie und die französische Bündnispolitik in den Jahren 1534/35*. Münster: Aschendorff, 1970.

Seifert, Arno. "Reformation und Chiliasmus. Die Rolle des Martin Cellarius-Borrhaus." *Archiv für Reformationsgeschichte* 77 (1986): 226–64.

* Selderhuis, Herman Johan. "Die hermeneutisch-theologische Grundlage der Auffassungen Bucers zur Ehescheidung." In Spijker, ed., *Calvin—Erbe und Auftrag*, pp. 229–43.

* ———. *Huwelijk en Echtscheiding bij Martin Bucer.* Leiden: Uitgeverij J. J. Groen BV, 1994. English translation: *Marriage and Divorce in the Thought of Martin Bucer.* Kirksville, Mo.: Thomas Jefferson University Press at Truman State University, 1999.

Skalweit, Stephan. *Reich und Reformation,* Berlin: Propyläen Verlag, 1967.

Sohm, Walter. *Territorium und Reformation in der hessischen Geschichte 1526–1555.* Marburg a. d. Lahn: Elwert, 1915. Reprint, Marburg a. d. Lahn: Elwert, 1957.

Specker, Hans Eugen, and Gerhard Weig, eds. *Die Einführung der Reformation in Ulm. Geschichte eines Bürgerentscheids.* Stuttgart: Kohlhammer, 1981.

Spijker, Willem van 't. "De invloed van Bucer op Calvijn blijkens de Institutie." *Theologia Reformata* 28 (1985): 15–34.

* ———. "De kerk in Bucers oecumenisch streven." In Frank van der Pol, ed., *Bucer en de kerk.* Kampen, 1991, pp. 10–54.

———. *De Ambten bij Martin Bucer.* Kampen: J. H. Kok N. V., 1970. English translation: *The Ecclesiastical Offices in the Thought of Martin Bucer.* Leiden: E. J. Brill, 1996.

* ———. "Calvin's Friendship with Martin Bucer: Did It Make Calvin a Calvinist?" In *Calvin and Spirituality,* ed. David Foxgrover. Grand Rapids, Mich.: Calvin Studies Society, 1998, pp. 169–86.

* ———. *Calvin. Biographie und Theologie.* Göttingen: Vandenhoeck & Ruprecht, 2001.

* ———. "Bucer's Doctrinal Legacy as Formulated in His Last Three Wills and Testaments." *Reformation and Renaissance Review* 3 (2001): 152–66.

———. "Recht und Kirchenzucht bei Martin Bucer." In Strohm, ed., *Martin Bucer und das Recht,* pp. 215–230.

Spitz, Lewis W. *The Religious Renaissance of the German Humanists.* Cambridge, Mass.: Harvard University Press, 1963.

Staehelin, Ernst. *Frau Wibrandis.* Bern, 1934.

Stafford, William S. "Domesticating the Clergy. The Inception of the Reformation in Strasbourg 1522–1524." Diss., Ann Arbor, Mich., 1976.

Stalnaker, John C. "Anabaptism, Martin Bucer, and the Shaping of the Hessian Protestant Church." *Journal of Modern History* 48 (1976): 601–43.

Stayer, James M. *Anabaptists and the Sword.* Lawrence, Kan.: Coronado Press, 1972.

Steitz, Heinrich. *Geschichte der Evangelischen Kirche in Hessen und Nassau, Teil I.* Marburg a. d. Lahn: Trautvetter & Fischer, 1961.

* Stephens, Peter. "The Church in Bucer's Commentary on the Epistle to the Ephesians." In Wright, ed., *Martin Bucer: Reforming Church and Community,* pp. 45–60.

———. *The Holy Spirit in the Theology of Martin Bucer.* Cambridge: Cambridge University Press, 1970.

———. *The Theology of Huldrych Zwingli.* Oxford: Clarendon, 1986.

Stierle, Beate. *Capito als Humanist.* Gütersloh: Gütersloher Verlagshaus, 1974.

Strasser, Otto Erich. "Die letzten Anstrengungen der Straßburger Theologen Martin Bucer und Wolfgang Capito, eine Union zwischen den deutschen Lutheranern und den schweizerischen Reformierten herbeizuführen." *Zwingliana* 6 (1934/37): 5–15.

Strohl, Henri. *Le Protestantisme en Alsace.* Strasbourg, 1950. Reprint, Strasbourg: Oberlin, 2000.

Strohm, Christoph. "Die Berufung auf kanonisches Recht, römisches Recht und Reichsrecht in der Auseinandersetzung um die Kölner Reformation 1543–1546." In Strohm, ed., *Martin Bucer und das Recht,* 123–45.

————, ed. *Martin Bucer und das Recht. Beiträge zum internationalen Symposium vom 1. bis 3. März 2001 in der Johannes a Lasco Bibliothek Emden.* Geneva: Librairie Droz, 2002.

Stupperich, Robert. *Der Humanismus und die Wiedervereinigung der Konfessionen.* Leipzig: Heinsius, 1936.

Thompson, Nick. "Martin Bucer's Assessment of the Canon of the Mass in the Era of Religious Colloquies." *Reformation and Renaissance Review* 3 (2001): 51–77.

Ulmann, Heinrich. *Franz von Sickingen.* Leipzig, 1872.

Varrentrap, Carl. *Hermann von Wied und sein Reformationsversuch in Köln.* Leipzig: Hirzel, 1878.

Vogt, Herbert. "Martin Bucer und die Kirche von England." Diss., Münster, 1966.

————. *Martin Bucer und Thomas Cranmer. Annotationes in octo priora capita Evangelii secundum Matthaeum.* Frankfurt: Athenäum-Verlag, 1972.

* Waldhoff, Stephan. "Der Evangelist des gewappneten Moses. Sebastian Francks Auseinandersetzung mit Martin Bucers Obrigkeitsverständnis." *Zeitschrift für Kirchengeschichte* 107 (1996): 327–54.

Wendel, François. *Calvin. Sources et évolution de sa pensée religieuse.* Paris: Presses Universitaires de France, 1950. 2d rev. ed., Geneva: Labor et Fides, 1985. German translation: *Calvin. Ursprung und Entwicklung seiner Theologie.* Neukirchen-Vluyn: Neukirchener Verlag des Erziehungswesens, 1968.

————. *L'église de Strasbourg. Sa Constitution et son Organisation 1532–1535.* Paris: Presses Universitaires de France, 1942.

————. *Le mariage à Strasbourg à l'époque de la Réforme 1520–1692.* Strasbourg: Imprimerie Alsacienne, 1928.

————. *Martin Bucer—Esquisse de sa Vie et de sa Pensée.* Strasbourg, 1951.

————. "Un document inédit sur le séjour de Bucer en Angleterre." *Revue d'histoire et de philosophie religieuses* 34 (1954): 223–33.

* Weyer, Michel. "Martin Bucer et les Zell. Une solidarité critique." In Krieger and Lienhard, eds., *Martin Bucer and Sixteenth Century Europe,* pp. 275–95.

Weyrauch, Erdmann. *Konfessionelle Krise und soziale Stabilität. Das Interim in Straßburg (1548–1562).* Stuttgart: Klett-Cotta, 1978.

————. "Strasbourg et la Réforme en Allemagne du Sud." In Livet and Rapp, ed., *Strasbourg au coeur religieux,* pp. 347–68.

Wiedeburg, A. "Die Freundschaft zwischen Bucer und Calvin nach ihren Briefen." *Historisches Jahrbuch* 83 (1964): 69–83.

Winckelmann, Otto. *Das Fürsorgewesen der Stadt Strassburg vor und nach der Reformation bis zum Ausgang des sechzehnten Jahrhunderts: Ein Beitrag zur deutschen Kultur- und Wirtschaftsgeschichte.* Leipzig: Heinsius, 1922. Reprint, New York: Johnson Reprint, 1971.

Wolfart, Karl. *Die Augsburger Reformation in den Jahren 1533/34.* Reprint. Aalen, 1972.

Wright, David F. "Martin Bucer and the *Decretum Gratiani.*" In Strohm, ed., *Martin Bucer und das Recht,* pp. 101–112.

* ————. "Martin Bucer in England—and Scotland." In Krieger and Lienhard, eds., *Martin Bucer and Sixteenth Century Europe,* pp. 523–32.

* ————. "Martin Bucer (1491–1551) in England." *Anvil* 9 (1992): 249–59.

* ————, ed. *Martin Bucer: Reforming Church and Community.* Cambridge: Cambridge University Press, 1994.

Youings, Joyce. *Sixteenth-Century England*. London: A. Lane, 1984.

* Zwierlein, Cornel. "Reformation als Rechtsreform. Bucers Hermeneutik der lex Dei und sein humanistischer Zugriff auf das römische Recht." In Strohm, ed., *Martin Bucer und das Recht*, pp. 29–81.

Index

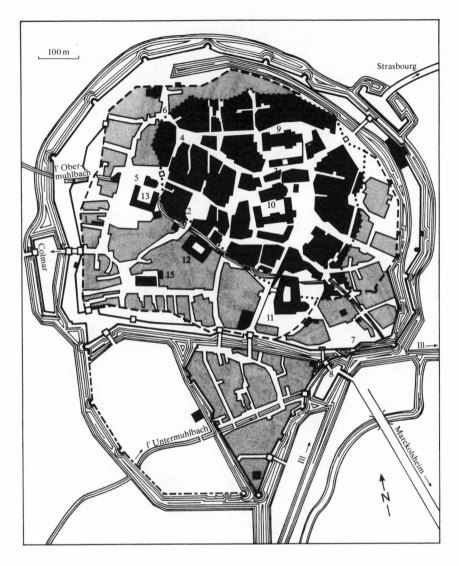

Sélestat (Schlettstadt)

1 Martin Bucer's house of birth
2 Town Hall
3 Cattle market (Viehmarkt)
4 Grain market (Kornmarkt)
5 Potters' market (Töpfermarkt)
6 Wine market (Weinmarkt)
7 Old Port: loading yard
8 New Port

9 City Church of St. George
10 Church of St. Fides (Sainte Foy)
11 Convent of Dominican nuns
12 Monastery of Dominican monks
13 Franciscan monastery
14 Latin school
15 Synagogue

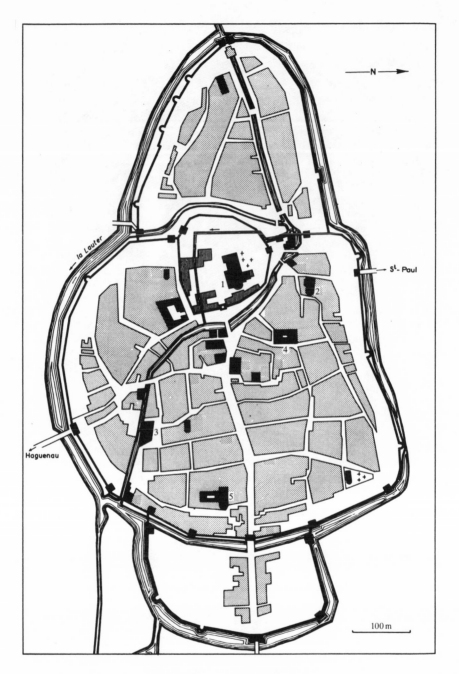

Wissembourg (Weissenburg)

1 Abbey of St. Peter and St. Paul   4 Augustinian monastery
2 City Church of St. John   5 Dominican monastery
3 Franciscan monastery

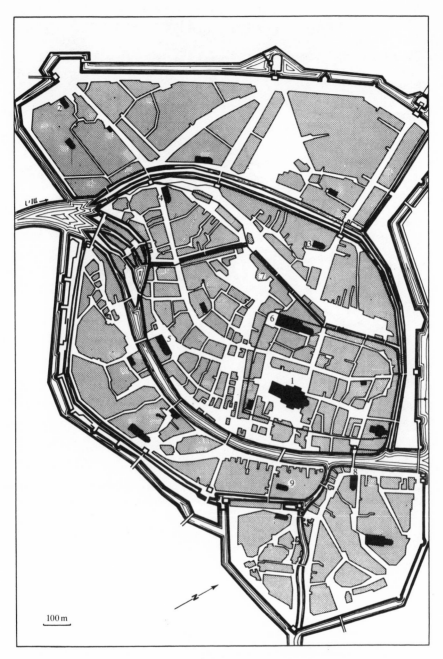

Strasbourg

1 Cathedral	4 Old St. Peter	7 Franciscan monastery
2 Sankt Aurelien	5 St. Thomas	8 Williamite monastery
3 Young St. Peter	6 Dominican monastery	9 Penitents of St. Magdalen

Landgraviate of Hesse from 1247 to 1567

The Development of the Landgraviate of Hesse from 1247 to 1567

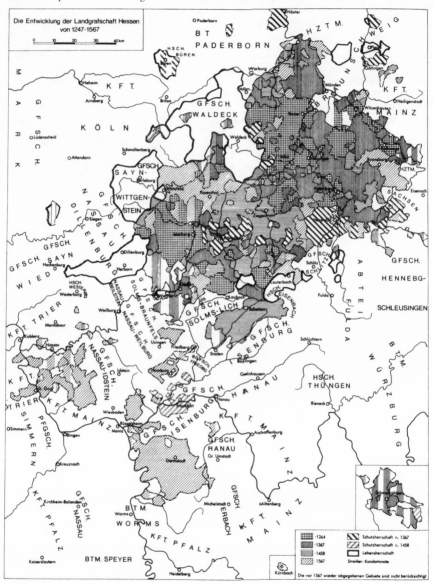

BTM (Bistum): bishopric
GFSCH (Grafschaft): county
HSCH (Herrschaft): dominion
HZTM (Herzogtum): Duchy
KFT (Kurfürstentum): electorate
PFGSCH (Pfalzgrafschaft): Palatine county
Schutzherrschaft: protectorate
Lehensherrschaft: fiefdom

Protectorate after 1367
Protectorate after 1458
Fiefdom
Vertical Stripes: Areas under Joint Rule

Areas relinquished before 1567 have not been
taken into account.

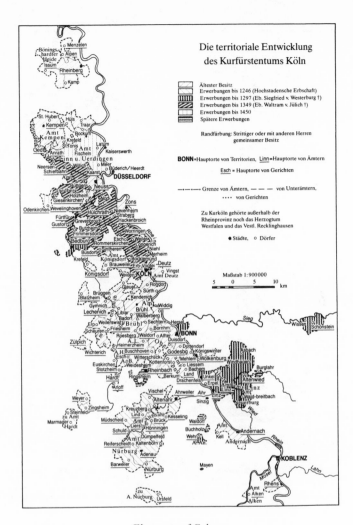

Electorate of Cologne

The Territorial Development of the Electorate of Cologne

Ältester Besitz: oldest dominions
Erwerbungen bis 1246: Acquired by 1246 (Hochstaden Inheritance)
Erwerbungen bis 1297: Acquired by 1297 (under Archbishop Siegfried von Westerburg)
Erwerbungen bis 1349: Acquired by 1349 (under Archbishop Waltram von Jülich)
Erwerbungen bis 1450: Acquired by 1450
Spätere Erwerbungen: Later Acquisitions

BONN: Capitals of Territories
Linn: Capitals of Districts (Ämter)
Esch: Capitals of Jurisdictions (Gerichte)

Grenze von Ämtern: District (Amt) Boundary
Grenze von Unterämtern: Subdistrict (Unteramt) Boundary
Grenze von Gerichten: Jurisdiction (Gericht) Boundary

Besides the Rhenish Province, the Duchy of Westphalia and the city of Recklinghausen with its surrounding region also belonged to the electorate of Cologne.

Städte: cities
Dörfer: villages

Maßstab: Scale

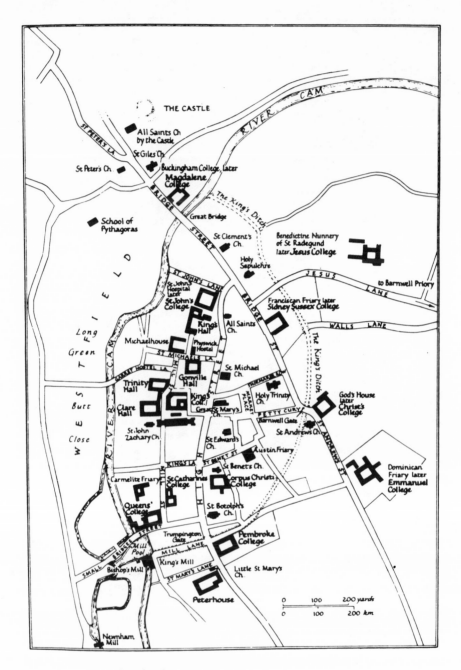

Cambridge in approximately the year 1500